MOVING INTO ADOLESCENCE

The Impact of Pubertal Change and School Context

SOCIAL INSTITUTIONS
AND SOCIAL CHANGE

EDITED BY

Peter H. Rossi
Michael Useem
James D. Wright

Bernard C. Rosen, **The Industrial Connection: Achievement and the Family in Developing Societies**

Paul Diesing, **Science and Ideology in the Policy Sciences**

James D. Wright, Peter H. Rossi, and Kathleen Daly, **Under the Gun: Weapons, Crime, and Violence in America**

Walter L. Wallace, **Principles of Scientific Sociology**

Robert C. Liebman and Robert Wuthnow (eds.), **The New Christian Right: Mobilization and Legitimation**

Paula S. England and George Farkas, **Households, Employment, and Gender: A Social, Economic, and Demographic View**

Richard F. Hamilton and James D. Wright, **The State of the Masses**

James R. Kluegel and Eliot R. Smith, **Beliefs About Inequality: Americans' Views of What is and What Ought to Be**

James D. Wright and Peter H. Rossi, **Armed and Considered Dangerous: A Survey of Felons and Their Firearms**

Roberta G. Simmons and Dale A. Blyth, **Moving into Adolescence: The Impact of Pubertal Change and School Context**

George Farkas, **Human Capital or Cultural Capital?**

Paula S. England, **Comparable Worth**

MOVING INTO ADOLESCENCE

The Impact of Pubertal Change and School Context

ROBERTA G. SIMMONS
DALE A. BLYTH

 1987

ALDINE DE GRUYTER
New York

ABOUT THE AUTHORS

Roberta G. Simmons is Professor of Sociology and Psychiatry at the University of Minnesota, and a Research Associate in Surgery. She has been a member of the governing Councils of the American Sociological Association, the Society for Research on Adolescence, and a member of the Advisory Sub-Panel for Sociology for the National Science Foundation. Dr. Simmons has published extensively and is author of: *Black and White Self-Esteem: The Urban School Child*; *Gift of Life: The Social and Psychological Impact of Organ Transplantation*; and was editor of *Research in Community and Mental Health*.

Dale A. Blyth is Professor of Human Development and Family Studies at Cornell University. He is executive secretary of the Society for Research on Adolescence. Dr. Blyth is also on the editorial boards of the *Journal of Early Adolescence* and the *Journal of Adolescence*. He has published numerous articles on adolescence and is author of *Philosophy, Policies and Programs for Early Adolescent Education: An Annotated Bibliography*.

ALDINE DE GRUYTER
A Division of Walter de Gruyter, Inc.
200 Saw Mill River Road
Hawthorne, New York 10532

Library of Congress Cataloging-in-Publication Data

Simmons, Roberta G.
    Moving into adolescence.

    (Social institutions and social change)
    Bibliography: p.
    Includes index.
    1. Youth—Wisconsin—Milwaukee—Psychology—
Longitudinal studies.   2. Adolescent psychology.
3. Puberty.   4. Articulation (Education). I. Blyth,
Dale A.   II. Title.   III. Series.
HQ796.S474   1987   305.2'35   86-32054
ISBN 0-202-30238-4 (lib. bdg.)

Printed in the United States of America
10 9 8 7 6 5 4 3 2 1

With love to our children,
Nicole and Janine
Jeremy, Heather, and Aaron
and with gratitude to our secretary and friend,
Barbara Ann Bailey

CONTENTS

IV. THE IMPACT OF SCHOOL ENVIRONMENT

V. FACTORS THAT MITIGATE OR AGGRAVATE
THE EARLY ADOLESCENT TRANSITION

VI. CONCLUSION

APPENDIXES

PREFACE

Missing from Shakespeare's chronicle of life periods is that of early adolescence. The individual is a "whining schoolboy" and then becomes "a lover." Yet in contemporary, western society, the individual moves not from childhood directly to late adolescence/young adulthood but into a period with vague but real rights and obligations of its own. Some historians have characterized adolescence as an invention of this century (Kett, 1977). Certainly adolescence is a period which takes on a very special character in our society.

This book represents a study of contemporary youngsters as they make the transition out of childhood into early and then middle adolescence.

In this book, we have investigated the impact of age, gender, pubertal timing, and timing of school transition on the self-image and social–psychological adjustment of white youth. Based on a random, stratified cluster sample, we interviewed 621 white youngsters in Grade 6 in 18 schools in Milwaukee in 1974. We then attempted to follow these students each year through Grade 10 in 1979. The study took advantage of a natural experiment. Side by side in Milwaukee were two school sequences. In one sequence, at entry to adolescence, children moved out of small kindergarten through sixth grade (K–6) schools into large, impersonal junior high schools in Grade 7. In the other sequence, at the same age in Grade 7, they remained in small, intimate kindergarten through eighth grade (K–8) schools. A key purpose of the investigation was to compare the short- and longer-term effects of these two environmental contexts on the early adolescent. The study is a quantitative one—using quantitative measurement and statistical analyses. A wide range of adjustment outcomes are investigated, with a focus on the self-image, in general, and self-esteem, in particular.

As the reader shall see, we found that the transition into adolescence does not involve widespread negative effects on average. However, adolescent transitions are difficult for some children under some circumstances, depending on (1) characteristics of the transition, (2) characteristics of the individual, and (3) the outcome area at issue.

In terms of the *characteristics of the transition, timing* appears critical. Many of the major findings from this study are compatible with a "developmental readiness hypothesis," which states that individuals can be thrust too soon out of childhood into adolescence before they are ready for the change. Short- and longer-term negative effects were associated with an early transition in Grade 7 into a large, impersonal junior high school. Children who remained in an intimate K–8 school two more years before moving into a large senior high did not evidence these negative effects. In addition, early pubertal development for girls, extremely early pubertal development for boys, early independence from parental supervision and chaperonage, and early dating all had problematic aspects.

The timing of school changes is also important in other ways. Many findings pointed to the importance of a "top dog," "bottom dog" effect, particularly in late childhood (Grade 6) and early adolescence (Grade 7). Many social-psychological advantages accrued when the children were the oldest students in the school, as did many disadvantages when they were the youngest in the school.

In addition to timing and relative status, the *"discontinutiy"* of the change appears important. A change is considered to be discontinuous when it is sudden and abrupt rather than gradual, and if it involves great difference between the pre- and posttransition periods. The transition out of elementary school to junior high school appeared to be an example of a sharp and difficult discontinuity.

While the timing and level of discontinuity of each individual change seems important for the adjustment of adolescents, also relevant was the *cumulation* of life changes at one point in time. Individuals who experienced a greater number of major life changes in early adolescence were at considerably greater risk, i.e., children who simultaneously experienced the transition into junior high school, pubertal change, early onset of dating, change of residence, and change in parents' marital status. Some of these findings are compatible with the "focal theory of change"—the hypothesis that it is easier for the youngster to be able to focus on one major transition at a time. They are also compatible with the idea of the need for an "arena of comfort"—the need for at least one area of life in which the individual can feel relaxed and comfortable, to which he or she can withdraw to become reinvigorated.

Reaction to adolescence appeared to be determined not only by the characteristics of the changes involved, but also by the *characteristics of the individual*. Our findings emphasized the continued importance of gender in the 1970's. On almost all key outcomes, boys and girls showed significant differences. Furthermore, females scored less favorably than males in terms of their self-image and appeared more vulnerable to the environmental and biological transitions of adolescence. This study also pointed to the importance of perceived good looks and a perceived favorable peer regard prior to the transition in enabling the youngster to cope well with the transition into junior high school. It also indicated that a history of school problem behavior hindered adjustment.

Finally, reactions to adolescent transition were not necessarily global and widespread. The *specific outcome area* was important. Negative changes were more evident in some areas than in others. The one realm in which there was a definite negative trend in adolescence involved conformity to adult standards and deviant behavior.

Furthermore, the different types of transitions had different types of effects. While school change and cumulative change affected global self-esteem and a student's Grade Point Average, pubertal timing did not influence global self-esteem, but rather had a narrow set of specific effects, particularly upon the body-image.

The book presents the details of this study of adolescent life transitions. While we have utilized statistical analyses, we have attempted to explain these analyses in a way that the reader who is not acquainted with one method or another can still follow the argument; we have tried in all chapters to summarize substantive findings clearly. However, the reader who is less interested in questions of studying change might find that for Chapters 4, 9, and 10, it is better to concentrate on the summaries.

Roberta G. Simmons
Dale A. Blyth

ACKNOWLEDGMENTS

We would like to express our gratitude toward many individuals who provided inspiration and help with aspects of this study. (Of course, the end result is our own responsibility.)

First, we wish to give credit to the granting agencies. This study has been funded by NIMH grants R01 MH30739 and grants from the William T. Grant Foundation as well as the assistance of The Boys Town Center for the Study of Youth Development at Omaha. In addition, the work of the senior author (R.G.S.) has been supported by a Research Development Award from the National Institute of Mental Health, #2 K02 MH41688 and by a Fellowship at the Center for the Advanced Study of the Behavioral Sciences at Stanford funded in part by the John D. and Catherine T. MacArthur Foundation. The University of Minnesota Computer Center has provided partial support through grants from the Supercomputer Institute.

Second, without Barbara Bailey, the secretary who has worked on this project from the beginning, it is unclear how we would have managed. She has been a totally committed research assistant, manager, secretary, editor, and friend throughout all stages. It is for this reason that she is one of the people to whom the book is dedicated.

Also, to be thanked for fine secretarial help and support are Connie Finnell and Dale's wife, Linda Blyth.

While we have dedicated this book to our children (who either have been or will be adolescents), we also wish to express gratitude to the rest of our families for their support, encouragement, and understanding.

Many research assistants have provided invaluable help over the years. In addition to those who are co-authors of chapters in the book, we wish to thank Debbie Felt, Joyce Hemphill, Scott Marino, Keith McGarrahan, Karen McKinney, Mary Jo Reef, Jennifer Richardson, Karen Thiel, Edward Van Cleave, and David Zakin. In additon, we are greatly indebted to the many staff, interviewers, and nurse-interviewers from the Wisconsin Survey Research Center for their skill and dedication. In particular, we are indebted to Ruth Wendle and June Held.

The Milwaukee Public School System and its Research Division are also to be thanked as are the children who participated and the parents who allowed and encouraged participation.

Three of our colleagues are important for the inspiration they provided and we wish to express thanks. Morris Rosenberg was the mentor of the senior author and responsible for our great interest in the self-image and for starting us down this road to further investigation of adolescence and the self-image. We are exceedingly grateful for his inspiration and for his own wonderful work. Betty Hamburg and Bert Brim are each to be thanked for encouraging this research and for bringing us together at many conferences with other persons studying adolescence and studying the life course. They both have helped to create exciting international communities focused on these relevant, intellectual issues.

Others of our colleagues have helped us with valuable criticism of our work; we wish to thank George Bohrnstedt, Jeanne Brooks-Gunn, Fred Damarin, Dorothy Eichorn, Mike Finch, Barbara Laslett, Geoffrey Maruyama, Steve McLaughlin, Jeylan Mortimer, Anne Petersen, Richard Savin-Williams, and Ron Schoenberg.

I

INTRODUCTION

INTRODUCTION

Substantial controversy has been generated within the behavioral sciences concerning the difficulty of adolescence as a transitional period. On the one hand, there are those who characterize the period as an exceptionally and necessarily stressful time in the life course. On the other hand, many investigators treat this view of adolescence as their straw man. To them, the supposed tumult of adolescence is just that—supposed and mythical. The purpose of this book is to study the transition from childhood into early and middle adolescence in order to investigate change along a wide variety of psychosocial dimensions with a particular focus on the self-image. For which of these dimensions, if any, is adolescence associated with negative consequences? Which types of children react with more distress at this age, and which types weather the changes most successfully? Furthermore, what aspects of the transition generate the most difficulty? Our primary focus will be on the role of pubertal change and school transition.

Overview and History

View of Adolescence as Tumultuous

Hall (1904) originally described the adolescent years as ones of "storm and stress." Later, Erikson (1959, 1968) characterized adolescence as a time of identity crisis, in which the youngster struggles for a stable sense of self. Psychoanalysts, such as Blos (1962, 1971) and Anna Freud (1958), have suggested that puberty sparks a resurgence of Oedipal conflicts for the boy and pre-Oedipal pressures for the girl (see Barglow and Schaefer, 1979). According to Elkind (1967), cognitive processes also contribute to adolescent difficulty. Adolescents become cognizant that others are formulating opinions of them, but they are unable to differentiate their own self-preoccupations from the perceived thoughts of their imaginary audience (adolescent "egocentrism"). They concentrate on their own faults and believe that these faults are as evident to others as to themselves.[1]

From the sociological point of view, adolescence traditionally has been described as a period of physical maturity and social immaturity (Davis,

1944). Because of the complexity of the present social system, children reach physical adulthood before they are capable of functioning well in adult social roles. The disjunction between physical capabilities and so-cially allowed independence and power and the concurrent status-ambi-guities are viewed as stressful for the adolescent in modern Western society (Mead, 1950; Benedict, 1954). It has been assumed that the need to dis-engage from parents during these years will result in high levels of rebellion and parent–child conflict. Higher rates of deviant behavior in adolescence than in childhood or than in adulthood (Greenberg, 1981) would appear to fit with this picture of difficult adjustment in the teenage years.[2]

The Tumult as Myth

Many empirical investigators, however, claim that for most youngsters these years are not marked by stress or turmoil (see Grinker, Grinker, and Timberlake, 1962; Offer, 1969; Offer, Ostrov, and Howard, 1981; Elkin and Westley, 1955, Douvan and Adelson, 1966; Douvan and Gold, 1966; Weiner, 1970; Bandura, 1972; Coleman, 1974, 1980; Rutter, 1980).

In some cases, the investigators compare levels on one or more variables across ages and fail to find that adolescents score more negatively than younger children (Attenborough and Zdep, 1973; Bowman, 1974; see Wy-lie's review, 1979). Alternatively, stability coefficients and/or factor structures over the years are compared, and no break is seen at the entry into adolescence (Monge, 1973; Dusek and Flaherty, 1981). In other cases, the issue is addressed in terms of the proportion of individuals affected. Whereas some children find adolescence difficult, the majority do not (Douvan and Adelson, 1966; Offer et al., 1981). Or the issue becomes one of severity. While adolescents show conflict with parents, the conflicts tend to be centered on minor issues related to appearance and not related to major values (Elkin and Westley, 1955; Campbell, 1969; Gold and Dou-van, Part IV, 1969; Feather, 1980; Hill, 1980; Montemayor, 1982). In still other research, the investigator notes that while there are likely to be specific problems at various ages, these problems neither generalize across variables nor persist throughout adolescence (Coleman, 1974).

Since a major focus of our research involves the self-image in adoles-cence, it should be noted that Wylie (1979), in reviewing studies in this area, concludes there is no patterned, consistent relationship of age to self-concept and no pattern across studies of increasingly negative self-images in adolescence. In fact, more recent reviews of large-scale lon-gitudinal studies report a consistent rise, and not a drop, in self-esteem as children move from early to late adolescence (McCarthy and Hoge, 1982; O'Malley and Bachman, 1983).[3] More at issue than what happens during adolescence is the fate of self-esteem and other aspects of the self-concept in the transition between childhood and early adolescence. While some studies show no age difference (Attenborough and Zdep, 1973; Coleman, 1974), others indicate a worsening near or upon entry to adolescence, that is, in Grades 6, 7, or 8 (or age 12–13) compared to earlier years (Piers and Harris, 1964; Katz and Zigler, 1967; Yamamoto, Thomas, and Karns, 1969; Jorgensen and Howell, 1969; Trowbridge, 1972; Soares and Soares, 1970; Eccles, Adler, Tutlerman, Goff, Kaczala, Meece, and Midgley, 1983; Eccles, Midgley, and Adler, 1984).[4]

These studies vary in their methodology. The longitudinal studies showing a rise in self-esteem during adolescence are large-scale and probably can be considered valid (O'Malley and Bachman, 1983). However, many of the studies comparing children to early adolescents are not so compelling. All are cross-sectional, and some have small samples (Piers and Harris, 1964; Katz and Zigler, 1967; Bohan, 1973). Only a few indicate they used random sampling (suburban sample: Katz and Zigler, 1967; Yamamoto *et al.*, 1969; national household sample: Attenborough and Zdep, 1973).

Our First Research: The Baltimore Study

In 1968, in collaboration with Morris Rosenberg, Simmons conducted a cross-sectional survey of 1,918 school children in Baltimore. Unlike many earlier studies, this one was large-scale and involved a careful random sample of 25 schools and the students within these schools (see Rosenberg and Simmons, 1972; Simmons, Rosenberg, and Rosenberg, 1973). Thus, the results of the study are generalizable to the population of Baltimore school children at the time. In addition, there were measures of both younger school-age children and of early and middle adolescents.

This study focused on the impact of age upon various dimensions of the self-image. According to this study, early adolescence appeared to be a disturbing period for the self-picture of children of both genders and of varying classes and races. The term "disturbing" was used to indicate any change in a direction presumed uncomfortable for the child. It was not meant to connote psychopathology or tumult. During early adolescence, compared to the years 8–11, the children exhibited heightened self-consciousness, greater instability of the self-image, slightly lower global self-esteem, lower opinions of themselves with regard to specific qualities they valued, and a reduced conviction that their parents, teachers, and peers of the same sex held favorable opinions of them. Early adolescents also showed more depressive affect than did younger children.[5]

The largest negative change appeared to occur among 12 year olds who had entered seventh grade, the first year of junior high school. In fact, the negative drop in self-esteem occurred only in that year, and then, as in many other studies, self-esteem rose (see O'Malley and Bachman, 1983). For most other self-variables, the negative trend continued to worsen throughout the *junior high school years*. In *senior high school,* the findings differed from one variable to another: some leveled off, others continued to worsen, and the scores improved for still others.

The clear pattern involved the early adolescent, junior high school years in which scores were more negative than they had been for younger children in elementary school. The only area that showed early adolescents to be more positive than younger children involved popularity with the opposite sex. In almost all cases, girls scored more negatively than boys on the self-image dimensions (see F. Rosenberg and Simmons, 1975; Simmons and F. Rosenberg, 1975).

While these data do not address the issue of whether early adolescence is tumultuous, they do suggest a negative impact on the self-image and that girls are particularly vulnerable. If these data are correct and early adolescence is a difficult time for the self-image, the question arises as to why. The most obvious answer is that pubertal development is the major determinant. The physiological changes of puberty and internal hormonal differences may challenge the view of the self in fundamental ways. However, in Baltimore at the time of the study (as in many other cities) a major change in environmental context also occurred at that age as well: the change from elementary to junior high school.

This move from a small, protected school environment into a much larger, more impersonal junior high school may be the child's first experience in coping with a "secondary-" rather than "primary-" type environment. The distinction between primary or intense and intimate relationships ("gemeinschaft") and secondary or impersonal and specific relationships ("gesellschaft") is a fundamental one and has been emphasized by many of the classic theorists in sociology (e.g., Toennies, 1887/1940; Cooley, 1912). The family typifies a primary-type environment, whereas large-scale bureaucracies are the quintessence of the secondary-type context (Weber, 1947). In our society, individuals have to learn to function, at some point, in large-scale organizational contexts, in "gesellschaft" rather than "gemeinschaft" environments (Toennies, 1887/1940). Nevertheless, the first transition into such an environment may be difficult. In elementary school, children usually have one teacher and one set of classmates; in the larger junior high, the adolescents' teachers, classmates, and even rooms are constantly being changed. While the elementary school resembles the comfortable primary-type context as does the family, the junior high with its impersonality, specialization, and greater emphasis on rules corresponds more closely to a bureaucratic environment.

In the Baltimore study, we made a first and somewhat imprecise attempt to ascertain the impact of pubertal development and of the environmental transition. Lacking an accurate measure of puberty, the Baltimore study simply compared the effects of age and environmental change upon the student's self-image and found that environmental context had a stronger effect than chronological age. In Grade 6, the last year in elementary school, 11 year olds were compared to 12 year olds based on the assumption that older children were more likely to have attained puberty. There were no differences, however, in the self-images of 11 and 12 year olds in Grade 6. Similarly in Grade 7, in junior high school, there were no differences between 12 and 13 year olds. However, 12 year olds in seventh grade (junior high school) scored more negatively than 12 year olds in Grade 6 (elementary school). Thus, making the transition to a traditional junior high school appeared to be a more significant factor affecting the child's self-image than age.

There were, however, no comparable, consistent differences at the point of transition into senior high school. Thus, according to the Baltimore data, transition into a new, larger environment is not sufficient to induce these effects. The young age at the junior high school transition, the fact that it was the first such transition, and/or the concurrence of environmental and pubertal change at the same time may have been the causal culprits.

In any case, the Baltimore study identified a key developmental year at the beginning of adolescence as disturbing for the self-image, showed females to be most vulnerable at this age, and suggested that part of the problem was due to a marked change in the child's environmental context at that point.

These results then, do not establish that early adolescence is a time of "storm and stress" but rather provide evidence of a negative turn for the self-image. It is possible that the negative self-image changes seen in the above findings reflect a greater accuracy of perception rather than intense distress among adolescents. According to other results, there is evidence that younger children's self-ratings of social and ethnic standings are inflated compared to those of adolescents (Simmons and Rosenberg, 1971; Rosenberg and Simmons, 1972, Chs. 4 and 6); it is also likely that young children's self-ratings in other spheres are similarly inflated. Nevertheless, for the adolescent, a less favorable self-rating, a lack of self-stability, and an intensified self-consciousness should evoke discomfort whether or not a greater accuracy of perception is involved.

It also should be noted again that some other studies fail to find comparable grade or age level differences in the self-image (Attenborough and Zdep, 1973; Coleman, 1974). Most studies, however, do not report whether or not early adolescents were attending junior high schools or when they made a transition into a large-scale school context.[6]

Limitations of the Baltimore Study

In attempting to ascertain whether the biological transition of puberty or the environmental discontinuity of the move into junior high school was responsible for self-image disturbance, we were frustrated by several limitations of the Baltimore study. First, it was a cross-sectional rather than longitudinal study. It compared Grade 6 to Grade 7 students, assuming no initial cohort differences; but cohort effects were certainly possible. Also without a longitudinal design, one cannot determine the number and type of children who change in a negative direction in these years—one can only compare resultant mean differences and distributions.

A second limitation of the Baltimore study (and of many prior studies) was the absence of an adequate measure of puberty. The individual's chronological age has been shown to be a poor indicator of physical development (see Tanner, 1962, 1971; Reynolds and Wines, 1948, 1951 Petersen and Taylor, 1980). Without a more direct indicator of pubertal change, it is impossible to understand the role of physical maturation.

A third limitation is that there was no comparison of types of schools in seventh grade; *all* seventh graders in Baltimore were attending junior high school, having moved from the protected elementary school. Ruth Benedict (1954) characterizes the transitions in modern Western society from childhood to adulthood as marked by great "discontinuity" of cultural expectations rather than by gradualism. The transition to junior high school appears to be an example of a sharp environmental "discontinuity". In Baltimore all children at this key point in the life cycle were subject to this discontinuity.

The Newer Milwaukee Study

The present study, which forms the core of this book, exhibits strengths that were missing in the original Baltimore research. It was designed specifically to overcome the limitations of the Baltimore survey. The study is longitudinal, not cross-sectional. It begins with a focus on the problematic transitional year at entry to adolescence. It first follows children from Grade 6 (the "last year of childhood") into Grade 7 (early adolescence), and then extensively remeasures them in Grades 9 and 10 (middle adolescence), thus covering a 5-year period. The short- as well as the long-term consequences of the transition into early adolescence, therefore, can be studied, including the transition into senior high school. In addition, the new study measured level and timing of pubertal development as carefully as possible within the constraints of school permission and the desire to avoid sample loss (see Chapter 2). Finally, in this study all children did not pass from elementary into junior high school in the key Grade 7 year. Milwaukee presented us with an excellent natural experiment. Side by side were two types of grade structure, with the schools roughly comparable in other respects (see Chapter 2). One type was the same as in Baltimore—children attended kindergarten to sixth grade in one school, switched to junior high school in Grade 7 (7–9), and then switched again in Grade 10 to senior high school (Grades 10–12). The other grade structure was based on a kindergarten through eighth grade school (K–8). Children remained in the same small elementary school from kindergarten through eighth grade and made their first transition into a larger, more impersonal school in ninth grade, when they entered a 4-year senior high school.

A kindergarten through eighth grade school might be expected to present the child moving from sixth to seventh grade with a less sudden change, both in terms of the impersonality of the environment and in terms of others' expectations for adultlike behavior on the child's part. Thus, in Grade 7 (at the entry to early adolescence) we can compare children who have stayed within the same small, intimate school to children who have made a transition into a large, more impersonal junior high school environment.

The later transition into senior high school for the two groups can also be compared. For the K–8 cohort, the movement into senior high school was their first transition into a large, impersonal context and occurred at a later age than did the junior high cohort's first such transition. The key question is whether it is easier for children to make their first major move into a large organization at a later rather than earlier age. For the youth in the junior high school cohort, who had to make two important school transitions, we can investigate whether the second change was easier or harder than the first.

The presence of two parallel grade structures in the same community provides an excellent opportunity to study the short- and long-term effects of major environmental change at entry to adolescence. The ability to differentiate short- and long-term consequences of this transition helps us to avoid the assumption that exposure to a stressor has only negative consequences. Erikson (1959) hypothesizes that a search for identity through experimentation in adolescence is important for good mental health later on in the life cycle (also see Peskin and Livson, 1972). The rapid choice of a comfortable identity too early in life has been termed "identity foreclosure" and is expected to have detrimental consequences later in the life course. Similarly, successful coping with the stressors of adolescence may prepare one for stresses later in life better than absence of challenge (Elder, 1974; Meichenbaum, 1977). While we have not yet followed the subjects of the Milwaukee study into adulthood, we have followed them into middle adolescence. Therefore, we can see which youngsters most successfully make the transition into senior high school: those who had no earlier junior high school transition to make, those who coped successfully with an early transition, or those who coped unsuccessfully.

Thus, the new study corrects for limitations of the Baltimore research by providing the strengths of a longitudinal design, detailed measures of pubertal development, and the presence of two alternate organizational contexts for comparison. The focus of the book will be to investigate the impact of school context, pubertal timing, and gender upon children as they move from late childhood to early and middle adolescence.

Determinants of Social–Psychological Outcomes

Environmental Discontinuity as a Determinant

Discontinuity in General

In a classic article, Benedict (1954) characterizes adolescence in American society as an example of a maximally discontinuous status transition. According to her, societies vary in degree of congruity of expectations between childhood and adulthood (also see Mead, 1950). In some societies, the socialization for one age-graded status prepares one for the next. In other societies, the expectations for a later age-role conflict with those of an earlier one, with the consequence that the individual is ill prepared for the later role. In the United States, for example, the child is socialized to be nonresponsible, submissive, and asexual, while the adult is expected to be responsible, dominant, and sexually active. Benedict hypothesizes that where expectations are very different, where there are no clear, formal rites of passage or mechanisms to bridge the gap, and where there is a long and unclear time of transition, the situation will be particularly disturbing. All of these characteristics are viewed by Benedict as applying to American society, and hence adolescence in America is seen as a difficult transitional period.

In our view, the transition is not from childhood to adulthood but from the status of child to the status of adolescent (see Blyth, 1977). Furthermore, adolescence can be subdivided into early, middle, and late adolescence; we shall study the first two of these subperiods. In addition, we are interested in differences not among societies but *within* our society. We, thus, utilize the Benedict hypothesis to predict that youth who experience more discontinuity in environmental context will manifest greater disturbance (see Elder, 1968; Glaser and Strauss, 1971).

School Discontinuity

The average youth spends at least 7 hours of each weekday in school—approximately 40% of his or her waking weekday hours. Thus, there is every reason to expect the nature of this environmental or ecological context to be important to the individual's adjustment (Bronfenbrenner, 1970; Hill, 1973).[7] However, save for our own work, a newer study by Eccles, Midgley, and Adler (1984) and research in Great Britain (Rutter and Hersov, 1977; Rutler, Maughan, Mortimore, Ouston, with Smith, 1979)[8] little is known from large-scale studies about the effects of school discontinuities on children's reactions (see this volume, Chapters 7 and 12). The present study compares the effects of two types of school environments, involving different levels of continuity and discontinuity during the status transition into early adolescence. The K–8 school provides maximum continuity during the transition—the child moves from Grade 6 to Grade 7 in the same small, elementary school. In contrast, the K–6/junior high school arrangement presents considerable discontinuity.

For the K–8 youngsters, the major environmental discontinuity comes later in middle adolescence between Grades 8 and 9 when they move into senior high school. For most girls and a substantial proportion of boys, this switch comes after the biological changes of puberty. Also, *for most youngsters, it follows rather than coincides with the change in definition of self from a child to a teenager.* Therefore, since it coincides with fewer other changes and since the child is older and more mature, one might expect less negative reaction to this environmental discontinuity than to the earlier Grade 7 transition of other youngsters into a junior high school.

History of School Grade Structures

The exact point at which youngsters first move into secondary school, and hence into large organizational environments, has changed drastically in the United States over the last 50 years and also differs radically from society to society[9] (see Blyth, 1977; Blyth, Simmons, and Bush, 1978; Blyth and Karnes, 1981). In the United States from 1900 to 1970, there was a dramatic decrease in the number of traditional 4-year high schools and a marked increase in the number of junior high schools. In the past two decades there has been a new movement into a middle school system in which the switch to a new school often precedes adolescence—that is, it occurs in Grade 5 or 6 (see Lipsitz, 1977). Unfortunately, this study does not have a middle school comparison.

Timing of Pubertal Development as a Determinant

There is no uniform environmental signal, then, that one has passed into adolescence. Although some children transfer into secondary school at the beginning of their teenage years, others do not. Similarly, the biological signals of adolescence are only loosely correlated with age. The timing of pubertal development varies; there has been a long history of studies comparing early, middle, and late developers (see Stolz and Stolz, 1951; Jones and Mussen, 1958; Faust, 1960; Dwyer and Mayer, 1968; Jones, Bayley, MacFarlane, and Honzik, 1971; MacFarlane, 1971; Peskin and Livson, 1972; Clausen, 1975; Petersen and Taylor, 1980; Livson and Peskin, 1980; Brooks-Gunn and Petersen, 1983).

The concept of asynchrony becomes relevant here (Eichorn, 1975; Blyth, Simmons, Bulcroft, Felt, Van Cleave, and Bush, 1981). For some youngsters, the level of pubertal development is average and typical for their age. Others are out of step, either earlier or later than most age peers or manifest a different pattern. This study also investigates the impact of different patterns of early, middle, and late development upon the student's reaction along a wide variety of dependent variables. We shall investigate whether pubertal change itself is stressful or beneficial, whether being different from peers leads to disturbance, whether early or late timing causes difficulty, and whether having attained puberty leads to different expectations from others and different levels of independent behavior for oneself.

Pubertal change, then, is not regarded as a simple biological phenomenon in its impact. It is also a process with a social meaning that mediates its effect. Not only is recency of change an issue, but also whether one is changing earlier, later, or at the same time as one's peers (Petersen and Taylor, 1980).

Gender

In this study, the effects of gender will be investigated as well as the effects of environmental discontinuity and pubertal timing. The classic studies that have explored the impact of pubertal timing, that is, the California longitudinal studies (Jones and Mussen, 1958; Jones et al., 1971; MacFarlane, 1971; Peskin and Livson, 1972; Clausen, 1975) and the Fels research (Kagan and Moss, 1962) indicate that boys and girls react differently to pubertal changes (see Hill and Lynch, 1983). The Baltimore study of Simmons et al. (1973) discussed earlier, also emphasizes the importance of gender differences. At issue in the current research, then, is the differential reaction of boys and girls to entry to adolescence. The first question to be investigated is whether girls are more vulnerable, that is, more likely to react negatively at this age, as suggested by the Baltimore survey. Other gender-specific responses will also be explored, as will the differences between boys and girls in their particular reaction to school and pubertal changes.

Part II of this book will deal with gender differences along all our outcome variables. Attention will focus on the extent to which boys and girls differ at this age, in general, and whether they change differentially as they move into adolescence. Part III will examine the effects of pubertal development for each gender, and Part IV will focus on the consequences of the two school types for each gender.

We now turn to a discussion of the dependent variables to be used in this study.

Outcome Variables

In terms of the outcome or dependent variables, the earlier Baltimore study concentrated on the self-image, in general, and self-esteem, in particular (Rosenberg and Simmons, 1972; Simmons, 1978; Simmons and F. Rosenberg, 1975). While the self-image is still of major concern in this new study and while self-esteem is considered of prime importance, many other dependent variables have been added as well. The aim is to investigate consequences of school environment and timing of pubertal development upon a wide set of outcome variables related to significant developmental tasks for adolescents. According to Havighurst (1953, p. 2) an individual developmental task is one "which arises at or about a certain period in the life of an individual, successful achievement of which leads to his happiness and to success with later tasks, while failure leads to unhappiness in the individual, disapproval by the society, and difficulty with later tasks." Table 1.1 lists the outcome variables and classifies them according to the "developmental tasks" of adolescence (Havighurst, 1953; Aldous, 1978).

TABLE 1.1. Dependent Variables—Tasks of Adolescence

1. **Establish Self-Image**

   A. *Global self-image*
      Self-esteem
      Self-consciousness
      Self-stability

   B. *Body-image*
      Perceive self as good looking
      Satisfaction with looks
      Satisfaction with weight
      Satisfaction with height
      Satisfaction with figure/muscles

   C. *Concern with body-image*
      Care about looks
      Care about weight
      Care about height
      Care about figure/muscle development

   D. *Perceived self-competence*
      Intelligence
      School work
      Athletic ability

   E. *Concern with competence*
      Value competence more than popularity and independence
      Care about intelligence
      Care about school work
      Care about athletic ability
      Care about independence from parents

   F. *Perceptions of gender role*
      Positive feelings about being a girl/boy
      Care about not acting like the opposite sex
      How often act like the opposite sex

   G. *Self-perception of depressive affect*

(*Continued*)

TABLE 1.1. *(Continued)*

2. **Intensifying Peer Relationships**

A. *Peer popularity*
Same sex
Opposite sex

B. *Value popularity*
Care about same sex
Care about opposite sex
Value popularity more than competence or independence
Value opposite sex popularity more than competence

C. *Dating behavior*

D. *Others' expectations regarding opposite sex relationships*
Parents expect dating
Same sex friends expect dating
Parents expect interest in opposite sex
Same sex peers expect interest in opposite sex

E. *Participation in activities*
Total in-school clubs and sports
Total out-of-school clubs and sports
Coed clubs (in and out of school)
Leadership in clubs and sports

3. **Establish Independence**

A. *Independence from parents*
Take bus without adult
Go places without parents permission
Parents' permission not required after dark
Left home alone
Times per month baby-sit
Part-time job
Perceived independence from parents
Decision making

B. *Perception that others expect older behavior*
Parents
Friends
Teachers

C. *Concern with independence*
Care about independence
Value independence more than competence or popularity

4. **Plan for Future**

A. *Educational, occupational, and marital aspirations*
Plan to go to college
Want to get married
Want to have children
SES of ideal job
SES of expected job
Expect to work regardless of family

B. *Perception that others expect career planning*
Parents
Teachers
Friends

TABLE 1.1. *(Continued)*

5. **Deal with Conformity/Deviance Issues**
   A. *Problem behavior*
   Problem behavior scale
   Probations/suspensions
   Truancy
   B. *Victimization*
   C. *Academic performance*
   GPA
   Reading achievement score
   Math achievement score
   D. *Perception that adults evaluate one highly*
   Parents
   Teachers
   E. *Perception of parent–peer relationship*
   Parents like close friends
   Close friends like parents

1. Achieving a New Self-Image

A primary task of early and middle adolescence is to achieve a new and positive sense of self in response to the many changes that occur at that age (Aldous, 1978). Perhaps most dramatic are the biological changes and the alterations in physical appearance that require a change in the *body image* and in the relevant self-evaluations. At a more global or general level, the adolescent should develop a new acceptance of the self as a person of worth (Aldous, 1978), that is, a favorable level of *self-esteem.* In addition, in Erikson's classic conception (1968), adolescence is a time to experiment with possible identities and ultimately to achieve a *stable,* specific picture of the self. It is also a time when *gender role identities* may assume increasing and changing importance and when the values one holds for oneself may be altered. The process of accomplishing this task of achieving a new self-image may be a difficult one; and, with these dependent variables, we attempt to measure the level of difficulty.

Not only may individuals develop low self-evaluations in the areas listed in Table 1.1 and show low stability of the self-picture, but they may also find that their changing view of themselves and their concern over others' opinions intrude on normal interaction and render them uncomfortably *self-conscious.* In sum, this study investigates whether environmental transitions and pubertal change affect the accomplishment of the tasks involving various aspects of the self-picture. It also explores the extent to which there are self-image problems in these regards in early and middle adolescence (see Rosenberg, 1965, 1979 and Rosenberg and Simmons, 1972 for a more detailed discussion of the dimensions of the self-image; also see this volume, Chapter 3).

2. Intensifying Peer Relationships

A second, major task of adolescence is to intensify intimate relations with peers and to learn to relate in new ways to members of the opposite sex, so that at a later age the individual will be emotionally prepared to leave his or her family of origin and set up a new family of procreation (Havighurst, 1953; Douvan and Adelson, 1966; Douvan and Gold, 1966; Berndt, 1982). Several related dependent variables are included: perceived peer popularity with the same and the opposite sex, valuation of peer popularity, dating behavior, participation in extracurricular activities, and perception of others' expectations concerning the opposite sex.

3. Establishing Independence

The adolescent has the task of developing independence (Douvan and Adelson, 1966; Aldous, 1978). Typically, at the beginning of adolescence, children are physically and emotionally dependent upon their parents, but by the end of adolescence they are capable of leaving their family of orientation and assuming responsibility for self and others. Subjects were asked whether their parents allow them to engage in a variety of independent behaviors, how highly they themselves value independence, and about relevant changes in the expectations of significant others (parents, friends, teachers).

4. Planning for Future

The pressure upon adolescents to make vital career and mate decisions is viewed by Erikson (1959) as part of the reason for their identity crisis. However, the need to select and prepare for a career and to begin plans for a family of one's own are more appropriately considered tasks of late adolescence rather than of the early and middle adolescent years being studied here. Nevertheless, young adolescents do begin to formulate aspirations in these regards; these aspirations are, therefore, measured. The extent to which significant others are applying pressure to begin occupational planning is also investigated.

5. Dealing with Conformity versus Deviance Issues

As a result of new levels of independence and as part of adolescent exploration and/or rebellion, the teenager has a much greater opportunity than before to engage in deviant behavior. A final task, or more accurately a final problem, results from this situation. The adolescent is confronted with adult pressure to conform to rules while also having to deal with peer and perhaps internal pressure to violate those rules (see Aldous, 1978). He or she may choose to strive for academic success or instead to engage in problematic or delinquent behavior in the school setting (see Jessor

and Jessor, 1977). Therefore, we have measured students' reported involvement in problem behavior in school, either as victims or perpetrators, their academic conformity as indexed by objective indicators of achievement (GPA, achievement tests), their perception of how highly key adult authority-figures (parents and teachers) evaluate them, and the extent to which they perceive parents and peers in conflict. It should be noted that while all of the variables placed in this "conformity/deviance" category have relevance for the underlying issue, the relevance is, in certain cases, somewhat loose. While GPA and achievement test scores can be studied as indicators of academic conformity, they also can be studied on their own right apart from this connection. Similarly, the opinions parents and teachers hold of the child are determined by and have consequences for many factors besides his or her conformity behavior.

Thus, this last task category is used more for convenience of organization than because of logical tightness. Nevertheless, these issues are highly relevant to the adolescent's life experience. Clearly, an investigation of the major consequences of environmental transition and pubertal change should deal with their impact upon problem behavior, academic performance, and parental and teacher evaluations. Findings for each of these key, but related, areas will be presented separately.

Summary

In summary, this study will follow students as they make a major life course transition from childhood into early adolescence. We will investigate the impact of timing of pubertal change and also the movement from an intimate, elementary school context into a large-scale secondary school environment. The first major movement into a large-scale organizational context may cause difficulty for the child, as may the dramatic changes of puberty. In addition, gender differences and changes in gender differences will be studied. Both short- and long-term consequences of transition will be of issue, since the students are followed for 5 years into middle adolescence. Consequences of the transition into senior high school will also be investigated.

Whether or not this newer study (1974–1979) replicates the earlier Baltimore study (1968) is of prime relevance. The Baltimore study suggests that early adolescence presents a disturbance for the self-image, that girls are more vulnerable than boys to this transition, and that a discontinuous change of environmental context into a junior high school may be responsible, in part, for negative effects. With an improved design this new study investigates consequences of gender, school context, and pubertal development upon a wide variety of dependent variables involving tasks of adolescence: (1) the need to form a new self-image; (2) to intensify peer relationships; (3) to establish independence; (4) to plan for the future; and (5) to deal with conformity versus deviance issues.

Footnotes

[1]See Kohlberg and Gilligan (1971) for other discussions of cognitive processes in adolescence compared to childhood. Also see the issue of *Daedalus* Vol. 100 (Fall 1971) for other general discussions of early adolescence.

[2]See Friedenberg (1959), Hamburg (1974), and Lipsitz (1977) for other discussions of the turmoil of adolescence. Also Hathaway and Monachesi (1963) show adolescents less likely to score "normal" on the MMPI than adults and more likely to show sociopathy or psychotic profiles (although less likely to show neurotic profiles).

[3]Also see Engel (1959), Long, Ziller, and Henderson (1968), Kaplan (1975). Hulbary (1975) and Bohan (1973) show contradictory results in cross-sectional studies.

[4]While Protinsky and Farrier (1980) show no age differences in self-esteem, they do show an increase in negative self-consciousness between childhood and early adolescence. Bohan (1973) shows a decline in self-esteem for girls but not boys after childhood. For Monge (1973), Dusek and Flaherty (1981), and Harter (1982), results are also mixed. Bowman (1974), however, shows an increase in self-esteem in his longitudinal (though not cross-sectional) samples as they move from Grades 4 and 6 to Grades 6 and 8.

[5]These findings replicated for black and white students and middle and working class (see Simmons *et al.,* 1973, Table 4). Offer *et al.* (1981) suggest that our results hold only for black and working-class youngsters; this appears to be a mistaken conclusion of some sort.

[6]Katz and Zigler (1967), who show a drop in self-image after Grade 5, conducted their study in elementary, and junior and senior high schools, as did Long *et al.* (1968) and Eccles *et al.* (1983, 1984). It also should be mentioned that very few relevant studies were conducted in large American cities: Soares and Soares (1970) research may have been so located; Attenborough and Zdep (1973) used a national, household sample. Eccles *et al.* (1983, 1984) studied the total population of two school districts in southeast Michigan. In a doctoral dissertation, Reid (1983) compared children from a seven-county metropolitan area who made a transition out of elementary school in either Grade 5, 6, or 7, with mixed results. In Grade 6 students in secondary schools had lower self-esteem than those in elementary school, but there was no difference in Grade 5 or 7. However, Grade 8 students, who had made an early transition (Grade 5 or 6) into middle school, had higher self-esteem than those who had made a Grade 7 transition into junior high school. If the middle schools were smaller and less impersonal than the junior high schools, these results would be compatible with our findings of higher self-esteem in small, elementary schools than in large junior high schools. However, no detail is given about school size.

[7]Smaller clinical studies document difficulties of transition in Great Britain on types of adjustment (see Hersov, 1960). Also see Metcalfe (1981) for a small, quantitative study and Reid (1983) for a larger, unpublished work. For discussions of the transitions into secondary school in Great Britain, see Nisbet and Entwistle (1966), and for discussion of the junior high school transition in the United States, see Hamburg (1974), Berkovitz (1979), and Lipsitz (1977).

[8]For studies investigating various aspects of school environments, see McDill and Rigsby (1973), Heyns (1978), Brookover, Beady, Flood, Schweitzer, and Wisenbaker (1979), Rutter *et al.* (1979), Epstein and McPartland (1976, 1979), Epstein and Karweit (1983), Gottfredson and Daiger (1979), Gottfredson, Joffe, and Gottfredson (1981), Lipsitz (1977), Hindelang and McDermott (1977), Moos (1978), Coleman, Campbell, Hobson, McPartland, Mood, Weinfeld, and York (1966),

Coleman, Hoffer, and Kilgore (1982), Eccles (1984), Reuman (1984), Feldlaufer (1984), and Midgley (1984). For discussion in this area, see Kelly (1968) and Schmiedeck (1979). For reviews of differences in the effects of middle versus junior high schools and of other school organizations, see Schonhaut (1967), Gatewood (1971), Lipsitz (1977), Blyth and Karnes (1981), and Educational Research Service (1983).

[9]For a discussion of cross-cultural differences, see Nisbet and Entwistle (1966); Rutter (1979); and Garnier and Hout (1981).

2

METHODS

Overview

The present study is based on a natural experiment in the Milwaukee public schools. The system is organized so that two structures or grade-level arrangements exist side by side. Some children attend a kindergarten through eighth grade school (K–8) and move into a 4-year senior high school in Grade 9, while other children attend kindergarten through sixth grade school (K–6) and make a first transition into a 3-year junior high school in Grade 7 and a second transition into a 3-year senior high school in Grade 10. Our research design is intended to take advantage of this natural arrangement, while considering the many factors that might interfere with appropriate comparisons. The situation in Milwaukee has provided the opportunity to study the natural ecology of early adolescence in two quite different school environments. Since it is not likely that one could experimentally manipulate and artificially create major change points in the lives of large numbers of children, this natural quasi-experimental design seemed optimal.

The study was conducted between 1974 and 1979 and had two major phases. The first phase examined the transition from late childhood into early adolescence using a 2-year longitudinal design. Students were followed from sixth grade in elementary school into the two types of contrasting seventh grade settings. After the original phase was completed, there was a brief interim in eighth grade where we simply maintained contact with subjects and continued collecting key physical measures. The second phase of the study, which took place over a 2-year period (ninth and tenth grade), was designed to study the transition into senior high school and to contrast the effects of a double transition in school environment versus a single change in school environments; that is, to contrast students who experienced both a junior and senior high transition to those who moved directly from elementary school to senior high school. This second phase also permitted the assessment of longer term effects— that is, whether students who had difficulty during the entry into adolescence in Grades 6–7 experienced continued problems in later years or managed to recover a year or two after the transition. Thus the entire study is a 5-year longitudinal design with major measurement points in sixth and seventh grade in 1974–1976 and then again in the second phase in Grades 9 and 10 in 1978–1979. Each of these phases of the research will be described later in this chapter along with the sampling design used.

Exploratory Nature of the Project

To understand the present study it is important to realize the exploratory nature of the work in early adolescence which was being undertaken in the mid-1970s. While research in early adolescence was beginning to increase, there was relatively little large-scale systematic work being done based on random samples. This study was specifically designed to follow up on the key findings of the earlier Baltimore study (Simmons *et al.*, 1973), particularly the effect of school transitions and pubertal changes on the development of the self-image. In addition, the current research expands upon the earlier work by investigating effects of transition and change upon other tasks of adolescence as well as upon the establishment of a new self-image.

This exploratory framework led to the creation of wide ranging, multi-topic survey interviews with students. While the self-image was investigated in some depth, we aimed for breadth of coverage for most other outcome areas. The object has been to examine the effects of major social and biological changes across areas that had been neglected in much of the previous work.

The exploratory nature of the work also affects the type of analytic approach that will be used. While theory and speculation suggested that school transitions and pubertal changes would have multiple impacts on early adolescents, we were not sure what dimensions would be affected or how strong such effects might be. Therefore, in order not to overlook potential impacts (a type 2 error), we elected to use a strategy with a generous level of significance (.10 level). We have tempered this strategy both by an awareness that some statistically significant results may not be substantively meaningful and by a focus on patterns of results rather than individual tests. Furthermore, in major analyses, in order to avoid exaggerating statistical significance, we have used Multivariate Analysis of Variance (MANOVAs) to investigate clusters of variables and Repeated Measures Analyses of Variance to inspect findings over time before running individual tests. In all cases we have tried to provide complete information so that the reader who wishes to impose a stricter standard may do so. In general, however, the exploratory mode has rendered us generous. Because of this orientation, patterns of negative findings (or the lack of an impact) have to be taken very seriously.

The First Phase:
From Late Childhood to Early Adolescence

The particular status transition studied in the first phase involves the move from late childhood into early adolescence. The research was designed to capture a reading of the psychosocial location of the children as they ended childhood (around sixth grade) and then again as they began adolescence. In actuality, there is no exact transition point between childhood and adolescence. The entry to adolescence in our society is ambiguous and some investigators recognizing early biological changes have placed onset as young as age 10. However, as sociologists we have chosen to emphasize social definitions; and, in that respect adolescence has started at least by the teen years and Grade 7.[1] At around this age the individual assumes a new status, one that is often described in terms of what it is not. The individual is no longer a child but not yet an adult. This transition into adolescence needs to be viewed both as role change and role acquisition—a process of becoming rather than a major leap between two quite different statuses. The degree of continuity or discontinuity in this process under different degrees of environmental continuity is what is under investigation. It is important to emphasize that we are studying the process of becoming an adolescent. This point is important since much early research has concentrated on individuals who are clearly adolescents (usually high school students) or in the process of becoming an adult (i.e., college students making the transition out of adolescence).

In this section we shall briefly describe the rationale and procedure used in selecting the original sample for the study, the site of the study, and some of the general characteristics of the sample. This discussion will be followed by a brief description of the characteristics of the schools involved and an analysis of the initial sample attrition.

Initial Design

In the Milwaukee Public Schools the official change from elementary to secondary schooling occurs between the sixth and seventh grades regardless of the type of school.[2] Figure 2.1 indicates the two types of school structures that we will compare. The first column in the figure presents the widely used pattern of grade level organization often known as the 6-3-3 plan. As noted previously, it involves spending 6 years in an elementary school, 3 years in a separate junior high school, and finally, transition into a final 3-year senior high school. Students in a 6-3-3 system begin their secondary school career in a totally new and, as we shall see, a very different type of school. The shift from being a sixth grader in a K–6 elementary school to a seventh grader in a 7–9 junior high school represents

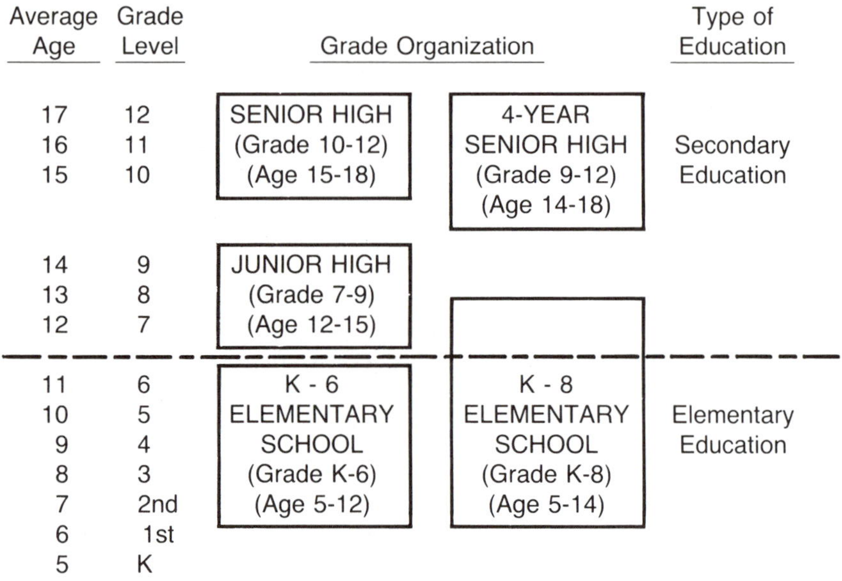

Average Age	Grade Level	Grade Organization		Type of Education
17	12	SENIOR HIGH (Grade 10-12) (Age 15-18)	4-YEAR SENIOR HIGH (Grade 9-12) (Age 14-18)	Secondary Education
16	11			
15	10			
14	9	JUNIOR HIGH (Grade 7-9) (Age 12-15)		
13	8			
12	7			
11	6	K - 6 ELEMENTARY SCHOOL (Grade K-6) (Age 5-12)	K - 8 ELEMENTARY SCHOOL (Grade K-8) (Age 5-14)	Elementary Education
10	5			
9	4			
8	3			
7	2nd			
6	1st			
5	K			

FIGURE 2.1. The two educational contexts under study in Milwaukee, Wisconsin.

a more discontinuous and less gradual change into secondary education and into early adolescence.

The school structure indicated by the second column in Fig. 2.1 is similar to the traditional 8-4 system popular during most of the first half of this century in the United States (see Blyth and Karnes, 1981). Since K–8 students stay within the same school in Grades 6 and 7, their educational environment during the transition into adolescence can be thought of as relatively more continuous than that of the students in a 6-3-3 pattern. Change is more gradual, less abrupt. Exactly how gradual and continuous, however, is an empirical question.

The same students were interviewed once in sixth grade and once in seventh grade in order to provide longitudinal data on the effects of the two grade-level arrangements. Ideally, of course, one would like to randomly assign students to the two different types of school contexts in order to ensure optimal comparability. In practice, such a course is not feasible. The quasi-experimental design possible in Milwaukee was the next best alternative.

The Urban Context of the Study

With a city population in 1970 of over 717,000 in an urban area (SMSA) approaching 1.5 million, the city of Milwaukee is the largest metropolitan and industrial area in Wisconsin and the twelfth largest city in the country.

According to 1970 Census figures, just over 77% of the population are native-born Americans with much of the remaining 23% coming from a range of European backgrounds (most notably German and Polish). The racial composition of the city at the beginning of the 1970s was predominantly white (84.4%), with a significant black population (14.7%) but a relatively small Spanish-speaking community (2.2%). These figures had changed by the 1980 census such that almost one-fourth of the population of the city was black (23.1%). The increase in the Spanish-speaking population of the city was less than 1%.

The Milwaukee Public Schools operated 120 elementary schools, 22 junior high schools, and 15 senior high schools in the mid-1970s and faced both declining enrollments and the issue of desegregation. Approximately 38% of the student population was black in 1974. A court-ordered desegregation plan with extensive busing was being developed during most of the first phase of the study but was not implemented until the interim period (when most subjects were in eighth grade). The public schools within the city ranged from large, older two-story buildings to modern one-story buildings and were in communities that ran from ghettolike high crime areas to more suburbanlike areas.

In summary, the research sites for the present study were representative of public schools within a large Midwestern city during the mid-1970s. The next section describes the selection of the initial sample of schools and students.

Rationale for and Selection of Sample Schools

The first step in the sampling procedure was to define the population of elementary schools from which subjects would then be selected. All public schools containing sixth graders within Milwaukee were classified as being either (1) a K–8 school (7%), (2) a K–6 school that explicitly fed into a 7–9 junior high school (74%), or (3) any of a set of other, idiosyncratic school types for sixth graders (19%) (see Table 2.1).[3]

Since all K–8 schools, but not all K–6 schools, were predominantly white, we stratified the schools in the population on the basis of the percentage of minority students in the school. Three broad classes of schools were defined: those with 0–20% minority, those with 21–42%, and those with 43–100% minority students (all of the latter schools were K–6 schools; see Table 2.1). The cutoff points selected represented major break points in the distribution. The size of the sixth grade class in 1973 was used as a second stratifying variable in selecting schools.

Principals at all seven K–8 schools were asked to participate; only one school principal refused to grant permission. A constrained, stratified random sample of K–6 schools was chosen from each of the other categories noted.[4] Two principals of the selected comparable K–6 schools also refused, and new schools were randomly drawn. In addition, one K–6 school

TABLE 2.1. The Process of Selecting Sample Schools

	K-8 grade schools feeding into 4-year high schools[a] percentage minority			K-6 grade schools feeding into 3-year junior high schools[a] percentage minority		
	0–20	21–42	43–100	0–20	21–42	43–100[c]
Schools meeting eligibility criteria[b]	5	2	None	46	3	19
Schools selected for study	4	2	None	6	2	4
Number of students in sixth grade	263	87		403	72	296
Number of students interviewed	231	66		352	54	22
Percentage of students who participated	88	76		87	75	75

[a]For the 116 Milwaukee public schools in Grade 6; 7% were K-8, 74% were K-6, and 19% were miscellaneous school types. Students were not selected from the miscellaneous school types since they represent a variety of idiosyncratic grade level patterns and/or feed into nonstandard schools.

[b]To be considered eligible, schools had to be clearly of one of the two grade level patterns noted and not have a heavy concentration of Spanish-speaking students.

[c]None of the students from this set of schools will be used in the current analyses since there are no comparable heavily black K–8 schools.

was randomly replaced because the junior high school it fed into was unwilling to participate in the study. Altogether 18 schools were included in the final sample: six K–8 schools, eight comparable K–6 schools, and four predominantly black K–6 schools (see Row 2 in Table 2.1).

The Sample of Students

Every sixth grade student in each of the sampled schools was invited to participate; thus every student *within* each stratum of the sample had an equal probability of being selected.

The percentage of students who actually participated did not differ by type of school. Signed parent consent was secured for 85% of the students in the K–8 and *comparable* K–6 schools, and these children were interviewed in the sixth grade. The response rate thus was very good. No rejections came from the students themselves once parental permission was obtained.

Table 2.1 (bottom two rows) presents a brief summary of number and percentage of students who were actually interviewed *while in sixth grade*. There were 924 students in the total sample in Grade 6, 703 of whom were from K–8 and comparable K–6 schools. Of these, 621 (88%) were white. For purposes of this book, the small number of black students in comparable types of schools made it necessary to limit analyses to only white students. Earlier publications have dealt with black–white differences in key areas (Simmons, 1978; Simmons, Brown, Bush, and Blyth, 1978). All subjects for this book, then, are white and come from sixth grade schools which could be expected to have a majority of white students.

Issues of Comparability and Representativeness

In order to claim that differences between children in K–8 and K–6 schools reflect differential reactions to school transitions rather than initial differences, we searched for possible initial demographic differences in the selected school *populations* using school records and census data. There were virtually no differences between the K–8 and comparable K–6 schools on a variety of characteristics (see Table 2.2). This lack of difference between school types, while not guaranteeing the comparability of the students, does provide evidence that the students should be as similar as possible given the fact that schools and not individual students had to be sampled. The students in both school types come from socioecon-

TABLE 2.2. Comparison of Sampled K-6 to K-8 Schools

Social characteristics	Totals	
	K-8	Comparable K-6 sample
Mean % minority	18.5	15.0
Range of % minority	2–38	0–41
Mean of median family income ($)[a]	11,267	11,213
Achievement[b]		
% Scoring below average	35.2	29.4
% Scoring above average	16.7	14.3
Mean % mobility[c]	20.7	24.9
Mean % children above age for grade	22.5	16.3
Mean number of sixth graders[d]	59.0	59.1
Mean % of teachers		
with B.A.	69.5	76.6
with only 1 year experience	10.8	3.6
Number of schools	6	8

[a]The median family income was obtained from the 1970 U.S. Census Reports and is based on the census tract within which the school was located.

[b]Achievement is measured by the percentile rank on the Composite Test of the Iowa Tests of Basic Skills. The group scoring below average is made up of those children whose percentile was less than 23. Those scoring above the seventy-seventh percentile were defined as above average.

[c]This is the percentage of students who either move into or out of the school during the school year.

[d]The value for one of the comparable K–6 schools is based on fifth grade figures for the 1973-1974 school year, since sixth grade figures are unavailable.

omically diverse populations.[5] This factor should be noted since wider generalizability of the findings is therefore permitted; certain other important, recent studies concentrate on more middle-class samples (Petersen, Schulenberg, Abramowitz, Offer, and Jarchow, 1984; Blyth *et al.*, 1981).

Once students were interviewed it was possible to compare the socioeconomic backgrounds and parents' marital status of the *sampled* students in each of the two environments (see Table 2.3). The overwhelming impression is one of remarkable similarity. The students in the K-6 schools are not statistically different from those students in K-8 schools in terms of occupational status, mother's and father's educational levels, and parents' marital status.

Our original sample is also quite representative of the population from which it was drawn. Overall we had permission from 82% of the parents to participate in the study (85% in the comparable school types used for this book). Still some selection bias is possible. Fortunately, data were

TABLE 2.3. Description of Comparable White Samples in Terms of Parents' Marital Status, Occupational Status of Head of Household, and Mother's and Father's Level of Education

Parameter	K-8	Comparable K-6	Total
Marital status			
Married	76.7%	76.1%	76.4%
Separated	1.6	2.6	2.2
Divorced	16.5	17.2	16.9
One or both parents deceased	5.2	4.1	4.6
N	(249)	(343)	(592)
Occupation of head of household			
Semi or unskilled labor	21.7%	27.1%	24.8%
Skilled labor	34.0	36.3	35.4
Lower white-collar job	25.1	28.6	27.1
Upper white-collar job	19.1	8.0	12.7
N	(235)	(325)	(560)
Father's education			
Less than high school diploma	6.7%	12.0%	9.8%
High school diploma	43.3	43.8	43.6
Business or technical school	12.2	18.5	15.9
College	25.0	21.7	23.1
Professional or graduate school	12.8	4.0	7.7
N	(180)	(249)	(429)
Mother's education			
Less than high school diploma	5.7%	12.5%	9.6%
High school diploma	55.5	56.4	56.0
Business or technical school	9.0	9.8	9.4
College	22.7	19.5	20.9
Professional or graduate school	7.1	1.7	4.0
N	(211)	(287)	(498)

TABLE 2.4. Comparison of Sample Students with Nonsample Students on
GPA, Days in Attendance, and Standardized Achievement Tests

	Population[a] mean (Standard Deviation)	Sample mean (N)	Nonsample mean (N)	Significance of difference between sample and nonsample
GPA	2.44 (.85)	2.45 (686)	2.34 (133)	(ns)
Number of days in attendance	162.4 (20.1)	164.0 (686)	153.8 (133)	(p < .001)
Achievement[b] scores				
Vocabulary	45.1 (27.0)	46.6 (680)	37.1 (143)	(p < .001)
Reading	40.7 (26.6)	41.7 (680)	34.6 (143)	(p < .01)
Arithmetic	37.0 (31.7)	38.0 (680)	31.0 (143)	(p < .01)

[a]Includes all students (white and minority) in sampled K–8 and comparable K–6 schools with less than 43% minority youth.
[b]Mean percentile score on particular subtests of the Iowa Tests of Basic Skills.

available on certain academic and achievement variables for all students (even those who refused to participate). A comparison of the sample of students who participated to the population from which it was drawn indicates that there are only very slight differences (see Table 2.4). A statistical comparison (using t-tests) between those in the study and those without parental permission indicates no significant differences in GPA but significantly greater standardized achievement scores and more days in school for those in the study. These differences are in the direction one would expect. More important, from our perspective, is the close extent to which the final sample means corresponded to the population means. Thus, while every sample has some biases, this particular sample appears representative in most dimensions, and the known biases appear relatively minor. The overall representativeness and diversity of the original sample is one of the particular strengths of the study.

In summary, a sample of students was selected which is (1) reasonably representative of the population in Milwaukee, a large urban–metropolitan area, and (2) is optimally comparable between the two kinds of school structures which are under study. As in any natural experiment, one can neither control all extraneous variables nor claim that there are no initial differences. However, as far as we are able to determine, there are no major demographic differences between the sample of students who represent the K-8 cohort and the K-6/junior high school cohort.

The Nature of the School Settings

In this section we briefly describe some of the main characteristics of two types of schools in sixth and then in seventh grade.

For sixth grade students, the K-8 and K-6 schools were reasonably similar in overall size, the number of students per grade level, and the distribution of white and nonwhite students. In particular, both the K-8 schools and the K-6 schools had a population of between 300 and 700 pupils, with the K-8 schools being slightly larger because they housed more grade levels.

The school day within both the K-8 and K-6 schools was organized quite similarly. In general, most students stayed in one classroom for the majority of the day with one primary teacher. They moved for special classes, such as gym or music, but in virtually all cases, the same classmates remained together throughout the day.

In the second year of the study, when the students made the transition into seventh grade, we begin to see dramatic differences in the nature of the schools students attended. Students in the K-8 elementary schools remained in the same building they had been in for sixth grade; they simply moved into a new classroom with a new teacher. In general these students still stayed within a basic homeroom classroom, although they occasionally went to other parts of the building or even outside the building for a specialty class (e.g., industrial arts or home economics). In several of the K-8 schools the seventh and eighth grade classrooms tended to be at one end of the building somewhat separated from the rest of the elementary school. While some students from other schools transferred in for the seventh grade in the K-8 buildings, this was generally a small percentage, and the overall character of the seventh grade class would probably be changed relatively little, if at all.

By contrast, the other students in the study finished their elementary school years in sixth grade and made a major transition into a junior high school containing Grades 7, 8, and 9. As the seventh graders in junior high schools, these students were at the bottom of the totem pole or, to mix metaphors, small frogs in a much larger pond. The junior high schools ranged in size from 808 to 1590 students with somewhere between 200 and 500 students at the seventh grade level within each building. This size is in marked contrast to the elementary schools they had come from (357–632 students) and is larger than *any* of the K-8 schools (which ranged from 323 to 694). As one might expect, the very nature of the school environment and the general atmosphere of the school was dramatically different in these junior high schools from either of the elementary types of schools. The buildings contained only early adolescents and a much larger set of peers from more diverse parts of the city. The geographical catchment areas for the junior high schools were generally five to eight times larger than those for the elementary schools.[6] This change in size and diversity had the effect of making it very difficult for a student to become acquainted with the other students even in their own grade level. This is in direct contrast to the seventh graders in the K-8 schools who could be expected to be acquainted with most, if not all, of the other seventh and eighth graders in the building (see later Table 7.4).

In addition to the changes in the size of the schools there are also some differences between the K-8 schools and the junior high schools in terms of the amount of movement and the general organization of the day. While the K-8 schools still tended to keep students in a self-contained classroom almost all of the day, two of them were somewhat departmentalized with a separate class for each period. By contrast, virtually none of the junior high schools had a primary teacher for the entire day. Rather, students were moved from one class to another throughout the day in a departmentmentalized system. Occasionally, the junior high schools would keep the same classmates together and send them as a unit to different teachers. In many cases in the junior high schools, however, both the students and the teachers would change from one period to the next.

In summary, as intended, the seventh graders in our study were in two quite different environments. The K-8 students were in environments of small size that were essentially identical to the ones they had been in the year before. By contrast, the students who had left the K-6 schools and entered the much larger junior high schools experienced a dramatic change in the nature of their environments during the seventh grade year. The schools were larger, had more students in a given grade-level than one could reasonably be expected to know, and the movement during the day involved contact with more students and teachers. In terms of the natural experiment, the seventh grade students in the two comparable types of schools did indeed experience quite different ecological settings at entry to adolescence.

Sample Attrition within the First Phase

The very nature of the longitudinal experiment made it impossible to avoid sample attrition from sixth to seventh grade. Because of the natural experiment involved, we decided to follow only those students who entered a seventh grade class within the public schools of the city of Milwaukee. Students who moved out of state or moved to a suburban area of the greater metropolitan region were not interviewed, although we attempted to locate them for our records. For some of the analyses in this book 10 students were also eliminated because they did not go into the type of school that we anticipated in Grade 7 (e.g., a student in a K-8 school who transferred to a junior high school for seventh grade or a student in a K-

6 school who transferred into a K-8 school). Such students were interviewed and will be included in analyses of gender effects and pubertal
effects but will not be in those analyses that directly compare the effect
of one school environment to the other.[7] There are, of course, other situations in which cases are removed from certain analyses because of
missing data, most significantly students missing pubertal data cannot be
included in the puberty analysis. This problem will be noted when we
discuss the creation of the various pubertal measures to be used.

The seventh grade students who were actually reinterviewed in 1975–
1976 represented 89% of the original sixth grade sample (see Appendix
A). No subjects were lost due to parental or student refusal. While 6.6%
of the original sample was lost because they left the city of Milwaukee
or the public school system, another 3% was lost because they went to
Milwaukee schools where we were not permitted to work. Other students
were lost from analyses because they had failed or skipped a grade (0.8%).
A few additional students (0.6%) had left the Milwaukee public school
system and were no longer on the central computer list, but we were
unable to determine where they went.

Differences between those students who did remain in the sample for
seventh grade and those who were lost were not significant in terms of
gender, mean self-esteem, mean GPA, or mean math and reading achievement scores. However, subjects who were lost did tend to have marginally
lower socioeconomic status ($p < .10$), came from separated or divorced
homes ($p < .001$), and reported a higher level of problem behavior at
school during sixth grade ($p < .01$).[8]

In summary, the seventh grade sample overall appears to be reasonably
comparable to the sixth grade sample with relatively few biases having
been introduced. The biases are in the direction one would expect in terms
of lower socioeconomic status and more problematic families being less
likely to stay in the sample. Even these differences were relatively slight.
The overall attrition rate for these white subjects was only 11% so that
the vast majority of students studied in sixth grade were studied again in
seventh grade. Thus sample loss in Grade 7 was not great.

Insofar as possible, analysis throughout this book have been based on
the largest, most representative sample possible, given the years that were
being studied. Where differences in effects were found between the early
and later years of the study, the analysis was redone just for those students
who remained in the sample for the entire time (the "longitudinal sample")
in order to make certain that the early–late difference was not due to
differential dropout. In fact, insofar as possible, all analyses were run
both for the largest sample possible and for the "longitudinal sample."
Very few differences in conclusions emerge either in Grades 6–7 or in the
later phase to be discussed subsequently. Those few differences are re-

ported. In addition, as will be noted, key findings involving the effects of pubertal timing and school transition were checked to see if they persisted in the middle and working classes.[9]

The Interim Year—Eighth Grade

After early analyses of the Grades 6–7 data, the decision was made to pursue a longer term follow-up of these students and to investigate their transition into senior high school in middle adolescence. Full funding for data collection was obtained (from National Institute of Mental Health and The William T. Grant Foundation) in time to collect data in Grades 9 and 10. Grade 8 became an interim year in which children were tracked and data in physical development were still obtained.[10]

The only unfortunate aspect of the interim in eighth grade is that the transition from eighth grade into a 4-year high school for the K-8 cohort can not be studied as precisely as one might wish. Because we are missing eighth grade data it is not possible to do a "clean" before (Grade 8) and after (Grade 9) comparison for the K-8 students as they make the transition out of their unique elementary arrangement into the first year of a 4-year high school. However, Grades 6, 7, and 9 data are available and thus change can be partially estimated.

The Second Phase—Entry into Middle Adolescence

The second phase of the project was originally designed to answer three basic questions. The first question dealt with the extent to which the dramatic differences in seventh grade environments might have longer lasting effects on students. Was the disruption caused by the transition to a junior high school, for example, likely to have effects in the later years of the junior high school and even into the high school years?

The second question we wished to address was whether or not the impact of the first transition would either facilitate or aggravate the transition into high school. That is, does the fact that students have already made a transition to a junior high school make it easier or more difficult for them to make the next transition into the larger senior high schools within the city?

A third area of inquiry also included in Phase 2, involved the issue of the relative long- or short-term effects of early and late physical development. In particular, we were interested in whether or not those students who had experienced early physical maturation would be significantly different from their average or late-developing peers in the ninth and tenth grade when most of the major changes in physical development were well underway for all students.

In this section we shall briefly discuss the nature of the school environments during the ninth and tenth grade and then move on to note the level and causes of attrition in these years and resulting potential biases.

The School Environments in Phase 2

The sampled students generally attended one of two basic types of schools in ninth grade. The K-8 students had transferred into 4-year high schools that were much larger (ranging from 973 to 2654) than the elementary school environment they had experienced. In order to put this change in a comparative framework: the transition of the K-6 youngsters out of elementary school into the junior high school involved an increase in school size of roughly two and a half times while the K-8 students who moved into 4-year high schools experienced an increase in size of roughly three and a half. Many of these 4-year high schools were also larger than the 3-year junior high schools that the K-6/junior high group of students attended in ninth grade (which ranged from 906 to 1435), although there was considerable overlap in size (see later Table 7.4).

The transition into a 4-year high school for the K-8 cohort also involved a dramatic increase in the number of students at a given grade level, in the geographic diversity from within the city, and, for the first time, in racial diversity. In the 4-year high schools there were between 200 and 600 students at any given grade level, so that it now became impossible to know everyone at their own grade level, let alone everyone in the school. The percentage of minority students in the school also increased dramatically for most K-8 students. In many cases students went from attending a largely white or clearly majority white school to attending a desegregated school, and, in a few cases, students changed into a majority nonwhite school.

In contrast, the students who started out in K-6 schools and were now in the ninth grade of the junior high schools experienced little or no change in school environments between seventh and ninth grade. The school size was likely to be quite similar to what they had been experiencing since seventh grade, and the number of students per grade level was also roughly the same. Although some students experienced a marked increase in the percentage minority in their school due to desegregation, all but two students were in schools that had no more than 52% minority students. This proportion was roughly comparable to what they had experienced in seventh grade.

In addition to these fundamental differences and similarities in environments for the different types of students, it is also important to note that we now have an almost complete reversal of relative rank in school for students in the two types of cohorts. In ninth grade the K-8 students, now in senior high school, experienced what it was like to be the youngest grade in a much larger and older environment. The junior high school cohort, however, had become the oldest students in their schools—the "top dogs" in the environment. In summary, ninth grade is a dramatic year of change for the K-8 cohort, while it is one of relative stability and increasing prestige for the junior high school cohort.

The movement into tenth grade once again sees a major reversal. In tenth grade the K-8 cohort of students continue in the large 4-year high schools; they continue to be moved from class to class in a departmentalized structure. By contrast the junior high school cohort now experiences its second transition, the transition into a 3-year high school which is somewhat larger and only slightly more departmentalized than the junior high schools they had experienced from seventh through ninth grade.

The Nature and Effect of Sampling Attrition during the Second Phase

In Grades 9 and 10, once again most sample loss was due to the students' leaving the Milwaukee public school system; relatively little was due to withdrawal of consent. In order to deal with the increase in chronic truancy, we attempted in these years to interview chronic absentees at home or in a convenient place if we could not schedule an interview at school.

In the ninth grade 58% of the original sixth grade sample of students was reinterviewed (see Appendix A). The reason, in most cases, that children were not reinterviewed was because they left the Milwaukee public school system. Of the original sample, 19% were located as having left the school district; 4.5% were no longer listed on the school system computer, and we were not able to further locate them. A few students had died or were institutionalized (1.4%). Some students that were within the Milwaukee system were not able to be interviewed because of noncooperating schools (9.3%) or habitual absence and failure to complete a home interview (1.9%). A little over 3% of all the parents or students did not grant permission for the second phase of the project.

In tenth grade the attrition rate was less severe, and we interviewed 51% of the original sixth grade sample. Once again the reasons for loss were quite similar to previous years. (A more detailed breakdown of the reasons for sample loss each year can be found in Appendix A.)

In summary, the attrition problems in the ninth and tenth grade were more severe than they had been in the first phase of the study. It is likely that the increased departure of students from the city school district was related to the implementation of the desegregation plan during the eighth grade.

In addition, in seventh grade, some students went to a different type of school or changed junior high schools or K-8 schools during the course of the study. While these students remain in the analysis that involve gender and puberty effects, they are not included in analyses that focus on a comparison of the two school types at issue (see Chapters 7 and 8).[11]

If one compares the ninth and tenth grade samples with the original sixth grade sample, we see that the students who are lost by ninth grade are slightly more likely to be males ($p < .10$), to come from separated or divorced families ($p < .10$), and have lower grade point averages ($p < .05$). There were, however, no longer differences between those in the sample and those out of the sample in terms of the average reported problem behavior at school. Furthermore, the math and reading achievement scores still did not differ significantly for those in and out of the sample.[12] The socioeconomic status of the head of the household was now *not* statistically different for the two groups possibly because some of the higher SES families had left the school district.

In the tenth grade a similar comparison indicates that the sample we obtained was different from the sample that had been lost only in terms of the marital status of parents ($p < .001$), the average GPA ($p < .01$), and problem behavior at school reported by the youths ($p < .05$). These biases were the same as those seen earlier in the study. In no case were the differences between the sample and nonsample particularly dramatic. The biggest difference was in marital status where 25% of the sample that had been lost came from divorced or separated parents as opposed to only 15% of those students that were reinterviewed in the tenth grade.

As indicated previously, analyses involving early years have been run both for the students who remain all 4 years in the study and for the larger group that is present at the relevant early time period. The few differences in conclusions that occur are reported. Some relevant analyses also control for social class and the Grade 6 score on key outcome variables (such as GPA and problem behavior).[13]

The Nature and Timing of Measurements

The major source of information in this study comes from face to face interviews with the adolescents. In the following sections we briefly comment on the nature of the adolescent interviews and other data sources that were used in this project. The measures of physical development will be discussed more extensively subsequently.

The Adolescent Interviews

The private interviews with adolescents were conducted in school during the course of the regular school day by professionally trained interviewers from the University of Wisconsin Survey Research Laboratory.

Fall and Spring Samples

Because it was considered likely that reactions to a transition may be greater in the first few months of a school year than at the end of the school year in Grade 6 and 7, the sample was essentially randomly divided so that roughly 50% of the students in a school would be interviewed in the fall (late October and November), and the other 50% would be interviewed in the early spring (March and April). In the later years of the study (Grades 9 and 10) the interview data were collected only in the spring of the year. This was the result of analyses that indicated the differences between the fall and spring samples in the early years did not justify the continued splitting of the sample (see Chapters 7 and 8).

Other Data Sources

In addition to interviewing each of the students in the schools, we also interviewed the principals of the schools in the sixth, seventh, and tenth grades in order to get a more direct understanding of the nature of the schools, school policies, and the comparability of schools.

It was possible with both parental and school district permission to have access to the course grades and achievement data that the school district collected systematically.

The standardized achievement test scores that were administered by the district changed during the course of our study. In each of the 3 years (Grades 6, 7, and 10), different achievement tests were administered to our students—in Grade 6: the Iowa Tests of Basic Skills (ITBS); in Grade 7: the Metropolitan Achievement Tests (MAT); and in Grade 10: Tests of Academic Skills (TASK). Each of these tests contains both reading and mathematic sections.

The tests are not equivalent forms but rather are age-graded nonequivalent forms. As a result, direct comparison of the raw scores from these tests is not possible. In order to make comparison possible, scores for both the reading and mathematics areas of each test were transformed to standard scores, which provided a ranking of each student in each domain for each year in terms of standard deviation units from the mean.

Measurement of the Tasks of Adolescence

Given the breadth of coverage and the strategy to search widely for factors affected by either the school transitions or changes in physical development, we elected (as noted in the first chapter) to organize our data in terms of the following tasks of adolescence: achieving a new self-image; intensifying peer relationships; establishing independence; planning for the future; dealing with conformity versus deviance issues.

Within each of these major tasks we have developed a number of particular measures (both scales and single-item indexes) that help to define various aspects of the tasks. The interested reader will find key information on each measure contained in the charts in Appendix G.

It should be noted that self-esteem and GPA were key outcome variables in our view. In this research the Rosenberg–Simmons self-esteem scale was used, which is a version of the Rosenberg self-esteem scale but for younger children. For many analyses, the items in this scale were combined, as in earlier work, in an additive scale (see Rosenberg and Simmons, 1972, and Simmons, Blyth, Van Cleave, and Bush, 1979 for reliability and validity information). For other analyses (to be identified) the scale was disaggregated and a measurement model constructed with the LISREL program (Jöreskog and Sörbom, 1981) in order to correct for reliability and correlated error (see Appendixes E and G). As one of our other key outcome variables, students' academic GPA was secured from central records (see Appendix G).

The Assessment of Physical Growth and Development

One of the primary objectives of this study is to investigate the effects of the physical changes of adolescence in conjunction with the effects of change in school environment. Reliable information about the students' physical growth was collected during the school day. A female registered nurse and assistant, who worked for the project and not for the school system, visited each school, removed the child from class for 15 minutes, performed the necessary measurements, and asked the necessary questions.

The measurement procedure had three components: a series of questions asked by the nurse, a series of anthropometric measures of the student secured by the nurse, and, third, a set of ratings recorded by both the nurse and the interviewer based on observation of the student. The interview questions dealt with many specific and general changes in the body from facial to underarm hair; information was also sought about onset of menstruation for girls. The anthropometric measures collected involved height, sitting height, weight (with calibrated scales), and shoulder width. These measurements were made using specialized equipment designed for the project and based on the work of Stolz and Stolz (1951). This equipment was transported to each school in order to ensure an accurate standing height and sitting height against a firm vertical surface. In all cases, several measurements were taken and the average then used. Due to the constraints of working within a school and the need for parental permission, the decision was made not to take any measurements that might be perceived as sensitive or to have the children remove any clothes other than shoes. Thus, it was impossible to secure self-perceived Tanner (1971) ratings or to directly observe the nude child's physical development. As noted earlier, both the person interviewing the student and the nurse performing the height and weight measurements completed a series of ratings on the child's physical characteristics immediately after seeing the child. Muscularity of body build, development of a figure, issues of comparative physical maturity, growth and distribution of facial hair, and presence of acne were among the items evaluated.[14]

In summary, procedures to assess the changing physical status and development of the students involved many components, all of which were noninvasive and generally nonembarrassing. These data were collected approximately every 6 months from students during the sixth and seventh grade and on a yearly basis thereafter. By repeating the same questions and procedures each year or every 6 months it was possible to obtain longitudinal data on these characteristics and to use procedures that tended to minimize unreliability. During the season in which the student was also interviewed with the larger survey, the physical assessment procedure took place about 2 weeks after the interview. It is important to note that the physical assessment was conducted at a separate time and by different individuals who wore their medical uniforms in order to encourage the respondent to reply honestly and to feel comfortable about confiding medical information. This procedure appeared to work quite well, even for males talking to female nurses. The next section describes how these data were translated into various measures of pubertal status and the relative timing of such development.

Creation of Pubertal Development Indexes

Having obtained a series of anthropometric ratings, self-perceptions, and observers' ratings of the physical changes occurring in our subjects over a period of years, we summarized these changes in a few ways. First, we attempted to determine whether or not the individual had achieved a certain point in his or her physical maturation. This approach might be described as a status view of physical change, insofar as it is a measure of physical status at a given point in time. This type of status measure is most appropriate when there are clear milestones that occur in puberty and which can be determined at any given time without information from prior or subsequent time periods. The classic example is, of course, the occurrence of menarche, which is a major and salient event for females (Brooks-Gunn, in press; Ruble and Brooks-Gunn, 1982; Koff, Rierdon, and Jacobson, 1981).

Where no such event occurs, measures of this type are difficult to obtain. For example, although the increase in height for males is an important aspect of physical development during puberty, there is no clearly defined point at which one can say that a boy has reached his maximum rate of height growth without a record of height over a fairly long period of time.

An alternative way of assessing the physical changes, and one on which this book relies heavily, is to examine the occurrence of the changes in development relative to the development of others. This relative timing perspective involves the placement of an individual's physical changes on a continuum relative to the changes of others or to the changes ultimately to be experienced by the individual. Measures of the relative earliness or lateness of physical maturation have been prominent in research in this domain (e.g., see Jones and Mussen, 1958; Mussen and Jones, 1957; Peskin, 1967; Clausen, 1975; Simmons, Blyth, and McKinney, 1983).

A decision has to be made about the standard of comparison when using a timing perspective. Most previous research has used a chronological definition of earliness or lateness, which implies that the child has reached a point in physical maturation prior to or later than would be expected for someone of that chronological age. An alternate definition, and the one used in this book, examines timing relative to the development of other individuals in the same grade level. Thus, the issue is not whether your physical development occurs at a young age, but whether it occurs before most others around have matured (early developer) or at a time after most others have attained physical maturation (late developer). Since it is likely that the psychosocial impacts of pubertal change depend, in part, on social comparison processes, we chose to use the more socially defined sense of timing (although grade at puberty and age at puberty will, of course, be highly correlated; see following and Blyth and Simmons, 1983).

Before describing the specific measures of pubertal development, it is important to recognize that there are a variety of physical changes that take place during puberty and that these changes vary enormously in both their visibility to others and their accessibility to measurement. Although these occur in a relatively well-established sequence (Tanner, 1971), physical development during early adolescence shows great individual variability. It is due to this variability that a social definition of pubertal timing is particularly relevant.

Procedure for Establishing Female's Physical Maturation Levels. As noted previously, the single most dramatic pubertal event of early adolescence for females is the onset of menstruation or menarche (Petersen and Taylor, 1980; Brooks-Gunn and Petersen, 1983). For most girls, menarche occurs relatively late in the process of physical development, after the period of peak height growth. Tanner (1971) has described five stages of breast and pubic hair development—menarche occurs approximately at the same time as the fourth stage. This means that the typical girl who has reached menarche has already experienced rapid growth and has changed dramatically with respect to breast development and the more visible signs of secondary sexual characteristics. The average age of menarche usually reported (Faust, 1977, p. 34) is 12.79 years with some variability across racial, ethnic, and socioeconomic groups. In our sample of white girls, the mean age for the onset of menarche was 12.75, a figure virtually identical to that reported in other studies.

Establishing the date of menarche. At every interview over the 5 years of the study girls were asked:

> Have you ever had a menstrual period or monthly bleeding, or haven't you had a period yet?
>
> IF HAS HAD A PERIOD, ASK: When did you have your first period?
>
>   ____ month   ____ year

Once an estimate of the date of the onset of menses had been established,[15] girls were classified (1) as to whether they had begun menstruation by the time of the current interview (an indication of current pubertal status) and (2) as having developed early or late relative to their same grade peers. In creating the second of these measures, the distribution was trichotomized into roughly equal thirds to permit the inclusion of not only the early and late developers but also the middle developers in all analyses. Furthermore, the cutting points established for the distribution were made relative to the natural school year breaks. Those girls who reached menarche prior to the beginning of seventh grade were classified as early developers, representing 38% of the sample. Girls labeled as middle developers reached menarche during seventh grade or the following summer (27%). Finally, girls who had not reached menarche prior to the beginning of eighth grade or did not reach menarche during the course of the study were considered late developers (35%). By the end of ninth grade only seven girls had not reached menarche, and all but one girl had reached menarche by the end of tenth grade.

In addition to this trichotomy, we also established a more extreme group of early and late developers based on a roughly 20-60-20 split; 19% of the girls (extreme early developers) had reached menarche by January of the sixth grade and 20% (the extreme late developers) reached menarche after January of eighth grade. These more extreme categories of early and late development allow us to examine whether or not differences occur only for people who are the most deviant from the norm; the less extreme split provides more cases for analyses in the early and late developing groups.[16]

It should be noted that care was taken to eliminate those subjects who were either extremely young or old for their grade so as not to bias the definitions of early and late development relative to those in the same grade.[17] Both early and late developers can be considered "off-time" in this aspect of their life-course trajectory; middle developers are "on-time" (see Eichorn, 1975).

Validity. The indicator of relative onset of menarche has been validated through inspection of correlations with other measured aspects of physical development as well as with subjects' self-perceptions and interviewer and nurse ratings (see Appendix B). As expected, in the sixth and seventh grade early developing girls were significantly taller, heavier, and less lean than their peers, and their rate of growth had begun to slow. They were also significantly more likely to report underarm hair, the presence of a figure, and an awareness of physical changes. Adult raters were more likely to perceive them as having acne, being heavier set, having a more developed figure, and looking more physically mature than their peers. By ninth grade many of these same relationships persist but to a lesser degree. By tenth grade, however, the early developers are somewhat shorter than the late developers while still weighing more and being less lean. The late developers in Grade 10 are the ones to indicate more awareness of recent physical changes. These correlations are all in the predicted direction and help to validate the indicators of female pubertal development used. In particular, one should note that the late developers are always slimmer and leaner than the early developers and eventually end up taller. Also, as one would expect, those girls defined as socially early maturers are just slightly older (4.8 months on the average) than those who are defined as late maturers.

Procedures for Establishing the Relative Timing of Development for Males. In order to develop a parallel measure of the relative onset of puberty for males, it was necessary to recognize both the fundamental differences in male and female development and the lack of a salient developmental event for males. Thus, no measure that we could select for relative onset of puberty in males would really be identical to that which we used for females. The best to be hoped was for a change that, on average, occurred at a roughly similar point of development (i.e., middle to late during the course of the pubertal process) and one that would have a great deal of salience for males. The spurt in height growth presumably has this significance for males, and the peak rate of height growth does occur middle to late in the pubertal sequence. Thus, we focused on the time during which the boy's rate of height growth was greatest.

It is unlikely that the adolescent is aware that he is at the moment of peak height growth and that this rate of growth is about to decline; however, one would expect that he is aware that his height has been changing with great speed. The importance of height for males in our culture and in some sports should make the rapid gain in height highly significant.

In order to establish the relative onset of puberty for males a two-step procedure was utilized. The first step involved plotting the rate of height growth over time in order to establish a peak period of growth. The second step involved utilizing that information along with other data in order to estimate the point of peak height growth for individuals for whom complete growth curves were absent. Both of these steps will be described briefly.

Plotting growth curves. The procedure used in identifying the peak rate of pubertal growth is a modification of that developed by Stolz and Stolz (1951) and later discussed in Faust (1977). Specifically this procedure involves: (1) calculating and plotting annual height growth rates for each subject at each of the time intervals for which we have data; (2) establishing an average rate of annual height growth by subtracting sixth grade height from tenth grade height and then dividing by the number of days between measures and multiplying this quotient by 365; (3) identifying the period of peak height growth by locating the period with the greatest rate of height growth; (4) identifying the period of onset of pubertal height growth by inspecting height growth rates for each period preceding the peak in a backward fashion and comparing them to the average annual rate of height growth over the entire period until a point is reached when the rate is less than or equal to the average rate (the first period of time following this point is then identified as the beginning of pubertal height growth); and, finally (5) establishing the point of postpubertal height growth by proceeding forward from the peak of height growth and comparing each rate with the average rate until a period is reached where the rate of height growth is less than or equal to the average (this point then identifies the end of the period of pubertal height growth).

Once a date was established for the peak period of height growth, it was possible to divide the cases into three groups using socially defined cutoff points. Once again we tried to establish a set of roughly equal size categories for early, middle, and late maturers. The early maturers were those males who reached their peak period of height growth before the spring of seventh grade. Of the sample, 34% met this criterion. Middle developers reached their peak period of height growth between spring of seventh grade and spring of eighth grade and represented 28% of the actually classified individuals. Late developers (38%) reached their peak period of growth after the spring of eighth grade or had not yet reached their peak period of growth by tenth grade.

With this procedure about 49% (158 out of 325) of the white males could be easily classified as having a clear peak followed by a significant decrease in the rate of height growth. In about 22% of the cases (73) no clear peak was discernible, and in the remaining 29% (94 cases) missing data made determination of the peak of height growth impossible.

Estimating point of peak height growth. In order to increase the number of classifiable cases, a series of discriminant analyses was utilized. During the preliminary phase a number of secondary indicators were used to discriminate among the *confirmed* early, middle, and late developing individuals. This analysis was performed separately for Grades 6, 7, 9, and 10. The variables used in each discriminant function analysis included height to weight ratios, sitting height to height ratios, weight, height, shoulder width, self-reported rate of height growth, self-reported rate of muscle growth, self-reported amount of physical change, self-reported presence of facial hair and voice change, nurse's and interviewer's ratings of acne, facial hair, muscle build, and overall physical maturity.

Based on the estimated discriminant functions, the program then computed the probability that each individual was an early, middle, or late developer. This was done separately for each of the 4 years. For example, in sixth grade an individual might be given a probability of .7 of being an early developer, a .2 of being a middle developer, and a probability of .1 of being a late developer. Estimated probabilities could be different in different years. When boys are younger the secondary data can discriminate the early from the middle and late developers fairly well, but not the middle from the late developers. In the later years of puberty, the late developers can be fairly easily discriminated from the middle and early developers.

Using these probabilities, we then averaged the four predictions, one for each year for each of the three pubertal groups, to give us an average probability that the subject is an early, middle, and late developer. Each male with an already confirmed pubertal timing pattern was then classified as an early, middle, or late developer based on the discriminant function analyses and the largest average probability of group membership, as long as the largest probability was at least .10 larger than the next largest probability (to make certain there really was some separation between the different pubertal timing groups). The result of the process up to this point was to predict, based on secondary information, the already known developmental group for each individual. This process proved quite successful with 83.4% of the individuals with known points of peak height growth being accurately classified using only the secondary data available.

Given this high degree of accuracy for classifying known subjects, we then applied the same estimated weights from the discriminant function analysis to those individuals for whom only secondary data were available (either because they were missing height data or because the height growth patterns they exhibited were unclear). Once again the probabilities were estimated for each year and averaged. Individuals were classified based on the average probabilities as either early, middle, or late developers. As a result of this process, we were able to classify 68% (113 out of 167) of the previously unclassifiable cases. Through this process a sample of

271 boys became available for analysis of pubertal effects, 158 classified according to their clear height growth patterns, and 113 classified using only secondary data.

The correlations between these pubertal timing measures for all subjects and various self-reported, measured, and stranger ratings of physical development were all high and in the directions expected. Given the highly effective discriminant function analysis, this association is to be expected but provides evidence of criterion validity (see Appendix C).

Although the procedure for classifying an adolescent male as to whether he is an early, middle, or late developer is very complex, we have every reason to believe that it accurately encompasses the kinds of physical changes that are taking place in the boys' lives at this time. Unfortunately, it is not a procedure that can be replicated in other studies without extensive longitudinal data on height.

Just as for girls, a more extreme split was also created and is used for certain analyses in Chapter 6. For boys, the extreme split exists only for those cases where a clear peak of height growth could be pin pointed with actual height curves.

Summary. The pubertal process is complex with multiple changes occurring during a few years. The present investigation emphasizes the timing of major pubertal events (i.e., menarche for females, peak rate of height growth for males) relative to others in the same grade level. This orientation is similar to the definitions of timing used in previous studies, although many of these other studies focus on timing relative to the chronological age rather than relative to grade level. Since these indexes will be highly correlated, findings would be similar but not identical (e.g., in the present data the correlation between the chronological age at menarche and the social indication of early and late maturity we used is .80, $p < .001$, and the correlation for boys between grade and age at peak height growth is .58, $p < .001$; see Blyth and Simmons, 1983).

This research then is one of a very few recent social–psychological investigations with a large random sample of early adolescents and careful pubertal measures (see Brooks-Gunn and Petersen, 1983; Dornbusch, Gross, Duncan, and Ritter, in press; Nottelmann, Sussman, Blue, Inoff-Germain, Dorn, Loriaux, Cutler, and Chrousos, in press).

Summary of Strengths and Weaknesses

In conclusion, it is appropriate to review the basic strengths and weaknesses of this study in terms of the sample, the overall design, the measures of key independent variables, and, finally, the measures of the tasks of adolescence.

The data are drawn from a representative random sample of public schools in a large metropolitan area with subjects from the full range of social class backgrounds. The original sample is clearly one of the strengths of the study, particularly in the early phase. Furthermore, the sample design took advantage of a natural experiment, allowing comparison of the effects of two major sequences of school environments. The combination of a systematic representative sample and the natural experiment gives this research unusual advantages.

While the sample is a major strength of the study, sample loss, particularly in the later phase (Grades 9 and 10), represents one of the study's limitations. We have attempted to identify and control for biases introduced by sample loss due to the fact that students were not followed if they went to schools outside of the system and due to the fact that the school-comparison analyses could not include students who changed schools at unscheduled times. However, some biases undoubtedly remain in the later years, and conclusions must be tentative on that account. Furthermore, because the sample at any given point in time is representative only of the students who entered the schools in sixth grade, it may not be representative of the entire student population in the later grade levels. For most analyses the maximum number of subjects available at that grade level will be used to minimize biases. Where these biases seem relevant to the analysis, they are discussed in the text.

Another major strength of the study is the long-term longitudinal design which allows for the assessment of both short-term and long-term effects of the different types of school transition. Nonetheless, it is important to note that it is a study of a single cohort and that, in itself, the design is not a sequential one (Nesselroade and Baltes, 1979). However, some cohort comparisons are possible because of an earlier, similar study (the Baltimore 1968 study), which utilized many of the same measures on another cohort of subjects of the same ages (although this earlier study was cross-sectional rather than longitudinal). We are able to compare the cohorts both in terms of general conclusions and in terms of certain specific findings. Particularly in the next set of chapters on gender differences we shall discuss cohort differences between the 1968 and 1974-1979 samples from two different cities. It is, of course, important to note that the results of this research can not be generalized beyond the metropolitan area that it represents or to time periods other than the mid- to late 1970s.

An additional strength of the study is the quality of measurement for key independent variables. The pubertal variables just described are particularly elaborate, carefully constructed, and validated. Similarly, the ability to compare the major contrasting types of school transitions and school environments clearly represents a major advantage. While we have not yet fully assessed the effects of all of the dimensions involved in physical change and in school transition, our approach represents a significant step in the study of social and biological determinants of adolescent adjustment.

In terms of the dependent variables, the study's strength lies in its breadth. We have examined a number of variables across a wide variety of tasks of adolescence so as to provide an initial exploration of the effects of school transition and pubertal change during early adolescence. In consequence, it was not always possible to have depth in particular areas. There is, however, sufficient depth in the measurement of aspects of the self-image, particularly in terms of the positive–negative dimension of self-evaluation.

In sum, this study investigates the extent and nature of the impact of the major social transitions and physical changes that occur in early adolescence. The sample is a representative one, and the quantitative measures focus on the perceptions and attitudes of the adolescents themselves.

Footnotes

[1]Glen Elder has referred to the entry into secondary schools as marking the "lower social boundary of adolescence" in the United States (Elder, 1968, p. 6).

[2]In all schools, a seventh grader is considered a secondary school student and is required to take particular classes common throughout the system (e.g., industrial arts and home economics).

[3]The third category can be divided into those schools that were missing one or more grade levels on either end (such as K–7 or 4–6 schools) and those that did not feed into a regular 3-year junior high school (such as a school with only seventh grade or with Grades 7–12). There were not enough of such schools to make a viable comparison, and it was felt that it would be more advantageous to eliminate these schools and maximize sample size in the two main school types. Schools that were heavily Spanish-speaking in composition were excluded from all three populations. This decision was based on the unknown validity of our instruments with this ethnic group, the difficulty of bilingual instruments, and the small proportion of such students in the city. Of the minority students in Milwaukee, 94% were black.

[4]By a constrained random sample we mean that a random sample of schools would be accepted only if the characteristics of the sample fell within certain predefined constraints (i.e., one standard deviation) for an acceptable representative sample. The constraints dealt with the mean of the median family income for the attendance area and the mean percentage of underachievers. If a randomly drawn sample within any strata of percentage minority did not meet the constraints, the entire sample of schools for that category was randomly redrawn. This procedure is utilized to ensure that a small random sample from a large population is not a biased sample simply by chance. In fact, the random sample of K–6 schools in this book did not need to be redrawn. Only the sample of heavily black schools (which is not used in this book) needed to be redrawn once.

[5]Social class background was measured by the head of household's occupation according to Hollingshead and Redlich (1958).

[6]In general this new diversity of peers did not affect racial balances. There were a few instances of students who had been attending a predominantly white sixth-grade school moving into a more integrated seventh-grade school. Nonetheless, the schools in seventh grade were, with one exception, majority white schools.

[7]White students in K–6 schools that were 43% or more minority (the noncomparable schools) are also included in the gender and puberty analyses but not in the school comparisons ($N = 27$).

[8]The few children who stayed in the sample but left their type of school also appeared more likely to come from broken families.

[9]See footnote 13 for a discussion of the difficulties of a similar procedure with parental marital status.

[10]Also, students were given a very brief self-administered questionnaire that contained a version of the self-esteem scale and a measure of the numbers of extracurricular activities.

[11]Analyses of school effects were conducted that included the students who changed schools in unscheduled ways along with the students who remained in the two school patterns of interest. Results for the unscheduled students did not form a generally interesting or consistent pattern and therefore, for the purpose of this book, only the two prime types are presented. As in the case of all other types of sample attrition, the children who by Grade 9 were in unexpected schools had originally scored lower in GPA in Grade 6. They did not distribute differently on gender, parents' socioeconomic, educational, or marital status. (See Chapters 7 and 8 for further discussion of this issue in relation to key findings. See Chapter 11 for indication that unscheduled school change in conjunction with other major changes may have negative effects on GPA and other variables, even when prior GPA is controlled.)

[12]However, in Grade 9, students who were still in our general sample but not in the expected school type (i.e., they had changed schools in an unexpected way) scored significantly lower in math achievement tests than students in the expected type of school.

[13]See Parts IV and V for analyses that control for the Grade 6 score of key outcome variables. In terms of parents' marital status for these white children, there were not really enough of the interviewed students living in one-parent families (particularly in Grades 9–10) for a separate analysis to see whether findings would be the same within this subgroup. Where exploratory analyses were run on this subgroup (a subgroup more susceptible to drop-out from the study), key significant findings did not appear to alter basic direction.

[14]It should be noted that these types of procedure have become more commonly used in similar research. See for example, work by Petersen, Tobin-Richards, and Boxer (1983).

[15]In cases of discrepancy, information secured closer to the time of reported menarche was given priority.

[16]For 49 girls, no clear date of menarche could be established even given the large number of data-points available. These girls were not reliable in reporting when menarche occurred and therefore were eliminated from the pubertal analyses.

[17]Students who were either much too old or too young for their grade level were eliminated from puberty analyses since we have used a social definition of relatively early or late pubertal timing. A student was defined as being much too old or too young if he or she were more than 1.96 SD away from the mean age for that grade. Eight females (7 too old and 1 too young) and 10 males (1 too young and 9 too old) were eliminated.

II

GENDER AND GRADE-LEVEL EFFECTS

Before looking at the impact of school transitions and pubertal change upon adolescents' social–psychological adjustment, we shall investigate differences between boys and girls over the 5-year period. In what ways do the genders already differ at the end of childhood, that is, in Grade 6? What happens to gender differences in early and middle adolescence (Grades 7, 9, and 10)? Do differences between the genders persist, intensify, or decrease during adolescence as compared to late childhood? Chapter 3 will focus on the nature and direction of gender differences for this 1974–1979 Milwaukee cohort and will compare these differences to those found in the original Baltimore cohort. Chapter 4 will address the changes boys and girls experience during adolescence and how these changes differ by gender.

Clearly these results have relevance not only for the developmental study of adolescence, but also for the large body of research on gender differences. It is to a brief consideration of this literature we turn first, before presenting the gender difference findings.

3

GENDER DIFFERENCES IN LATE CHILDHOOD AND EARLY ADOLESCENCE*

Sparked by the Women's Movement, in the past decade there has been an upsurge of research on the social and psychological differences between males and females. Almost all of the major issues in this literature remain controversial (see Hoffman, 1977). In order to set our study in context, it is relevant to review some of these issues. First, whether or not specific differences between the sexes exist is often controversial. Maccoby and Jacklin (1974) in their review of the development of sex differences conclude that all but a few well-accepted differences are mythical. However, critics of their review challenge many of their conclusions on grounds ranging from insufficiency of present evidence to inaccuracy of interpretation (Block, 1976, 1984; Petersen, 1980; Stockard and Johnson, 1980).

Second, and a key question for us (to be dealt with in Chapter 4): Is there intensification of gender differences in adolescence (Hill and Lynch, 1983)? That is, as children enter adolescence do the differences between the sexes increase? The evidence is certainly not clear on this issue either.

Third, even if one accepts the existence of certain social–psychological differences or that the difference between the genders changes in adolescence, the suggested reasons for these findings remain controversial. The nature versus nurture controversy is nowhere more evident (Maccoby and Jacklin, 1974; Hoffman, 1977). Are the differences biological/genetic in origin? Or are they instead produced by culturally based differences in socialization and sex-role patterning? To what extent did gender differences first arise and then persist because of their evolutionary advantage? On the one hand, some scholars theorize that there was an evolutionary advantage for societies when the female was child caretaker and more nurturant in orientation, and when the physically stronger male was the food securer and more aggressive (Pleck and Pleck, 1980; Rossi, 1968, 1977). Chodorow (1978), however, criticizes this line of reasoning, noting that the bioevolutionary argument can apply only to a subset of societies with subsistence economies, but not to the many societies where both men and women work close to home, close to each other, and to children.

*By Roberta G. Simmons, Diane Mitsch Bush, and Dale A. Blyth.

Whether or not there was an initial evolutionary advantage, the *present day* determinants of gender differences remain unclear and controversial. There is disagreement over the impact of biological factors, of socialization and cultural values, and of differential opportunity and discrimination.[1]

If differences that exist are in good part due to socialization, cultural values, and discrimination, then efforts for change should be successful. The extent to which change has occurred since the rise of the Women's Movement is also unclear. Evidence from Mason, Czajka, and Arber (1976), Thornton and Freedman (1979), Cherlin and Walters (1981), and Thornton, Alwin, and Camburn (1983) suggests that attitudes toward women in public life (work and politics) have become more egalitarian in recent years.[2] However, attitudes toward women's and men's roles in the home have changed less, and there is evidence that other gender differences have persisted at least into the 1970s (Bush, Simmons, Hutchinson, and Blyth, 1977; Lueptow, 1980a, 1984; also see Broverman, Vogel, Broverman, Clarkson, and Rosenberg, 1972; Herzog, 1982).[3]

Finally, in addition to controversy over the existence and determinants of gender differences and over the degree of change occurring at present, there is ideological disagreement over the direction of change that is desirable. For some, the simple goal of equality of opportunity has been superceded. Equal entry into male-dominated positions is no longer regarded as sufficient by many feminists. Simple acceptance of male values for the society (masculinization) is viewed as questionable. More desirable would be a change in societal values for both sexes, such that greater emphasis was placed on traditional female values—that is, altruism, intimacy, interpersonal connection (Mednick, Tangri, and Hoffman, 1975; Gilligan, 1982b; Hoffman, 1977).

Issues To Be Investigated

It is not the object of this book to deal with all of these controversial issues, although they provide a context for the subset of issues that we shall explore. Our aim is to investigate some of the social–psychological differences between males and females during one life-course transition. To what extent and in what ways do the genders differ in late childhood (Grade 6), at the entrance into adolescence (Grade 7), and in middle adolescence (Grades 9–10)? A central question then involves the developmental impact of adolescence on the genders. Furthermore, to what extent have gender differences narrowed or widened between 1968 and the years of this study, 1974–1979; that is, from a period before the resurgence of the Women's Movement to a time after the Movement had gained much prominence?

In investigating these issues, we shall focus on the five task areas identified in Chapter 1. To what extent do boys and girls differ (1) in their establishment of a positive self- and body-image, (2) in the degree of their investment and success in interpersonal relationships to same and opposite-sex peers, (3) in the development of independence, (4) in establishment of future aspirations, and (5) in resolution of conformity-related concerns? Thus, we will examine neither the full range of traits, personality characteristics, and socialization experiences thought to differentiate males and females, nor the attitudes toward adult occupational or marital equality between the genders.[4] However, linkages to issues not directly measured here will be made as gender differences in the five task areas are presented. This chapter will focus on the extent to which the sexes differ along the above task-dimensions; Chapter 4 will address whether differences increase in adolescence.

We are interested not only in the *level* and *direction of gender differences,* but also whether one or the other sex is more vulnerable at this age, that is, *whether one gender scores more negatively* than the other on these outcome variables. As noted in Chapter 1, in the earlier Baltimore study females scored more negatively on a variety of self-image dimensions including attitude toward one's own sex; and, in fact, there was indication that these sex differences were wider in adolescence than in childhood (Simmons *et al.,* 1973; F. Rosenberg and Simmons, 1975; Simmons and F. Rosenberg, 1975). Our earlier analysis of some of the data from the current longitudinal study also supports this view (Bush *et al.,* 1977).

However, as suggested previously, the literature is in conflict on this point. On the one hand, in agreement with our work, females show significantly lower self-esteem in nationally representative samples of high school seniors by O'Malley and Bachman (1979) and Conger, Peng, and Dunteman (1977). Furthermore, evidence of lower self-confidence among females, at least in task areas, is cited or shown by Hoffman (1975c), Bush and Simmons (in press), Eccles and Hoffman (in press), Mednick *et al.* (1975, Ch. 3), Offer *et al.* (1981), and Hathaway and Monachesi (1963).[5]

On the other hand, O'Malley and Bachman (1979) suggest that the male–female difference, while present, is not substantial enough to reach statistical significance unless sample sizes are large; Maccoby and Jacklin (1974, Ch. 3) and Wylie (1979) in reviewing the literature state there are few global self-image differences before college age, but that females show less task self-confidence, particularly at college age.[6] Yet, Block (1976) reanalyzes Maccoby and Jacklin's data and concludes there is evidence of lower self-esteem among younger girls (Petersen, 1980).

On more serious indicators of vulnerability, for example, mental illness, in general, and depression, in particular, there is evidence that *adult women* are more at risk than men.[7] This study does not identify mental health disorders or serious depression; however, we do measure "depressive affect," that is, the extent to which individuals perceive themselves as generally happy or unhappy. Whether preadolescent and adolescent girls already indicate greater vulnerability in terms of depressive affect will be investigated.

However, Kessler and McRae (1981) present evidence that sex differentials in depression among adults are becoming smaller in recent years. This chapter will investigate whether there is a cohort difference in relative risk along a wide variety of variables. The Baltimore cross-sectional sample in 1968 will be compared to the Milwaukee longitudinal sample from 1974–1979. One of the questions at issue is whether the relative vulnerability of females in 1968 persisted into the middle to late 1970s along the same variables. Of course, differences between the two cohorts cannot be attributed with certainty to the time of measurement since the city and area of the country differ as well.

The urban context of our research should be noted as well as the time frame of the study and the age period investigated. Both Milwaukee and Baltimore are very large cities. While Maccoby and Jacklin (1974) and Wylie (1979) report few gender differences in self-image in the studies they review, none of the studies cited shows *all* of the following characteristics present in our research: (1) a focus on early or middle adolescents; (2) use of a self-report rather than external rating of self-image; (3) a *large* random sample or total population; (4) a large city as study site; and (5) a sample representing the full range of the class structure.[8]

In summary, this chapter will investigate gender differences in late childhood and early to middle adolescence with a particular focus on the extent to which one sex is more at risk than the other. In addition, a comparison between 1968 and 1974–1979 urban samples will explore the degree to which traditional gender differences have persisted or changed since the resurgence of the Women's Movement.

Method

Most of the methodological issues relevant for this chapter have been discussed in Chapter 2. However, a few points should be noted.

Statistical Analyses

First, Multivariate Analyses of Variance (MANOVAs) have been performed in order to see whether gender is significantly related to the different clusters of variables identified in Table 1.1. One-way ANOVAs were then run for each variable each year, with gender as the independent variable. While the MANOVA is a suitable analysis to summarize the existence of effects across sets of dependent variables in any one year, a Repeated Measures Design can summarize the effects for one variable across years. Most of the statistical results from a Repeated Measures analysis are presented in Chapter 4. However, the significance of the gender effect over the 4 points in time for each variable is also presented here.[9]

Controls for Social Desirability

A special Analysis of Covariance has been performed on Grade 7 data to investigate whether the gender-difference findings would persist if social desirability and tendency to reveal true feelings were controlled. Although there is some inconsistency, prior literature indicates that females are more likely to answer in a socially desirable fashion and to be willing to disclose their feelings.[10]

In this study also, girls are slightly more likely to score high on social desirability, as measured by questions from Crowne and Marlowe (1964) ($r = .09$, $p < p < .10$). They also score higher on a scale that measures perceived tendency to reveal true feelings ($r = .12$, $p < .05$).[11] However, all of the significant differences to be presented in Grade 7 persist when these two variables are controlled. In other years the necessity to keep the questionnaire within length prevented the inclusion of the items for these two variables.

Table 3.1 presents the MANOVAs for the various variable clusters. Before turning to individual outcome variables, we wish to make certain that we do not exaggerate the meaning of specific statistically significant results. The MANOVA allows us an overall sense of the extensiveness of gender differences. In fact, gender differences are widespread. Almost all variable clusters in all task areas show significant gender differences each year from Grade 6–10. For more detail, we address each of the task areas in turn.

Findings

Establishing a Positive Self-Image

Table 3.1 indicates significant gender differences for all self-image clusters for all years. In each grade females and males show significant differences in global self-image, body-image, valuation of body-image, perceived self-competence, valuation of competence, and gender-role attitudes.

In order to determine the direction of these differences between boys and girls, Table 3.2 presents the means of each variable within each of the clusters. The first cluster involves global self-image variables. The meaning of these variables will be discussed first, followed by the ways boys and girls differ.

TABLE 3.1. MANOVAs—Relationship of Variable Clusters to Gender

	Grade 6 (621)		Grade 7 (553)		Grade 9 (361)		Grade 10 (314)	
	Canonical	p	Canonical	p	Canonical	p	Canonical	p
I. Establish Self-Image								
A. *Global self-image*	.26	< .001	.25	< .001	.27	< .001	.22	< .01
1. Self-esteem								
2. Self-consciousness								
3. Self-stability								
B. *Body-image*	.31	< .001	.28	< .001	.42	< .001	.32	< .001
4. Perceive self as good looking								
5. Satisfaction with looks								
6. Satisfaction with weight								
7. Satisfaction with height								
8. Satisfaction with body build								
C. *Concern with body-image*	.31	< .001	.38	< .001	.52	< .001	.47	< .001
9. Care about looks								
10. Care about weight								
11. Care about height								
12. Care about body build								
D. *Perceived self-competence*	.23	< .001	.30	< .001	.28	< .001	.25	< .001
13. Perceive self as smart								
14. Good at school work								
15. Good at sports								
E. *Concern with competence*	.25	< .001	.21	< .001	.17	< .05	.29	< .001
16. Value competence versus popularity and independence								
17. Care about being smart								
18. Care about school work								
19. Care about good at sports								

	r	p	r	p	r	p	r	p
F. *Gender role attitudes*								
20. Positive feelings about being own gender	.65	< .001	.66	< .001	.60	< .001	.62	< .001
21. Care about not acting like opposite sex								
22. How often act like opposite sex								
G. 23. *Depressive affect*	—		—		—		—	
II. Intensify Peer Relationships								
A. *Peer popularity*	n.s.		n.s.		n.s.		n.s.	
1. Same sex								
2. Opposite sex								
B. *Value popularity*	.15	< .01	.29	< .001	.32	< .001	.25	< .01
3. Care about same sex popularity								
4. Care about opposite sex popularity								
5. Value popularity more than competence or independence								
6. Value opposite sex popularity more than competence								
C. *Dating behavior*	.12	< .05	n.s.		n.s.		n.s.	
7. Dating behavior								
7a. Opposite sex popularity[a]								
D. *Others' expectations regarding opposite sex relationships*	.38	< .001	.27	< .001	.12	< .10	n.s.	
8. Parents expect to date								
9. Same sex friends expect dating								

(Continued)

TABLE 3.1. (Continued)

	Grade 6 (621)		Grade 7 (553)		Grade 9 (361)		Grade 10 (314)	
	Canonical	p	Canonical	p	Canonical	p	Canonical	p
10. Parents expect interest in opposite sex					—	—	—	—
11. Same sex peers expect interest in opposite sex					—	—	—	—
E. *Participation in activities*								
12. Total in-school clubs and sports	.22	< .001	.21	< .001	n.s.	—	.16	< .05
13. Total out-of-school clubs and sports								
14. Coed clubs (in and out of school)								
15. Leadership in clubs and sports					—	—	—	—
III. **Establish Independence**								
A. *Independence from parents*								
1. Take bus without adult	.47	< .001	.59	< .001	.57	< .001	.56	< .001
2. Go places without parents permission								
3. Parents permission not required after dark								
4. Left home alone								
5. Times per month baby-sit								
6. Part-time job								
7. Perceived independence from parents					—	—	—	—
8. Perceived independent decision making								

58

B. *Perception that others expect older behavior*	.20	< .001	.16	< .01	.15	< .05	.18	< .05
9. Parents								
10. Friends								
11. Teachers				.12	< .05	.12	< .10	.13	< .10
C. *Value independence*	n.s.		.12	< .05	.12	< .10	.13	< .10
12. Value independence								
13. Value independence vs. competence and popularity								
IV. **Plan for Future**								
A. *Educational, occupational, and marital aspirations*	.26	< .001	.26	< .001	.32	< .001	.25	< .01
1. Plan to go to college								
2. Want to get married								
3. Want to have children								
4. SES of ideal job								
B. *Perception that others expect career planning*	.19	< .001	n.s.		.22	< .001	.16	< .10
7. Parents								
8. Teachers								
9. Friends								
V. **Deal with Conformity/Deviance Issues**								
A. *Problem behavior*	.33	< .001	.33	< .001	.28	< .001	.25	< .001
1. Problem behavior scale								
2. Probations/suspensions[b]								
3. Truancy								

(Continued)

TABLE 3.1. (Continued)

	Grade 6 (621)		Grade 7 (553)		Grade 9 (361)		Grade 10 (314)	
	Canonical	p	Canonical	p	Canonical	p	Canonical	p
B. 4. *Victimization*	—	—	—	—	—	—	—	—
C. *Academic performance*	.26	< .001	.31	< .001	—	—	.24	< .001
5. GPA								
6. Reading achievement score								
7. Math achievement score					—	—		
D. *Perception that adults evaluate one highly*	.11	< .05	n.s.		.12	< .10	.15	< .05
8. Mother[c]								
9. Teachers								
E. *Perception of parent-peer relationship*	.09	< .10	.13	< .01	n.s.		.15	< .05
10. Parents like close friends								
11. Close friends like parents								

[a]This item is also used in the "Dating Behavior" Cluster.
[b]There is some overlap between the problem-behavior scale and the probations-suspensions variable, since the probations-suspensions variable is one of four items in the scale.
[c]For all MANOVA analyses, the "Perception that adults evaluate one highly" cluster uses mother's evaluation rather than parent's evaluation in order to minimize that impact of missing data from children without fathers.

TABLE 3.2. Self-Image Variables—Means for Boys and Girls[a]

	Grade 6 Boys (335)	Grade 6 Girls (286)	Grade 7 Boys (294)	Grade 7 Girls (258)	Grade 9 Boys (183)	Grade 9 Girls (178)	Grade 10 Boys (164)	Grade 10 Girls (150)	Repeated measures ANOVA[b] four point in time sex effect $p \leq$
I. Establish Self-Image									
A. *Global self-image*									
1. Self-esteem	3.68	3.03*	3.75	3.02*c	4.30	3.41*c	4.28	3.60*c	.001
2. Self-consciousness	1.76	2.15*c	1.78	2.07*c	1.95	2.25*c	1.96	2.16****c	n.s.
3. Self-stability	1.81	1.49*	1.80	1.53**	1.95	1.54*	1.97	1.61**	.001
B. *Body-image*									
4. Perceive self as good looking	2.88	2.61*c	2.88	2.62*c	2.91	2.66*c	2.96	2.75*c	.001
5. Satisfaction with looks	3.24	3.08***c	3.24	3.07*c	3.20	2.99*	3.20	3.02*	.001
6. Satisfaction with weight	2.86	2.59*c	2.86	2.72***c	3.02	2.44*c	2.95	2.53*c	.001
7. Satisfaction with height	3.20	3.16	3.14	3.14c	3.21	3.07****c	3.23	3.26c	n.s.
8. Satisfaction with body build	3.16	2.73*c	3.03	2.76*c	3.03	2.55*c	2.96	2.64*c	.001
C. *Concern with body-image*									
9. Care about looks	2.84	2.84	2.86	2.96c	2.89	3.11**c	2.91	2.99c	n.s.
10. Care about weight	2.70	2.95*	2.56	3.11*	2.48	3.32*	2.46	3.17*c	.001
11. Care about height	2.65	2.40*c	2.58	2.42***	2.36	2.26	2.24	2.09****c	.05
12. Care about body build	3.04	2.74*c	2.85	2.91	2.75	3.33*	2.68	3.15*	.001
D. *Perceived self-competence*									
13. Perceive self as smart	3.02	2.95****c	3.01	2.95****c	3.01	2.97	3.05	2.97c	n.s.
14. Good at school work	3.00	3.01	2.98	2.98c	2.91	2.95	2.94	2.89	n.s.
15. Good at sports	3.21	2.88*c	3.17	2.78*c	3.07	2.69	2.99	2.65*	.001

(Continued)

61

TABLE 3.2. (Continued)

	Grade 6		Grade 7		Grade 9		Grade 10		Repeated measures ANOVA[b] four point in time sex effect $p \leq$
	Boys (335)	Girls (286)	Boys (294)	Girls (258)	Boys (183)	Girls (178)	Boys (164)	Girls (150)	
E. *Concern with competence*									
16. Value competence versus popularity and independence	.43	.34***	.44	.38	.44	.42	.49	.45	n.s.
17. Care about being smart	3.53	3.50c	3.47	3.41	3.27	3.22	3.24	3.25	n.s.
18. Care about school work	3.57	3.65	3.53	3.59	3.26	3.29c	3.15	3.30***	n.s.
19. Care about good at sports	3.28	2.92*	3.10	2.81*	2.88	2.61**	2.91	2.49*	.001
F. *Gender role attitudes*									
20. Positive feelings about being own gender	3.54	3.20*c	3.49	3.24c	3.45	3.33****	3.53	3.44	.001
21. Care about not acting like opposite sex	2.55	1.96c	2.64	1.97c	2.64	2.08*	2.54	1.95*	.001
22. How often act like opposite sex	1.30	2.50*c	1.26	2.38*c	1.24	2.20*c	1.27	2.22*c	.001
G. 23. *Depressive affect*	1.93	1.75***	2.00	1.82***c	1.92	1.69****c	2.12	1.78*c	.05

[a]According to a One-Way Analysis of Variance: *$p < .001$; **$p < .01$; ***$p < .05$; ****$p < .10$.

[b]The Repeated Measures ANOVA was based on those cases for which we have data at all four points in time. The means are based on the largest number of cases each year.

[c]There are homogeneity of variance problems here.

62

Global Self-Images

In general, we have adopted Gardner Murphy's (1947) definition of the self-concept, as "the individual as known to the individual." So defined, the self-concept has several dimensions (Rosenberg, 1965, 1979), and one would expect negative changes in many of these to be disturbing or uncomfortable for the individual. In terms of the global self-image, the first dimension and most important variable for this entire book is self-esteem,[12] that is, the individual's global positive or negative attitude toward him or herself.[13] The second dimension measures individual's sense of self-stability—how sure they are that they know what kind of person they are, how often they feel confused about what they are really like, and how frequently they change from liking to disliking the way they are. Lecky (1945) and Rosenberg (1979) hypothesize that an unstable sense of self will be very disturbing and that persons are highly motivated both to maximize their level of self-esteem and to establish stable self-pictures. Erikson (1959) in his theories of life stages posits that adolescence is a time of identity search, and, in some cases, identity crisis. Therefore his theory, as well as many others (Hall, 1904; A. Freud, 1958), would predict that feelings of self-stability would be volatile during adolescence. The variable of "stability versus instability of self" is as close as we come to measuring the extent to which the subjects believe they are unclear about their identity.[14] The third global dimension of the self-image involves the degree of uncomfortable self-consciousness individuals report they feel in social situations.

For these first three dimensions, Table 3.2 (Rows 1–3) shows that females scored significantly more negatively than males in all 4 years. They score lower in self-esteem,[15] lower in sense of self-stability, and higher in self-consciousness. According to a 4-point-in-time Repeated Measures Design, the sex effect is significant in general over the years for self-esteem and stability ($p < .001$); and, according to one-way ANOVAs, it is significant each year for all three variables.

It should be noted that the greater vulnerability of girls in these regards is already present in Grade 6, a period we have termed "the last year of childhood."

In several instances (especially in Grades 7–10), girls and boys demonstrate significant differences in homogeneity of variance. In all these cases, girls show greater variance in scores than do boys. Thus, while on the average girls score more unfavorably than boys, they also exhibit greater variability of response.

Body-Image

Given the dramatic physical changes of adolescence, the incorporation of a new body-image should be a major task of adolescence (Aldous, 1978).

Several studies have indicated that females, including adolescents, are less satisfied with their physical appearance than are males (Offer *et al.*, 1981; Clifford, 1971; Schwab and Harmeling, 1968; White and Wash, 1965). Table 3.2 (Rows 4–8) demonstrates that in our study girls rate themselves as less good looking than do boys and indicate they are less satisfied with their looks, weight, and body build, although there are no clear gender differences for satisfaction with height. Except for satisfaction with height, both the Repeated Measures and the one-way ANOVAs each year indicate statistically significant results. There are also some significant homogeneity of variance differences between boys and girls, with girls always showing the greater variance.

Once again, then, adolescent girls demonstrate more difficulty with their self-picture than do adolescent boys. The difference pre-dates adolescence and is present in Grade 6.

We measure not only self-ratings of physical appearance but also the value placed on it. Students were asked how much they "cared about" several key characteristics, including aspects of their looks. It was pre-dicted that in adolescence girls would begin to care more about their looks than would boys, given the greater emphasis placed on female physical appearance in the larger culture.[16] Traditionally, the larger culture has emphasized the importance for the female to secure a mate and for the male to attain occupational success. In securing a mate, physical ap-pearance has traditionally been thought to play a particularly important role for women. As adolescents prepare for adult roles, one might expect their value systems to diverge in line with these traditional expectations.[17]

In fact, in preadolescence (Grade 6), boys and girls do not differ in their valuation of looks, and boys are the ones who care more about body build (Table 3.2, Rows 9 and 12). In the early adolescent years, starting with Grade 7, as predicted, girls begin to care more than boys about looks and about body build, although the differences reach statistical significance only in Grade 9. In all years girls care significantly more about their weight (Row 10) and boys care more about height (Row 11) (the ANOVA is sig-nificant for height in all but Grade 9). For all these areas, except valuation of looks in general, the Repeated Measures Design also indicates a sig-nificant sex effect.[18]

Thus, after Grade 6 at the same time that girls rate their appearance more negatively than do boys, they also place higher value on looks, weight, and body build. Rosenberg (1979) has shown that it is particularly disadvantageous psychologically for individuals to rate themselves low on characteristics about which they care a great deal; their overall self-esteem is then in jeopardy. Girls are more likely to find themselves in this situation than boys. On the average, boys apparently are not so likely as girls to be in the position of caring a great deal about an aspect of their looks with which they are dissatisfied.

Figure 3.1 shows, for example, that 28% of Grade 7 girls but only 8%

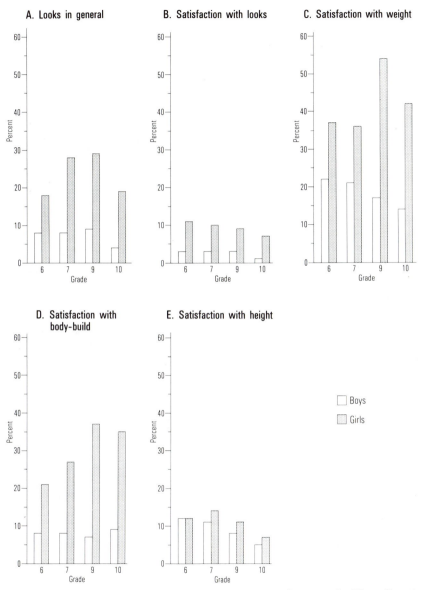

FIGURE 3.1. Percentage of boys and girls who care "a great deal" or "pretty much" about an aspect of their physical appearance with which they are dissatisfied.

of Grade 7 boys are in this situation of caring "a great deal" or "pretty much" about their looks at the same time as they are "dissatisfied" with these looks. Similar results are found in all other grades for attitude toward looks in general and for satisfaction with weight and body build. The reverse effect is not shown for satisfaction with height, the only body-image dimension that adolescent boys value more highly than do girls.

It is our hypothesis that girls who care a great deal about an aspect of their appearance but are dissatisfied will be at particular risk in terms of their self-esteem. In other words, dissatisfaction with appearance will be more highly related to low self-esteem for girls who care a great deal about appearance than for girls who care less. While we do not have enough cases in the various valuation categories to test this hypothesis for Grades 9 and 10, Table 3.3 presents the results for Grades 6 and 7. For girls, this hypothesis is generally, but not completely, confirmed. For example, in Row 1 the unstandardized regression coefficient of self-esteem on rating of looks is 1.18 ($p < .001$) for girls who care "very much" about their looks but only .52 for those who care less. These results are replicated for girls in Grade 7 for this indicator and in both Grades 6 and 7 for "satisfaction with looks" and "satisfaction with weight" and for "satisfaction with body build" in Grade 6. It is not replicated for satisfaction with body

TABLE 3.3. Effect of Perceived Physical Appearance Upon Self-Esteem Among Students Caring More Versus Those Caring Less About Physical Appearance—Unstandardized Regressions: Dependent Variable Self-Esteem

	Grade 6			Grade 7		
	How much care about that aspect:			How much care about that aspect:		
Aspects of physical appearance	Not care	Care pretty much	Care very much	Not care	Care pretty much	Care very much
Girls[a]						
How good looking	.52***	.69**	1.18*	.52****	1.34*	1.37*
Satisfaction with looks	.19	.78*	1.01*	.67***	1.30*	1.41*
Satisfaction with weight	.12	.27****	1.33***	.04	.69**	.56*
Satisfaction with body build	.23	.35****	.50**	.88**	1.04*	.22
Satisfaction with height	.21	.08	.31****	.72*	.22	.69**
Boys[b]						
How good looking	.63***	1.02*	.28	.37	.66***	.74****
Satisfaction with looks	1.02*	.74**	.42****	.43	.56*	.56****
Satisfaction with weight	.27****	.38***	.53**	.38***	.53**	.88*
Satisfaction with body build	.55**	.21	.24	.84**	.23	.10
Satisfaction with height	.17	.19	.55**	.08	.04	−.25

[a]Grade 6, $N = 286$; grade 7, $N = 259$.
[b]Grade 6, $N = 335$; grade 7, $N = 294$.
*$p \leqslant .001$; **$p \leqslant .01$; ***$p \leqslant .05$; ****$p \leqslant .10$

build in Grade 7, nor is it replicated for satisfaction with height in Grade 7, the aspect of body-image about which girls care the least. For boys, no consistent pattern emerges across variables.[19]

In summary, the results do indicate: (1) Girls are more likely than boys to be in the position of caring a great deal about their looks at the same time as they find themselves wanting in this area; (2) there is evidence that girls in this position are particularly likely to score low in overall self-esteem (the effect of self-rating of looks upon self-esteem is higher for girls who care a great deal about their looks than for other girls); and (3) overall, girls score lower than boys in self-esteem.

The finding of a significant sex difference in the process linking looks and self-esteem may be related to the fact that females are supposed to care more about appearance in our society than are males.[20] Broverman *et al.,* (1972) have found that a typical clinician's picture of a "mentally healthy adult woman" included a concern with her appearance whereas appearance was not considered central for "mentally healthy men."

Self-Competence

On the one hand, prior studies have shown that girls receive higher grades than boys in early years (see Maccoby and Jacklin, 1974). On the other hand, investigators have suggested that girls have less self-confidence in their coping ability (see Hoffman, 1975a; Mednick *et al.,* 1975, Ch. 21; Offer *et al.,* 1981; Dusek and Flaherty, 1981). While we did not ask students about their perceptions of their overall competence, as did Offer *et al.,* (1981), we did ask them to rate themselves in areas of academic and athletic competency, and we secured objective ratings of their school performance. Later in this chapter we shall examine objective gender differences in academic performance. At this point, self-perceived competencies are of concern. The students have been asked to rate themselves as to how smart they are, how good at school work, and how good they are at sports. The Repeated Measures Design shows no overall gender difference for self-rating of intelligence or success at school work, but does indicate a significant difference in rating of athletic ability. As would be expected, boys rate themselves significantly higher than girls each year on athletic ability (Table 3.2, Row 15). In Grades 6 and 7 only, boys are significantly more likely to rate themselves as smart. Thus, whatever gender differences occur relative to these specific competencies favor boys.

If traditional gender-role differences hold, one might expect boys to value general competence more than girls. All students were asked:

Which would you most like to be? Would you like to be

_____ able to do things for yourself
_____ well liked, or
_____ the best in the things you do?

When this variable is dichotomized so that valuation of competence is opposed to all else, the Repeated Measures Design and most of the ANOVAs show no significant sex effect (Table 3.2, Row 16).[21]

In addition, there are almost no significant sex differences in valuation of intelligence or school work (Rows 17 and 18). As might be expected, boys value athletic skill significantly more than girls in all years (Row 19).

Thus, girls are at risk in terms of their global self-image and body-image. Where there are differences in self-perceptions of intellectual and athletic competency, these differences also favor boys.

Sex-Role Self-Image

Several earlier studies conducted prior to the Women's Movement indicated that females regard their own sex-role with less favor than do males. Females are more likely to wish they had been born a member of the opposite sex, to feel it is better to be a male than to be a female, and to denigrate the characteristics that stereotype their own gender.[22]

According to Wylie (1979), theorists have suggested that females have lower opinions of themselves for the following reasons related to a woman's role:[23]

> social and economic dependence, minority group status, segregation, and relative powerlessness; cultural ideology that calls women inferior, accords them less prestige with age and derogates their bodies. . . .(p. 259)

In light of such negative cultural evaluations of women, two central goals of feminist ideology and movements have been to enhance the evaluations of women by both genders and to alter the social structure such that both sexes might be less constrained by rigid roles. Learning one's gender role is a key aspect of adolescent socialization and is important in the creation of a new self-image. The question is whether girls moving out of childhood into adolescence in the mid-to late 1970s still find themselves limited and constrained by a less desirable gender role.

In order to measure attitudes toward one's gender role, the students were asked first of all:

> How do you feel about being a girl (boy)? Is it great, good, fair or poor to be a girl (boy)?

Table 3.2 (Row 20) shows that in all years, girls in this study are less likely than boys to say it is "great" to be a member of their own sex, although the difference does not reach statistical significance in Grade 10, according to the ANOVA analysis. The Repeated Measures analysis indicates an overall significant sex effect.

Students were also asked:

> How important is it for you *not* to act like a [member of the opposite sex: boy, girl]? Very important, pretty important, somewhat important, not at all important?
>
> How often do you act like a [the opposite sex: girl, boy]? Very often, pretty often, not very often, not at all.

Hartley (1959) hypothesized that gender-role demands for boys are enforced much earlier and more strictly than they are for girls (see Eccles and Hoffman, in press). At young ages, it is permissible for a girl to be a tomboy but not for a boy to be a sissy (Chodorow, 1978). Weitzman (1979, p. 14) suggests that the situation may change in adolescence. However, in our data (Table 3.2, Rows 21 and 22), in all 4 years girls are significantly more willing than boys to admit that they have acted like the opposite sex, and boys are significantly more likely to consider it very important to avoid behaving like the opposite sex. The Repeated Measures sex effects are also significant. This difference precedes adolescence but persists through the adolescent years.

Where there are significant differences between the sexes in variance for these variables, girls once again show greater variance in scores than boys (especially in Grades 6 and 7).

In summary, this study conducted in the mid-1970s indicates that for both boys and girls, being male is viewed as more desirable than being female. It is not only less desirable *to be* a girl, but behavior that resembles that of females has negative connotations.[24] Once again, the more negative self-rating of girls predates the adolescent years.

Self-Perception of Depressive Affect

As noted earlier, there is evidence that adult women are more at risk than men in terms of clinical depression.[25] Rutter (1980) in his review of his own and other studies views adolescence as the period in which these mental health disorders for females begin to emerge:

> During early and middle childhood there is little difference between the sexes in rates of emotional disturbance, however measured. . . . However, during adolescence this picture changes; mood disturbances become increasingly common in girls and in adult life depression is twice as common in women as in men. (p. 59)

Maccoby and Jacklin (1974), on the other hand, conclude from their literature review that it is not early adolescence but later in the college years that sex differences disadvantageous to women begin to occur. However, Maccoby and Jacklin do not review the literature for mental health disturbances, depression, or even for "depressive affect." As mentioned earlier, we do not measure serious depression but "depressive affect" or general level of happiness or unhappiness.

In this area, the exact measure of depression appears to have considerable effect on the existence and direction of gender differences among adults. Newmann (1984) examines the different items in the PERI depression scale and shows that while females score more unfavorably than males in terms of feelings of sadness, gender differences are much smaller for more severe symptoms, such as suicidal impulses. In fact, in her study, men were slightly more likely than women to report thinking about suicide; national statistics indicate higher actual (but not attempted) suicide rates among men as well. At the other extreme, using measures of general happiness and satisfaction rather than measures of sadness, Gurin, Veroff, and Feld (1960), Bradburn and Caplovitz (1965), Campbell, Converse, and Rodgers (1976), and Veroff, Duovan, and Kulka (1981) show virtually no overall gender differences among adults, and Duncan and Duncan (1978) find women to be happier.[26] Our measures closely resemble the happiness and satisfaction measures used by this last set of investigators.

On these measures, we, like the foregoing investigators, also fail to show females at risk in terms of depressive-affect, despite the earlier findings indicating their more negative self-image scores. In fact, in all 4 years, findings indicate that preadolescent and adolescent girls are significantly less "depressed" or "more happy" than boys (Table 3.2, Row 23). The Repeated Measures Analysis indicates an overall significant sex effect. Once again, in several cases, girls show significantly greater variance than do boys on these measures.

It is possible that these findings simply reflect a measurement difference between a scale of this type (asking about happiness) and other measures in the literature that focus on sadness or psychopathology. It is also possible that the pattern of female depression develops later than early or middle adolescence.

Intensification of Peer Relations

A major task of adolescence is to develop intimate relationships with peers and to begin learning how to relate to the opposite sex. During the years of adolescence, children change from individuals whose prime emotional attachments are to their parents, into persons capable of leaving their parents and establishing families of their own. Attachments to peers, particularly opposite sex peers, can provide an emotional bridge between these two orientations (Youniss, 1980; Seltzer, 1982, Berndt, 1982).

There are theoretical and empirical reasons to expect gender differences in this area. Theoretically, adult females have been described as playing the expressive and nurturant roles in the traditional family; males, the instrumental or task-oriented role (Parsons and Bales, 1955). Whether or not the reason for this division of labor has bioevolutionary roots, a division of labor in which adult women assume the prime parental role has characterized our society. It has been hypothesized that females have developed greater needs for intimate relationships than males as an outcome of this division of labor and the consequent differential socialization of boys and girls (Chodorow, 1978). Similarly, the hierarchy of values for girls and boys is expected to be different, with sociability assuming higher primacy for females and competence higher primacy for males.[27]

While some prior research supports these hypotheses, there is controversy in this area as in many of the other issues involving gender roles. Several studies indicate that girls are more sociable and rate themselves as more invested and/or skillful in interpersonal relationships than do boys, or that they score higher on self-reported need for affiliation.[28] From Maccoby and Jacklin's review (1974), however, one could conclude that the existence of gender differences in this area depends on the aspect of sociability investigated. They suggest that girls form smaller, more intimate groups of friends (pp. 225–226), and that they rate themselves higher on *social competence* and interest in social activities (pp. 158–160; 214).[29] However, they maintain there is no evidence that the genders differ in regard to orientation to interpersonal cues, dependency on caretaker, willingness to remain alone, striving for social reinforcement, or time spent with playmates (Chapter 6).[30] In addition, there are insufficient data on gender differences in altruistic or nurturant behavior (see Stockard and Johnson, 1980).

We have not measured the full range of sociability-related issues but concentrated on those dimensions most closely related to self-evaluation and self-values. Subjects were asked how well liked they were by same sex and opposite sex peers and how much they cared about these types of popularity. They were also asked about participation in extracurriccular activities in school, about "dating" behavior, and parental expectations concerning dating.

Perceived Peer Popularity

There are virtually no significant differences between the sexes on perceived popularity with same or opposite sex peers. Table 3.1 shows no significant MANOVA differences, and Table 3.4 (Rows 1 and 2) shows no significant Repeated Measures sex effects and almost no significant ANOVAs. In general, then, boys and girls report equal levels of peer popularity.

Valuation of Peer Popularity

Although adolescent girls in our sample do not rate themselves more favorably on interpersonal popularity, there *is* evidence that they care more about same sex evaluations than do boys. The MANOVA analysis indicates significant gender differences each year for valuation of peer popularity (Table 3.1). More specifically, girls care significantly more than do boys whether same sex peers like them in every grade (Table 3.4, Row 3). The Repeated Measures Design also indicates an overall significant sex effect for this variable. When the same question is asked concerning valuation of opposite sex popularity, almost no significant differences appear (Table 3.4, Row 4). In Grades 6 and 7 when asked whether they care most about independence, competence, or being well liked, girls are significantly more likely than boys to say they place the highest premium on being well liked (Table 3.4, Row 5).[31] In Grade 9 they are significantly more likely to say they place greater value on opposite sex popularity than upon competence (Row 6).[32] The Repeated Measure sex effect is significant for the first of these two questions but not for the question involving opposite sex popularity.

Thus, there is some evidence that girls are more invested than boys in peer relationships in general, but not specifically in opposite sex popularity. Once again, the differences that occur are already present in Grade 6 and pre-date adolescence.

Dating Behavior

There is evidence that boys begin to date earlier than girls. (See Appendix G for information about dating scale.) In Grades 6 and 7 boys score significantly higher on the dating scale (Table 3.4, Row 7). However, the difference in dating almost disappears by Grade 10. Furthermore, parents expect significantly more dating and interest in the opposite sex for boys than girls in Grades 6, 7, and 9.[33] (See MANOVA Analysis in Table 3.1 and ANOVAs and Repeated Measures on Table 3.4, Rows 8 and 10.) By Grade 10, however, parents no longer expect boys to date more. It should be noted that it is possible for boys to begin dating earlier than girls, even if dating is mostly among same-age peers. Such a pattern could be produced by several different boys dating only a few girls.[34]

Participation in Extracurricular Activities

There are few significant differences between boys and girls in terms of in school or out of school participation or leadership in clubs or sports activities and no significant Repeated Measures sex effects (Table 3.4, Rows 12, 13, and 15).[35] However, in Grades 6 and 7 girls are more likely than boys to report participating in coed activities (Row 14).[36]

In summary, in terms of establishing peer relationships, girls indicate neither greater popularity than boys nor greater concern with the opposite sex. As predicted, however, they are more invested in same-sex popularity. There are also differences between the sexes in the nature of their involvement with the opposite sex in pre- and early adolescence (Grades 6 and 7). Girls' interactions with boys are more likely to be set in the formal organizational context of an extracurricular activity, while boys are more likely to begin the independent, less supervised activity of dating.

Establishing Independence

The question is whether this difference in dating patterns reflects an overall tendency for boys to be allowed earlier independence. The need to establish physical independence is the third task of adolescence upon which we focus. Like sociability, independence can be defined in a variety of ways. When the issue is one of independence training, Hoffman (1975 a, b, c, 1977) and Eccles and Hoffman (in press) claim that boys receive more of such training than girls. Weitzman (1979), based on her literature review, hypothesizes that parents punish dependency behavior in boys but not girls (pp. 19–20). However, Maccoby and Jacklin (1974, pp. 320–323) report there is no consistent evidence across studies to suggest that one sex receives more reinforcement for dependency than the other.[37] When the issue involves a personality or behavior trait, some investigators report boys score higher on independence (Nesselroade and Baltes, 1974; Hoffman, 1975a, b, c), but Maccoby and Jacklin (1974, Ch. 6) report no gender difference in the tendency to seek close contact with adults or in the tendency for children to resist separation from parents.

In our study, we have primarily investigated the extent to which parents allow children to engage in certain specific independent behaviors, for example, taking a bus alone, going places at night without parental permission, being left home alone, holding a part-time job. In other words, are they permitted to hold jobs and are they permitted freedom from supervision and from chaperonage? There is evidence in the literature that boys are allowed independence of this type earlier than girls (Maccoby and Jacklin, 1974, p. 319; Block, 1976; Ch. 2; Weitzman, 1979).

Chaperonage

Our data also indicate that boys are allowed earlier independence from chaperonage than girls. The MANOVA analysis (Table 3.1) shows significant gender differences in independence all 4 years ($p < .001$). According to most of the one-way ANOVAs and the Repeated Measures Design, boys were significantly more likely to be allowed to go places without parental permission, to go out after dark without parental per-

TABLE 3.4. Peer Relationship Variables—Means for Boys and Girls[a]

	Grade 6		Grade 7		Grade 9		Grade 10		Repeated measures ANOVA[b] four point in time sex effect $p \leq$
	Boys (335)	Girls (286)	Boys (294)	Girls (258)	Boys (183)	Girls (178)	Boys (164)	Girls (150)	
II. Intensification of Peer Relationships									
A. *Peer popularity*									
1. Same sex	3.14	3.13	3.06	3.14***c	3.09	3.10c	3.04	3.08	n.s.
2. Opposite sex	2.32	2.36	2.64	2.67c	2.94	2.90	3.00	2.97	n.s.
B. *Value popularity*									
3. Care about same sex popularity	2.96	3.12***	2.79	3.12*	2.57	2.96*	2.58	2.76***	.001
4. Care about opposite sex popularity	2.09	2.21****	2.43	2.45c	2.86	2.82	2.93	2.79c	n.s.
5. Value popularity more than competence or independence	.20	.30**c	.21	.40*c	.20	.20	.15	.14	.05
6. Value opposite sex popularity more than competence	1.83	1.85	1.85	1.87	1.77	1.86***c	1.84	1.90c	n.s.
C. 7. *Dating behavior*	1.01	.91****	1.20	1.10****	1.65	1.56	1.77	1.75	n.s.

74

D. *Others' expectations regarding opposite sex relationships*

8. Parents expect to date	−.48	−2.19*	−.12	−1.51*c	.75	.34****c	1.05	1.19c	.001
9. Same sex friends expect dating	−.15	−.26	.47	.42c	.81	.96c	1.13	1.32c	n.s.
10. Parents expect interest in opposite sex	.07	−.12*	.10	−.03***	—	—	—	—	.05
11. Same sex peers expect interest in opposite sex	.16	.25****	.26	.30	—	—	—	—	.01

E. *Participation in activities*

12. Total in-school clubs and sports	1.04	.92	.95	.79c	.87	.99	.88	1.35*c	n.s.
13. Total out-of-school clubs and sports	.57	.53	.56	.58c	.56	.57	.57	.63c	n.s.
14. Coed clubs (in and out of school)	.58	.79**c	.93	1.23****c	—	—	—	—	n.s.
15. Leadership in clubs and sports	.30	.27	.26	.18****c	.46	.43	.27	.30	n.s.

[a]According to a One-Way Analysis of Variance: *$p < .001$; **$p < .01$; ***$p < .05$; ****$p < .10$.
[b]The Repeated Measures ANOVA was based on those cases for which we have data at all four points in time. The means are based on the largest number of cases each year.
[c]There are homogeneity of variance problems here.

mission, and to be left home alone. Where differences were not statistically significant (in certain grades and for being allowed to take a bus without an adult), they were in the same direction[38] (Table 3.5).

Jobs

While self-ratings of independence did not distinguish boys and girls (Table 3.5, Row 7), their part-time job pattern did (Table 3.5, Row 6). The only independence behavior significantly more frequent among females was baby-sitting. As might be expected, girls were more likely to baby-sit (for other than their own siblings) in all 4 years ($p < .001$ for all ANOVAs and for the Repeated Measures sex effect). However, boys were significantly more likely to hold other types of part-time jobs outside the home in all 4 years ($p < .001$ for all ANOVAs and for the Repeated Measures sex effect).[39] Thus, the type of work for money was gender-role determined with girls more likely to baby-sit and boys more likely to hold other types of jobs.

Significant Others' Expectations

We also asked the students each year about the expectations of their significant others—parents, teachers, and friends—in regard to acting older.[40]

Boys in all 4 years are more likely than girls to report that parents expect "much older" behavior from them this year (Table 3.5, $p < .05$ all 4 years; Repeated Measures sex effect: $p < .001$). Friends' and teachers' expectations show hardly any significant gender effects, but the entire cluster involving significant others' expectations indicates significant gender effects all 4 years (Table 3.1).

In summary, there is evidence that boys are allowed earlier independence than girls in terms of being released from chaperonage (they seem to be allowed to date earlier, to go places without seeking permission, to remain alone). They also report parents as expecting older behavior from them. All of these differences are already evident in Grade 6.

Setting Future Aspirations

The MANOVA analysis indicates significant gender differences all 4 years for the cluster of variables involving aspirations (Table 3.1). Traditional gender-role patterns suggest that girls will be less likely than boys to wish to work at an occupation continuously through their adult lives, and boys will be less oriented to marriage and children. In fact, in sixth and seventh grade, males *were* significantly less likely to want to get married (Table 3.6, Row 2) or to have children (Row 3).[41] However, these

TABLE 3.5. Independence Variables—Means for Boys and Girls[a]

	Grade 6		Grade 7		Grade 9		Grade 10		Repeated measures ANOVA[b] four point in time sex effect $p \leq$
	Boys (335)	Girls (286)	Boys (294)	Girls (258)	Boys (183)	Girls (178)	Boys (164)	Girls (150)	
III. Establish Independence									
A. Independence from parents									
1. Take bus without adult	.98	.96	1.26	1.21	—	—	—	—	n.s.
2. Go places without parents permission	.19	.11**	.24	.15**	.39	.31	.59	.44**	.001
3. Parents permission not required after dark	.33	.16*	.53	.20*	.37	.22**	.47	.25*	.0001
4. Left home alone	2.13	2.04	2.39	2.34	2.83	2.75**** [c]	2.89	2.77*** [c]	.05
5. Times per month baby-sit	.42	1.81* [c]	.80	2.81* [c]	1.09	3.45* [c]	.62	2.68* [c]	.001
6. Part-time job	.28	.16* [c]	.37	.20* [c]	.45	.22* [c]	.50	.32* [c]	.001
7. Perceived independence from parents	3.05	3.06	3.01	3.03	3.15	3.14	3.13	3.21	n.s.
8. Perceived independent decision making	2.15	2.18	2.21	2.18	2.42	2.29**** [c]	2.37	2.37	n.s.
B. Perception that others expect older behavior									
9. Parents	3.26	3.10***	3.38	3.14**	3.49	3.25**	3.38	3.08** [c]	.001
10. Friends	2.73	2.92** [c]	2.81	2.92	2.83	2.86	2.86	2.77	n.s.
11. Teachers	3.42	3.20**	3.44	3.43	3.80	3.70	3.61	3.58	n.s.
C. Value independence									
12. Value independence	3.37	3.36 [c]	3.25	3.27	3.27	3.45***	3.16	3.34***	n.s.
13. Value independence vs. competence and popularity	.37	.36	.34	.24*** [c]	.36	.35	.36	.38	.07

[a] According to a One-Way Analysis of Variance: *p < .001; **p < .01; ***p < .05; ****p < .10.

[b] The Repeated Measures ANOVA was based on those cases for which we have data at all four points in time. The means are based on the largest number of cases each year.

[c] There are homogeneity of variance problems here.

77

TABLE 3.6. Aspirational Variables—Means for Boys and Girls[a]

	Grade 6		Grade 7		Grade 9		Grade 10		Repeated measures ANOVA[b] four point in time sex effect $p \leq$
	Boys (335)	Girls (286)	Boys (294)	Girls (258)	Boys (183)	Girls (178)	Boys (164)	Girls (150)	
IV. Plan for Future									
A. *Educational, occupational, and marital aspirations*									
1. Plan to go to college	.65	.63	.53	.59	.39	.52***	.38	.58*	.001
2. Want to get married	.69	.78***c	.74	.82***c	.89	.87	.90	.90	n.s.
3. Want to have children	.62	.74*c	.69	.76*****	.88	.84	.86	.87	n.s.
4. SES of ideal job	2.90	3.33*c	2.86	3.38*c	2.82	3.37*c	3.04	3.37*c	.001
5. SES of expected job	2.56	3.02*	2.59	3.17*	2.54	3.09*	2.58	3.03*	.001
6. Expect to work regardless of family	—	—	—	—	—	—	—	—	.001
B. *Perception that others expect career planning*									
7. Parents	2.88	2.58*	2.93	2.79***	3.50	3.30*	3.47	3.37	.01
8. Teachers	2.46	2.34	2.78	2.76	3.44	3.57****	3.36	3.53****c	.10
9. Friends	2.27	2.28	2.28	2.27	2.46	2.45	2.60	2.62	n.s.

[a]According to a One-Way Analysis of Variance: *$p < .001$; **$p < .01$; ***$p < .05$; ****$p < .10$.
[b]The Repeated Measures ANOVA was based on those cases for which we have data at all four points in time. The means are based on the largest number of cases each year.
[c]There are homogeneity of variance problems here.

78

differences disappeared by Grades 9 and 10 when almost everyone wanted to marry (91%) and have children (87%) (Table 3.7).

In terms of educational and occupational plans, girls were more, not less, oriented than boys to college in Grades 9 and 10 (Row 1),[42] and virtually all youth, regardless of sex, expected to hold some occupation (see Table 3.7). Desired occupations, unfortunately, were not coded into traditionally female and traditionally male ones (see Lueptow, 1981, 1984;

TABLE 3.7. Future Aspirations by Gender

	Percentages							
	Grade 6		Grade 7		Grade 9		Grade 10	
Aspirations	Boys	Girls	Boys	Girls	Boys	Girls	Boys	Girls
Expect to go to college								
Percentage	65	63	53	59	30	52***	38	58*
(*N*)	(326)	(277)	(277)	(248)	(174)	(169)	(159)	(141)
Do you want to have a job when adult?								
Percentage yes	100	96	100	98	100	99	100	100
	(335)	(286)	(294)	(259)	(183)	(178)	(164)	(150)
How long do you expect to work when adult?[a]								
Percentage all the time even if I have children	—	25	—	24	—	18	—	17
		(279)		(256)		(183)		(164)
Percentage all the time except when I have young children	—	37	—	41	—	57	—	54
		(279)		(256)		(183)		(164)
Ever want to get married (%)	69	78**	74	82***	89	87	91	91
	(306)	(282)	(274)	(251)	(172)	(175)	(180)	(154)
Ever want children (%)	62	74*	69	76***	88	84	87	88
	(301)	(281)	(265)	(250)	(172)	(174)	(180)	(156)
(Among those who wish to work either all the time after have children or after children are no longer young) Do you want to work full or part-time?								
Percentage Full-time	—	56	—	44	—	65	—	77
		(106)		(89)		(96)		(78)

[a]The multiple choice alternatives were "___ Just until I get married, ___ just until I have children, ___ all the time except when I have young children, or ___ all the time, even if I have children." (A card was used.)

*$p < .001$; **$p < .01$; ***$p < .05$.

Eccles and Hoffman, in press). They were, instead, coded according to the Hollingshead index of occupational prestige (Hollingshead and Redlich, 1958). Girls were significantly more likely to aspire to white-collar jobs, while a high proportion of boys plan for blue-collar work (especially "skilled labor").

The major distinction between the sexes in this area lies in the timing of the work. Girls did not usually plan a life-time, uninterrupted, career.[43] Only 25% of Grade 6 females planned to work continuously regardless of the age of their children, and this proportion decreased to 17% by tenth grade despite maturation and societal changes between 1974–1979 (Table 3.7). In fact, fewer girls in this sample aspired to work when they had young children than actually do so in the adult population—in 1977 Hoffman reported that 35% of white mothers with preschool children were working.[44] On the other hand, depending on grade in school, 62–75% of the girls expect to work all of the time in their adult life except when they have young children.

Thus, while middle adolescent boys and girls are similar in their desire for marriage and family, girls' occupational aspirations remain very different from those held by boys in 1978–1979. Work for the majority of girls was seen as a temporary activity to be given up at least temporarily when children are born.[45]

Others' Expectations for Career Planning

The MANOVA analysis indicates significant gender differences for the cluster of variables involving others' expectation of career planning in all but Grade 7. However, parents and teachers differ in the direction of their expectations. Parents are perceived to expect more career planning for boys than girls in all 4 years (Table 3.6, Row 7, Repeated Measures sex effect: $p < .01$; ANOVAs $p < .05$ in Grades 6, 7, and 9). However, in Grades 9 and 10, teachers are perceived to expect more career planning from girls (Row 8). The perceived expectations of friends in this regard show no significant gender differences.

In any case, parental expectations for career planning complement gender differences in parental expectation for dating early (Table 3.4, Row 8), and for acting older (Table 3.5, Row 9). In all cases, parents are perceived as expecting older and more independent behavior for boys, and this difference is evident as early as Grade 6. Parents may be generally more protective toward girls than toward boys.

Dealing with Conformity-Related Issues

Adolescents have been described as under great pressures to deviate from adult prescriptions, and the last set of dependent variables all have some relationship to conformity-deviance issues. However, they also have relevance for other issues as well; we shall place them in relevant contexts in the literature.

School Problem Behavior and Victimization

Since there are higher rates of juvenile delinquency and adult crime among males than females (Boesel, Crain, Dunteman, Ianni, Martinolich, Moles, Spivak, Stalford, and Wayne, 1978; Bush, 1983), since boys have been found to be more physically aggressive than girls and less compliant to adults (Maccoby and Jacklin, 1974),[46] since there is some evidence that boys have greater problems with impulse control (Block, 1976) and a greater propensity to risk-taking behavior (Hill and Lynch, 1983),[47] we expected to find males scoring higher in school problem behavior. While the school system did not allow us to ask questions about criminal behavior, we were able to ask students the extent to which in the last year they had gotten in trouble at school, were always getting into trouble with teachers, had been sent to the principal's office, had been suspended from school, had been placed on probation, and had been truant. Overall, in all 4 years boys were more likely to be behavior problems in school than girls (except for Grade 9 truancy) (Table 3.8, Rows 1–3).[48] The MANOVA analysis indicates significant gender effects for the cluster in all 4 years (Table 3.1, $p < .001$; the Repeated Measures sex effects are significant save for truancy, as are most of the ANOVAs [Table 3.8, Rows 1–3]).

It also appears that the victims as well as the perpetrators are more likely to be males than females. Our data agree with prior research on this point (see Boesel et al., 1978, p. 99). We asked youngsters in Grades 7, 9, and 10 if they had been subject to threats of being hurt or beaten, if they had experienced theft of objects costing more than a dollar, or if they had actually been beaten or seriously hurt. A victimization scale (described in Appendix G) was constructed based on these items (see Blyth, Thiel, Bush, and Simmons, 1980). Table 3.8 (Row 4) shows that in all measured years boys reported significantly more victimization than girls (Repeated Measures sex effect: $p < .01$; ANOVAs: $p < .10$, $p < .01$, $p < .01$).

Thus, problem behavior in adolescence involves males more in both roles—as perpetrators and as victims.

Academic Performance

The absence of behavior problems is one indicator of conformity. Being a good student can be regarded as another type of conformity. In fact, Hoffman (1975c) has posited that girls' school performance is motivated

TABLE 3.8. Conformity Variables—Means for Boys and Girls[a]

	Grade 6		Grade 7		Grade 9		Grade 10		Repeated measures ANOVA[b] four point in time sex effect p ≤
	Boys (335)	Girls (286)	Boys (294)	Girls (258)	Boys (183)	Girls (178)	Boys (164)	Girls (150)	
V. Deal with Conformity/Deviance Issues									
A. Problem behavior									
1. Problem behavior scale	6.83	5.68*	6.57	5.42*[c]	6.55	5.83*	6.50	5.65*	.001
2. Probations/suspensions[d]	1.17	1.03*[c]	1.18	1.05*[c]	1.31	1.22	1.37	1.25****	.001
3. Truancy	1.17	1.08***[c]	1.28	1.19[c]	2.05	2.41***[c]	2.55	2.54	n.s.
B. Victimization	—	—	.39	.32****	.46	.33**	.40	.26**	.01
C. Academic performance									
5. GPA	2.39	2.68*	2.24	2.67*	2.08	2.36**	1.73	2.13*	.001
6. Reading achievement score	−.29	−.11***	.11	.16[c]	—	—	.10	.24	.10
7. Math achievement score	−.27	−.34	.02	.13	—	—	.24	.26	n.s.
D. Perception that adults evaluate one highly									
8. Parents	1.03	.99	.82	.95	.73	.82	.59	.97*[c]	n.s.
9. Teachers	2.89	2.99***[c]	2.89	2.97****	2.81	2.90****[c]	2.83	2.99**[c]	.05
E. Perception of parent-peer relationship									
10. Parents like close friends	3.43	3.49	3.38	3.53****[c]	3.34	3.43	3.36	3.53**	.01
11. Close friends like parents	3.38	3.51***	3.36	3.53**	3.33	3.39[c]	3.45	3.49	.05

[a]According to a One-Way Analysis of Variance: *p < .001; **p < .01; ***p < .05; ****p < .10.
[b]The repeated measures ANOVA was based on those cases for which we have data at all four points in time. The means are based on the largest number of cases each year.
[c]There are homogeneity of variance problems here.
[d]There is some overlap between the problem-behavior scale and the probations-suspensions variable, since the probations-suspensions variable is one of four items in the scale.

more by need for adult approval than by need for achievement (see Stein and Bailey, 1975); and Cross (1975) has noted:

> The many explanations offered [for girls' high grades in school] include the frequent observations that girls tend to be more conscientious, conforming, and docile in the classroom. (p. 343)

In fact, as we discussed previously (Table 3.2, Rows 17 and 18), girls in our data set care somewhat more about their school work than boys (although the differences reach significance only in Grade 10) but not more about being smart.

However, the issue of gender and achievement has a substantial history in the literature, independent of the issue of conformity. The question has been raised as to whether females' traditionally lower occupational achievement could have led to and/or has been the result of a lower need for achievement or a lower academic ability (Horner, 1968; Maccoby and Jacklin, 1974; Tresemer, 1977; Stockard and Johnson, 1980). Considerable data indicate, however, that girls do not show lower academic ability. At least in early years they earn higher grades than boys (Maccoby and Jacklin, 1974; Cross, 1975; Lueptow, 1980a; Eckland and Alexander, 1980). While some studies suggest that girls score lower than boys in need for achievement when a projective test involves same sex individuals (see McClelland, 1953; Veroff, McClelland, and Ruhland, 1975), Maccoby and Jacklin (1974) conclude that there are no consistent gender differences in need for achievement across measures.[49] They also note, however, that when a situation of competition is activated,[50] boys score higher than girls in need for achievement.

Maccoby and Jacklin (1974) and Stockard and Johnson (1980) conclude that females' lower occupational attainments have been directly due to gender norms and discrimination rather than through intervening variables such as lower ability or lower need for achievement. We have not measured need for achievement, but we have measured grades in school and find, as have earlier investigators, that girls have significantly higher GPAs all 4 years (Table 3.8, Row 5) and that the Repeated Measures sex effect is significant: $p < .001$.

Some investigators suggest that as they get older, girls traditionally have held back in their performance perhaps because of a "motive to avoid success."[51] Girls have been afraid that others would perceive them as less feminine if their achievement were higher than that of boys. Maccoby and Jacklin (1974) note that many studies fail to replicate Horner's work, and there is some evidence that the gender difference in this regard may be decreasing (Hoffman, 1975a, Ch. 13). In any case, our data show that Grade 10 girls are still outperforming their male counterparts in GPA.

In addition to GPA, we have indications of verbal and math ability based on standardized achievement tests administered by the school system in Grades 6, 7, and 10.[52] Prior literature has indicated that boys score higher in math ability tests and spatial relations while girls score higher in the verbal area, and that these gender differences become more pronounced in adolescence than earlier.[53] However, based on newer studies, recent reviewers regard these math–verbal differences as less clear than do earlier investigators and reviewers.[54] In our data, in all years girls score higher in reading achievement, although the difference is significant only in Grade 6 (Table 3.8, Row 6; Repeated Measures sex effect: $p < .10$). However, our data show no significant gender differences in the math achievement tests (Row 7). The direction of differences follows no clear pattern either—in Grade 6 girls do worse, in Grade 7 they do better, and in Grade 10 there is virtually no difference. We cannot determine the extent to which these results are muddied by the fact that the school system used a different test each year.[55]

In any case where there are significant differences in the academic area, they favor girls. Girls have earned higher GPAs and score higher in verbal achievement tests. (The MANOVA analysis indicates a significant gender effect across all these academic performance variables each year; see Table 3.1.) The relationships of these objective facts to the self-image analogs presented earlier are very interesting (Table 3.2, Rows 13 and 14). Despite their lower scores, it is boys who rate themselves as "smarter," and there are no significant differences in self-ratings of "good at school work." These results are compatible with studies that show that boys attribute poor performance to "bad luck," while girls attribute their failures to lack of ability (Dweck, Davidson, Nelson, and Enng, 1978; Stipek, 1984; Frieze, Whitley, Hansuy, and McHugh, 1982; Bush and Simmons, in press; Bush, in press).[56] While we cannot be certain that girls' higher academic performance is an indicator of an underlying tendency to conform, the results are at least compatible with such an interpretation.

Adults' Evaluation

Conformity to adults' prescriptions could be expected to result in higher evaluations by these adults and in indications of less conflictful relationships with adults. The MANOVA analyses in regard to "Perception That Adults Evaluate One Highly" and "Perception of Parent–Peer Relationships" indicate significant differences in most, but not all, years (Table 3.1). Teachers in all 4 years are perceived as rating the girls more highly (Table 3.8, Row 9; Repeated Measures sex effect: $p < .05$).[57] For parents, there are no significant differences before Grade 10, but by Grade 10 parents are seen as rating girls significantly higher. In fact, in Grade 6, the "last year of childhood," the slight difference that occurs is in boys' favor.

After this point in all the adolescent years (Grades 7, 9, and 10) the differences favor girls even where not significant.

In addition to perceived evaluations, we used multiple-choice questions to ask students: "How much do your parent(s) like your close friends?" "How much do your close friends like your parent(s)?"

According to these indicators of perceived parent–child conflict, or absence of conflict, girls again score more "favorably." That is, in all years girls perceive parents and friends to like one another better than do boys. Although differences reach significance according to the ANOVA analysis in only some years, the Repeated Measures sex effect is significant for both variables across years.[58]

Thus, in general, adolescent girls appear to conform more to adult prescriptions than do boys—they are less likely to be involved in school behavior problems, they are more likely to perform well in school, are more likely to see parents and teachers as rating them highly, and are more likely to perceive their parents and friends to be in concert.

However, the issue of relationships with parents is more complex than these data suggest. In Grades 9 and 10 we collected a considerable amount of additional data on the parent–child relationships, on parent–child conflict, and on disengagement from parents (Tables 3.9 and 3.10). First, we, like other investigators (Hill, 1980; Montemayor, 1982), show that the responses of only a minority of students indicate severe conflict with parents (Table 3.9). From 4 to 22% of students indicate they argue "very much" with parents (depending on the issue and the gender); only 8–18% see "not very much" or "not any" agreement with parents on important issues. Larger proportions report not engaging in activities with parents and failing to seek their advice (Table 3.10). However, save for playing games with parents and seeking advice about same or opposite sex peers, it is still the minority who fall in the most "disengaged" category. On the other hand, the majority of youth report enjoying the company of close friends more than that of parents.

In terms of gender differences (Tables 3.9 and 3.10), girls do not always show closer relationships with parents. In fact, girls report arguing more frequently with parents,[59] agreeing with them less, finding their advice less helpful, and preferring the company of friends. On the other hand, girls *are* more likely to report seeking parental advice about problems with best friends and about dates. No gender difference is shown either in frequency of participation in activities with parents or in likelihood of seeking advice about future aspirations or about grades in school.

While it cannot be said, then, that boys have more daily conflict with parents or are more disengaged from parental advice and activities, adolescence for boys does appear to be a more independent and less protected time than for girls. Part of this independence involves a greater

TABLE 3.9. Levels of Conflict by Grade—Extent to Which Boys and Girls Argue with Parents

	Grade 9						Grade 10					
	Boys (N = 177)			Girls (N = 173)			Boys (N = 185)			Girls (N = 153)		
Conflict with parents	Very much	Some-what	Not very/ Not at all	Very much	Some-what	Not very/ Not at all	Very much	Some-what	Not very/ Not at all	Very much	Some-what	Not very/ Not at all
Verbal arguments with parents												
IN GENERAL, how much do you and your parents argue?												
Percentage arguing:	4	36	60	17	38	45	6	39	55	10	44	46
How much do you and your parents argue about WHEN YOU CAN GO OUT WITH YOUR FRIENDS?												
Percentage arguing:	10	30	60	17	22	61	7	24	69	12	24	64
How much do you and your parents argue ABOUT DOING CHORES AROUND THE HOUSE?												
Percentage arguing:	10	34	56	17	33	50	8	33	59	12	34	54
How much do you and your parents argue ABOUT YOUR CHOICE OF FRIENDS?												
Percentage arguing:	2	22	76	10	15	75	3	17	80	5	11	84
How much do you and your parents argue ABOUT WHEN YOU HAVE TO BE HOME AT NIGHT?												
Percentage arguing:	14	29	57	22	24	54	14	29	57	17	28	55
Share parents' opinions												
How much do you AGREE WITH YOUR PARENTS' IDEAS about the important things in life?												
Percentage agreeing:	15	77	8	13	69	18	14	77	9	15	71	14

TABLE 3.10. Extent to Which Boys and Girls Participate with Parents and Seek Parental Advice

	Grade 9						Grade 10					
	Boys (N = 177)			Girls (N = 173)			Boys (N = 185)			Girls (N = 153)		
	Very often	Some-what	Not very/Not at all	Very often	Some-what	Not very/Not at all	Very often	Some-what	Not very/Not at all	Very often	Some-what	Not very/Not at all
Participation in activities with parents												
How often do you and your parents play games together? Percentage:	7	43	50	9	44	47	4	44	52	10	38	52
How often do you and your parents work together on projects around the house? Percentage:	20	47	33	18	41	41	16	53	31	14	50	36
How often do you and your parents go places and do things together away from home? Percentage:	29	50	21	33	41	26	20	58	22	29	41	30
Seek advice of parents	Always	Usually	Not very/Almost never	Always	Usually	Not very	Always	Usually	Not very	Always	Usually	Not very
How much do you GO TO YOUR PARENTS FOR ADVICE? Percentage:	12	55	33	14	45	41	12	56	32	15	46	39
	Always helpful	Usually helpful	Not very/Almost never									
How much do you find your parents' advice HELPFUL in deciding what you should do? Percentage saying:	12	80	8	12	69	19	13	84	3	8	82	10

(Continued)

TABLE 3.10. (Continued)

	Grade 9				Grade 10			
	Boys (N = 177)		Girls (N = 173)		Boys (N = 185)		Girls (N = 153)	
	Yes	No	Yes	No	Yes	No	Yes	No
If you were worried about what you were going to do after high school . . . Percentage who would talk to your parents:	92	8	88	12	90	10	87	13
If you were worried about a problem you were having with your best friend . . . Percentage who would talk to your parents:	43	57	51	49	48	52	62	38
If you were worried about your grades at school . . . Percentage who would talk to your parents:	77	23	74	26	77	23	73	27
If you were worried about going out with a girl (boy) . . . Percentage who would talk to your parents:	28	72	37	63	24	76	43	57
	Parents	Close friends	Parents	Close friends	Parents	Close friends	Parents	Close friends
Who do you enjoy being with the most . . . your parents or your close friends? Percentage:	34	66	19	81	28	72	21	79

likelihood for boys to behave in ways that violate rules. Girls are less likely to be involved in antisocial behavior and more likely to conform to school expectations and to do well academically. Once again, these sex differences are already present in sixth grade, prior to adolescence proper.

Change Over Time

The findings just presented indicate considerable traditional gender-role differentiation among adolescents in a large Midwestern city in the mid- to late 1970s: Girls rate themselves and their sex less highly than do boys; girls value appearance and same-sex popularity more; boys are allowed earlier independence and are expected by parents to act in older ways; girls view a job as a temporary activity to be halted when they have young children; boys conform less to adult prescriptions related to school. The question is whether these differences were even larger in an earlier cohort. In Tables 3.11A and 3.11B, gender differences on many of these same variables are presented for the Baltimore cohort measured in 1968 before the Women's Movement had gained widespread acceptance.[60] In this table the Milwaukee results are weighted to counteract the fact that we had oversampled from K-8 school types (see Chapter 2). (However, the direction of significant findings, unless otherwise indicated, remains the same whether or not the Milwaukee sample is weighted.) Of course, we are comparing not only two different time cohorts, but two different cities and regions of the country.

Comparison of the two studies shows, first of all, that most gender differences are in the same direction. As can be seen in the bottom rows of Tables 3.11A and B, the vast majority of male–female differences that are statistically significant in either study are in the same direction in both.

Second, among variables where statistically significant gender differences are found in one or both studies, no consistent reduction of traditional gender differences is evident from the time of the first to the second study. This conclusion is verified whether we look at the bulk of these variables in which gender differences persist in the same direction or at the few variables where direction changes. Among the variables where gender differences persist in the same direction, the number of cases in which there are larger male–female differences in the 1968 Baltimore study is about the same as the number in which there are greater differences in the later Milwaukee study. Where differences are discrepant in direction between the two studies, there is also no clear pattern: Differences are not more traditional in one versus the other study.

Furthermore, in comparing the Baltimore and Milwaukee studies, one sees no more evidence of widespread lessening of traditional gender-role attitudes in Grades 9–10 (1978–1979) than in Grades 6–7 (1974–1975). Even though the children have grown older by Grades 9 and 10 and more his-

TABLE 3.11A. Comparison of 1968 Baltimore Study to 1974–1979 Milwaukee Study—Grades 6 and 7[a]

	Grade 6						Grade 7					
	Baltimore (1968)			Milwaukee (1974-1975)			Baltimore (1968)			Milwaukee (1975-1976)		
	Boys	Girls	Diff.[c]	Boys	Girls	Diff.	Boys	Girls	Diff.	Boys	Girls	Diff.
Weighted N	—	—		(1518)	(1336)		—	—		(1394)	(1235)	
Unweighted N[b]	(36)	(38)		(335)	(286)		(47)	(55)		(249)	(259)	
I. Establish Self-Image												
A. *Global self-image*												
1. Self-esteem	3.56	2.97	+.59	3.75	3.07*	+.68	3.17	2.79	+.38	3.80	2.90	+.90
2. Self-consciousness	2.53	2.22	+.31	1.78	2.20*	-.42	2.38	3.14*	-.76	1.80	2.05*	-.25
3. Self-stability	1.92	1.03*	+.89	1.84	1.49*	+.35	1.64	1.16***	+.48	1.82	1.49*	+.33
B. *Body-image*												
4. Perceive self as good-looking	2.76	2.58	+.18	2.91	2.64*	+.27	2.65	2.44****	+.21	2.89	2.63*	+.26
5. Satisfaction with looks	3.14	2.92	+.22	3.30	3.06**	+.24	3.06	2.96	+.10	3.26	3.06*	+.20
6. Care about good looks	2.58	3.34*	-.76	2.92	2.81	+.11	3.09	3.24	-.15	2.90	3.01	-.11
C. *Perceived self-competence*												
7. Perceive self as smart	3.11	2.95****	+.16	3.06	2.96*	+.10	2.96	2.84	+.12	3.02	2.97**	+.05
8. Good at sports	3.36	2.92**	+.44	3.27	2.90*	+.37	3.08	2.74***	+.34	3.19	2.79*	+.40
D. *Concern with competence*												
9. Value competence vs. popularity and independence	.33	.37	-.04	.38	.34***	+.04	.42	.15**	+.27	.45	.39**	+.06
10. Care about being smart	3.56	3.58	-.02	3.56	3.50**	+.06	3.49	3.44	+.05	3.46	3.44	+.02
11. Care about good at sports	3.30	3.03	+.27	3.30	2.96*	+.34	3.53	3.13**	+.40	3.08	2.83*	+.25
E. *Gender role attitudes*												
12. Positive feelings about being own gender	3.55	3.32	+.23	3.60	3.21*	+.39	3.60	3.36****	+.24	3.54	3.25*	+.29
13. Care about not acting like opposite sex	2.61	2.14****	+.47	2.59	2.01*	+.58	2.45	2.48	-.03	2.63	2.04*	+.59
14. How often act like opposite sex	1.18	2.54*	-1.36	1.28	2.48*	-1.20	1.16	2.12*	-.96	1.26	2.36*	-1.10
F. 15. *Depressive affect*	1.91	1.86	+.05	1.80	1.75	+.05	2.21	1.98	+.23	2.00	1.85*	+.05

II. Intensification of Peer Relationships

	M	F	Diff	M	F	Diff	M	F	Diff	M	F	Diff
A. Peer popularity												
16. Same sex	3.22	3.24	−.02	3.21	3.17	+.04	3.00	3.17	−.17	3.09	3.14***	−.05
17. Opposite sex	2.65	2.73	−.08	2.35	2.34	+.01	2.71	2.71	±.00	2.66	2.64	+.02
B. Value popularity												
18. Care about same sex popularity	2.86	3.34**	−.48	2.99	3.12***	−.13	2.74	3.16**	−.42	2.82	3.18*	−.36
19. Care about opposite sex popularity	2.52	2.68	−.16	2.08	2.21*	−.13	2.96	3.00	−.04	2.51	2.48	+.03
20. Value popularity more than competence or independence	.33	.50	−.17	.22	.27**	−.05	.34	.65**	−.31	.18	.34*	−.16
C. Participation in activities												
21. Total in-school clubs and sports	1.12	.86	+.26	1.07	.86*	+.21	.56	.50	+.06	.79	.58*	+.21
22. Total out-of-school clubs and sports	1.00	.92	+.08	.61	.50*	+.11	1.04	.51**	+.53	.61	.51**	+.10
23. Leadership in clubs and sports	.63	.58	+.05	.33	.26*	+.07	.53	.49	+.04	.26	.14*	+.12
III. Establish Independence												
24. Value independence vs. competence and popularity	.33	.13***	+.20	.40	.40	±.00	.23	.20	+.03	.37	.26*	+.11
IV. Plan for Future												
25. Plan to go to college	2.11	2.04	+.07	2.20	2.18	+.02	2.03	2.19	−.16	2.14	2.18***	−.04
26. Want to get married	.66	.82	−.16	.70	.83*	−.13	.71	.85****	−.14	.75	.85*	−.10
V. Deal with Conformity/Deviance Issues												
Perception that adults evaluate one highly												
27. Mother	3.28	3.13	+.15	3.55	3.46*	+.09	3.15	3.16	−.01	3.44	3.48	−.04
28. Father	3.18	3.18	±.00	3.53	3.43*	+.10	3.28	3.13	+.15	3.40	3.39	+.01
29. Teachers	3.09	2.97	+.12	2.93	3.02***	−.09	2.72	2.85	−.13	2.90	2.97	−.07
Number of variables showing significant differences in one or both studies[d]			24						21			
Of these, how many show gender differences in same direction in both studies?			18						20			

[a] According to a One-Way ANOVA, *p < .001, **p < .01, ***p < .05, ****p < .10.

[b] The Milwaukee sample was weighted to better reflect the population proportions in computing means. However, significance levels were interpreted based on unweighted Ns, since the weighting procedure inflates the ''N.''

[c] The female mean is subtracted from the male mean. Therefore, a positive difference indicates a higher male score; a negative difference a higher female score.

[d] Since the entries in Rows 9, 20, and 24 are dummy variables based on the same question and therefore not independent, only two out of three are included in this tally (Rows 9 and 20). If males and females are tied in one study but not the other, differences are treated as if in different directions for this tally.

TABLE 3.11B. Comparison of 1968 Baltimore Study to 1974–1979 Milwaukee Study—Grades 9 and 10ᵃ

	Grade 9						Grade 10					
	Baltimore (1968)			Milwaukee (1977–1978)			Baltimore (1968)			Milwaukee (1978–1979)		
	Boys	Girls	Diff.	Boys	Girls	Diff.	Boys	Girls	Diff.	Boys	Girls	Diff.
Weighted N	—	—		(953)	(931)		—	—		(957)	(829)	
Unweighted Nᵇ	(45)	(37)		(183)	(178)		(32)	(12)		(164)	(150)	
I. Establish Self-Image												
A. Global self-image												
1. Self-esteem	3.50	3.03	+.47	4.34	3.24**	+1.10	3.75	2.91	+.84	4.30	3.42*	+.88
2. Self-consciousness	2.44	3.19**	−.75	2.00	2.26*	−.26	2.38	2.50	−.12	2.04	2.19*	−.15
3. Self-stability	1.45	1.22	+.23	1.98	1.47*	+.51	1.16	.75	+.41	1.91	1.53	+.38
B. Body-image												
4. Perceive self as good-looking	2.65	2.50	+.15	2.92	2.62*	+.30	2.76	2.67	+.09	2.95	2.70*	+.25
5. Satisfaction with looks	2.98	2.77****	+.21	3.20	2.97*	+.23	3.13	2.90****	+.23	3.19	2.99*	+.20
6. Care about good looks	3.18	3.14	+.04	2.88	3.08**	−.20	3.09	3.50****	−.41	2.90	2.95	−.05
C. Perceived self-competence												
7. Perceive self as smart	3.00	2.86	+.14	3.03	2.98***	+.05	2.91	3.10	−.19	3.06	2.96*	+.10
8. Good at sports	3.07	2.73**	+.34	3.08	2.57*	+.51	2.91	2.75	+.16	3.01	2.53*	+.48
D. Concern with competence												
9. Value competence vs. popularity and independence	.25	.22	+.03	.47	.47	±.00	.42	.48	−.06	.52	.48	+.04
10. Care about being smart	3.62	3.38****	+.24	3.32	3.23*	+.09	3.41	3.25	+.16	3.24	3.23	+.01
11. Care about good at sports	3.40	2.86**	+.54	2.93	2.51*	+.42	3.12	2.92	+.20	2.86	2.39*	+.47
E. Gender role attitudes												
12. Positive feelings about being own gender	3.59	3.38	+.21	3.45	3.32****	+.13	3.47	3.60	−.13	3.54	3.43	+.11
13. Care about not acting like opposite sex	2.66	2.32***	+.34	2.64	2.14*	+.50	2.62	2.70	−.08	2.52	2.00	+.52
14. How often act like opposite sex	1.10	1.91	−.81	1.23	2.19*	−.96	1.04	2.10*	−1.06	1.28	2.19*	−.91
F. 15. *Depressive affect*	1.91	1.89	+.02	1.92	1.70*	+.22	2.40	2.00	+.40	2.10	1.79*	+.31

II. Intensification of Peer Relationships

A. Peer popularity												
16. Same sex	3.16	3.11	+.05	3.08	3.07	+.01	3.07	3.08	-.01	3.07	3.03	+.04
17. Opposite sex	3.02	2.75***	+.27	2.94	2.88	+.06	2.93	3.00	-.07	3.01	2.91	+.10
B. Value popularity												
18. Care about same sex popularity	2.91	3.16****	-.25	2.63	2.99*	-.36	2.75	3.33***	-.58	2.61	2.79***	-.18
19. Care about opposite sex popularity	3.22	2.86****	+.36	2.86	2.75**	+.11	3.16	3.33	-.17	2.97	2.77*	+.20
20. Value popularity more than competence or independence	.59	.62	-.03	.20	.19	+.01	.19	.75*	-.56	.12	.12	±.00
C. Participation in activities												
21. Total in-school clubs and sports	.49	.44	+.05	.88	.96	-.08	.31	.64	-.33	.74	1.14*	-.40
22. Total out-of-school clubs and sports	1.16	1.08	+.08	.60	.55	+.05	1.38	.92	+.46	.55	.57	-.02
23. Leadership in clubs and sports	.64	.54	+.10	.34	.22*	+.12	.53	.75	-.22	.26	.28	-.02
III. Establish Independence												
24. Value independence vs. competence and popularity	.16	.16	±.00	.33	.34	-.01	.19	.08	+.11	.36	.40	-.04
IV. Plan for Future												
25. Plan to go to college	2.36	1.93**	+.43	2.22	2.44*	-.22	2.18	2.14	+.04	2.35	2.53*	-.18
26. Want to get married	.93	.92	+.01	.89	.89	±.00	.86	.92	-.06	.91	.90	+.01
V. Deal with Conformity/Deviance Issues												
Perception that adults evaluate one highly												
27. Mother	3.04	3.24	-.20	3.39	3.36	+.03	3.19	3.25	-.06	3.26	3.40*	-.14
28. Father	3.12	3.29	-.17	3.27	3.32	-.05	2.93	3.38****	-.45	3.16	3.26**	-.10
29. Teachers	2.93	2.92	+.01	2.83	2.91****	-.08	2.86	2.92	-.06	2.81	2.99**	-.18

Number of variables showing significant differences in one or both studies[a]: 20   21

Of these, how many show gender differences in same direction in both studies?: 17   15

[a] According to a One-Way ANOVA. *p < .001, **p < .01, ***p < .05, ****p < .10.

[b] The Milwaukee sample was weighted to better reflect the population proportions in computing means. However, significance levels were interpreted based on unweighted Ns, since the weighting procedure inflates the "N."

[c] The female mean is subtracted from the male mean. Therefore, a positive difference indicates a higher male score; a negative difference indicates a higher female score.

[d] Since the entries in Rows 9, 20, and 24 are dummy variables based on the same question and therefore not independent, only two out of three are included in this tally (Rows 9 and 20). If males and females are tied in one study but not the other, differences are treated as if in different directions for this tally.

torical time has passed by 1978–1979, gender differences are persistent. In both studies, in both early and middle adolescence, girls' self-image, body-image, view of their own intelligence, and, for the most part, attitude toward their own sex is more negative than that of boys. In both studies, boys value sports more than do girls, and girls value same sex popularity more than do boys. Furthermore, if we compare the absolute scores for females in the Baltimore and Milwaukee studies, there is no evidence that females are developing a more positive attitude toward being a girl.

Within this larger picture, however, there are some suggestions of change in self-values. Traditionally girls place higher value on looks and same sex popularity than do boys (see Tables 3.11A and B, Rows 6, 18, and 20). Sex differences in these regards are generally larger in the earlier Baltimore study than in the later Milwaukee study (but with the exception of Grade 9 in Rows 6 and 18).[61]

In addition, in the Baltimore study, in Grades 9 and 10 boys were more likely to expect to go to college than girls. In the later Milwaukee study, in Grades 9 and 10 girls were the ones more likely to expect to attend college. These findings fit with other research on 1970s cohorts.[62] They are also consistent with Cross's (1975) report that both sexes are now being graduated from high school with equal frequency compared to earlier male advantage and her projections that the gender difference in college attendance will be closing in the near future as women attend in higher proportions.[63]

In summary, our comparison of gender differences in two cohorts separated by 6–11 years suggests that overall far less has changed than might be expected, although there are some hints of change even in these data. Lueptow (1980a, 1984), Duncan and Duncan (1978), and Nesselroade and Baltes (1974) also report much persistence of differences over time. Again it should be noted that we have not measured some of the attitudes that have shown change among adults in other studies.[64]

While we have measured occupational aspirations in the Milwaukee study and shown that most girls do not project an unbroken career line, we have no comparable measure in the earlier data. Lueptow (1984) reports somewhat of an increase between 1964 and 1975 in female occupational aspirations, and others suggest an increase in college women's occupational goals and commitment (see Weitzman, 1979; Cross, 1975; Veroff et al., 1981) as well as in the proportion of women working (Eccles and Hoffman, in press). On the other hand, investigators do report persistent gender differences in occupational values (Herzog, 1982; Lueptow, 1980a, 1984) and in sex-typing of jobs actually held rather than desired (Eccles and Hoffman, in press; Lueptow, 1981).

It is, of course, possible that *we* would have seen larger gender-role changes had we been able to compare two cohorts from the same region of the country. The Midwest may be slower to exhibit change than either coast. Other studies that report relatively little change were also from the Midwest: Lueptow's studies (1980a, 1981) were conducted in Wisconsin, while Duncan and Duncan's (1978) samples were from Detroit.

It also should be noted that most of the studies demonstrating change utilized adult samples; our studies, Lueptow's research (1980a), and that of Nesselroade and Baltes (1974) were based on adolescents, and all showed persistence over time. Early and middle adolescence may be developmental periods when gender differences are temporarily intensified or more stereotyped (Hill and Lynch, 1983). This issue will be dealt with more directly in Chapter 4.

Summary

In summary, these data collected in the mid to late 1970s indicate persistence of many gender differences related to tasks of adolescence. On most of the variables measured in both a 1968 cohort in Baltimore and a 1974–1979 cohort in Milwaukee, male–female differences remain in the same direction with little indication of narrowing. This pattern of persistence has occurred despite the growth of the Women's Movement throughout the 1970s. Within the larger context of persistence, there are some suggestions of change in specific areas: Whereas middle adolescent boys were more likely than girls to aspire to college in the earlier study, girls are more likely to express such aspirations in the later research. In addition, the tendency for girls to value looks and same-sex popularity more than boys may have been reduced.

A need to construct a new self-image when confronted with the major physical and social changes of puberty can be regarded as one task of adolescence. Although the literature is controversial on this point, we find evidence that girls scored lower than boys in global self-esteem. Girls also scored less favorably in terms of stability of the self-picture, self-consciousness, body-image, and attitude toward one's own sex. At the same time as girls rated their appearance less favorably, they were more likely to care about their looks, in line with traditional gender-role values. Ranking low in an area about which one cares a great deal would be expected to have greater global repercussions than ranking low in an area that is not highly valued. In fact, this combination of body-image dissatisfaction and high valuation of appearance tended to be particularly detrimental to the overall self-esteem of girls.

A second task of adolescence involves the intensification of close peer relationships. According to traditional views, females are socialized for greater involvement in expressive activities with others, males for greater instrumental activity. Therefore, it has been predicted that girls will be more sociable than boys. The controversy in the literature over this issue makes it clear that the exact method of defining sociability is crucial to the results. We have shown that adolescent and preadolescent girls placed higher value on same-sex popularity than do boys, although they were no more likely to perceive themselves as popular.

A third task of adolescence is the need to attain a higher degree of independence. Again the controversy in the literature makes clear the importance of the precise type of independence measured. On issues related to chaperonage and parental supervision, boys were allowed earlier independence than girls. Boys were allowed to date earlier, while girls were more likely to be involved in coed activities in a more supervised setting (i.e., coed clubs). Boys were also left alone and permitted to go places without parental permission more. Similarly, parents were perceived as expecting their sons to act older, to date earlier, and to plan for careers earlier than their daughters.

A fourth task involved the establishment of plans for adulthood. While this is primarily a task of later adolescence, these youngsters had started to form future aspirations. Although girls had relatively high educational aspirations and although most expected to work for a good part of their lives, only a small minority of girls expressed the desire to work continuously, even when they had young children.

Finally, a set of variables clustered loosely around conformity/deviance issues was examined. In adolescence there is greater opportunity and greater pressure for youngsters to deviate from adult prescriptions. Boys were more likely than girls to be involved in deviant behavior in school contexts both as perpetrator and victim. Adults, particularly teachers but also parents (in Grade 10), were perceived as evaluating boys less highly than girls (although the data do not support the simple conclusion that boys have a more conflictful relationship with parents than girls).

Boys also earned lower GPAs in school and scored lower on verbal achievement tests than did girls. It should be noted that despite their lower school achievement, boys did not rate themselves any lower than girls in intelligence or even in competence at school work. Our data do not show girls of this cohort scoring lower than boys in math achievement tests, as has been demonstrated in some earlier literature.

Whether one or the other gender was at a disadvantage in adolescence was a key question guiding this analysis. In terms of the *self-image,* girls clearly appeared at a disadvantage throughout the age period. However, girls did not score more unfavorably than boys on a depressive affect or happiness scale, and girls indicated fewer school behavior problems. It should be noted that there are investigators who claim that boys are generally more vulnerable than girls (Rutter, 1981). However, there is evidence emerging from other research which indicates that while boys may react more negatively to stressors in childhood, this pattern reverses in adolescence (Bronfenbrenner, in press; Werner and Smith, 1982). Our findings of more negative self-images for female pre-adolescents and adolescents are compatible with this latter view.

Another key question was whether boys and girls changed differentially in adolescence. This question guides the entire analysis of Chapter 4. However, at this point we should note that almost all key gender differences were already present by Grade 6.[65] A key issue for future investigation is to discover how far back into childhood such sex differences exist.

Footnotes

[1]See Bardwick (1971), Maccoby and Jacklin (1974, Part 3), Hoffman (1975a,b,c, 1977), Lipman-Blumen and Ticameyer (1975), and Eccles and Hoffman (in press). See Mussen (1969), Meyer (1980), and Matteson (1975) for discussions of the psychological mechanisms involved in sex-role identification and socialization. See Weitzman (1979) for a discussion of the role of the mass media, school textbooks, and other cultural factors in gender-role socialization.

[2]Also see Helson (1975), Duncan and Duncan (1978), Lueptow (1980a, 1981), Herzog (1982), Veroff et al. (1981), and Stockard and Johnson (1980).

[3]For current cohorts of adolescents, boys are more conservative in many of their gender-role attitudes than are girls (Herzog, 1982; Braito and Klundt, 1984; Bush, 1985; MacCorquodale, 1984).

[4]See Maccoby and Jacklin (1974), Petersen (1980), and Duncan and Duncan (1978).

[5]Also see Lenney (1977), Veroff et al. (1981), and Mackie (1983) for findings relevant to adults.

[6]Also see Engel (1959), Piers and Harris (1964), Rosenberg (1965), Carlson (1965), and Drummond, McIntire, and Ryan (1977).

[7]See Silverman (1968), Bamber (1973), Gove and Tudor (1973), Pearlin (1975), and Ross, Mirowsky, and Ulbrich (1983).

[8]See, however, Drummond et al.'s (1977) study of 500 youngsters from Grades 2 to 12 in an urban school district in central Maine. Self-esteem differences between the genders do not show up.

[9]As noted in Chapter 2, when analyses involve all 4 years of data (as in the Repeated Measures design), only those students for whom we have data at all time periods can be used. However, when we are looking at one grade at a time, we utilize all cases available that year. Since our best sample in Grades 6 and 7 involves the largest number of cases, we do not wish to eliminate students who were missing in later years from these analyses of early results. However, unless otherwise indicated, the direction of significant findings remains the same whether or not these cases are eliminated.

[10]Hill and Lynch (1983), Block (1976), Stockard and Johnson (1980), and Maccoby and Jacklin (1974, pp. 209–10).

[11]Do you usually tell people what things you really like, or .... ( )
Do you usually *not* tell people what things you really like? .... ( )

When you are unhappy, do you tell other people, or .... ( )
Do you keep it to yourself? .... ( )

When you are unhappy, do you think you *should*
    Tell other people how you feel, or .... ( )
    Keep your feelings to yourself? .... ( )

A kid told me: "I usually show other people how I really feel."
How about you? Do you . . .
    Usually show people how you really feel .... ( )
    Sometimes show people how you really feel .... ( )
    Never show people how you really feel? .... ( )

A person who keeps his feelings to himself usually doesn't tell others
what he really thinks and feels inside. How much do you keep your
feelings to yourself?
    Very much .... ( )
    Pretty much, or .... ( )
    Not very much? .... ( )

[12]See Rosenberg (1965, 1979), Rosenberg and Simmons (1972), and Simmons *et al.* (1977) for a discussion of the importance of self-esteem for emotional disturbance and overall adjustment.

[13]See Savin-Williams and Demo (1983) for a critical discussion of self-esteem as a global construct.

[14]See Matteson (1975) and Mednick *et al.* (1975).

[15]The difference between boys and girls varies from 35 to 59% of a standard deviation unit over the 4 years of measurement, a proportion substantially higher than that found by O'Malley and Bachman (1979).

[16]Clifford (1971), Rosenbaum (1979), and Rand and Hall (1983). See also Maccoby and Jacklin (1974, p. 214).

[17]Much theory and research on gender-role socialization contends that pressure to attract a future husband intensifies for girls at early adolescence (Bernard, 1975; Huston-Stein and Higgins-Trenk, 1978; Hill and Lynch, 1983; Bush, 1985).

[18]In the cases where there are significant homogeneity of variance differences, girls had greater variability in response than boys in all but one case.

[19]See Lerner and Karabenick (1974) for compatible findings.

[20]Morgan (1970), Broverman *et al.* (1972), Bem (1974), Bernard (1975), and Stockard and Johnson (1980).

[21]It should be recalled that these results are for white students only. For gender comparisons that include black students as well, see Bush *et al.* (1977).

[22]See McKee and Sheriffs (1957, 1959), Watson and Johnson (1972, p. 378), Kohlberg (1966), Hathaway and Monachesi (1963), Rosenkrantz, Vogel, Bee, Broverman, and Broverman (1968), Bem and Bem (1973), Simmons and F. Rosenberg (1975), F. Rosenberg and Simmons (1975), and reviews in Wylie (1979), Maccoby and Jacklin (1974), Weitzman (1979), and Bush (1985).

[23]See Hacker (1951), Bardwick (1971), and Carlson (1965).

[24]It should be noted we measured neither the extent to which male and female stereotypes were still held for a variety of characteristics, nor the extent of masculinity, femininity, or androgeny in gender self-ratings (see Weitzman, 1979; Broverman *et al.*, 1972; Mednick *et al.*, 1975; Stockard and Johnson, 1980, p. 167–168).

[25]Silverman (1968), Bamber (1973), Gove and Tudor (1973), Pearlin (1975), Radloff and Rae (1981), and Gove and Swafford (1981).

[26]Other investigators, who do find females to be at a disadvantage, seem to be using mild to moderate indicators of psychopathology rather than measures of happiness. Kessler and McRae (1981) show women to be at a disadvantage on a screening scale of psychophysiological symptoms. Similarly, Gurin *et al.* (1960)

and Veroff *et al.* (1981) show women to be at a disadvantage in terms of measures of actual or impending "nervous breakdowns," seeking professional help, and/ or feeling overwhelmed. However, Dusek and Flaherty (1981) show no gender differences among adolescents on an adjustment scale based on the following bipolar adjectives: relaxed–nervous, steady–shaky, refreshed–tired, stable–unstable, healthy–sick, happy–sad.

[27]Gilligan (1982a) finds that girls and women are more concerned with socioemotional aspects of moral dilemmas (responsibility to others), while males focus more on instrumental elements and abstract rights.

[28]Carlson (1965), Douvan and Adelson (1966), Sherman (1975), Matteson (1975), F. Rosenberg and Simmons (1975), Simmons and F. Rosenberg (1975), Block (1976), Hoffman (1977), Weitzman (1979), Petersen (1980), Offer *et al.* (1981, Ch. 4), and Dusek and Flaherty (1981). Also see Gilligan (1982b), Lueptow (1980b), Wylie's review (1979, pp. 317–28), and Hill and Lynch (1983).

[29]Also see Whiting and Whiting (1975), Lever (1978), Bell (1981), Rubin (1983), and Thorne (1984).

[30]Block (1976) raises some questions about these conclusions based on sampling and measurement.

[31]In addition, girls show significantly greater variance on this question than do boys.

[32]Where there are significant homogeneity of variance differences, boys show greater variability than girls.

[33]Where there are significant homogeneity of variance differences, girls show more variability than boys.

[34]See Bowerman and Kinch (1959) for evidence of girls' beginning dating earlier than boys.

[35]In Grade 7, we see the only case in which gender differences are significant using either weighted or unweighted means but the direction of differences is reversed with weighted versus unweighted (compare Table 3.4, Row 13 to Table 3.11, Row 22).

[36]Also, girls show significantly greater variability in response to this question than do boys.

[37]Also see Duncan and Duncan (1978), Lueptow (1980a, 1984), and Block's criticisms (1976).

[38]Tests for homogeneity of variance on these items revealed that girls showed significantly greater variance in terms of being left home alone.

[39]Tests for homogeneity of variance showed girls with significantly greater variance on the baby-sitting variable and boys on the other part-time jobs variable.

[40]See Appendix G for details about the construction of the score.

[41]Where there are significant homogeneity of variance problems, boys show greater variance than girls.

[42]Cross, in 1971, showed similar findings, although it was noted that boys were actually more likely to attend college than girls, and that they were more likely to aspire to completion of 4 years of college and to obtain graduate degrees.

[43]In 1974–1979, we assumed that boys did hold such aspirations and did not ask this question. In future studies, no such assumption could be made.

[44]See Kennedy (1985, Ch. 4) for estimates of the proportion working in 1980.

[45]Some recent studies of high school seniors indicate aspirations for more continuous work on the part of females (see Corder and Stephan, 1984; Braito and Klundt, 1984; and Herzog, 1982). For studies of other aspirations of other age groups, see Stockard and Johnson (1980), Weitzman (1979), and Cross (1975). For a study of occupational values and aspirations in a nonrandom sample of 600 eleventh grade boys and girls, see Tittle (1981).

[46]Also see Gilligan (1982b), Nesselroade and Baltes (1974), and Hoffman (1977).

[47]Hoffman (1977) questions whether greater male aggression (and presumably risk taking) seen cross-culturally have not evolved due to the gender-oriented division of labor with females oriented to child-rearing activities and males assigned more dangerous tasks farther from home. Also see Matteson (1975) and Sherman (1975).

[48]Where there are significant differences in variance on these variables, Grade 6 and 7 boys show greater variance than girls, but in Grade 9 the situation is reversed.

[49]Some of the studies reviewed show girls with higher achievement needs. Lueptow (1980c) also shows girls to have higher achievement orientations, but the person in the relevant question is male rather than same sex. See Nesselroade and Baltes (1974) for a study in which boys are more achievement oriented.

[50]Block (1976, Ch. 2) finds that boys' parents encourage competition more than do girls' parents.

[51]Horner (1968, 1970); see also Coleman (1961), Weitzman (1979), and Stockard and Johnson (1980).

[52]See Chapter 2 for details.

[53]Maccoby and Jacklin (1974), Sherman (1975), Weitzman (1979, p. 69), Nesselroade and Baltes (1974), and Eckland and Alexander (1980).

[54]See Fox (1977), Petersen (1980), and Becker and Jacobs (1983). Also see Plake, Hoover, and Loyd (1980), and Sherman (1980) for discussion of gender-bias in test items in mathematical tests.

[55]The causes for the gender differences in verbal, spatial relations, and perhaps math abilities are in controversy (see Petersen, 1980). The extent to which they are genetic or affected by differential socialization and different sex-role norms is in doubt. While Kagan (see Maccoby and Jacklin, 1974, pp. 311–312, 495) shows that mothers of female infants engage them more in certain types of vocalizations, Maccoby and Jacklin (1974) conclude there is no consistent difference in verbal stimulation of female and male infants across studies. With regard to adolescence, Fennema (1977) finds no sex differences in math achievement test scores when math background (number and type of course) is controlled.

[56]Hoffman (1975c) also reports that girls underestimate their academic ability. Also see Cross (1975).

[57]Although there are significant differences in variance, there is no clear pattern of one gender showing greater variability over the years.

[58]Although there are significant differences in variance, there is no clear pattern of one gender showing greater variability over the years.

[59]Also see Montemayor (1982).

[60] Missing variables were not measured in the Baltimore study.

[61]An earlier analysis of the Grades 6 and 7 data reports that when students had to rank the values of popularity, independence, and competence, the later Milwaukee study suggested that girls in the 1970s might be placing relatively higher value on competence than they were in 1968 (Bush et al., 1977–1978). However, when data from Grades 9 and 10 are added, the pattern is much less consistent (see Row 9 of Tables 3.11A and 3.11B). While in Grade 7 and 9 Milwaukee girls value competence more than Baltimore girls, in Grade 10 (and Grade 6) there is no distinction. Similarly, if one compares the difference between boys and girls in Grades 7 and 9, there is less traditional gender difference in the Milwaukee study. However, in Grade 10 (and Grade 6) there is more traditional gender difference in Milwaukee, with boys placing more value on competence than girls.

[62]See Rosen and Aneschensel (1978) and Macke and Morgan (1978).

[63]She notes that girls are more likely to be content with a 2-year college, however, while boys are more likely to aspire to a 4-year degree and beyond.

[64]For example, general approval of married women and mothers working (Yankelovitch, 1974; Helson, 1975; Thornton *et al.*, 1983; Thornton and Freedman, 1979; Cherlin and Walters, 1981; Mason and Bumpass, 1975; Mason *et al.*, 1976); approval of women participating in politics (Duncan and Duncan, 1978, Ch. 12; Mason and Bumpass, 1975); approval of equal pay for equal work (Yankelovitch, 1974); sex-typing of jobs and job aspirations (Lueptow, 1981; Herzog, 1982); approval of equality within marriage (Thornton *et al.*, 1983; See Mason and Bumpass, 1975; Yankelovitch, 1974); approval of the assignment of household chores according to gender (Duncan and Duncan, 1978, Ch. 8, 10; Mason, and Bumpass 1975; Mason *et al.*, 1976); need for achievement (Lueptow, 1984); need to avoid success (Hoffman, 1975a, Ch. 13); rates of major mental illness (Kessler and McRae, 1981).

[65]Nesselroade and Baltes (1974) also show that their gender differences were present by age 12.

4

TRENDS OVER TIME AND CHANGES IN GENDER DIFFERENCES DURING ADOLESCENCE*

Boys and girls show clear and persistent gender differences. Most of these differences, however, are already present in Grade 6. One question dealt with in this chapter is whether these gender differences intensify in adolescence. Another issue is whether boys or girls demonstrate evidence of disturbance as they move out of Grade 6 into the adolescent years.

Several ways of studying change are relevant here. In order to discover whether disturbance occurs and, if so, whether it increases during the adolescent years, both the *degree* and the *direction* of change are relevant. Measures of amount of absolute change over time will be examined as indicators of stability/instability; and the direction of changes in means will be investigated to determine whether reactions are positive or negative. The first question at issue, then, is whether there is stability or instability as youngsters enter adolescence? Second, do boys differ from girls in terms of stability at the time of the adolescent transition? Third, are changes in means that do occur negative in direction for either gender?[1]

Finally, in order to investigate the issue of gender intensification in adolescence, we shall see whether the mean scores of boys and girls become increasingly different with time. The question is whether initial differences become greater in early adolescence.

General Stability (Correlations)

The issue of stability and changes at entry to adolescence should be put in context. Before examining the degree of change of boys and girls upon transition into adolescence (Grades 6–7), we shall present the general level of correlation for our different outcome variables across the 5-year period of the study. These correlations indicate the overall level of rank-order stability, the extent to which the youngsters who score higher than their peers on an outcome at one point in time also score higher at a later point.

*By Roberta G. Simmons, Richard Burgeson, Dale A. Blyth, and Diane Mitsch Bush.

103

In a longitudinal study of adolescents, Dusek and Flaherty (1981) show average 1-year correlations for their variables of .48 to .52, although they *do not* present these correlations separately for males and females. Similarly, Table 4.1 (Column 1) shows average 1-year correlations for our variables for both genders combined. These 1-year correlations range between .19 and .79 with the modal correlation between .40 and .49.[2] Thus, some outcome variables show very high rank-order stability during adolescence; some show very little. The highest correlations involve GPA, scores on reading and math achievement tests, and self-estimates of athletic ability and of frequency of acting like the opposite sex. Variables with the lowest correlations include victimization, perceived expectations of others (significant others' expectation that one should act older this particular year, friends' and teacher's expectations about career planning, and friends' expectations about interest in the opposite sex), and dummy variables based on comparative valuation of competence, independence, and peer popularity.

Four-year correlations between the Grade 6 scores ("the last year of childhood") and Grade 10 (middle adolescence) are also shown in Table 4.1 (Column 2) and vary from .02 to .75, with the majority of correlations between .15 and .29. Variables with the highest correlations once again include GPA, achievement test scores, and self-ratings of sports ability and of frequency of acting like the opposite sex. Self-ratings of looks, satisfaction with weight, and reported school problem behavior are also highly correlated. Most variables that measure the self-image—global and specific self-ratings—demonstrate significant and moderate-size correlations in the range of .20–.39. On the other hand, variables that show very low correlations over the 4 years involve opposite sex popularity, valuation of opposite sex popularity, and peer and parent expectations about dating. Since interest in the opposite sex is a new phenomenon in adolescence, it is not surprising to find low correlations on these variables between Grades 6 and 10. Children who were the most concerned with the opposite sex in Grade 6 are not necessarily the same ones who are most concerned in Grade 10. Certain items measuring independence also show very low correlations over the 4-year interval (being left home alone, perceived independence in decision making), presumably because almost all children are attaining high independence in these regards.

In general, there is a moderate but not exceptionally high level of stability from childhood through middle adolescence on most of the outcome variables at issue. Objective academic scores demonstrate very high rank-order stabilities; self-image ratings, moderate stability; and self-values and perceived expectations of others, relatively low stabilities. Thus, two types of instability appear to characterize adolescence: The first involves society's expectations of appropriate behavior for the child; the second concerns the aspects of themselves that youth value, the areas about which they care.

TABLE 4.1. Stability by Gender and Year—Boys ($N = 161$) and Girls ($N = 149$)

	Average 1-year correlations[a] both genders (1)	Grade 6–10 correlations[b] both genders (2)	Mean absolute change (Standard Deviations)[c]			
			Grades 6–7		Grades 9–10	
			Boys (3)	Girls (4)	Boys (5)	Girls (6)
I. Establish Self-Image						
A. *Global self-image*						
1. Self-esteem	.54	.36[x]	1.18 (1.15)	1.28 (1.21)	1.06 (1.13)	1.17 (1.18)
2. Self-consciousness	.48	.25[x]	.71 (.71)	.56 (.63)	.52[ooo] (.64)	.55[++++] (.67)
3. Self-stability	.40	.22[x]	.88 (.78)	.75 (.78)	.87 (.82)	.80 (.82)
B. *Body-image*						
4. Perceive self as good-looking	.49	.40[x]	.28* (.45)	.39 (.52)	.12[o] (.33)	.30 (.48)
5. Satisfaction with looks	.46	.18[x]	.46 (.57)	.38 (.54)	21[o] (.41)	.18 (.41)
6. Satisfaction with weight	.58	.40[x]	.56 (.67)	.62 (.74)	.43[o] (.54)	.42 (.56)
7. Satisfaction with height	.42	.14*[xx]	.60 (.63)	.52 (.63)	.36[oo] (.56)	.49[+++] (.65)
8. Satisfaction with body build	.51	.38[x]	.47 (.57)	.54 (.61)	.35[o] (.49)	.35 (.55)
C. *Concern with body-image*						
9. Care about looks	.40	.12[xxx]	.53 (.62)	.56 (.67)	.45 (.56)	.50 (.59)
10. Care about weight	.54	.17[x]	.67 (.68)	.63 (.73)	.55[oo] (.62)	.44 (.58)
11. Care about height	.48	.27[xxx]	.60 (.66)	.58 (.70)	.56 (.63)	.49 (.65)

(Continued)

TABLE 4.1. (Continued)

| | Average 1-year correlations[a] both genders (1) | Grade 6–10 correlations[b] both genders (2) | Mean absolute change (Standard Deviations)[c] | | | |
| | | | Grades 6–7 | | Grades 9–10 | |
			Boys (3)	Girls (4)	Boys (5)	Girls (6)
12. Care about body-build	.50	.17[x]	.64 (.65)	.67 (.73)	.45° (.52)	.42 (.58)
D. *Perceived self-competence*						
13. Perceive self as smart	.44	.32[x]	.22 (.43)	.23 (.44)	.17 (.38)	.21 (.44)
14. Good at school work	.43	.26[x]	.26*** (.46)	.36 (.50)	.26 (.44)	.34 (.50)
15. Good at sports	.62	.42[x]	.42 (.53)	.40 (.57)	.33°°°° (.51)	.34 (.49)
E. *Concern with competence*						
16. Value competence vs. popularity and independence	.25	.08	.42 (.50)	.40 (.49)	.35°°° (.48)	.31 (.46)
17. Care about being smart	.31	.18[x]	.42*** (.55)	.56 (.61)	.42 (.54)	.49 (.63)
18. Care about school work	.36	.15[xx]	.39 (.54)	.40 (.60)	.37 (.53)	.41 (.56)
19. Care about good at sports	.44	.20[x]	.64 (.75)	.66 (.68)	.47°° (.69)	.51 (.64)
F. *Gender role attitudes*						
20. Positive feelings about being own gender	.44	.20[x]	.40 (.52)	.48 (.61)	.33°°° (.53)	.35 (.53)

21. Care about not acting like opposite sex	.41 (.57)	.43 (.64)	.49 (.58)	.49 (.72)	.39[x]	.47
22. How often act like opposite sex	.45 (.58)	.18° (.40)	.59 (.65)	.33* (.58)	.54[x]	.69
G. 23. *Depressive affect*	.71 (.74)	.61 (.69)	.74 (.74)	.64**** (.74)	.25[x]	.42

II. Establish Peer Relationships

A. *Peer popularity*

1. Same sex	.20[++++] (.40)	.14° (.36)	.29 (.47)	.35 (.49)	.15[xx]	.45
2. Opposite sex	.18 (.39)	.22° (.42)	.42 (.58)	.53 (.57)	.08	.46

B. *Value popularity*

3. Care about same sex popularity	.50 (.62)	.46° (.61)	.67 (.74)	.63 (.77)	.16[xx]	.39
4. Care about opposite sex popularity	.46 (.58)	.42° (.52)	.66 (.68)	.74 (.73)	.02	.46
5. Value popularity more than competence or independence	.09 (.29)	.16° (.37)	.38 (.49)	.35 (.48)	.19[x]	.34
6. Value opposite sex popularity more than competence	.14 (.35)	.21 (.41)	.14 (.34)	.16 (.37)	.09	.33

C. 7. *Dating behavior*

7. Dating behavior	.30 (.51)	.25° (.48)	.41 (.58)	.47 (.58)	.24[x]	.49

D. *Others' expectations regarding opposite sex relationships*

8. Parents expect to date	2.03[+++] (2.19)	1.38 (1.56)	1.84 (2.23)	1.94**** (1.80)	.09	.38

(Continued)

TABLE 4.1. (Continued)

	Average 1-year correlations[a] both genders (1)	Grade 6–10 correlations[b] both genders (2)	Mean absolute change (Standard Deviations)[c]			
			Grades 6–7		Grades 9–10	
			Boys (3)	Girls (4)	Boys (5)	Girls (6)
9. Same sex friends expect dating	.30	.10[x]	1.85 (1.54)	1.68 (1.62)	.99[o] (1.03)	1.17 (1.29)
10. Parents expect interest in opposite sex[d]	.33	—	—	—	—	—
11. Same sex peers expect interest in opposite sex[d]	.19	—	—	—	—	—
E. *Participation in activities*						
12. Total in-school clubs and sports	.47	.16[xx]	.96 (1.01)	.86 (.90)	.76 (.99)	1.01[+++] (1.08)
13. Total out-of-school clubs and sports	.50	.29[x]	.47 (.67)	.50 (.65)	.50 (.73)	.50 (.70)
14. Coed clubs (in and out of school)[d]	.38	—	—	—	—	—
15. Leadership in clubs and sports	.39	.20[x]	.28 (.45)	.24 (.43)	.21 (.41)	.24 (.43)
III. **Establish Independence**						
A. *Independence from parents*						
1. Take bus without adult[d]	.38	—	—	—	—	—

2. Go places without parents permission	.41	.22^x	.22 (.42)	.14 (.34)	.27^{oo} (.44)	.26 (.44)
3. Parents permission not required after dark	.41	.23^x	.35*** (.48)	.21 (.41)	.29 (.45)	.19 (.39)
4. Left home alone	.37	.10	.57 (.71)	.60 (.69)	.18° (.44)	.25 (.46)
5. Times per month baby-sit	.53	.27^x	.71 (1.22)	2.01 (1.86)	.94 (1.46)	1.68 (1.72)
6. Part-time job	.31	.15^{xx}	.31**** (.46)	.23 (.43)	.38^{oooo} (.49)	.31 (.46)
7. Perceived independence from parents	.32	.14^{xx}	.41 (.55)	.50 (.59)	.35^{oooo} (.52)	.40 (.54)
8. Perceived independent decision making	.26	.09	.53**** (.57)	.44 (.56)	.42^{ooo} (.54)	.34 (.48)
B. *Perception that others expect older behavior*						
9. Parents	29	.17^{xx}	.81**** (.76)	.77 (.76)	.89 (.75)	.71 (.67)
10. Friends	26	.17^{xx}	.78 (.71)	.73 (.66)	.69^{oooo} (.69)	.63 (.66)
11. Teachers	29	.03	.88 (.75)	.79 (.73)	.77 (.79)	.75 (.72)
C. *Value independence*						
12. Value independence from parents	35	.12^{xxx}	.61 (.66)	.65 (.71)	.49° (.58)	.42 (.57)
13. Value independence vs. competence and popularity	22	.14^{xx}	.42 (.50)	.33 (.47)	.33 (.47)	.33 (.47)

(*Continued*)

TABLE 4.1. (Continued)

| | Average 1-year correlations[a] both genders (1) | Grade 6–10 correlations[b] both genders (2) | Mean absolute change (Standard Deviations)[c] | | | |
| | | | Grades 6–7 | | Grades 9–10 | |
			Boys (3)	Girls (4)	Boys (5)	Girls (6)
IV. Plan for Future						
A. *Educational, occupational, and marital aspirations*						
1. Plan to go to college	.53	.30^x	.31**** (.46)	.23 (.43)	.21^{oo} (.41)	.15 (.36)
2. Want to get married	.59	.23^x	.20**** (.41)	.10 (.30)	.05° (.21)	.06^{+++} (.25)
3. Want to have children	.59	.16^{xx}	.21 (.41)	.13 (.34)	.07^{oo} (.25)	.10^{+++} (.30)
4. SES of ideal job	.47	.26^x	.58 (.77)	.69 (.94)	.50^{ooo} (.76)	.48 (.71)
B. *Perception that others expect career planning*						
7. Parents	.40	.15^{xx}	.62 (.68)	.73 (.67)	.37° (.52)	.38 (.51)
8. Teachers	.24	.12^{xxx}	.77 (.78)	.89 (.77)	.52° (.70)	.50 (.69)
9. Friends	.25	.09	.89 (.75)	.68 (.70)	.70 (.75)	.73^{+++} (.72)
V. Deal with Conformity/ Deviance Issues						
A. *Problem behavior*						
1. Problem behavior scale	.65	.41^x	1.08*** (1.02)	1.01 (.89)	1.30 (1.13)	.94^{++++} (1.07)

110

2. Probations/ Suspensions	.31	.16[xx]	.17* (.46)	.05 (.24)	.34° (.56)	.21 (.43)
3. Truancy	.54	.13[xxx]	.21 (.55)	.19 (.56)	.87° (1.16)	.69 (1.06)
B. 4. Victimization[d]	.19	—	—	—	—	—
C. Academic performance						
5. GPA	.74	.51[x]	.48 (.36)	.50 (.41)	.59°° (.44)	.58 (.49)
6. Reading achievement score[d]	.71	.75[x]	—	—	—	—
7. Math achievement score[d]	.61	.68[x]	—	—	—	—
D. Perception that adults evaluate one highly						
8. Mother	.50	.28	.63 (.85)	.54 (.75)	.44°°° (.75)	.37 (.66)
9. Teachers	.33	.25[x]	.31**** (.49)	.22 (.43)	.34 (.50)	.27 (.45)
E. Perception of parent– peer relationship						
10. Parents like close friends	.38	.16[xx]	.45 (.58)	.47 (.67)	.36 (.51)	.44 (.55)
11. Close friends like parents	.43	.16[xx]	.57** (.63)	.43 (.57)	.42° (.55)	.26 (.49)

[a] The Grades 6–7 and the Grades 9–10 correlation for the total samples available those years are averaged.
[b] F-test: [x]$p \le .001$; [xx]$p \le .01$; [xxx]$p \le .05$; [xxxx]$p \le .10$.
[c] Repeated Measures Analysis of Variance (two time periods: grades 6–7 and grades 9–10).
Sex effect: *$p \le .001$; **$p \le .01$; ***$p \le .05$; ****$p \le .10$.
Time effect: °$p \le .001$; °°$p \le .01$; °°°$p \le .05$; °°°°$p \le .10$.
Sex-by-time interaction: +$p \le .001$; ++$p \le .01$; +++$p \le .05$; ++++$p \le .10$.
[d] This variable was not measured at all four points in time. Therefore, the Repeated Measures Analysis could not be run. The average 1-year correlations was based on only one correlation.

Stability upon Entry to Adolescence (Degree of Absolute Change)

Correlations tell us whether the children who score high on a variable at one point in time are also the ones who score high at the second point in time. Comparison of correlations across subgroups, however, raises well-known difficulties, because the size of a correlation is influenced not only by the strength of the association but also by differences in variances on each variable within subgroups. In addition, correlations can be sizable even when children are changing a great deal, as long as the rank order among the children remains fairly stable across the variables. While gender- and grade-specific correlations are presented in Appendix D and are briefly discussed below, the main focus is more directly on degree of absolute change.[3]

One-year *absolute* change scores are constructed for each variable at the entry to adolescence (Grade 6–7) and in middle adolescence (Grade 9–10).[4] That is, *the direction of change at this point is ignored*, to be dealt with more specifically in the latter half of this chapter. Right now we wish to know whether children are changing a lot or a little, regardless of direction. For each variable, a mean absolute change score can be computed in different subgroups as well as the standard deviation around that mean.[5] If there is little stability, both the mean and the standard deviation of absolute change should be high; conversely, if stability is high, both the mean absolute change and standard deviation will be low.

A Repeated Measures Analysis of Variance was performed for each variable with the Grade 6–7 absolute change as the first "time period" and the Grade 9–10 absolute change as the second "time period." This analysis indicates whether there are significant gender effects, significant differences between Grade 6–7 and 9–10 change (called "time" effects), and significant gender by time interactions. Only children with measures in Grades 6, 7, 9, and 10 can be included. The results are presented in Columns 3–6 of Table 4.1.

Absolute Change at Entry to Adolescence

First, absolute change at the entry to adolescence (Grade 6–7) can be compared to absolute change in middle adolescence (Grade 9–10) for each gender. In Table 4.1, Column 3 can be compared to Column 5 for males; Column 4 to Column 6 for females. It is obvious for both genders that there is more absolute change (less stability) upon entry to adolescence than in middle adolescence. The focus here is on significant "time" effects. Of the 62 variables tested, there were 42 with significant time or time by gender effects. For males, 36 of these variables show higher mean absolute change scores from Grade 6 to 7 than from Grade 9 to 10. For females, 33 variables demonstrate higher mean absolute change in Grades 6–7, and only 9 variables demonstrate higher mean absolute change in Grades 9–10. As one would expect, comparison of the standard deviations leads to the same conclusion—that there is greater variability of absolute change during early adolescence (in Grades 6–7). For males the Grade 6–7 standard deviations of change are higher for 34 of these same variables; while the Grade 9–10 standard deviations are higher for only 7 variables. For females, the comparable figures are 31 versus 10 variables.[6] Several key variables show no significant difference in degree and variability of change between the two time periods: global self-esteem, perceived self-stability, academic self-rating, and depression.

Interpretation of these data raises some difficulty. There is clearly greater instability between Grades 6 and 7 than between Grades 9 and 10. However, without data prior to Grade 6, it is difficult to know whether the entry to adolescence, as a new phase in the life course, is causing the greater instability and change. The other possibility is that younger children in general show less stability on these measures than do older children.

Girls versus Boys

In Chapter 3, we showed that girls scored more negatively on many outcomes in all 4 years. However, despite that indicator of greater vulnerability, girls clearly do not show greater instability between Grades 6–7 than do boys (Column 3 versus 4). Here, we are focusing on significant gender effects and a comparison of boys to girls at the same time period. Out of the 62 variables tested, 22 showed significant gender or gender by time effects. Of these variables, boys showed higher mean absolute change scores for 17 variables in Grade 6–7; girls for 5. If standard deviations are compared, the comparable figures are 14 and 5.[7] In Grade 9–10 the division is closer to an even one, although girls show higher change on a few more variables (Column 5 versus 6). In terms of mean absolute change, boys score higher on 9 variables, girls on 13; in terms of standard deviation the figures are 10 versus 12.

In general, the outcome variables on which boys show greater absolute change involve independence, problem behavior, and parent/peer relations, while girls change more on several self-image variables. However, once again, it should be noted that there is no difference in absolute change between boys and girls on some key variables, for example, self-esteem, perceived self-stability, or GPA.

The question arises as to whether ceiling and floor effects could be introducing artifacts into these relationships. In some special cases it is possible. If both genders are moving in one direction and one gender starts out closer to the extreme in that direction, then this latter group has less room to move and a lower change score could result. Similarly, if over all 4 years the children are moving in one clear direction, the Grade 9 youngsters will find themselves closer to the ceiling or floor and will have less room to continue moving. This problem could result in lower change scores for the Grade 9–10 students than the Grade 6–7 ones. If the children are not generally moving with any such clear direction, then the fact that we are using absolute change scores should help prevent these artifacts. Where there are significant differences, we have examined each variable individually to see whether it would fall into these special categories where ceiling and floor artifacts are possible. Even if all such variables were removed from the analysis, the foregoing conclusions would hold. That is, many more variables show significantly greater changes in Grade 6–7 than 9–10, and girls are not generally more unstable than boys.

As noted already, gender-specific correlations were also run at each time period (see Appendix D). In general, an inspection of these correlations leads to the same conclusions.[8] Grade 6–7 correlations are lower than Grade 9–10 correlations, suggesting more instability at the time of entry to adolescence than later. Correlations for girls are not generally lower than those for boys. While theoretically subgroup differences in variance could be distorting these results, there are no significant differences in variances over time.[9] Thus, the differences between the Grade 9–10 and Grade 6–7 correlations could not be due to such an artifact. It is also unlikely that the gender-related conclusions are due to differences in homogeneity of variance.[10]

In sum, these findings indicate higher instability in early than in later adolescence and no difference in stability between girls and boys.

Direction of Change (in Mean Levels)[11]

A relatively high level of change and instability provides one indicator of disturbance upon entry to adolescence. This indicator ignores direction of change. It is clearly also important to examine the direction of change. Widespread change in a negative direction would certainly indicate disturbance. Means can be compared over the 4 years of the study to determine whether change is positive or negative for boys and for girls. A four point-in-time Repeated Measures Analysis will be used to identify significant changes over time; where change is significant, the direction will be determined.

Positive versus Negative Changes over Time

In the earlier (Baltimore) study, evidence of a negative turn in adolescence was presented (Simmons *et al.*, 1973; see Chapter 1 in this volume). Early adolescents scored, on the average, less highly than younger children on many of the variables we have measured here. The purpose of this volume is to determine whether these findings will be replicated and whether gender, school context, and pubertal development affect this change. At this point, overall trends will be examined, ignoring for the moment school context and pubertal change.

Table 4.2 presents the results of a four point-in-time Repeated Measures Analysis for all of the outcome variables with gender and time (grade in school) as independent variables. The gender effects have already been discussed in Chapter 3 (see Tables 3.2, 3.4, 3.5, 3.6, and 3.8). According

TABLE 4.2. Effects of Gender and Grade in School—Levels of Significance for Four Point-in-Time Repeated Measures Analysis ($N = 310$)[a]

	Between subjects gender (p)	Within subjects (p)	
		Time (grade in school)	Gender x-time
I. Establish Self-Image			
A. *Global self-image*			
1. Self-esteem	< .001	< .0001	n.s.
2. Self-consciousness	n.s.	< .0001	n.s.
3. Self-stability	< .001	< .05	n.s.
B. *Body-image*			
4. Perceive self as good-looking	< .001	< .10	n.s.
5. Satisfaction with looks	< .001	< .01	n.s.
6. Satisfaction with weight	< .001	n.s.	< .0001
7. Satisfaction with height	n.s.	n.s.	n.s.
8. Satisfaction with body build	< .001	< .01	< .05
C. *Concern with body-image*			
9. Care about looks	n.s.	n.s.	n.s.
10. Care about weight	< .001	n.s.	< .0001
11. Care about height	< .05	< .0001	n.s.
12. Care about body build	< .001	< .10	< .0001
D. *Perceived self-competence*			
13. Perceive self as smart	n.s.	n.s.	n.s.
14. Good at school work	n.s.	< .0001	n.s.
15. Good at sports	< .001	< .0001	n.s.
E. *Concern with competence*			
16. Value competence vs. independence and popularity	n.s.	< .01	n.s.
17. Care about being smart	n.s.	< .001	n.s.
18. Care about school work	n.s.	< .001	n.s.
19. Care about good at sports	< .001	< .0001	n.s.
F. *Gender role attitudes*			
20. Positive feelings about being own gender	< .001	< .10	< .10
21. Care about not acting like opposite sex	< .001	< .10	n.s.
22. How often act like opposite sex	< .001	< .0001	< .0001
G. 23. *Depressive affect*	< .05	< .01	< .10

(Continued)

TABLE 4.2. *(Continued)*

	Between subjects gender (p)	Within subjects (p)	
		Time (grade in school)	Gender x-time
II. Establish Peer Relationships			
A. *Peer popularity*			
1. Same sex	n.s.	< .05	< .10
2. Opposite sex[b]	n.s.	< .0001	< .05
B. *Value popularity*			
3. Care about same sex popularity	< .001	< .0001	n.s.
4. Care about opposite sex popularity	n.s.	< .0001	< .01
5. Value popularity more than competence or independence	< .05	< .0001	< .05
6. Value opposite sex popularity more than competence	n.s.	n.s.	n.s.
C. 7. *Dating behavior*	n.s.	< .0001	n.s.
D. *Others' expectations regarding opposite sex relationships*			
8. Parents expect to date	< .001	< .0001	< .0001
9. Same sex friends expect dating	n.s.	< .0001	n.s.
10. Parents expect interest in opposite sex	< .05	< .0001	< .01
11. Same sex peers expect interest in opposite sex	< .01	< .05	n.s.
E. *Participation in activities*			
12. Total in-school clubs and sports	n.s.	< .05	< .01
13. Total out-of-school clubs and sports	n.s.	n.s.	n.s.
14. Coed clubs (in and out of school)	n.s.	n.s.	n.s.
15. Leadership in clubs and sports	n.s.	n.s.	n.s.
III. Establish Independence			
A. *Independence from parents*			
1. Take bus without adult	n.s.	< .0001	n.s.
2. Go places without parents permission	< .001	< .0001	n.s.
3. Parents permission not required after dark	< .0001	< .0001	< .05
4. Left home alone	< .05	< .0001	n.s.
5. Times per month baby-sit	< .001	< .0001	n.s.
6. Part-time job	< .001	< .0001	n.s.
7. Perceived independence from parents	n.s.	< .0001	n.s.
8. Perceived independent decision making	n.s.	< .0001	< .10
B. *Perception that others expect older behavior*			
9. Parents	< .001	< .05	n.s.
10. Friends	n.s.	n.s.	n.s.

TABLE 4.2. (Continued)

	Between subjects gender (p)	Within subjects (p)	
		Time (grade in school)	Gender x-time
11. Teachers	n.s.	< .0001	n.s.
C. *Value independence*			
12. Value independence	n.s.	n.s.	< .10
13. Value independence vs. competence and popularity	< .10	n.s.	n.s.
IV. Plan for Future			
A. *Educational, occupational, and marital aspirations*			
1. Plan to go to college	< .001	< .0001	n.s.
2. Want to get married	n.s.	< .0001	n.s.
3. Want to have children	n.s.	< .0001	< .01
4. SES of ideal job	< .001	n.s.	n.s.
5. SES of expected job	< .001	n.s.	n.s.
B. *Perception that others expect career planning*			
7. Parents	< .01	< .0001	n.s.
8. Teachers	< .10	< .0001	n.s.
9. Friends	n.s.	< .0001	n.s.
V. Deal with Conformity/ Deviance Issues			
A. *Problem behavior*			
1. Problem behavior scale	< .001	n.s.	n.s.
2. Probations/ suspensions[c]	< .001	< .0001	n.s.
3. Truancy	n.s.	< .0001	n.s.
B. 4. *Victimization*	< .01	n.s.	n.s.
C. *Academic performance*			
5. GPA	< .001	< .0001	n.s.
6. Reading achievement score	< .10	< .0001	< .05
7. Math achievement score	n.s.	< .0001	< .05
D. *Perception that adults evaluate one highly*			
8. Mother	n.s.	< .0001	n.s.
9. Teachers	< .05	< .001	n.s.
E. *Perception of parent–peer relationship*			
10. Parents like close friends	< .01	n.s.	n.s.
11. Close friends like parents	< .10	n.s.	n.s.

[a]Students for whom we have interviews at all four points in time.

[b]This item is also used in the "dating behavior" cluster.

[c]There is some overlap between the problem-behavior scale and the probations variable, since the probations variable is one of four items in the scale.

to Table 4.2, there are also a great many significant time effects; that is, mean levels do change over time.

The question is the direction of significant differences. In fact, comparison of the means for each gender shows no consistent negative turn on those variables where there are significant time effects (see Tables 3.2, 3.4, 3.5, 3.6, and 3.8).[12]

Self-Image

As youngsters move from Grade 6 into adolescence, there is no clear trend of negative change in the self-image variables (see Table 3.2). For some self-image variables there is improvement with age: self-esteem and stability of the self-picture. For many of these variables, there are no significant differences: satisfaction with looks, with height, and rating self as smart. For most other variables the pattern with age is inconsistent. Only self-evaluation of athletic ability clearly declines with age for both genders.

Peer Relationships

The only clear change in peer relationships involves the opposite sex (Table 3.4). As would be expected, dating and perceived opposite sex popularity increase with age. There is some, not totally consistent, tendency for perceived popularity with the same sex to decline after childhood. The effects on participation in extracurricular school activities are not clear in direction and there are no significant time differences in leadership or participation in out-of-school activities.

Independence

As would be expected, adolescents report an increase in many specific independence behaviors and an increase in others' expectations of older behavior from them (Table 3.5).

Plans for the Future

Compared to sixth graders, adolescents report an increased desire to marry and to have children. But after sixth grade, there is a decrease in the numbers planning to go to college (Table 3.6).

Conformity-Related Issues

Several, but not all, variables in this cluster do show a negative change after Grade 6 (Table 3.8). In the achievement area, GPAs decline. (National Achievement test score averages rise with age, but they are designed to do so.) While the overall school problem behavior scale indicates no worsening, there is an increase in the proportion of students reporting probations and suspensions and truancy.[13] Also, parents and teachers are perceived as evaluating students, particularly males, less highly in adolescence than in Grade 6. (There is no change in the extent to which parents and peers are perceived to like one another.)

In summary, when school context and pubertal development are ignored, no clear trend of negative change is found after Grade 6 upon entry into adolescence. In fact, the key variable of self-esteem rises with age, as has been found in several other studies (McCarthy and Hoge, 1982; O'Malley and Bachman, 1983). Issues related to conformity to adult standards show the most consistent negative change after Grade 6: GPAs decline; probations and suspensions increase; and perceived parental evaluations, particularly of boys, decline. (All of these particular patterns occur for both middle- and working-class children.)

Gender-Role Intensification

On the one hand, it has been hypothesized that early adolescence is a time of intensification of gender-related expectations (Hill and Lynch, 1983; also see Block, 1979.) That is, boys and girls become increasingly differentiated, especially with regard to traditional gender-role expectations. Boys find it particularly important to act masculine; girls to act feminine. Later on in adolescence when they feel more secure with their new age and gender roles, some of these differences may be reduced.

On the other hand, Kohlberg (1966) hypothesizes that as children move from early to late childhood and develop more cognitive flexibility, they will become more flexible in issues related to gender role as well (Meyer, 1980). It is possible that such an increase in flexibility could extend into adolescence and yield a reduction in gender-role differences.

The prior literature is sparse on this issue. Block (1976) claims that if the studies reviewed by Maccoby and Jacklin (1974) are regrouped by age of subject, more studies of older than younger children show gender differences. Werner and Smith (1982) suggest that boys are more vulnerable to insult in childhood, but girls become more vulnerable in adolescence. In contrast, Nesselroade and Baltes (1974) conclude from their work that gender differences are established by age 12 and do not increase or change. Wylie (1979), in her review of the literature dealing with overall self-regard, sees few consistent age or gender differences.

Gender-Role Expectations

The most direct test of the gender-intensification hypothesis involves measures of gender-role expectations. According to the hypothesis of gender intensification, the early adolescent has an increased need to conform to traditional gender-role expectations. With multiple-choice questions, we asked the students how important it was for them not to act like the opposite sex, and how frequently they did act like the opposite sex. We predicted that in early adolescence students would be most likely to find it important not to act like the opposite sex and least likely to admit that they ever do so. If Grade 6 is considered the last year of childhood, reluctance to act like the opposite sex should be greater in the years that follow. Table 4.3 presents the trends for subjects for whom we have data at all four points in time.[14]

The trends are in the direction predicted by the intensification hypothesis. First, both boys and girls show an increase after Grade 6 in the degree to which it is important to them not to act like the opposite sex, with a peak in Grade 7 for boys and in Grade 9 for girls. After that, by Grade 10, there is a decrease in concern with this issue. The effect of time and of gender are each statistically significant according to a four point-in-time Repeated Measures Analysis. The gender-intensification hypothesis predicts a temporary increase in concern with acting like the proper gender in early adolescence, and these findings tend to support such a hypothesis.

One might also expect that, as they move into adolescence, students of both genders will be less likely to admit they ever act like the opposite sex. In fact, girls follow such a pattern. In Grades 7, 9, and 10 they are less likely than they were in Grade 6 to admit they ever act like boys.

TABLE 4.3. Gender-Role Expectations—Means for Boys and Girls with Data at All Time Points

	Means							
	Boys (N) = 161)				Girls (N = 149)			
	Grade 6	7	9	10	Grade 6	7	9	10
Care about not acting like the opposite sex[a]	2.58	2.67	2.63	2.53	1.93	1.95	2.07	1.96
How often act like the opposite sex[b]	1.28	1.28	1.24	1.28	2.61	2.45	2.20	2.22

[a]According to a four point-in-time Repeated Measures Design, there is no significant gender-by-time interaction. There is a significant time effect ($p \leq .10$) and gender effect ($p < .001$).

[b]According to a four point-in-time Repeated Measures Design, there is a significant gender-by-time interaction ($p < .0001$), a significant time effect ($p < .0001$), and a significant gender effect ($p < .001$).

Whether this is a temporary change is unclear, since there are no measures after Grade 10. Boys, on the average, however, show little change on this variable with age. Even in childhood (Grade 6), boys are unwilling to admit acting like a girl, and thus there is little room for them to change. The four point-in-time Repeated Measures Analysis indicates a significant time by gender interaction, showing that the patterns of change over time are significantly different for boys and girls.

Thus, for the variables that measure gender role concerns most directly, there is some evidence in support of the gender-intensification hypothesis.

Across the Other Variables

If one looks at our data in terms of trends (see Chapter 3, Tables 3.2, 3.4, 3.5, 3.6, and 3.8), there is no clear pattern of increasing or decreasing gender difference between means over many variables as boys and girls move into adolescence. Insofar as males and females are behaving differently over the years, the four point-in-time Repeated Measures Analysis should show significant gender-by-time interaction effects. Gender intensification, of course, is only one such way the sexes could react differently to adolescence. Thus, we look first for significant gender by time effects and then compare means to see if the direction of effects is in line with the gender-intensification hypothesis.

In Table 4.2, the four point-in-time Repeated Measures Analysis indicates several significant gender-by-time interaction effects. That is, the males and females do show effects different from one another over time, particularly in terms of body-image and peer and opposite sex popularity. Thus, while on most measures the genders do not appear to change differentially with time, there is a subset of variables where such changes are evident.

The issue here is whether traditional gender differences become greater in early adolescence. Therefore our interest is primarily in variables where we have already seen clear-cut gender differences. Among the variables in which there were significant gender by time interaction effects, the following fit this criterion of showing clear-cut gender differences: satisfaction with weight, satisfaction with body build, caring about weight, caring about body build, caring about popularity (versus competence and independence), and being allowed to go out after dark without permission. All of these six variables exhibited clear-cut gender differences in Chapter 3 and will be examined first for gender intensification.

The four relevant body-image variables are shown in Table 4.4 for students with measures at all four points in time. The gender-intensification hypothesis predicts an increase in traditional gender differences after Grade 6 with a peak in early adolescence, followed by a narrowing of difference

TABLE 4.4. Variables Over Time by Gender

| Variable | Subjects with data at all time periods (means and differences in means) | | | |
	Grade 6	Grade 7	Grade 9	Grade 10
A. Satisfaction with weight				
Boys	2.81	2.87	3.01	2.96
Girls	2.54	2.67	2.43	2.52
Difference	.17	.20	.57	.44
B. Care about weight				
Boys	2.75	2.61	2.49	2.45
Girls	2.99	3.11	3.33	3.17
Difference	− .24	− .50	− .84	− .72
C. Satisfaction with body build				
Boys	3.16	2.98	3.03	2.96
Girls	2.68	2.71	2.53	2.64
Difference	.48	.27	.50	.32
D. Care about body build				
Boys	3.09	2.84	2.77	2.70
Girls	2.82	3.01	3.31	3.15
Difference	+ .27	− .17	− .54	− .45
E. Value popularity more than competence or independence				
Boys	.205	.179	.179	.147
Girls	.297	..355	.203	.152
Difference	− .092	− .176	− .024	− .005
F. Parent permission not required after dark				
Boys	.306	.494	.344	.469
Girls	.154	.195	.181	.248
Difference	.152	.299	.163	.221

sometime later (perhaps by Grade 10). For each of the four body-image variables, the gender difference does increase at some point after Grade 6 in the traditional direction, and in all four cases the peak difference occurs in Grade 9.

The clearest patterns involve satisfaction with weight and valuation of weight. In Grade 6 girls are already more dissatisfied than boys with their weight and already care more about their weight. The gender difference then increases steadily until Grade 9 and then begins to narrow in Grade 10 (Table 4.4[A] and [B]). For valuation of body build, girls come to care more than boys only after Grade 6 with the peak difference in Grade 9 and a slight narrowing in Grade 10 (Table 4.4[D]). Satisfaction with body build does not follow so clear a pattern (Table 4.4[C]).

The other two relevant variables are shown in Table 4.4[E] and [F]. Girls always place higher value on peer popularity than boys; the peak difference occurs in Grade 7 and narrows each year after that. A similar, but less clear, pattern is shown for boys' greater ability to go out without permission after dark.

In the case of the foregoing variables, we have been dealing with areas in which traditional gender differences are to be expected. The other variables with gender-by-time interactions are not ones where we found or expected clear-cut gender differences, and therefore it is not too surprising that no consistent pattern of increasing or decreasing gender discrepancy is evident. It is interesting that in Grades 6, 7, and 9 parents of boys are perceived as expecting them to date more, but in Grade 10 the situation reverses and girls are expected to date more. Also, in late childhood and early adolescence, girls are more likely than boys to want children, but by Grades 9 and 10 almost everyone wants children and there is very little gender difference (see Table 3.6).

In summary, there is some, but not overwhelming, support for the gender-intensification hypothesis. When directly asked how important it is not to act like the opposite sex and how frequently they do act in this way, subjects (especially girls) show a pattern of mean changes generally in line with the hypothesis. That is, it becomes most important not to act like the opposite sex in early adolescence. When we looked for increasing male–female differences on variables that in Chapter 3 had shown clear-cut gender effects, we found no significant gender-by-time differences for most such variables. There were significant differences involving six variables, four of which were body-image variables. For these six variables, the patterns are roughly, but not perfectly, in line with the gender-intensification hypothesis. Traditionally, females care more about body image and peer popularity than do males. As hypothesized, these differences between the genders become particularly large in early adolescence compared to childhood.

It is possible that a study of behavioral differences would show more powerful support of the gender-intensification hypothesis than the attitudinal comparisons measured here. It is also possible that ceiling and floor effects and regression to the mean are counteracting and masking gender-differentiation effects. Boys and girls are already quite different in Grade 6, and there may not be enough room on our measures for them to demonstrate increases in differentiation.

Conclusion

This chapter has focused on three issues: (1) the general level of instability upon entry to adolescence; (2) the degree of negative change at this time; and (3) the extent of gender intensification during early adolescence. Analysis of degree of absolute change as a measure of instability over time is somewhat suggestive of difficulty. For both genders, measures of 1-year change indicate greater instability upon entry to adolescence (between Grades 6 and 7) than in middle adolescence (between Grades 9 and 10). Whether these lower stabilities are evidence of an early adolescence disturbance or simply of less consistency at younger ages, however, is unclear due to lack of data before Grade 6.

While girls showed less favorable scores on many of these variables, they do not demonstrate less stability than boys either from Grades 6 to 7 or from Grades 9 to 10. Neither in areas where they were at a disadvantage and could have used improvement, nor in areas where they scored similarly to males did girls indicate more absolute change than boys.

In terms of a more direct indicator of adolescent disturbance, there is no consistent evidence of a *negative change* in adolescence on our outcome variables for either gender when school environment and pubertal development are ignored. The key variable of self-esteem shows improvement, not disturbance, with age. Outcomes related to conformity to adult standards are the most likely to show negative change in adolescence: GPA declines, the proportion of probations and suspensions increase, and perceived parental and teacher evaluations worsen, especially for boys. Whether children react more negatively if they are undergoing pubertal change or early school transitions are issues dealt with in the next two parts of this book.

The third concern of this chapter has involved the issue of intensification of gender difference. In Chapter 3 we showed clear and significant mean differences between adolescent boys and girls in this sample. Most of these differences were already present in Grade 6. The issue here is whether males and females diverge even more in traditional ways as they move out of childhood into adolescence. There is some evidence of such a process in terms of a few variables, particularly body-image variables and valuations of peer popularity. In early adolescence, the difference between boys and girls becomes larger, with girls coming to care even more about their looks and popularity. However, for most variables, if such a process is occurring, it is not strong enough to be reflected in a simple comparison of means for boys and girls over the 5 years.

On the other hand, direct questions about gender-role behavior do elicit some evidence of gender intensification. When they move into early adolescence, both boys and girls become more likely to indicate that it is important not to act like the opposite sex. Also, girls become more unwilling to admit that they ever do act like boys. Boys are never very willing to admit acting like girls, so there is little room for increase in unwillingness upon entry to adolescence.

Up to this point the focus has been on age and sex differences in general. The question now is whether pubertal timing (Part III) or school type (Part IV) affects responses on these variables.

Footnotes

[1]One could also ask if there are changes in factor structures of the variable between childhood and early adolescence for either sex (see Mortimer *et al.*, 1982). Many of the variables used here are not multiple-item measures. For those key ones that are, the issue has been dealt with in Chapter 12 (see Monge, 1973; Dusek and Flaherty, 1981).

[2]The 1-year correlations between Grades 6 and 7 and Grades 9 and 10 are averaged.

[3]See Duncan (1975) and Markus (1979) for discussion of different ways to study change.

[4]That is, the Grade 6 score is subtracted from the Grade 7 score and the sign of the difference is ignored. Similarly, the Grade 9 score is subtracted from the Grade 10 score and the sign is ignored. Thus an increase of 0.2 points is treated the same as a decrease of 0.2 points.

[5]If we were not to ignore direction and compute raw change scores, then children changing in a positive direction would counteract those changing in a negative direction, and the mean raw change score would not give a meaningful estimate of degree of change or stability. The standard deviation around the raw change score would give such an estimate; however, children who changed in the opposite direction from the mean would be given greater weight than children who changed the same amount in the direction of the mean. Raw change scores also correlate negatively with the initial Time 1 score, raising additional problems for subgroup comparisons (Bohrnstedt, 1968). However, the conclusions to be reported here generally hold if the standard deviations around the raw change scores are inspected instead of the absolute change scores and standard deviations.

[6]For both boys and girls, one of these variables shows equal standard deviations.

[7]There are three variables that show no difference in standard deviations.

[8]Appendix D presents correlations based on the largest possible sample available for each period. However, the findings are very similar and the conclusions the same if they are based on only those cases for which there are 4 years of data.

[9]According to an *F*-Max test from the Repeated Measures four points-in-time analysis, no differences in variance across the 4 years of measurement show statistical significance at the .05 level or better (Nie, Hull, Jenkins, Steinbrenner, and Bent, 1975).

[10]We have concluded that girls do not exhibit greater instability than boys since they do not show a pattern of lower correlations. It should be recalled that girls show greater variance on many of these variables (see Chapter 3).

[11]Quite clearly there are a number of methodologies for analyzing change— e.g., repeated measures of variance, analysis of computed change scores, analysis of trajectories of change (e.g., Rogosa *et al.*, 1982). Repeated Measures Analysis of Variance, examination of change trajectories or direct analysis of raw change via regression will all yield the same results when one is examining raw change

over two time points. These different methods will yield somewhat different results when three or more time points are examined simultaneously, since each method summarizes the data in subtly different ways.

In addition, one may be interested in more theoretical issues that involve controlling for initial differences (e.g., using analysis of covariance with the Time 1 score as the covariate and the change score as the dependent variable). When this is the case, the results of analysis may also be different.

In succeeding chapters we make use of a number of procedures for analyzing change depending on the questions we are interested in answering. In this chapter we focus on changes in mean levels over time using Repeated Measures Analysis of Variance.

[12]The means in these tables are based on the largest possible sample each year. However, unless otherwise indicated, conclusions presented remain the same if based on only those cases where there are 4 years of data. The Repeated Measures Analysis of Variance, of course, analyzes the responses only of those students on whom we have data in all years.

[13]Victimization was not measured in Grade 6; therefore, comparisons that involve the last year of childhood cannot be made.

[14]Chapter 3 presents means for all subjects measured at each grade level.

III

THE IMPACT OF PUBERTAL TIMING AND PHYSICAL CHARACTERISTICS

Introduction

This volume began with the question whether movement into adolescence is difficult; and, if so, along which dimensions, for which types of youngsters, and for what reasons. We have seen that adolescent girls appear to be at some disadvantage, particularly with respect to self- and body-image, while boys are more likely to be involved in behavior that deviates from adult norms. By and large, however, movement out of childhood into adolescence did not reveal general negative effects for either gender when level of pubertal development or type of school context was ignored. The only dimensions where general negative change was evident involved nonconformity behavior and lower grades in school.

Yet, in the cross-sectional study that sparked this research, negative effects upon entry to adolescence were evident (Simmons *et al.,* 1973), and we speculated that the onset of puberty or the entry into junior high school may have been the causal culprits. This part of the volume explores the impact of timing of pubertal development upon students' social–psychological reaction, first for girls and then for boys.

Pubertal Development as a Control Factor

Before tackling this central task, however, we shall expand the discussion of gender differences by taking pubertal development into account. Tobin-Richards, Boxer, and Petersen (1983) suggest that gender differences at any age may be due to differences in level of pubertal development between boys and girls rather than to a distinction in sex-role experiences in our society. As noted in Chapter 2, girls enter puberty about a year earlier than boys, on the average, and thus any male–female comparison in a given school grade involves a contrast between more developed girls and less developed boys.

In order to investigate this issue, we inspected the means for boys and girls on all outcome variables (as listed in Tables 3.2–3.6 and 3.8), first for early developers and then for middle and late developers. In general, differences between boys and girls that were significant in Tables 3.2–3.6 and 3.8 persist in the same direction within each pubertal-timing group. Occasionally, a finding will disappear or change for one or two of the four grades within one of the developmental groups, but not with any pattern and not involving the variables emphasized most in Chapter 3.[1]

The only cases where controlling for pubertal timing has a notable effect involve satisfaction with height and onset of dating behavior. In general, data in Chapter 3 showed boys to be more satisfied with their physical appearance than girls. Boys also cared less about physical appearance. The one body-image area about which boys cared more than girls was their height. Interestingly, we find that male–female differences in satisfaction with height are affected by stage of pubertal development (Table III.1). Up until Grade 10 *early and middle developing* boys are *more* satisfied with their height than are early and middle developing girls. In all years, however, *late developing* boys are *less* satisfied with their height than are late developing girls. The explanation becomes clear when we consider the actual height differences among developmental groups and the social meaning of these height differences.

For boys, the later the development the shorter they are, even in high school (see Table III.2B). In addition, in reflection of societal standards, the shorter the boy, the less satisfied he is with his height ($r = .32–.43$ depending on the year, $p<.001$). Thus, late developing boys are particularly likely to be short and therefore particularly likely to be dissatisfied with the one aspect of body-image that matters most to them. For girls, by Grades 9 and 10 late developers are, in fact, taller than their early developing counterparts; and, in any case, late developing girls are no less satisfied with their height than are early developing girls (Table III.1).

TABLE III.1. Satisfaction with Height—Means for Boys and Girls According to Timing of Pubertal Development

Grade[a]	Early developers		Middle developers		Late developers	
	Boys	Girls	Boys	Girls	Boys	Girls
6**+ +	3.37	3.17	3.30	3.16	2.91	3.18
	(90)	(80)	(76)	(69)	(103)	(88)
7+	3.37	2.99	3.11	3.06	2.94	3.37
	(90)	(69)	(73)	(69)	(103)	(86)
9*+	3.36	2.88	3.34	3.02	3.00	3.24
	(55)	(52)	(50)	(48)	(69)	(66)
10	3.26	3.37	3.23	3.12	3.16	3.37
	(58)	(43)	(52)	(43)	(73)	(60)

[a]According to a Two-Way ANOVA within each grade: *gender main effect is significant, $p \leqslant .10$; **pubertal timing main effect is significant, $p \leqslant .01$; the two-way interaction is significant, +$p \leqslant .001$, + +$p \leqslant .01$.

TABLE III.2A. Median Weight (in Pounds) for Girls and Boys According to Timing of Pubertal Development

Grade	Early developers	Middle developers	Late developers
Girls			
6 (Fall)	113.88	98.62	86.12
7 (Fall)	122.81	108.00	96.50
9	134.50	126.00	116.91
10	132.62	127.06	122.96
Boys			
6 (Fall)	99.75	90.88	79.25
7 (Fall)	115.00	99.90	85.75
9	145.38	135.50	115.08
10	153.38	149.06	128.50

Therefore, the gender difference in regard to satisfaction with height is contingent on stage of pubertal development.

Gender differences in dating behavior are also contingent on pubertal stage. Once again late developing boys turn out to be a special group. When pubertal development was ignored, we found that in all years boys dated more than girls, although differences reached significance only in Grades 6 and 7 (see Table 3.4). In Grade 6 only, we see a statistically significant interaction between pubertal development and gender in influencing dating behavior (two-way ANOVA, $p<.05$). Among early and middle developers, boys are still more likely to date than are girls. However, late developing boys are less likely to date in Grade 6 than are late developing girls.[2]

In general, then, with the foregoing two exceptions, the gender differences reported earlier do not appear to be due to the slower developmental

TABLE III.2B. Median Height (in Millimeters) for Girls and Boys According to Timing of Pubertal Development[a]

Grade	Early developers	Middle developers	Late developers
Girls			
6 (Fall)	1559.75	1510.00	1476.00
7 (Fall)	1600.12	1573.00	1539.83
9	1636.25	1616.50	1636.50
10	1643.00	1631.00	1650.25
Boys			
6 (Fall)	1521.00	1488.50	1439.00
7 (Fall)	1607.50	1545.25	1481.33
9	1732.00	1719.50	1649.75
10	1749.75	1748.50	1705.50

[a]A millimeter = .04 in.

clock of boys versus girls. Boys and girls who develop *earlier* than other children in their class still differ on average from one another, as do *late* developing boys and girls. Boys still show more favorable self- and body images than girls, more favorable sex-role evaluations, less concern with body image and same sex popularity, and more independent and non-conformist behaviors.

While we are interested in pubertal development as a potential modifier of gender differences, our main question involves the impact of pubertal change itself upon adolescents' social–psychological reaction. It is to this issue we now turn.

Footnotes

[1]For example, findings disappear or change in the following instances where there were originally significant differences: depressive-affect, Grades 6–7—middle developers; self-perception as smart, Grades 6–7—late developers; value opposite sex popularity versus competence, Grade 9—early developers, late developers; parents expect interest in opposite sex, Grade 6—late developers; left home alone, Grade 9—late developers; parents expect career plans, Grade 7—middle developers; teachers expect career plans, Grade 10—early developers; truancy, Grade 10—early developers; reading achievement, Grade 6—early developers.

[2]It should also be noted that while Grade 6 boys, in general, are more likely than girls to perceive that their parents expect them to be interested in the opposite sex, late developing boys are no more likely than late developing girls to report this type of expectation.

5

THE SOCIAL–PSYCHOLOGICAL EFFECTS OF PUBERTY ON WHITE FEMALES[1]

Pubertal change, as a process, is both a biological and a social phenomenon. While our society has no ceremonies triggered solely by onset of puberty, pubertal change still serves as a visible signal that the child has reached a new period in the life course. It makes evident to all that the individual has attained or is attaining sexual maturity, and it acts as a cue to significant others that a new set of rights and obligations is relevant, and that a new and different age-role should be assumed. However, it is only one of the social criteria entitling the individual to be labeled an adolescent rather than a child in our age-graded society. In fact, the entry to adolescence is ambiguous, in large part, because actual age, personal maturity, and physical maturity do not coincide in the same way for all youth. There is great asynchrony in patterns across and within individuals (Eichorn, 1975). Youngsters of the same age vary greatly in their level of pubertal development with large minorities "off-time" or deviant in comparison to their peers. In the literature these "off-time" youngsters have been termed "early" and "late" developers (Petersen and Taylor, 1980).

Because puberty is both a physical and social set of events, several alternate hypotheses have been proposed linking pubertal change and social–psychological reactions. The question is which of these hypotheses is best supported by the data.

Hypothesis 1: *Pubertal Change Will Have Negative Consequences (or "Stressful Change" Hypothesis).* The major reason for expecting a negative impact is that change itself is viewed as inherently stressful. In this case, the internal endocrine changes as well as dramatic alterations in physical appearance are seen as major stressors (see Petersen and Taylor, 1980). According to this reasoning, the negative impact of pubertal change should be relatively immediate and short-lived, diminishing as the girl adjusts to her new physiology and self-image. In this view, the period of psychological disturbance should start and end earlier for early developing girls than for later developing girls, but both will exhibit signs of distress close to the time of maximum change. No predictions are made about any longer lasting effects of being an early versus late developer.

Hypothesis 2: *Pubertal Change Will Have Some Positive Consequences (or "Adult Resemblance" Hypothesis).* If change occurs in such a way that the adolescent's appearance more closely approximates that of an adult and hence grants her the prestige of adult status, then the change may be advantageous (see Faust, 1960).

Hypothesis 3: *The Timing of Pubertal Change Is the Critical Factor.* Pubertal development, in and of itself, cannot be labeled as positive or negative. Subsumed under this conceptualization are two distinct lines of thought.

3A. The Deviance Hypothesis. First, being part of a minority and deviant relationship to peers is stressful, so puberty will have the greatest impact on two deviant groups: the early developers who are changing when few others are doing so, and late developers who lag behind the rest of their peer group (see Gold and Tomlin, 1975; Petersen and Taylor, 1980). The groups that are "off-time" will react negatively.

According to both Hypothesis 1 and this Hypothesis (3A), *early developers will exhibit negative effects during and just after pubertal change.* However, the two hypotheses do not yield identical predictions for late developers. According to Hypothesis 1, the late developers also will show negative effects during and just after greatest pubertal change. In contrast, according to Hypothesis 3A, the later developers *will* demonstrate negative reactions before they change because they are in the minority. Once they experience pubertal change and join the majority, negative effects will no longer be evident.

3B: Developmental Readiness Hypothesis (or "Stage Termination" Hypothesis). A second line of thought that emphasizes timing stems from the psychodynamic school. According to this approach, not having enough time in a life stage (i.e., childhood) will have negative consequences that will extend into the next life stage (see Peskin and Livson, 1972; Petersen and Taylor, 1980). Therefore, early pubertal development will be disadvantageous during adolescence insofar as it shortens the latency period. The latency period, generally thought of as extending from ages 6 to 12, is supposed to be a period of ego development. The period is characterized by absence of sexual experience and by the presence of ego dominance, reality organization, and integration. If the latency period with these gains for ego development is prematurely cut short or interrupted, then the individual will experience adolescence as a time of difficulty. On the other hand, late development will cut short the period of adolescence, thereby not allowing the individual enough time to adjust prior to the interruption of adulthood, and the late developer will show more difficulty during adulthood. This conception fits with Erikson's notion of an identity crisis (1968), his key idea being that adolescence should be a time of experimentation with new identities; if adolescence is too short, there may be identity foreclosure (i.e., premature affixing of one's self-image).

Since our research extends only to middle adolescence, we are not in a position to test this last hypothesis about adulthood. However, several theorists have noted that what is a short-run disadvantage for the adolescent may turn out to be a long-run advantage for the adult. Because an adolescent crisis is likely to enhance experimentation by the individual, it may have long-term advantages (Peskin and Livson, 1972; Peskin, 1973; Livson and Peskin, 1980; Haan, 1977).

Our study does focus, however, on the immediate and short-term effects of pubertal development during early and middle adolescence. In terms of adolescence, the previous hypotheses are not necessarily mutually exclusive. During the teenage years, it is possible that pubertal development affects various outcome variables and adolescent tasks differently, and that both negative and positive consequences can be found.

The primary source from which we have extrapolated and derived the foregoing conceptualizations and hypotheses is the California longitudinal research.[2] The major studies in the past that have investigated the impact of pubertal development on females have been these California longitudinal studies: the Berkeley Growth Study, the Berkeley Guidance Study, and the Oakland Growth Study (e.g., Jones and Mussen, 1958; Jones et al., 1971; MacFarlane, 1971; Peskin and Livson, 1972; Clausen, 1975). In fact, these and other studies have provided some evidence that pubertal change is stressful at the time it occurs, particularly when those who are changing thereby become part of a minority in relation to their peers (see Petersen and Taylor, 1980). That is, girls who reach puberty earlier than most of their peers (early developers) initially show more negative reactions to their bodies,[3] less popularity with same-sex peers,[4] lower degrees of sociability,[5] less leadership,[6] and lower levels of general happiness.[7] Such girls are described as bigger than most of their male and female classmates and as feeling unattractive as a result (Stolz and Stolz, 1951; Dwyer and Mayer, 1968–1969). In addition, early developing girls have indicated more interest in the opposite sex (Dwyer and Mayer, 1968–1969). On the other hand, there is some evidence that once pubertal changes are far behind and early developing girls move into adulthood, they actually attain higher levels of well-being than do other girls (Peskin and Livson, 1972; Livson and Peskin, 1980).

Our sample has the advantage of being more recent than the California and other major longitudinal studies.[8] Our sample is also larger than most early U.S. studies and more representative and diverse than the Fels, Terman, or Berkeley Growth Studies. As a random sample from a major metropolitan center, it permits good generalizability back to a large population. The findings reported here are complemented by other U.S. longitudinal studies being conducted simultaneously with ours from Anne Petersen's laboratory and from the Gross–Dornbusch–Duke group (see Brooks-Gunn and Petersen, 1983).[9]

With the advantage of this sample, the purpose of the present research is to further investigate whether pubertal development has a patterned impact on the social–psychological status of the girls during adolescence. And, if so, in what direction? Is pubertal change stressful? Does early development have unfavorable consequences? Aside from the negative–positive dimension, do early developing girls who resemble adult women more than their peers also approximate adult behavior and attitudes more? Are they expected to act older by teachers, peers, and parents? If there are effects of early pubertal development, are they short lasting or do they persist into middle adolescence even after almost all girls have reached menarche?

Finally, upon which of our outcome variables is pubertal development likely to have an effect? If there are effects, are they global and extensive affecting a wide variety of outcome variables, or are they specific to a few variables or variable clusters.

Definition of Pubertal Variables

While most of the measurement issues relevant to this analysis are dealt with in Chapter 2, a few points should be noted. Measurement of puberty is dealt with in several ways in this chapter, all based on timing of menarche:[10]

1. *Presence or absence* of onset of menstruation (menarche) by the time of any one survey interview. This measure is useful in Grades 6 and 7 only; by Grades 9 and 10 almost all girls had reached menarche.

2. *Developmental timing.* Based on date of menarche, girls are placed as closely as possible into three equal size groups, and classified as early, middle, or late developers *relative to other students in their grade.*[11] According to this split, 34% of girls are early developers relative to peers, having attained menarche prior to Grade 7; 29% are middle developers, attaining menarche in Grade 7 or the following summer; and 37% are late developers, reaching menarche subsequent to the start of Grade 8. This split allows enough cases for data analysis.

3. *Extreme early and late development.* In order to better test the deviance hypothesis and to more closely approximate the California longitudinal studies and the present research by Gross, Dornbusch, Duke and others (Gross, 1984; Duke, Carlsmith, Jennings, Martin, Dornbusch, Siegel-Gorelick, and Gross, 1982; Dornbush *et al.,* in press), we have also attempted to trichotomize the distribution close to a 20%, 60%, 20% split. Extreme early developers relative to peers attained menarche before January of Grade 6 (19%), middle maturers between that January and December of Grade 8 (61%), and late maturers, after January of Grade 8 (20%).

4. *Recency of menarche.* Number of months between menarche and the interview that year.

The bulk of the chapter deals with the first two measures, especially the second. However, at the end of the chapter, we attempt additional tests of the "deviance hypothesis" and the "stressful change" hypothesis by using the last two measures.

Findings

Nature of the Impact: Specific or General

Table 5.1 presents multivariate analyses of variance relating developmental timing (early, middle, or late) to our various outcome variable clusters. Despite theories of adolescent "storm and stress" (Hall, 1904; Anna Freud, 1958) and the implications of the California longitudinal studies as well as the popular literature, we show relatively few clusters with significant pubertal effects. In particular, timing of pubertal development has almost no significant effects on the global self-image clusters. Significant effects primarily involve the body image and independence. To a lesser extent, clusters involving gender-role attitudes, dating behavior, and valuation of peer popularity are impacted.

The effects of pubertal development for girls then are specific rather than pervasive. We shall now turn to these specific effects. We will look not only at those clusters where there are effects, but also at specific outcome variables that appear influenced in a consistent and statistically significant way by early, middle, and late developmental timing or by the presence or absence of menstruation. We shall also indicate key areas where pubertal timing has no impact. The general conclusion is that the effects of pubertal timing are limited. However, given the widely held view that its effects are considerable, we shall mention all consistent and significant findings.[12]

Specific Effects

One-way analyses of variance have been run. Where the puberty effects are significant, values will be presented (Tables 5.2–5.6). The values to be presented are deviations from the grand mean of a dependent variable, as secured from a Multiple Classification Analysis for the different pubertal subgroups. If the values are positive, then the score for that pubertal subgroup (e.g., early developer) is higher than the overall mean on the dependent variable; if the value is negative, then the score for that group is below the overall mean.

In addition to this general analysis, we have performed a second analysis that controls for height and weight. Early developing girls are heavier than late developers in all years; early developers begin adolescence by being the tallest (Grades 6 and 7) but end up shorter than late developers by Grade 10. In order to see whether pubertal effects are due to these

TABLE 5.1. MANOVAs—Relationship of Variable Clusters to Timing of Pubertal Development (Early, Middle, Late Development) for Girls[a]

Cluster	Grade 6 (N=237)		Grade 7 (N=225)		Grade 9 (N=166)		Grade 10 (N=146)	
	Significant canonicals	p	Canonical	p	Canonical	p	Canonical	p
Establish Self-Image								
Global self-image	n.s.		n.s.		n.s.		.26	< .10
Body image	.27	< .10	.28	< .05	n.s.		.38	< .01
Concern with body-image	n.s.		n.s.		.35	< .01	n.s.	
Perceived self-competence	n.s.		n.s.		n.s.		n.s.	
Concern with competence	n.s.		n.s.		n.s.		n.s.	
Gender-role attitudes	n.s.		.19	< .10	n.s.		n.s.	
Depressive affect	—		—		—		—	
Intensify Peer Relationships								
Peer popularity[b]	n.s.		n.s.		n.s.		n.s.	
Value popularity	n.s.		n.s.		.28	< .10	n.s.	
Dating behavior	n.s.		n.s.		.25	< .01	n.s.	
					.18	< .05		
Others' expectations regarding opposite sex relationships	n.s.		n.s.		n.s.		n.s.	
Participation in activities	n.s.		n.s.		n.s.		n.s.	

136

Establish Independence				
Independence from parents	n.s.	.30	n.s.	n.s.
Perception that others expect older behavior	.22 $< .10$	.22 $\leq .05$	.23	.29 $\leq .05$
Value independence	.22 $< .05$	n.s. $< .10$	.23 $< .05$	n.s.
Plan for Future				
Educational, occupational, and marital aspirations	n.s.	n.s.	n.s.	n.s.
Perception that others' expect career planning	n.s.	n.s.	n.s.	n.s.
Deal with Conformity/Deviance Issues				
Problem behavior	n.s.	n.s.	n.s.	n.s.
Victimization	—	—	—	—
Academic performance	n.s.	n.s.	n.s.	n.s.
Perception that adults evaluate one highly	n.s.	n.s.	n.s.	n.s.
Perception of parent–peer relations	n.s.	n.s.	n.s.	n.s.

[a]See Table 3.1 for a list of variables in each cluster each year.
[b]The peer popularity and dating cluster contain a common item—opposite sex popularity. See Table 3.1.

height and weight differences or whether height and weight differences
are masking or suppressing pubertal effects, an Analysis of Covariance
and Multiple Classification Analysis has been performed with height and
weight as covariates. Where findings change consistently once these controls have been instituted, this fact will be mentioned. Where a pattern
of significant findings has emerged, adjusted deviations from the grand
mean frequently will be presented in bar-graph form.[13]

Self-Image

Global Measures. One key area in which pubertal timing has virtually
no significant effect involves the global self-image. Not only does the
overall cluster fail to show significant results in Grades 6, 7, or 9 (Table
5.1), but there are no significant effects involving self-esteem or stability
of the self-picture and no consistent effects over the years involving self-
consciousness (Table 5.2). In light of the widespread changes occurring
during these years, it has been posited that the adolescent has the task
of developing a new stable and positive self-image (see Chapter 1). Thus,
in line with prior literature, one might have expected that those girls in
sixth and seventh grade who are changing physically earlier than their
peers and becoming bigger and heavier than most age-mates would demonstrate impaired self-esteem, increased self-consciousness, instability of
the self-picture, and greater depressive-affect.[14] Nevertheless, level and
timing of pubertal development appears to have little or no significant
impact on these variables in our study, not even on the key variable of
self-esteem. This lack of effect is true whether or not height and weight
are controlled (except for the one significant finding for self-consciousness
in Grade 10 shown in Table 5.2).

Body-Image Variables. While pubertal development does not seem to
affect the global or overall dimensions of the self-picture, the body image
is affected. Table 5.1 shows significant relationships for the cluster of
body-image variables over several years. The specific variables within the
cluster indicate interesting relationships to pubertal development. We
suggested earlier that a major task of adolescence is to incorporate the
dramatic physical changes of puberty into a favorable body image. As
noted, we asked respondents to report how satisfied they were with their
height, weight, and figure; we also asked them how much they cared about
each of these dimensions.

Overall, early developers are less likely to be satisfied with these specific
physical characteristics than are late developers and are more likely to
care about these characteristics. Table 5.2 (Variables 6–12) shows the
significant effects of pubertal development—both of presence/absence of
menstruation and of early, middle, late developmental timing. Let us look
at satisfaction with weight first. Table 5.2 (Variable 6) indicates that in

both Grades 6 and 7, girls who have begun menstruating (periods present) are significantly less satisfied with their weight than are girls who have not begun menstruating (periods absent). Similarly, in all years early developers are the least satisfied with their weight and late developers the most satisfied.[15] Once height and weight are controlled, however, these significant differences disappear in all but Grade 10.

Thus, the reason for early developers' greater dissatisfaction with weight appears clear. As shown in Table III.2A, early developers are heavier and fatter than late developers. Moreover, heavier girls are more dissatisfied with their weight. The Pearson's correlations between weight and satisfaction with weight range from $-.47$ to $-.54$ ($p<.0001$) over the 4 years of the study. The fact that the significant difference between early and late developers usually disappears when actual weight is controlled indicates that it is the early developing girls' greater weight that is the primary culprit in causing dissatisfaction.

Girls who have matured earlier show significantly greater dissatisfaction with their height in Grades 7 and 9, just as they do with their weight (see Table 5.2).[16] Thus, whichever way we measure pubertal development, girls who have matured earlier tend to be more dissatisfied with their height and weight than are later maturers. The level of a girl's satisfaction with her figure shows a more complex pattern, however.

In Grades 9 and 10, when almost all girls—late maturers as well as early maturers—have a figure, the early maturers are less satisfied with their figure, just as they are less satisfied with their height and weight. In Grade 6, however, the findings are somewhat different. There are no significant differences before height and weight are controlled. But once height and weight are controlled, differences emerge. In sixth grade when early developers are probably the only ones to have much of a figure (see Chapter 2, Appendix B), they are the ones to show greater than average satisfaction with their figure.

The bars in Figure 5.1 and other figures in this chapter show the adjusted deviations from the grand mean of a variable for a specific year for a particular developmental subgroup, controlling for height and weight. Only statistically significant relationships are presented. Where bar graphs are not shown for a grade, the results are not significant.[17] If the bars rise above the middle line, then the scores for that subgroup as a whole are significantly higher than the mean for the total sample of girls; similarly, if the bars descend below the center line, that subgroup is scoring significantly below the mean.

Thus, in Grade 6, the bars for the girls who have begun menstruating rise above the line and indicate greater than average satisfaction with figure once height and weight are controlled (Figure 5.1A). Girls who have not started menstruating indicate less than average satisfaction in Grade 6; their bars descend below the line.[18]

TABLE 5.2. Self-Image Variables—Deviations from Grand Mean According to Timing of Pubertal Development for Girls[a]

	Presence (P)/absence (A) of menstruation				Early (E), middle (M), late (L) development											
	Grade 6		Grade 7		Grade 6			Grade 7			Grade 9			Grade 10		
	P (59)	A (218)	P (119)	A (131)	E (80)	M (69)	L (88)	E (69)	M (69)	L (87)	E (52)	M (48)	L (66)	E (43)	M (43)	L (60)
A. Global self-image																
1. Self-esteem	n.s.		n.s.		n.s.			n.s.			n.s.			n.s.		
2. Self-consciousness	n.s.		n.s.		n.s.			n.s.			n.s.			−.07**	+.23	−.13
3. Self-stability	n.s.		n.s.		n.s.			n.s.			n.s.			n.s.		
B. Body-image																
4. Perceive self as good-looking	n.s.		n.s.		n.s.			n.s.			n.s.			−.12*[b]	−.08	+.13
5. Satisfaction with looks	n.s.		n.s.		n.s.			n.s.			n.s.			n.s.		
6. Satisfaction with weight	−.43*	+.11	−.19*	+.17	−.26*	+.02	+.22	−.16***	−.05	+.17	−.20**	−.09	+.22	−.35*	−.03	+.25
7. Satisfaction with height	n.s.		−.15*	+.14	n.s.			−.17*	−.09	+.21	−.14**	−.08	+.16	n.s.		
8. Satisfaction with body build	n.s.		n.s.		n.s.			n.s.			−.19***	+.03	+.12	−.15*	−.10	+.17
C. Concern with body-image																
9. Care about looks	n.s.		n.s.		n.s.			n.s.			n.s.			n.s.		
10. Care about weight	+.20***	−.05	+.14**	−.12	n.s.			n.s.			+.21*	+.14	−.26	+.30*[b]	+.13	−.29
11. Care about height	+.21**	−.06	n.s.		n.s.			−.04***	+.21	−.14	n.s.			n.s.		
12. Care about body build	n.s.		n.s.		n.s.			n.s.			n.s.			n.s.		
D. Perceived self-competence	+.36*	−.10	n.s.		+.17**	+.07	−.22	n.s.			+.22*	+.15	−.27	+.24*	+.13	−.25

13. Perceive self as smart	n.s.	n.s.	n.s.	−.10*** +.04 +.06	n.s.	n.s.
14. Good at school work	n.s.	n.s.	n.s.	n.s.	n.s.	n.s.
15. Good at sports	n.s.	n.s.	n.s.	n.s.	n.s.	n.s.
E. Concern with competence						
16. Value competence versus popularity and independence						
17. Care about being smart	n.s.	n.s.	n.s.	n.s.	n.s.	n.s.
18. Care about school work	−.06*** +.06	n.s.	n.s.	n.s.	n.s.	n.s.
19. Care about good at sports	n.s.	n.s.	n.s.	n.s.	n.s.	n.s.
F. Gender-role attitudes						
20. Positive feelings about being own gender	−.09** +.08	n.s.	n.s.	+.18 +.16	n.s.	n.s.
21. Care about not acting like opposite sex	+.24* −.06	n.s.	n.s.	−.02** +.18 +.16	+.16*** −.15 −.02	n.s.
22. How often act like opposite sex	n.s.	n.s.	n.s.	n.s.	n.s.	n.s.
G. 23. *Depressive-affect*	n.s.	n.s.	n.s.	−.10*** +.22 −.08	n.s.	n.s.

[a]Deviations from the mean are reported in cases where the unadjusted relationship (with height and weight uncontrolled) are statistically significant ($p \leq .10$). Where no deviations are reported, findings do not reach significance. A One-Way ANOVA and MCA (multiple classification analysis) are used each year. $*p \leq .01$; $**p \leq .05$; $***p \leq .10$.

[b]Homogeneity of variance problem in cases where F is significant.

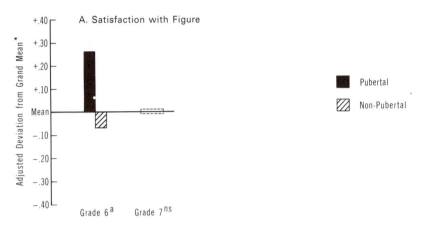

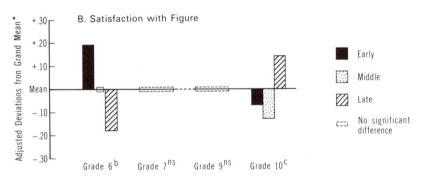

FIGURE 5.1. Pubertal development and satisfaction with figure for girls, with height and weight controlled: adjusted deviations from the grand mean. Note: *A separate grand mean is used for each year and each variable and an Analysis of Covariance performed. Significance: of relationship between puberty and variable: [a] $p \leq 0.01$; [b]$p \leq 0.05$: [c] $p \leq 0.10$: [ns] not significant.

In short, in Grade 6 the more developed, menstruating girls are generally more satisfied with their figures.[19] It is interesting that this early advantage reverses by Grade 9–10, when early developers are less satisfied with their height, weight, and figure than are late developers.[20] The fact that the early developers in ninth and tenth grade are shorter and stockier and the late developers are taller and slimmer helps to explain these findings.[21] As noted earlier, heavier girls are more dissatisfied with their weight. They are also more dissatisfied with their figure: Pearson's correlations between actual weight and satisfaction with figure range from $-.29$ to $-.42$ in the different grades ($p< .0001$).

One could conclude that by ninth and tenth grades the late developer approximates the current American ideal of female beauty better than her early developing peer—she is tall and slim and now has a figure.[22] The early developing girl starts out in sixth grade with the advantage of a figure when her peers have none but with the disadvantage of being heavier and bigger than all of her age-mates, boys and girls alike. Then in middle adolescence (Grades 9 and 10) she finds herself somewhat shorter and fatter than the other more recently developed girls in her class.

Not only are the early developing girls more dissatisfied with specific aspects of their physical self, but in general they care more about them (see Table 5.2, Variables 10–12). Menstruating girls indicate significantly greater than average concern with weight, height, and body build in Grade 6 and with weight in Grade 7. Similarly, early developers care significantly more than late developers about body build in Grades 6, 9, and 10; height in Grade 7; and weight in Grades 9 and 10.[23] (They also care more about height in Grades 9–10, although the difference only reaches significance once height and weight are controlled.) In general, then, early developing girls care more about height, weight, and figure than do late developing girls.

We have already shown in Chapter 3 that those girls who care a great deal about their physical appearance and who are dissatisfied with this appearance are more likely to be at risk in terms of their self-esteem. That is, the effect of body-image satisfaction upon self-esteem was generally greater for girls who cared more about their body image than for girls who cared less (see James, 1950; Rosenberg, 1967). In this case, it is the early developers and the physically more mature girls who not only rate themselves as more unsatisfactory on physical characteristics but care a great deal about these very characteristics.

The question arises whether these attitudes toward specific aspects of the body generalize to the overall evaluation of one's looks. In fact, by middle adolescence (Grade 10) early developers do show a more negative attitude toward their overall looks, just as they do to their weight, height, and figure. They are significantly less likely than late developers to perceive themselves as generally good looking (see Table 5.2, Variable 4). Whether or not the same difference shows up in earlier years depends on whether we look at the largest sample possible or the sample present all 4 years (the "longitudinal sample"). In the largest sample, in early adolescence (in Grades 6, 7, and 9), there are no significant differences among early, middle, and late developers in terms of overall rating of looks or in overall satisfaction with looks (Table 5.2, Variables 4 and 5). However, in the longitudinal sample, the early developers' view of themselves as significantly less good-looking begins in Grade 7 and persists in Grades 9 and 10.[24]

Gender Role Attitudes. In Grade 7, level of pubertal development relates significantly to the cluster of gender role attitudes (Table 5.1). The one gender-role variable showing several significant relationships to pubertal development measures positive or negative attitude toward being a girl. However, no consistent pattern of findings appears over the years. In Grade 7 the late developers have the most favorable attitudes toward being a girl (Table 5.2, Variable 20). In Grade 9 it is the early developers who have the most favorable attitude.

Same- and Opposite-Sex Peer Relations

As noted earlier, a major task of adolescence is to intensify intimate relationships and to begin to relate to members of the opposite sex.

According to Table 5.1, timing of pubertal development is unrelated to clusters involving peer popularity or participation in activities. A closer look at specific variables within these clusters (Table 5.3) shows no consistent relationship to girls' club or leadership behavior[25] or to the value they place on same-sex popularity.[26]

On the other hand, pubertal development does significantly affect a girl's relationships with the opposite sex. With only one exception over the 4 years, girls who are physically most mature indicate greater popularity and more dating with the opposite sex than those who are least mature, although results do not always reach significance and results are not always linear.[27] Table 5.3 (Variables 6 and 7) shows results that do reach statistical significance. Once height and weight are controlled, a few other significant findings emerge; for example, we see in Figure 5.2A and B that sixth and seventh grade girls who have begun menstruating are significantly more likely to perceive themselves as popular with the opposite sex and more likely to date than girls who have not attained menarche.[28]

As indicated in Appendix B, girls who have begun menstruating in sixth and seventh grade and early developers are more likely to have a developed figure than their later maturing peers. It seems likely that the presence of a figure makes the girls who have attained menarche more attractive to boys. It is unclear whether, in addition, the heterosexual interests of the menstruating girls themselves are increased by their perception of their own figure or by internal endocrine activity.[29]

It is interesting that early developing girls still date more or indicate higher opposite-sex popularity than late developers in ninth and tenth grade (Figure 5.2 C and D; Table 5.3). By this time late developing girls presumably have a visible figure and should also be attractive to boys. Perhaps the early start at opposite-sex relations has made the early developers more skilled and more comfortable in dealing with boys.

In sixth and seventh grade, there is also some evidence that early developing girls *care* more about opposite-sex popularity than do late developing girls. Once height and weight are controlled, some significant differences appear in this direction, although the findings are not always linear. In answer to the question of how much they care about boys' opinions of them in Grade 6, and in answer to the question of whether they would prefer to be well-liked by boys or good at the things they do in Grade 7, early developing girls place greater value on opposite-sex popularity than do late developing girls ($p < .10$).[30] Similarly, in Grade 7, girls who have begun to menstruate are more likely than nonmenstruating girls to place higher value on opposite-sex popularity than on competence ($p < .10$).[31]

By ninth and tenth grade, earlier developing girls no longer set higher value on relations with boys than do later developing girls.[32]

In summary, early developing girls and girls who have attained menarche indicate greater popularity and more active relationships with boys. This pattern begins in sixth grade and persists into tenth grade.[33] In addition, early developing girls appear to care more about these opposite-sex relationships in early adolescence (sixth and seventh grade) but not in middle adolescence (ninth and tenth grade).

Thus, while early development appears to be a disadvantage for a girl's body-image, it is an advantage in terms of increased popularity with the opposite sex.

Independence

In addition to establishing a favorable body-image and to learning how to relate to the opposite sex, another central task of adolescence, as we have noted earlier, is to develop greater independence from parents.

According to Table 5.1, some clusters in the area of independence do relate significantly to pubertal timing. In terms of actual independent behavior allowed by parents, the cluster reaches significance only in Grade 7, but specific variables show consistent, significant patterns in Grade 6 as well. The findings are presented in Table 5.4. On a variety of measures in sixth and seventh grade, girls who have begun menstruating indicate significantly more independence than girls who have not yet menstruated. That is, the girls who have begun menstruating indicate greater than average independence, whereas their counterparts score below average. Specifically, the girls who have attained menarche are significantly more likely to be able to take the bus alone in sixth grade, more likely to be left alone in Grades 6 and 7 when parents are not home, more likely to baby-sit in sixth and seventh grade, and more likely in sixth grade to perceive that they make their own decisions. Similarly, significant findings show early developers more likely than late developers to take the bus alone in Grade 6 and to be left home alone more in Grade 7.

In addition to being allowed more independent behavior, there is some evidence that earlier developers face higher expectations from adults in

TABLE 5.3. Peer Relationship Variables—Deviations from Grand Mean According to Timing of Pubertal Development for Girls[a]

| | Presence (P)/absence (A) of menstruation | | | | Early (E), middle (M), late (L) development | | | | | | | | | | | |
| | Grade 6 | | Grade 7 | | Grade 6 | | | Grade 7 | | | Grade 9 | | | Grade 10 | | |
	P (59)	A (218)	P (119)	A (131)	E (80)	M (69)	L (88)	E (69)	M (69)	L (87)	E (52)	M (48)	L (66)	E (43)	M (43)	L (60)
A. *Peer popularity*																
1. Same-sex popularity	n.s.		−.05***	+.05	n.s.			n.s.			n.s.			n.s.		
B. *Value popularity*																
2. Care about same-sex popularity	n.s.		n.s.		n.s.			n.s.			n.s.			n.s.		
3. Care about opposite-sex popularity	n.s.		n.s.		n.s.			n.s.			n.s.			n.s.		
4. Value popularity more than competence or independence	n.s.		n.s.		n.s.			n.s.			n.s.			n.s.		
5. Value opposite-sex popularity more than competence	n.s.		n.s.		n.s.			+.04***[b]	+.04	−.06	−.11*[b]	+.16	−.02	n.s.		

146

C. Dating behavior					
6. Dating behavior	+.14*** −.04	n.s.	n.s.	n.s.	+.02***[b] +.13 −.11
7. Opposite-sex popularity	n.s.	n.s.	n.s.	+.15*** −.11 −.03	n.s.
D. Others' expectations regarding opposite-sex relationships					
8. Parents expect to date	n.s.	n.s.	n.s.	n.s.	n.s.
9. Same-sex friends expect dating	n.s.	n.s.	n.s.	n.s.	+.19*** +.24 −.30
10. Parents expect interest in opposite sex	n.s.	n.s.	n.s.	n.s.	n.s.
11. Same-sex peers expect interest in opposite sex	n.s.	n.s.	n.s.	n.s.	n.s.
E. Participation in activities[c]					

[a] Deviations from the mean are reported in cases where the unadjusted relationship (with height and weight uncontrolled) are statistically significant ($p \leq .10$). Where no deviations are reported, findings do not reach significance. A one-way ANOVA and MCA are used each year. $*p \leq .01$; $**p \leq .05$; $***p \leq .10$.

[b] Homogeneity of variance problem in cases where F is significant.

[c] No specific variables in this cluster show statistically significant relationships.

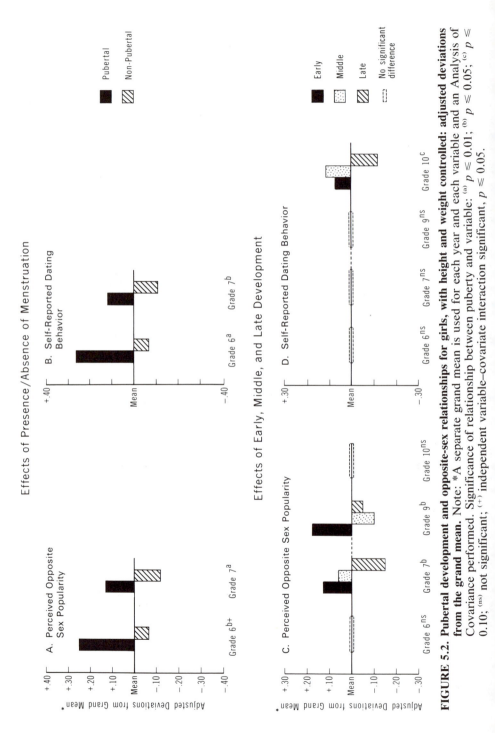

FIGURE 5.2. Pubertal development and opposite-sex relationships for girls, with height and weight controlled: adjusted deviations from the grand mean. Note: *A separate grand mean is used for each year and each variable and an Analysis of Covariance performed. Significance of relationship between puberty and variable: [a] $p \leq 0.01$; [b] $p \leq 0.05$; [c] $p \leq 0.10$; [ns] not significant; [+] independent variable–covariate interaction significant, $p \leq 0.05$.

148

TABLE 5.4. Independence Variables—Deviations from Grand Mean According to Timing of Pubertal Development for Girls[a]

(2nd)	Presence (P)/absence (A) of menstruation				Early (E), middle (M), late (L) development											
	Grade 6		Grade 7		Grade 6			Grade 7			Grade 9			Grade 10		
	P (59)	A (218)	P (119)	A (131)	E (80)	M (69)	L (88)	E (69)	M (69)	L (87)	E (52)	M (48)	L (66)	E (43)	M (43)	L (60)
A. *Independence from parents*																
1. Take bus without adult	+.32*	− .09	n.s.		+.23**	− .03	− .19	n.s.			n.s.			n.s.		
2. Go places without parents permission	n.s.		n.s.		n.s.			n.s.			+.12***	− .10	− .03	n.s.		
3. Parents permission not required after dark	n.s.		n.s.		n.s.			n.s.			n.s.			n.s.		
4. Left home alone	+.19**	− .05	+.09**	− .09	n.s.			+.03*	+.19	− .18	n.s.			n.s.		
5. Times per month baby-sit	+.52**	− .14	+.34**	− .32	n.s.			n.s.			n.s.			n.s.		
6. Part-time job	n.s.		n.s.		n.s.			n.s.			n.s.			n.s.		
7. Perceived independence from parents	n.s.		n.s.		n.s.			n.s.			n.s.			n.s.		
8. Perceived independent decision making	+.14**	− .04	n.s.		n.s.			n.s.			n.s.			n.s.		
B. *Perception that others expect older behavior*																
9. Parents	n.s.		+.12**	− .11	n.s.			+.10*	+.20	− .24	n.s.			n.s.		
10. Friends	n.s.		n.s.		n.s.			n.s.			n.s.			n.s.		
11. Teachers	n.s.		n.s.		+.10**	+.15	− .21	n.s.			n.s.			− .03*	+.36	− .24
C. *Value independence[b]*																

[a]Deviations from the mean are reported in cases where the unadjusted relationship (with height and weight uncontrolled) are statistically significant ($p \leq .10$). Where no deviations are reported, findings do not reach significance. A one-way ANOVA and MCA are used each year. *$p \leq .05$; **$p \leq .01$; ***$p \leq .10$.

[b]No specific variables in this cluster show statistically significant relationships.

149

Grades 6 and 7 (Table 5.4, Variables 9 and 11). In both Grades 6 and 7, teachers are more likely to be perceived as expecting older behavior of early and middle developers than of late developers, although the difference reaches significance only in Grade 6. Similarly, in Grade 7 parents are perceived as significantly more likely to expect older behavior of early and middle developers than of late developers and of menstruating than of nonmenstruating girls. Also, in Grade 6, once height and weight are controlled, more mature girls (menstruating girls, early developers) indicate they care more about independence from parents ($p \leq .05$).[34]

These effects of pubertal development disappear in almost all instances by ninth and tenth grade, although ninth grade early developers are still the most likely to report they can go places without parents' permission ($p < .10$).

Thus, in sixth and seventh grade, girls who look older (i.e., those who have attained menarche) are also allowed to act older—that is, to be more independent. By tenth grade, when early developers no longer look older than their peers (since almost all girls have attained menarche), pubertal development history no longer affects the level of independence allowed.

Plans for the Future

Table 5.1 shows no significant relationships between pubertal timing and clusters in the area of future plans, nor are there specific variables that relate in a consistent and significant direction (Table 5.5). However, just as teachers are perceived as expecting older behavior of more physically mature girls in Grade 6, they are also perceived as expecting more career planning from Grade 6 girls who have reached menarche (Table 5.5, Variable 8).

Conformity Issues

The adolescent has to choose whether to conform or not to adult rules and standards. While Table 5.1 indicates no significant relationship between pubertal timing and clusters in this sphere, some specific variables do show consistent and significant relationships, but only in Grades 6 and 7.

School Problem Behavior. Significant findings related to problem behavior in school appear primarily after height and weight are controlled and for the variable "presence/absence of menstruation" (see Figure 5.3, Table 5.6, Variables 1–3). Girls who have begun menstruating in sixth or seventh grade show more behavior problems at school. Figure 5.3 shows that, in sixth grade, girls who have begun menstruating are significantly more likely than average to have been put on probation or suspension and to score high on a "problem behavior scale."[35] In Grade 7, these girls

TABLE 5.5. Aspirational Variables—Deviations from Grand Mean According to Timing of Pubertal Development for Girls[a]

| | Presence (P)/absence (A) of menstruation | | | | Early (E), middle (M), late (L) development | | | | | | | | | | | |
| | Grade 6 | | Grade 7 | | Grade 6 | | | Grade 7 | | | Grade 9 | | | Grade 10 | | |
	P (59)	A (218)	P (119)	A (131)	E (80)	M (69)	L (88)	E (69)	M (69)	L (87)	E (52)	M (48)	L (66)	E (43)	M (43)	L (60)
A. *Educational, occupational, and marital aspirations*																
1. Plan to go to college	n.s.		n.s.		−.07***	−.04	+.09	n.s.			n.s.			n.s.		
2. Want to get married	n.s.		n.s.		n.s.			n.s.			n.s.			n.s.		
3. Want to have children	n.s.		n.s.		n.s.			n.s.			n.s.			n.s.		
4. SES of ideal job	n.s.		n.s.		n.s.			n.s.			n.s.			n.s.		
B. *Perception that others expect career planning*																
7. Parents	n.s.		n.s.		n.s.			n.s.			n.s.			n.s.		
8. Teachers	+.21***	−.06	n.s.		n.s.			n.s.			n.s.			n.s.		
9. Friends	n.s.		n.s.		n.s.			n.s.			n.s.			n.s.		

[a] Deviations from the mean are reported in cases where the unadjusted relationship (with height and weight uncontrolled) are statistically significant ($p \leq .10$). Where no deviations are reported, findings do not reach significance. A One-Way ANOVA and MCA are used each year. *$p \leq .05$; ***$p \leq .01$; **$p \leq .05$; ***$p \leq .10$.

151

TABLE 5.6. Conformity Variables—Deviations from Grand Mean According to Timing of Pubertal Development for Girls[a]

	Presence (P)/absence (A) of menstruation				Early (E), middle (M), late (L) development											
	Grade 6		Grade 7		Grade 6			Grade 7			Grade 9			Grade 10		
	P (59)	A (218)	P (119)	A (131)	E (80)	M (69)	L (88)	E (69)	M (69)	L (87)	E (52)	M (48)	L (66)	E (43)	M (43)	L (60)
A. *Problem behavior*																
1. Problem behavior scale	n.s.		n.s.		n.s.			n.s.			n.s.			n.s.		
2. Probations/suspensions[b]	+.06*[c]	−.02	n.s.		n.s.			n.s.			n.s.			−.09***[c]	+.14	−.05
3. Truancy	n.s.		n.s.		n.s.			n.s.			n.s.			n.s.		
B. 4. Victimization	n.s.		n.s.		−.17**	−.05	+.20	n.s.			−.02**	−.13	+.11	n.s.		
C. *Academic performance*																
5. GPA	n.s.		−.10**	+.09	n.s.			−.15***	−.03	+.14	n.s.			n.s.		
6. Reading achievement score	n.s.		−.14**	+.13	n.s.			−.21**	−.06	+.21	n.s.			n.s.		
7. Math achievement score	n.s.		−.15**	+.13	n.s.			−.19**	−.03	+.18	n.s.			n.s.		
D. *Perception that adults evaluate one highly*[d]																
E. *Perception of parent–peer relationship*																
10. Parents like close friends	n.s.		n.s.		n.s.			n.s.			+.15***[c]	−.19	+.02	n.s.		
11. Close friends like parents	n.s.		n.s.		n.s.			n.s.			n.s.			n.s.		

[a] Deviations from the mean are reported in cases where the unadjusted relationship (with height and weight uncontrolled) are statistically significant ($p \le .10$). Where no deviations are reported, findings do not reach significance. A One-Way ANOVA and MCA are used each year. $*p \le .01$; $**p \le .01$; $***p \le .05$; $***p \le .10$.

[b] There is some overlap between the problem-behavior scale and the probations-suspensions variable, since the probations-suspensions variable is one of four items in the scale.

[c] Homogeneity of variance problem in cases where F is significant.

[d] No specific variables in this cluster show statistically significant relationships.

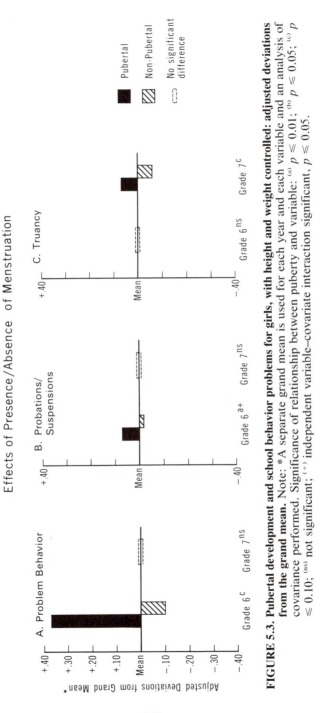

Effects of Presence/Absence of Menstruation

FIGURE 5.3. Pubertal development and school behavior problems for girls, with height and weight controlled: adjusted deviations from the grand mean. Note: *A separate grand mean is used for each year and each variable and an analysis of covariance performed. Significance of relationship between puberty and variable: [a] $p \leq 0.01$; [b] $p \leq 0.05$; [c] $p \leq 0.10$; [ns] not significant; [+] independent variable–covariate interaction significant, $p \leq 0.05$.

153

are more likely than average to report skipping school. The girls who have not attained menarche score below average in these school behavior problems. While the relationship between problem behavior and *early, middle, and late development* was not found to be significant, the findings are in the same direction as those reported for *presence/absence of menstruation;* that is, early developing girls in sixth and seventh grade are more likely to exhibit problem behavior in school than are late developers.

School Performance. Not only do pubertal girls show more school problem behavior in Grades 6 and 7, they also indicate less high performance in academic areas (Table 5.6, Variables 5–7). Insofar as a positive performance in school can be regarded as conformity to adult rules and standards, there is indication that early developing girls are conforming less. Only Grades 6 and 7 are presented, since no significant findings occur later. Table 5.6 indicates that in seventh grade more mature girls (menstruating girls, early developers) are significantly less likely to show academic or intellectual success than less mature girls (nonmenstruating, late developers), according to several indicators. More mature girls have significantly lower GPAs and score lower in reading and math achievement tests in Grade 7, and early developers score significantly lower in math achievement tests in Grade 6 as well. It should be noted that the scores for GPA and achievement tests have been secured directly from school records.

It is possible that girls who are more developed than their peers are distracted from their school work and are more likely to be tempted into deviant behavior because of their more intense relationships with boys. An alternate hypothesis is that they find pubertal changes stressful, and this stress is reflected in their academic behavior. Or finally, it is conceivable that nonpubertal (nonmenstruating) girls are compensating for their lack of popularity with the opposite sex by investing themselves in their school work.

Whatever the explanation, this consistent effect of early pubertal development on academic success and on school behavior problems has disappeared in our sample by ninth and tenth grades. The difference between adolescents in Grades 6–7 and those in Grades 9–10 on these variables may be less substantial than first appears, however. As we noted previously, this analysis utilized all cases measured each year. However, we also repeated all analyses in this book, utilizing only those individuals who provided data for all 4 years; that is, individuals who did not drop out of the study in later years. In general, up until now the statistically significant differences reported for the total sample have not been substantially different from the result in the 4-year subsample in terms of the direction of findings. When we look only at those students for whom we have data for 4 years, however, one set of findings is altered: The menstruating girls in Grade 7 no longer clearly earn lower GPAs.[36]

In fact, if we look directly at differences in this realm of school behavior between students who remained in our sample for 4 years and students who dropped out, an interesting phenomenon is revealed. Table 5.7 presents this comparison by showing means in GPA and school behavior problems for the two groups. As can be seen in Table 5.7, the early developers in Grades 6 and 7 show significantly lower GPAs and more school behavior problems if they are in the group that will drop out of the sample than if they are in the group that remains for all 4 years. However, among middle and late developers, there are no significant differences along these variables between those who later drop out and those who remain. Parallel findings are evident if we investigate the drop-outs for menstruating and nonmenstruating girls.

TABLE 5.7. Differences in Grade Point Average (GPA) and School Problem Behavior between Girls Who Remain in Sample for 4 Years of Measurement and Those Who Drop Out

	Girls (unadjusted means)		Significance of difference between means (F-test)
	In sample for 4 years	Drop out	
GPA (Grade 6)			
Early developers	2.86	2.33	.001
Middle developers	2.84	2.59	n.s.
Late developers	2.85	2.70	n.s.
GPA (Grade 7)			
Early developers	2.86	2.10	.0001
Middle developers	2.78	2.48	n.s.
Late developers	2.89	2.81	n.s.
School problem behavior (Grade 6)			
Early developers	5.41	6.47	.01
Middle developers	5.43	5.74	n.s.
Late developers	5.67	5.43	n.s.
School problem behavior (Grade 7)			
Early developers	5.37	5.81	n.s.
Middle developers	5.31	5.61	n.s.
Late developers	5.41	5.21	n.s.
GPA (Grade 6)			
Menstruation present	2.96	2.39	.004
Menstruation absent	2.82	2.56	.006
GPA (Grade 7)			
Menstruation present	2.87	2.17	.0001
Menstruation absent	2.82	2.75	n.s.
School problem behavior (Grade 6)			
Menstruation present	5.38	6.38	.06
Menstruation absent	5.55	5.62	n.s.
School problem behavior (Grade 7)			
Menstruation present	5.36	5.77	n.s.
Menstruation absent	5.38	5.21	n.s.

Thus, these findings indicate that we have greater sample loss among these particular early developing girls who are having school problems and not doing well academically in Grades 6 and 7. The question arises whether parents have deliberately removed these specific girls from the city public schools.

As discussed in Chapter 2, children with lower GPAs and higher levels of school problems are more likely to leave the city public school system. Thus, it is not surprising that some of our results in this specific area will change when we concentrate just on those children who remain in the school system for 4 years.[37]

These results showing less high academic scores among the early developers are interesting in that there is some literature suggesting that children who become early developers do better in academics, not only in adolescence, but even earlier.[38] Many of these findings were based on British data and on earlier cohorts;[39] and investigators suggested that poverty or early health problems might be responsible both for late development and less high academic achievement. More recent American studies conducted parallel to our own have shown no clear relationship between early, middle, and late development and academic scores for females.[40]

It should also be noted that there is some evidence in the literature that late development in girls is associated with the ability to do well in spatial relationships, an ability usually associated with males (see Petersen, 1983; Newcombe and Bandura, 1983; Newcombe, Bandura, and Taylor, 1983). Hypotheses to explain this association range from differences in brain lateralization to differences in types of athletic and other experience. We do not have measures of spatial relationships to report here, so we cannot determine whether the academic advantage of late developing girls in our cohort is even greater for spatial visualization.

Relationship with Parents. Our data indicate basically no significant, consistent effect of pubertal timing on girls' relationship with parents either before or after height and weight are controlled (see Table 5.6). In addition to the variables depicted in Table 5.6, for 2 years out of the 4 (Grades 9–10) we administered an additional battery of questions about the parent–child relationship. These variables are listed in Tables 3.9 and 3.10 and focus on conflict with parents and engagement with parents (joint participation, seeking parental advice). When pubertal timing was related to these variables, only a few significant relationships were found.[41] In all cases the middle developers indicated the most negative relationships and the difference between early and late developers was slight.

Thus, we do not demonstrate major differences between early and late developers in terms of relationship with parents. However, we have not measured behavioral interaction as have John Hill and his colleagues,[42] who show that the actual behavioral interactions between father, mother, and daughter in a laboratory task (as well as some related self-report measures) are related in subtle ways to her pubertal level (Hill, Holmbeck, Marlow, Green, and Lynch, 1985). With the few indicators we have included, we show no relationship of level of pubertal development to the child's perception of parental evaluation nor to perceived compatibility between peers and parents.

The Deviance Hypothesis Examined More Closely

Up to this point the data have indicated several disadvantages for early developing girls in terms of adjustment (more unfavorable body-images, more school problem behavior, and lower academic success) and few disadvantages for late developing girls aside from lower perceived popularity with boys. The "deviance" hypothesis predicts that early developing girls would show signs of negative adjustment in Grade 6 and the beginning of Grade 7 when they were in the minority, while late developing girls would be at a disadvantage in later years when they were in the minority. The high level of adjustment of the late developing girls throughout all 4 years is incompatible with this hypothesis.

Middle Developers

The deviance hypothesis could also lead one to predict that middle developers (who are never deviant) will score the most favorably in all years. In fact, if one examines Tables 5.2–5.6, there are 21 significant relationships on variables that have a clear positive or negative meaning.[43] In only 2 of these relationships do middle developers score the most positively (positive attitude toward one's gender Grade 7 and victimization Grade 9). Furthermore, if anything, middle developers in Grades 9 and 10 indicate more problems with parents. In sum, there is no evidence that middle developers are in an advantageous position.

Extreme Early and Late Developers

Thus, neither the middle or late developers follow a pattern consistent with the deviance hypothesis. However, measurement problems may be responsible for these findings. In order to have enough cases to compare, the analysis up to this point has been based on an early–middle–late trichotomy that divided the girls as closely as possible into equal thirds. Therefore, many of the late developing girls were members of a sizable rather than a small minority. It may be only those girls who are very atypical for their grade-level that react negatively. We therefore have reexamined our findings, splitting our distribution to make it more comparable to the 20%, 60%, 20% split used by the California longitudinal studies and by Ruth Gross and colleagues (Gross, 1984; Duke et al., 1982; Dornbusch et al., in press) (see Chapter 2).

Basically, the findings described persist when extreme puberty is investigated, both before and after height and weight are controlled, although they do not always reach significance. Extreme late developers are still more satisfied with their height, weight, and figure in Grades 9 and/or 10; extreme early developers care most about aspects of appearance all 4 years. Compared to extreme late developers, extreme early developers demonstrate more opposite-sex popularity and/or dating in all years. Also, extreme early developers show less academic success and frequently more problem behavior in the early grades; and, finally, there are no consistent significant effects of puberty upon global self-image or perceived evaluation of self by parents or teachers.

To further test the deviance hypothesis in a way that is less dependent upon the statistical significance of each separate finding, we used the following logic. If early, middle, and late development had no consistent positive or negative effect, then each of the three groups should score the most negatively on approximately 33% of the variables. However, if the deviance hypothesis is accurate, then the following findings should appear: (1) in Grades 6 and 7 the extreme early developers should be the ones to score most negatively on the dependent variables by and large; and (2) at least in Grade 9 the extreme late developers should be the ones to score the most negatively. By Grade 10 all but one of the late developers had attained menarche, so there was virtually no minority of girls left.

Depending on the year, there were from 25 to 27 dependent variables that carried a positive or negative meaning in terms of adjustment (e.g., high versus low self-esteem, a favorable versus unfavorable body image, high versus low GPA).[44] In each case, one group (early, middle, or late developers) demonstrates the most negative mean score.[45] The proportion of variables on which extreme early developers score most negatively in Grades 6 and 7 can be compared to the 33% that would be expected by chance. Similarly, in Grades 9 and 10, the proportion of times the extreme late developer scores most negatively can also be compared to a base probability of 33%. A one-tail significance test based on the binomial expansion was performed. In Grade 6, as predicted, extreme early developers score most negatively 62% of the time (16/26), a proportion significantly higher than 33% ($p < .01$).[46] However, no significant differences in the predicted direction were found in Grades 7, 9, or 10. In fact, in Grade 9 the extreme late developers scored more negatively on only 28% of the outcome variables (7/25); in Grade 10 on only 37% (10/27). Thus, the extreme early developers showed negative effects significantly more often than one would expect by chance in Grade 6 when they were in the minority; however, the late developers do not show a disproportionate number of negative effects at the time when they are more likely to be in the minority.[47]

The Eighth Grade

One of the limitations of this study is that we are lacking measures in Grade 8. By spring of Grade 9 the bulk of extreme late developers (31/35) have finally attained menarche. Thus, they have finally left the minority of amenarcheal girls. Although their atypical late development is likely to be fresh in their minds, there are too few cases (4) to isolate just those girls who are still without periods in Grade 9, whereas in Grade 8 there would still be a considerable number of amenarcheal late developers. While we do not have many eighth grade measures, we do have one version of global self-esteem.[48] In fact, however, whether a girl is an extreme early, middle, or extreme late developer has no significant effect upon global self-esteem in Grade 8. Once again, then, we show no evidence of negative effect when extreme late developers are in the minority.

The Change Hypothesis Examined More Closely

In this chapter, we have investigated whether the effects of pubertal change are in line with any of several alternate hypotheses. We have just shown that our data do not clearly support a deviance hypothesis; although absence of eighth grade data prevents a conclusive test for girls. The issue here is whether the data contradict or support the hypothesis that major change is inherently stressful and is likely to have negative consequences ("stressful change hypothesis"). According to this hypothesis, the early developers would show more difficulty in Grade 6 and perhaps Grade 7 as they do; the middle developers would be the ones with the greatest problems in Grade 7, and the late developers would have difficulty in Grades 8 and 9 and perhaps Grade 10. Only the first of these three predictions appears to be confirmed.

However, there is one other way the problem can be addressed more directly for girls. We can categorize girls in terms of the recency of menarche. In Grades 6 and 7 we have computed the number of months between menarche and the interview that year and placed the girls in the following categories according to the time of menarche: Menarche was 13 or more months earlier than the interview; 7–12 months earlier; 4–6 months earlier; 5–3 months earlier; 0–3 months later than the interview; 4–6 months later; 7–12 months later; and 13 or more months later.[49] We then plotted the means of all dependent variables that carried a positive–negative meaning against this new variable. A series of one-way ANOVAs were run giving us an overall test of significance plus a test of significance for curvilinearity.[50] Since almost all girls have attained menarche by Grades 9 and 10, the analysis is irrelevant at that time.

Out of the 27 dependent variables in Grade 6, only 2 were significantly related to recency of menarche ($p \leq .10$) according to the one-way AN-OVA, and only 1 showed a significant curvilinear relationship. Out of the 28 dependent variables in Grade 7, only 1 showed a significant relationship according to the one-way ANOVA, and two showed significant curvilinear relationships.[51] No particular variable was affected in both Grades 6 and 7.[52]

Thus, these tests suggest that recency of menarche or recency of pubertal change has little effect upon girls' adjustment. In general, the analysis contradicts the hypothesis that menarcheal change is necessarily an important stressor at the time it occurs.

Social Class and Pubertal Change

If pubertal change has social meaning, then it is possible that the meaning may differ according to the social class of the child. In fact, Clausen (1975), analyzing data from the original California studies, showed that the impact of early development varied according to the social class of the youngster. One might expect that the earlier entry to adulthood for working-class children would lead them to regard early development more favorably than would their middle-class peers. That is, early development will be more of an advantage and late development more of a disadvantage for working than for middle-class girls. Also, early pubertal development will be more likely to result in "older" behavior and attitudes and in expectations for older behavior among working-class students.

Clausen's (1975) results were in line with these predictions for boys but not for girls, and we shall discuss the issue for boys in Chapter 6. To test these hypotheses for girls with our data, two-way analyses of variance were run for all our outcome variables each year with pubertal timing and social class (middle versus working)[53] as the independent variables. For the effect of pubertal timing to be different for the two social class groups, statistically significant interactions would have to be evident. There are very few such significant interactions in Grades 6, 7, and 9 (4 out of 68, 1 out of 69, and 4 out of 63 outcome variables, respectively, each year).[54] Furthermore, no particular outcome variable was affected in more than 1 out of the 4 years. However in Grade 10, we find 9 significant interactions and 7 of these involve either the acceptance of typically adolescent values or the perception that others hold older expectations of them.[55] In relation to others' expectations the original hypothesis gains some support. Among working-class girls early developers are more likely than late developers to perceive that their parents and friends expect them to act older whereas in the middle class no such clear difference occurs.[56]

In most regards, the social class of the child does not appear to modify the effect of pubertal timing on the girl.

Summary and Discussion

This chapter has focused on the impact of pubertal development on white girls as they move from Grades 6–10. We now turn to a summary of findings in light of the initial questions and guiding alternative hypotheses. Menarche has served as the major indicator of female puberty although, of course, we recognize that pubertal development is a process involving biological changes in several related areas (see Chapter 2). Even so, we have defined pubertal development in a few different but obviously interconnected ways: (1) the attainment of menarche by the time of the interview in question; (2) early, middle, or late development compared to that of peers in one's grade; (3) extreme early, middle, and extreme late development compared to one's grade peers; and (4) recency of menarche to the interview in question. Regardless of the particular measure, the overall picture is similar.

How Substantial Are the Effects of Pubertal Development?

Our findings indicate that the effects of pubertal development upon the adolescent girl are specific rather than global and extensive. Despite theories of adolescent "storm and stress" (Hall, 1904) which imply that pubertal changes will negatively affect the self-image, overall adjustment, and relations with parents, we show little or no consistent impact of pubertal development in these areas. That is, pubertal development had no consistent effect on global self-esteem, overall levels of depression–happiness, degree of self-consciousness, or on perceived evaluation by parents; and early and late developers differ little in their self-reported affective relationships with parents.

In terms of the adolescent identity crisis (Erikson, 1968), pubertal development in our studies also shows no relationship in early or middle adolescence (Grades 6–10) to perceived stability of the self-picture, a measure of the extent to which the individual is confused or changes attitudes about her own identity. However, we have not utilized instruments devised by Marcia (1966, 1980) and others (Adams and Montemayor, 1983) to measure identity formation, and it is possible these measures would have been more responsive to pubertal timing. It is possible, however, that Erikson's identity crisis is more appropriate to a later stage of adolescence than that measured here. All in all, in Grades 6–10, there are a great number of outcome variables uninfluenced by the level of timing of pubertal development.

The effects of pubertal development, as we have said, are specific rather than pervasive. The following areas are the ones affected in a consistent and significant way by pubertal development: specific (but not always general) aspects of the girl's body-image, relationships with members of the opposite sex, level of independence, expectations by adults for older behavior, academic performance, and extent of problem behavior in school. (It should be noted that we have not studied the effects of pubertal timing on the moodiness that supposedly characterizes adolescence.)

Is Pubertal Development Advantageous or Disadvantageous?

Whether or not pubertal development has an effect and on what specific dimensions are only two of the questions to which the study was addressed. We also were interested in whether pubertal change and, in particular, early pubertal change is an advantage or disadvantage for the girl. Prior literature suggested that early development was a disadvantage for girls, at least initially. Our results are mixed, indicating that the effect of early development depends on the particular dimension at issue. On the one hand, early development appears to be a disadvantage for the girls' body image, school performance, and school behavior. On the other hand, it appears to be an advantage in terms of popularity with the opposite sex and in terms of allowed independence, if such can be considered advantageous.

The disadvantages are particularly evident when we look at the girl's body image. The early developing girl is generally more dissatisfied with her height and weight, and by ninth and tenth grade, she is also more dissatisfied with her figure. At the same time, she cares more than her later developing peer about these very characteristics. In Chapter 3 we have shown that, for the girls, caring a great deal about an area in which they evaluate themselves unfavorably can be particularly distressing (James, 1950; Rosenberg, 1967). This dissatisfaction of the early developers with their body image seems to be due in part to the fact that they end up shorter and heavier than their later developing peers.

In sixth and seventh grade, early developers are also at a disadvantage academically. They are less likely to earn good grades and/or to score well on standardized achievement tests. They are also more likely to show behavior problems at school. We suggested that the early maturer's greater involvement with boys may have distracted them from school work and tempted them to deviate from school rules. Evidence has been presented in early publications (Simmons *et al.*, 1979) that girls who date early are more likely to be the ones to score low in achievement tests, to have low GPAs, and to rate themselves as causing school behavior problems. However, an alternate hypothesis is that the late maturers compensate for their lack of popularity with the opposite sex by expending more energy on their school work.

Despite the above disadvantages of early development, the girl who matures more rapidly also experiences some advantages. She is more likely to perceive herself as popular with the opposite sex, and at least initially, she is likely to be allowed greater independence from her parents. As noted, it is unclear, however, whether earlier dating is an advantage or a disadvantage. In a prior analysis, Simmons *et al.* (1979) indicated that dating in early adolescence has a negative impact on girls' self-esteem.[57] Many early adolescent girls do not appear emotionally ready for this type of behavior. Findings from Douvan and Adelson (1966) also support this conclusion.

It is interesting that pubertal girls react negatively to aspects of their own physical appearance, while boys react positively to the appearance of the pubertal girl. Early developing girls appear to focus on their heavier weight. Boys, on the other hand, may be responding to figure development with the result that the early developer dates more.

Are Early Developing Girls More Adultlike?

Aside from the issue of whether early development is an advantage or disadvantage, there is another question that is also relevant. That is, do girls who reach puberty earlier and therefore resemble adult women more also approximate adult attitudes and behavior earlier? As we have seen, there are several ways in which girls who look older also act older. Girls who have attained menarche are more likely to date in Grades 6 and 7. In Grades 6 and 7 they are also more likely to be allowed independence from parents and to report that parents and/or teachers expect older behavior or career planning. In addition, in sixth grade only, girls who have attained puberty are more likely than their counterparts to report that teachers expect occupational planning of them (Table 5.5, Variable 8). In all of these respects except dating behavior, differences disappear in Grades 9 and 10 when almost all girls have reached puberty, and physical differences are no longer so dramatic. Furthermore, girls who mature the earliest physically also are more likely than those who mature latest to adopt typically adolescent values; that is, they are more likely to care about their body-image, about opposite-sex relationships, and about independence in Grades 6 and/or 7.

How Long-Lasting Are the Effects of Pubertal Development?

A further question addressed in this analysis involves the timing of the impact of pubertal development. Does the impact of pubertal development occur at the time of the change only, or are there lasting effects of being an early, middle, or late developer? The California longitudinal studies (Jones, 1965; Peskin, 1973) suggest that there are both immediate and long-term effects of early and late development. We, of course, cannot look yet at the long-range consequences in adulthood. However, we have compared girls at early and middle adolescence. Our data show many more consistent, significant effects of pubertal development in Grades 6–7 than in Grades 9–10. The differences between early and later developers in independence behavior are present almost exclusively in Grades 6–7—that is, only in those years when the early developers look more adult than other girls. Differences in academic behavior and school problems, and perceived adult expectations also seem to occur only in early adolescence.

The fact that there is a differential dropout from the sample, however, makes these last findings difficult to interpret. Girls who are doing less well in school or who are showing problem behavior appear to be less likely than other girls to remain in the sample for 4 years. Had they remained in the sample, we might have continued to find greater deviance and lesser academic success among early developers in ninth and tenth grade, and we might have been less apt to conclude that many of the effects of pubertal development are short-lived.

While for some outcomes, the impact of pubertal development may be short-lived, there are certain effects that do continue into middle adolescence. An unfavorable body image among early developers persists into ninth and tenth grade in reflection of actual physical differences that also persist (primarily greater heaviness). However, the effects of pubertal development on opposite sex relations last even after the physical cues that triggered them have disappeared. Earlier developing girls perceive themselves to be more popular with boys and/or to date more not only in sixth and seventh grade but also in ninth and tenth grade. Presumably, the early figure development attracted boys in sixth and seventh grade, but by ninth and tenth grade almost all girls have a figure. The early dating may have provided the early developing girl with skills that persist into later years and help to maintain her popularity. Also, her early view of herself as attractive to boys itself may help to perpetuate this attractiveness.

Which Alternative Hypotheses Fit the Data Better?

In the beginning of this chapter, several alternative hypotheses were introduced in order that we might investigate which appear to fit better with the data: (1) the hypothesis that change is stressful and will have negative consequences at the time it occurs; (2) that change leading to closer approximation of adult status will be positive in its impact ("the adult resemblance" hypothesis); (3) that being off-time in comparison to changing peers will have negative effects (the "deviance" hypothesis); and (4) change that comes too early and truncates a necessary developmental period will cause difficulty in the next developmental sequence (the "developmental readiness" hypothesis).

It is our conclusion that the "developmental readiness" hypothesis appears to fit better than the alternative hypotheses. First, pubertal change is neither universally positive nor universally negative at the time it occurs for girls; rather there are some favorable and some unfavorable consequences depending on domain, and there are many areas where puberty has no effect at all. Second, deviance is not always negative. While early developers show negative effects when they are in the minority, deviant, late developers do not exhibit comparable effects when they are in the minority (but missing data in Grade 8 limit this last conclusion).

The developmental readiness hypothesis suggests that early entry into a new period in the life course may be more difficult at least over the short term than a more gradual and later entry. According to our results, early maturers who have changed and reached menarche when the majority of their peers have not are more likely than others to respond unfavorably to their body characteristics and to show short-term negative reactions in school. The middle and later developing girls, whose exit from childhood and entry into adolescence has been more protracted, do not show such negative effects at the time of menarche.

These findings also suggest the importance of another element; that is, the cultural desirability of the change that is taking place. Change that meets cultural standards should have positive consequences. Thus, the reactions seen here may be due in part to the failure of the early developing girl to approximate the current U.S. ideal of feminine beauty. The changes at first lead her to be bigger than all her male and female peers and then on average to be shorter and heavier than the later developing girls. The result is that she is less likely to resemble the female ideal than is the late developing tall and slim girl.[58] As Petersen and Taylor (1980) note, the impact of the biological changes of puberty depends on the social and cultural context in which it occurs.

More discussion of these issues will be possible after we examine the effect of pubertal timing on boys in the next chapter. Later chapters will deal with the effects of pubertal timing in concert with school and other changes (Part V).

Footnotes

[1]See Simmons et al. (1983) for an earlier version of this chapter.

[2]For more recent studies being conducted simultaneously with ours, see Brooks-Gunn (1984), Brooks-Gunn and Warren (ms.), Brooks-Gunn and Petersen (1983), Gross (1984), Duke et al. (1982), Dornbusch et al. (in press). Major studies are being conducted by Anne Petersen, Jeanne Brooks-Gunn, and Duke, Gross, and Dornbusch and collaborators.

[3]Stolz and Stolz (1944).

[4]Jones and Mussen (1958); Faust (1960); Dwyer and Mayer (1968–1969).

[5]Peskin and Livson (1972).

[6]Jones and Mussen (1958).

[7]Early developers have been described as cheerless and whining by Peskin and

Livson (1972), submissive and listless by Jones and Mussen (1958), and in a greater degree of undisguised crisis and unrest by Peskin (1973).

[8]See also Kagan and Moss (1962), Moss and Kagan (1972) and Crandall (1972) for reports from the Fels research and Oden (1968) concerning the Terman study of the gifted. Also see Stone and Onqué (1959) for a review of other early longitudinal studies.

[9]See Greif and Ulman (1982) for a review of studies of the psychological impact of menarche. We do not investigate attitude toward menarche.

[10]See Chapter 2 for more discussion.

[11]It should be noted that relative timing of menarche refers to the time a girl reaches menarche relative to other girls in her grade level. It is not in any way adjusted for chronological age. That is, an early maturer is not necessarily maturing at an earlier chronological age than her peers. On the aggregate level, however, early maturers will have reached menarche at a lower mean chronological age than late maturers. See Chapter 2 for more discussion. The percentages based on this same split that were reported in Simmons et al. (1983) were based on black and white girls. The percentages here are reported for white girls only.

[12]As noted in Chapter 2, the data presented represent the total number of cases available each year. In this way, we approximate the original random sample as closely as possible. This strategy provides more confidence in the generalizability of the results to the public school population from which we drew the sample. Therefore, in sixth grade before any dropout occurs, the data are the most generalizable. In subsequent years, we cannot generalize to children who left the Milwaukee school system, but only to those who remain. In order to make certain that differences in results between early and late years are not due to the fact that some children have dropped out of the study, we have run all analyses reported here for that subset of children present for interviews in all 4 years (Grades 6, 7, 9, and 10). In cases where the results are different, we will report and discuss them. In other cases, it can be assumed that the results are the same.

[13]It should be noted that the analysis of covariance controls only for the linear element of height and weight. However, we have done a separate analysis controlling for the ponderal index which is a measure of leanness (technically it is height/weight^{-33} or the ratio of height to the cubic root of weight.) We find essentially the same results when we control for ponderal index as when we control for height and weight as individual variables. The direction of findings is almost always virtually identical, although differences may reach significance in one case but not the other.

[14]See Berzonsky and Lombardo (1983) for a retrospective study in which late adolescent females who reported early maturing were more likely to be classified as in identity crises. While we do not measure identity crisis, a similar variable involves "stability of the self-picture."

[15]As noted earlier, presence/absence of period can be investigated only in Grades 6 and 7.

[16]In the longitudinal sample (the students present in all 4 years of the study) the findings are reversed in Grade 10; however, early developers are most satisfied with height ($p < .10$, but there are also significant homogeneity of variance problems). In the full sample used earlier, there are no significant differences.

[17]As noted already, almost all girls were menstruating by Grades 9 and 10, so that presence/absence of menstruation no longer is a relevant variable.

[18]See Tobin-Richards et al. (1983), Brooks-Gunn and Warren (ms.), Brooks-Gunn (1984) for other evidence that breast development is regarded positively by young girls.

[19]However, a test for homogeneity of variance also indicates that there is sig-

nificantly more variance among girls who have begun menstruating; that is, they show more variability in satisfaction with figure than do girls who have not reached menarche. For all relationships reported in this chapter, we have tested for homogeneity of variance. In analysis of variance and covariance, if there are homogeneity problems and the independent variables are dichotomous and the cell sizes unequal, there may be problems in interpreting the significance of differences between means. The reported level of significance will provide a more liberal test than is sought if the group with the smallest N also has the largest variance (Glass, Peckham, and Sanders, 1972). The sixth grade results here for onset of menarche, where there are departures from homogeneity, have this type of pattern. As a result, the statistical significance of these results should be considered tentative.

[20]Also see Tobin-Richards *et al.* (1983) and Dornbusch *et al.* (in press) and literature cited earlier for similar findings.

[21]As noted already, in almost all cases when weight and height are controlled, the initial significant relationship between pubertal development and satisfaction with weight is reduced below the level of statistical significance, as is the ninth grade relationship between pubertal development and a girl's satisfaction with her figure.

[22]See Gross (1984), Jouard and Secord (1954), Tobin-Richards *et al.* (1983), Faust (1983) and Lerner and Spanier (1980, Ch. 8). In adulthood, however, original timing of development is no longer related to height (Faust, 1977, p. 15).

[23]In tenth grade, early developers show significantly less variance than others in the degree to which they care about their weight. Not only do they care more about their weight then, but they show relatively little variability in the degree to which they care. The question arises, however, whether the level of significance of difference reported already is accurate given the fact that there is not homogeneity of variance on this variable in tenth grade. Although the interpretation of the effects of departures from homogeneity of variance on tests of significance is fairly clear for dichotomous independent variables, this is not the case for trichotomous independent variables. Based on the literature available to us at this time, we are unsure how various patterns of cell Ns and variances may affect tests of significance for differences when there are more than two categories. Thus, where there are departures from homogeneity for longitudinal puberty, the statistical results should be viewed as tentative.

[24]In Grade 6, in both the longitudinal and the full sample, the findings are in the same direction although not significant—late developers regard themselves as better looking than early developers.

[25]However, Jones and Mussen (1958) found that early developers were less likely to be leaders or popular with the same sex.

[26]Although the value–popularity cluster relates significantly to developmental timing in Grade 9, only one variable is affected significantly. Although findings involving valuation of opposite sex popularity are significant in Grades 7 and 9, they are not consistent in direction over the two time periods (see Table 5.3, Variable 5).

[27]The one exception involves the following finding: in Grade 6, the usual pattern of early developers dating more than middle and late developers surfaces only after height and weight are controlled and is not statistically significant. However, that same year girls who have attained menarche are seen to date significantly more than their less developed peers, both before and after the controls for height and weight.

[28]It should be noted that, in Grade 7, girls who have begun menstruating show significantly more variance (or variability) in dating behavior than girls who have not attained menarche. For dichotomous independent variables in analysis of var-

iance and analysis of covariance, departure from homogeneity of variance does not seriously affect tests of significance for differences between means as long as the subgroup Ns are equal. In the seventh grade data for onset of menarche, the subgroup Ns are nearly equal (1:1.09). As a result, we feel that the departures from homogeneity do not seriously affect any interpretation of mean differences between subgroups. For a more complete discussion of the assumptions underlying analysis of variance and analysis of covariance, see Glass et al. (1972). The relationships between timing of pubertal development and perceived opposite-sex popularity in seventh grade and dating behavior in tenth grade also have problems with homogeneity of variance. See Footnote 23 for a discussion of the issue of homogeneity of variance relevant to this case.

[29]The findings that menstruating girls have higher rankings on opposite-sex popularity and dating than do nonmenstruating girls seem to be consistent with predictions from sociobiology (Wilson, 1978, pp. 121–128). Reproductively mature females can be expected to be more popular and date more than reproductively immature females, since it is to the reproductive advantage of the species for attention to be focused on physically mature females.

[30]In terms of valuation of opposite sex popularity over competence in Grade 7, there are homogeneity of variance problems. For further discussion of homogeneity of variance as it is relevant here, see Footnote 23.

[31]There are homogeneity of variance problems for valuation of opposite-sex popularity over competence. For further discussion as it applies here, see Footnote 28.

[32]In fact, in ninth grade, a significant finding somewhat reversed in direction appears both before and after controls are instituted, with middle developers most likely and early developers least likely to value this type of popularity. See Table 5.3, Variable 5.

[33]Dornbusch et al. (1981) report that they failed to find a significant relationship between dating and pubertal development. However, it is our opinion that their dating behavior measure is not so good as ours, since they used only a single-item indicator that asked whether or not the adolescent had ever been on a date (1981, p. 180). The reader should note that a similar measure was used in the Baltimore study (discussed earlier) and was found not to be valid. Basically, this is a phenomenological issue, that is, adolescents engage in various forms of heterosexual interaction that they do not label as dating, but which adults do.

[34]In Grade 6 menstruating girls score $+.21$ above average in caring about independence, while nonmenstruating girls score $-.06$ below average ($p \leq .05$). Similarly, early developers in Grade 6 score .22 above average while late developers score $-.15$ below average ($p \leq .05$).

[35]However, menstruating girls show significantly more variance on these two variables than girls who have not attained menarche. See Footnote 19 for a discussion of homogeneity of variance as it is relevant to these cases.

[36]The achievement test score differences remain in the same direction, however, although findings are no longer statistically significant.

[37]In fact, we are more likely to classify "early developers" as drop-outs for an artifactual reason. If girls attain menarche by Grade 6 we can classify them as "early developers." If they subsequently leave the sample they are still retained in the analysis in Table 5.7 as drop-outs. However, if girls who have not attained menarche in Grade 6 leave the sample, we are unable to classify them in terms of developmental timing; we do not know if they will be middle or late developers. They therefore become "missing cases" instead of drop-outs and are not included in the Table 5.7 analysis. Thus, whatever the fact, it looks like a higher proportion of early developers than later developers are "drop-outs." This artifactual problem

is not a consideration for the variable "Presence/Absence of Menstruation" and the findings using this variable are more valid.

[38]See Gross (1984), Douglas (1964), Douglas and Ross (1964), Douglas, Kiernan, and Wadsworth (1977), and Tanner (1971).

[39]Freeman (1936), Stone and Barker (1937), Douglas and Ross (1964), Nisbet, Illsley, Sutherland, and Douse (1964), and Poppleton (1968).

[40]See Gross (1984) for recent analysis of the U.S. Health Examination Survey collected on 7000 children in the 1960s and data from Anne Petersen's study of middle-class girls (Petersen, personal communication).

[41]In Grade 9, they involved argument about going out with friends ($p < .10$), argument about choice of friends ($p < .05$), argument about nighttime curfew ($p < .10$), and frequency of going places with parents ($p = .10$). In Grade 10, they involved argument about going out with friends ($p < .05$), argument about nighttime curfew ($p < .01$), and willingness to talk to parents about problems with friends ($p < .10$).

[42]See Steinberg and Hill (1978) and Hill and Lynch (1983).

[43]In some cases the same variable is significant for more than 1 year. Dating and independence variables are not included here since it is not clear that early behavior of this type has a positive meaning (see Simmons et al., 1979; in press b), nor do we include parents' and close friends' liking of one another. However, inclusion of these variables would not change the foregoing conclusion. (See footnote 44 for a total list of positive-negative variables.)

[44]The following variables are included: self-esteem, self-consciousness, perceived stability of the self-picture, depressive-affect, perception of self as good-looking, satisfaction with looks, height, weight, and body build, perception of self as smart, as good at sports, and in school work, positive attitude to own sex, perceived same and opposite sex popularity, participation in school activities, and in out-of-school clubs, leadership positions, school problem behavior, level of victimization, probation or suspension, truancy, GPA, reading and math achievement scores and perceived evaluation by parents and by teachers.

[45]A tie was counted as not confirming the hypothesis.

[46]In contrast, in Grade 6 on only 7/26 of the variables do the extreme late developers score most negatively. The extreme late developers at that time in Grade 6 are simply part of the majority of nonpubertal girls.

[47]The previous analysis did not control for height and weight. A parallel analysis that investigates the impact of puberty controlling for height and weight yields essentially the same conclusions, although with these controls added, the disadvantage for extreme early developers in Grade 7 also reaches statistical significance ($p < .05$). Another parallel analysis using the less extreme pubertal split also yields the same conclusions.

[48]In Grade 8 the measure was secured in brief questionnaires rather than by interview, as in other years.

[49]If a girl's first period occurred the same month and year as the relevant interview but it was unclear whether it preceded or succeeded the interview, we categorized the girl as "0." If the starting point was clear, the girl was categorized as $+.5$ or $-.5$.

[50]The Breakdown Program in SPSS subtracts R^2 (the linear component of the relationships of the independent and dependent variable) from Eta^2 (the overall relationship) securing an estimate of the nonlinear component. An F-test is then run to determine the significance of the nonlinear element.

[51]The Grade 6 variables affected are happiness with weight (one-way ANOVA $p < .001$) and dating behavior (one-way ANOVA $p < .01$; test of nonlinearity: $p < .05$). As girls move toward menarche they become less satisfied with their weight,

and in general, this dissatisfaction with weight continues to grow after menarche. Also, those girls most close to menarche date least. In Grade 7, completely different variables are affected: positive–negative attitude to being a girl (one-way ANOVA, $p < .01$; test of nonlinearity: $p < .01$), and perceived parental evaluation (test of nonlinearity: $p < .10$). Girls' attitude toward how good it is to be a female drops right after menarche and then slowly starts to rise again. Girls' perception of their parents' opinion of them reaches a peak 3–6 months prior to menarche and then drops, rising again shortly postmenarche and then levelling off.

[52]A polynomial test for curvilinearity in regression was also run for each variable and showed no significant relationships in either Grade 6 or 7.

[53]The occupation of the head of household in the child's home was classified by the Hollingshead Index as blue collar versus white collar.

[54]In Grade 6 stability, perceiving oneself good at school work, perceiving oneself as smart, and problem behavior were affected. In Grade 7 satisfaction with figure was affected; and in Grade 9, self-consciousness, satisfaction with looks, leadership, and perceived teachers' evaluation.

[55]That is, the extent to which the girls care about looks, height, and body build, and desire to get married and to have children; the extent to which they perceive that parents and friends expect older behavior. In Grade 10 perceived same-sex popularity and positive feelings toward one's own gender also show significant class/pubertal-timing interactions.

[56]In terms of perceiving that parents expect them to act older, blue-collar early developers show a mean of 3.18 while blue-collar late developers show a mean of 2.92. White-collar early developers show a mean of 2.58 versus 3.27 for white-collar late developers. Similar means are found in regard to the perception that friends expect one to act older (2.93 versus 2.68; 2.25 versus 2.95, respectively).

[57]However, see Chapter 12.

[58]Faust (1977) notes that the differences in height and weight between early and late developing girls disappear by adulthood.

6

THE SOCIAL–PSYCHOLOGICAL
EFFECTS OF PUBERTY ON WHITE
MALES*

We have found that timing of pubertal development does not have extensive ramifications for girls. However, it does affect girls' body image, peer relationships, and may have some impact upon others' expectations for older behavior. The question is whether boys react similarly. The same set of alternate hypotheses will guide the analysis:

1. *Change Hypothesis.* Change is generally stressful when it occurs in adolescence. Therefore pubertal change will have negative consequences close to the time it occurs. Early developers will show negative effects in Grades 6 and 7; late developers in Grades 9 and 10.
2. *Adult Resemblance Hypothesis.* (a) Greater approximation to adult status should confer prestige and be beneficial. Therefore, early developers should benefit in early adolescence, while there will be few differences in later adolescence when all have attained puberty. (b) Students who look older (early development in Grades 6 and 7) will be treated as older and may therefore adopt adolescent-type values earlier. In later adolescence when all have attained puberty, few differences will appear.
3. *Deviance Hypothesis.* Being different from the majority of one's peers in adolescence is detrimental social–psychologically. That is, being asynchronous in biological development will have negative effects. Therefore, early developers will show negative effects in Grades 6 and 7; late developers in Grades 9 and 10.
4. *Developmental Readiness Hypothesis or "Stage Termination" Hypothesis.*[1] Children who move into a new age-status early are likely to exhibit negative effects during the next few years due to lack of developmental readiness (e.g., in psychoanalytic terms, due to premature termination of the latency period). Thus, early developers will show negative effects for at least Grades 6 and 7 and perhaps longer. However, since boys develop later than girls on average,

*By Roberta G. Simmons, Dale A. Blyth, and Richard A. Bulcroft.

171

these effects should be less obvious for them. According to our classification, early developing girls have attained menarche prior to the beginning of seventh grade; while early developing boys exhibit their peak rate of height growth before spring of seventh grade. Thus, fewer of the early developing boys than girls experience substantive pubertal development prior to the entry to Grade 7.

Finally, an additional hypothesis has emerged from the analysis of the girls' data:

5. *Cultural Ideal Hypothesis.* Certain aspects of physical appearance are culturally valued in our society—for boys, greater height and muscularity. Other aspects are devalued—being heavy and fat. Since pubertal development is associated with being tall and muscular, early developers should benefit, particularly in early years. Insofar as pubertal development is associated with greater heaviness, early developers may suffer in those same years along certain dimensions. In later years, once most boys attain puberty, differences will disappear.

Prior Literature

The California longitudinal studies are the most important early investigations of the effects of male pubertal development on psycho–social variables.[2] Evidence from these and other researches has led many investigators to conclude that early pubertal development has positive ramifications for the boy in general (see Mussen and Jones, 1957, 1958; Eichorn, 1963; Weatherley, 1964; Jones, 1965; Frisk, Tenhunen, Widholm, and Hortling, 1966; Clausen, 1975; Runyan, 1980, Comas, 1982). Early developing males are said to show more favorable self-images,[3] more positive or more athletic body-images,[4] more peer popularity and leadership in general or in athletics,[5] more independence,[6] more maturity,[7] fewer problems with parents,[8] and higher IQ and achievement test scores.[9]

Some of the positive effects shown in the Oakland Growth Study seem to last until age 33 (Jones, 1965); although few remain at age 38 (Clausen, 1975). However, Peskin (1967) utilizing the Berkeley Guidance Study reports negative aspects of early development as well. Early developers become more rigid and conformist in adulthood, suggesting a foreclosed identity search in adolescence (see Clausen, 1975).

While the general picture of positive effects for early developing boys seems to pervade the literature, there is evidence of some mood disturbance, increased anxiety, and decreased activity and exploration among early developers at the time of puberty in the Berkeley Guidance Study (Peskin, 1967). Furthermore, some studies suggest no effects at all upon key variables such as the self-image (Apter, Galatzer, Beth-Halachmi, and Laron, 1981; Mussen and Boutourline-Young, 1964).

Most of the studies just cited are based on very small and nonrandom samples and/or involved adolescents who grew up several decades ago. In addition to our research, the major, more contemporary, surveys of pubertal timing among early adolescent boys are the studies being conducted by Anne Petersen and collaborators (Tobin-Richards *et al.*, 1983; Petersen *et al.*, 1983), and the research from Duke, Gross, and Dornbusch (Dornbusch, Carlsmith, Gross, Martin, Jennings, Rosenberg, and Duke, 1981; Duke *et al.*, 1982).[10] Preliminary analyses from the Petersen and Duke/Dornbusch/Gross studies suggest far fewer effects of pubertal timing on boys than has customarily been assumed, perhaps indicating cultural change. However, there is current evidence that early developing boys have a more favorable body image,[11] do better in academics,[12] hold more adult aspirations,[13] and are more involved in deviant behavior.[14]

Definition of Pubertal Variables

Pubertal Development

As described in Chapter 2, the measure of pubertal development for boys is based primarily on rate of height growth. Height growth curves were plotted for each boy and the rates of height growth over time calculated. Where possible, the period of most rapid height growth was determined. A boy then could be classified as an early, middle, or late developer based on the timing of his peak rate of height growth compared to the distribution among peers. For boys whose curves were unclear or for whom there was too much missing data, classification was based on a discriminant function analysis, utilizing a number of secondary indicators (see Chapter 2).

As with the girls, we trichotomized the boys into approximately equal numbers of early, middle and late developers. Among boys, 34% were classified as early developers and attained the peak rate of height growth before the spring of Grade 7; 28% were classified as middle developers, the peak rate of height growth occurring between the spring of Grade 7 and the end of Grade 8; 38% were classified as late developers with a peak rate of height growth occurring after Grade 8. In addition, there was another split used to isolate the more extreme early and late developers (see later in the chapter). The bulk of the chapter will utilize the first split in order to maximize cases in each category. A second, special analysis will then use the more extreme split to test the deviance hypothesis more precisely.

Findings

Nature of the Impact: Specific or General

Using multivariate analyses of variance, Table 6.1 indicates which clusters of variables are impacted significantly by pubertal timing and which are clearly not. As in the case of the girls, the effects are not extensive. Rather they appear concentrated in a few specific areas, in large part the same areas that we saw for girls—clusters related to body image, opposite-sex relationships, and others' expectations for older behavior.

Tables 6.2–6.6 present all individual variables that show significant effects for one or more years. If a variable is missing, pubertal timing has no significant effect for boys any year. (See Table 1.1 for total list of variables.) Findings that show consistency will be discussed. In order to determine whether findings emerge or disappear when height and weight are controlled, an analysis of covariance has been run for all variables with height and weight as the covariates. Where a consistent pattern of findings emerge, they will be presented in bar-graph form. Where findings disappear consistently, this fact will be mentioned.[15]

We shall examine the findings, as we have in earlier chapters in terms of the tasks of adolescence.

Specific Effects

Self-Image

Global Measures. One of the major tasks of adolescence, as discussed in the literature, is to develop a new and favorable self-image in the face of the multiple changes occurring in these years. Yet, whether one is an early, middle, or late developer has no significant effect on the cluster involving global self-image in any year (Table 6.1 MANOVA Analyses). If we switch to a one-way analysis of variance and an analysis of covariance, we find no significant effects in any of the 4 years, either before or after controlling for height and weight, upon our key variable of global self-esteem or upon level of self-consciousness or level of depressive-affect; and there are virtually no effects upon stability of the self-concept either (Table 6.2A).[16]

Body-Image. The effects of pubertal development appear to be concentrated largely on body image, just as they were for girls. Table 6.1 shows significant effects for the cluster of body-image satisfaction variables in Grades 6, 7, and 9 and for the cluster involving concern with body image in Grade 10.

Careful inspection of the one-way analysis of variance and of the analysis of covariance controlling for height and weight indicate that many of the significant effects disappear when height and weight are controlled and there is some inconsistency in direction of findings before the controls are instituted. Before height and weight are controlled, early developers are significantly more satisfied with their height than late developers in Grades 6, 7, and 9 (Table 6.2B). Their greater satisfaction with height is undoubtedly because they are taller (see Table III.2), since significant differences disappear when height and weight are controlled.[17]

In Grades 7 and 9 the early developers are significantly happier than late developers with their muscle development (Table 6.2B). When height and weight are controlled, early developers still show these advantages over late developers (although the difference involving satisfaction with muscles is then significant only in Grade 9).

As noted previously, pubertal boys are taller, heavier, and more muscular than nonpubertal counterparts (Table III.2). Given the cultural value placed on male height and muscularity, it is not surprising that they appear happier with their height and muscles (see Jourard and Secord, 1954). It is also not surprising that many of these differences disappear in Grade 10 when most boys have reached puberty and the height and muscular differences between early, middle, and late developers are beginning to decrease.[18]

However, these very specific satisfactions do not generalize to a greater overall satisfaction with looks among early developers. Whatever significant differences exist in satisfaction with looks or self-rating of looks are in the opposite direction. Before height and weight are controlled, in Grade 7 late developers are more likely to rate themselves as good-looking than early developers, and in Grade 9 late developers indicate they are more satisfied with their looks. Controlling for height and weight destroys even these two significant differences. These general dissatisfactions may then be due to the fact that early developers are heavier and late developers leaner. For both males and females in our society heaviness is devalued, even though at the same time male muscularity is prized (Richardson, Hastorf, Goodman, and Dornbusch, 1961; Richardson and Royce, 1968; Blyth *et al.*, 1981a).[19]

Thus, early developers are happier with their height and muscles for the years when they are taller and more developed muscularly than their peers. However, these specific feelings do not generalize to an overall satisfaction with looks. Also, the items comprising "value placed on physical appearance" do not relate in a consistent way to early, middle, or late development even in Grade 10, the one year the cluster shows significant differences (Tables 6.1, 6.2C).

Perceived Self-Competence. In terms of perceived self-competence, there are few significant findings either at the cluster level or at the individual variable level (Tables 6.1, 6.2D). While the Grade 9 cluster is significant, there are no significant effects for the three individual indicators

TABLE 6.1. MANOVAs—Relationship of Variable Clusters to Timing of Pubertal Development (Early, Middle, and Late Development) for Boys[a]

	Grade 6		Grade 7		Grade 9		Grade 10	
Cluster	Significant canonicals (271)	p	Canonicals (266)	p	Canonicals (174)	p	Canonicals (183)	p
Establish Self-Image								
Global self-image	n.s.		n.s.		n.s.		n.s.	
Body-image	.31	<.001	.35	<.0001	.45	<.0001	n.s.	
	.19	<.05					n.s.	
Concern with body-image	n.s.		n.s.		n.s.		.33	<.001
							.21	<.10
Perceived self-competence	n.s.		n.s.		.25	<.10	n.s.	
Concern with competence	n.s.		n.s.		n.s.		n.s.	
Gender-role attitudes	n.s.		.20	<.10	n.s.		.30	<.01
Establish Peer Relationships								
Peer popularity[b]	.17	<.05	n.s.		n.s.		n.s.	
	.11	<.10						
Value popularity	n.s.		n.s.		n.s.		n.s.	
Dating behavior	.15	<.10	n.s.		n.s.		n.s.	
Others' expectations regarding opposite-sex relationships	n.s.		n.s.		.20	<.10	n.s.	
Participation in activities	n.s.		n.s.		n.s.		n.s.	

Establish Independence								
Independence from parents	n.s.		n.s.		n.s.		n.s.	
Perception that others expect older behavior	n.s.		n.s.		n.s.		n.s.	
Plan for Future								
Educational, occupational, and marital aspirations	n.s.		.30	= .01	n.s.		.31	<.10
Perception that others expect career planning	n.s.		.19	<.10	n.s.		.23	<.10
Deal with Conformity/ Deviance Issues								
Problem behavior	n.s.		n.s.		n.s.		n.s.	
Academic performance	n.s.		n.s.		n.s.		n.s.	
Perception that adults evaluate one highly	n.s.		n.s.		n.s.		.23	<.10
Perception of parent–peer relations	n.s.		n.s.		n.s.		.21	= .10

[a]See Table 3.1 for a complete list of variables in each cluster.
[b]The Peer popularity and Dating cluster contain a common item—opposite-sex popularity—see Table 3.1.

TABLE 6.2. Self-Image Variables—Deviations from Grand Mean According to Timing of Pubertal Development for Boys[a]

	Grade 6			Grade 7			Grade 9			Grade 10		
	Early (91)	Middle (77)	Late (103)	Early (90)	Middle (73)	Late (103)	Early (55)	Middle (50)	Late (69)	Early (58)	Middle (52)	Late (73)
A. *Global self-image*												
Self-stability	n.s.			n.s.			-.36**	+.11	+.19	n.s.		
B. *Body image*												
Perceive self as good-looking	n.s.			-.05***	-.04	+.08	n.s.			n.s.		
Satisfaction with looks	n.s.			n.s.			-.04***	-.07	+.08	n.s.		
Satisfaction with height	+.20*	+.12	-.26	+.24*	-.02	-.09	+.15*	+.13	-.21	n.s.		
Satisfaction with body build	n.s.			+.12***o	-.09	-.04	+.11*	+.09	-.15	n.s.		
C. *Concern with body image*												
Care about weight	n.s.			n.s.			n.s.			+.20*	+.11	-.22
Care about body build	n.s.			n.s.			n.s.			-.14**	+.23	-.05
D. *Perceived self-competence*												
Good at sports	n.s.			n.s.			n.s.			+.17*	+.08	-.18
E. *Concern with competence*												
Care about being smart	n.s.			n.s.			n.s.			+.05***	+.10	-.11
Care about good at sports	n.s.			n.s.			n.s.			+.08**	+.21	-.20
F. *Gender-role attitudes*												
Positive feelings about being own gender	n.s.			+.12**o	-.14	-.01	n.s.			n.s.		
Care about not acting like opposite sex	n.s.			n.s.			n.s.			-.20**o	+.12	+.07
How often act like opposite sex	n.s.			n.s.			+.16**o	-.12	-.04	+.16*o	-.09	-.06
G. *Depressive-affect*	n.s.			n.s.			n.s.			n.s.		

[a]Deviations from the mean are reported in cases where the unadjusted relationship (with height and weight uncontrolled) are statistically significant (p ≤ .10). Where no deviations are reported, findings do not reach significance. A One-Way ANOVA and MCA are used each year.
*p < .01; **p < .05; ***p < .10; ohomogeneity of variance problem.

comprising the cluster and no consistency in direction of findings across these variables. In Grade 10, however, early developers rate themselves as best in athletics, late developers rate themselves as worst ($p < .01$). These results are compatible with the greater happiness of early developers with their muscle development in prior years. More muscular at a younger age, early developing boys undoubtedly have a head start in the athletic arena, and by Grade 10 this advantage is reflected in their athletic self-image.

In terms of values in the competence area, the clusters of variables show no significant effects any year (Table 6.1), although there are some individual significant differences in Grade 10 (Table 6.2E). Late developers indicate they care less than their peers either about being smart or about being good at athletics.[20] While it is difficult to explain the former finding, it is not surprising that individuals less adept at athletics should come to care less about athletic success (Rosenberg, 1979).

Gender-Role Attitudes. In Grade 7 and Grade 9 the cluster involving a boy's attitude toward his sex-role is significantly related to developmental timing. As noted earlier, there are three items in this cluster.

How do you feel about being a boy? Is it
____ Great
____ Good
____ Fair, or
____ Bad to be a boy

How important is it for you NOT to act like a girl? Would you say it is
____ Very important for you NOT to act like a girl
____ Pretty important for you NOT to act like a girl, or
____ Don't you care

Would you say you act like a girl
____ Very often
____ Sometimes
____ Not very often, or
____ Never

There is some, though not overwhelming, indication that early developers are more at ease with the sex-role issue (Table 6.2F). In Grade 7, they are significantly more likely than others to feel positive about being a boy. In Grade 10 they are least likely to insist on the importance of not acting like the opposite sex[21] and in Grades 9 and 10 most likely to be willing to admit they sometimes act like a girl. As noted earlier (Chapter 3), boys are much more likely than girls to emphasize the importance of not acting like the opposite sex. Behavior labeled "feminine" is a threat to masculinity for boys, whereas "masculine" behavior among girls is of less concern. These findings suggest that at least in Grades 9 and 10 early developing boys may be more comfortable with their masculinity than other boys and less threatened by admitting to opposite-sex behavior.[22]

In summary, there is no evidence in these few significant findings involving the self-image that the period closest to rapid pubertal change is more negative for the self-picture. To the contrary, early developers show some positive effects in the years (Grades 6 and 7) of their most rapid changes—they are more satisfied with their height and muscularity and feel more positively about being a boy. And while they do indicate more negative attitudes toward their looks in general in Grade 7, this dissatisfaction persists in Grade 9, a period when they are changing less than later developing peers. Evidence suggests this latter dissatisfaction stems more from their heavier weight than from rapid change per se.

Also, for the change hypothesis to be confirmed, late developers in Grades 9 and 10 should show negative effects that were absent in earlier years, since these are the years of greatest change for them. However, satisfaction with athletic ability is the only self-image variable that follows such a pattern, with late developers significantly less satisfied with their athletic ability in Grade 10 only. It is less likely that this dissatisfaction stems from pubertal change than from their muscular disadvantage in prior years.

There is little support in these findings for the deviance hypothesis or the developmental readiness hypothesis either, both of which would require fairly widespread negative impact upon early developers in Grades 6 and 7. Such negative impact is absent for the most part. Neither does a new negative reaction appear for late developers in Grade 9, as required by the deviance hypothesis. (It is in this grade, for the first time that late developers would be likely to be in the minority.)

However, the findings do lend some weak support to both the adult resemblance hypothesis and cultural ideal hypothesis. Particularly in the early years when the early developers are more likely than their peers to be adult-looking and tall and muscular; they react positively to these aspects of their body image as well as to their gender role.

Same and Opposite-Sex Peer Relationships

A second major task of adolescence, in addition to developing a positive self-image, is to intensify intimate relationships with peers and to build relationships with members of the opposite sex. The ability to develop such relationships prepares one for disengagement from parents and toward the establishment of a new, procreative family. For girls, we noted that pubertal development had little effect upon relationships with same-sex peers but that early developing girls began dating sooner.

There are very few significant differences in this realm either in the

TABLE 6.3. Peer Relationship Variables—Deviations from Grand Mean According to Timing of Pubertal Development for Boys[a]

	Grade 6			Grade 7			Grade 9			Grade 10		
	Early (91)	Middle (77)	Late (103)	Early (90)	Middle (73)	Late (103)	Early (55)	Middle (50)	Late (69)	Early (58)	Middle (52)	Late (73)
A. *Peer popularity*												
B. *Value popularity*												
Care about opposite-sex popularity	+.01***	+.17	−.14	n.s.			n.s.			n.s.		
C. *Dating Behavior*	+.12**	+.06	−.14	n.s.			n.s.			n.s.		
D. *Others' expectations regarding opposite sex relationships*												
Parents expect to date	n.s.			+.17***	+.21	−.30	+.40***	−.09	−.25	n.s		
Same-sex friends expect dating	n.s.			n.s.			n.s.			n.s.		
E. *Participation in activities*												
Total in-school clubs and sports	n.s.			n.s.			n.s.			+.15**o	+.32	−.33

[a]Deviations from the mean are reported in cases where the unadjusted relationship (with height and weight uncontrolled) are statistically significant (p ≤ .10). Where no deviations are reported, findings do not reach significance. A One-Way ANOVA and MCA are used each year.
*p < .01; **p < .05; ***p < .10; ohomogeneity of variance problem.

MANOVA Cluster Analysis or in the individual analyses of variance. In Grade 6 only, do we find significance (Table 6.1 Opposite-Sex Cluster). Early developing boys in Grade 6 do date significantly more than late developers (Table 6.3C): Early developers date .12 above the grand mean and late developers − .14 below the grand mean; $p < .05$. In other years, significant relationships are absent, and early developers are no longer the ones to date the most; middle developers, if anyone, seem to have an advantage.

Thus, for a short time at least, early developing youngsters of both sexes are more likely than their peers to be involved with the opposite sex. Whether the explanation lies with their physical appearance or with hormonal differences can not be determined from these data. It is possible that an increase in libido is pushing them in this direction. It is also possible that youngsters who look older and developed (1) are allowed more independence of this type by their parents and (2) are seen as more attractive by the opposite sex.

It is interesting, in this light, that the one year late developing boys are dating significantly less (Grade 6) is the one year they also indicate that they place lower value on opposite-sex popularity than do their more developed peers (Table 6.3B).[23]

Others' Expectations Regarding Opposite-Sex Relationships. Only in Grade 9 does this cluster of variables show significant puberty effects (Table 6.1), and over the 4 years only two specific relationships reach significance (Table 6.3D). However, in both cases, significant others (parents, friends) are perceived as expecting more dating from early and middle developers than from later developers. Those who look older earlier are expected to act older. Part of this effect is probably due to the fact the early developers are taller. For once height and weight are controlled, early developers in Grade 7 are no longer more likely to perceive that their friends expect them to date.[24] In Grade 9, however, regardless of whether height and weight are controlled, parents of early developers are seen as expecting most dating; parents of late developers least dating.[25]

Independence

Disengagement from parents during adolescence helps to prepare for later movement into adulthood. This disengagement involves not only emotional independence but also the ability to be physically independent. In addition, then, to developing a favorable self- and body-image and to learning how to relate to the opposite sex, the establishment of greater physical as well as emotional independence from parents has been regarded as a central task of adolescence. The establishment of this independence does not develop solely out of parent–child conflict but is often carefully encouraged by parents and teachers as part of the socialization process.

As noted earlier, we asked several questions to determine the extent to which the student is allowed independence in daily activities and the extent to which he or she is encouraged to act older. The question is whether the boys who look older are treated as older in these respects as they were in dating. As mentioned in Chapter 5, there is some evidence of this phenomenon for girls. However, the data for boys in Tables 6.1 and 6.4 do not support this hypothesis for allowed independence behaviors. There are no significant clusters under the independence rubric, and there are virtually no significant differences regarding specific allowed independence behaviors.

There are some individually significant findings involving others' perceived expectations for older behavior (Table 6.4B). In Grades 7 and 9 friends are more likely to expect older behavior from early and middle developers than from late developers. However, there are no significant findings for teachers, and the Grade 10 findings for parents are in the opposite direction. As far as friends are concerned, in Grade 7 once again, just as with dating expectations, part of the relationship appears to be due to the fact that early developers are taller. Once height and weight are controlled, the early developers in Grade 7 no longer are more likely to perceive their friends as expecting older behavior of them. (In Grade 9, however, the original relationship persists when height and weight are controlled.)

Thus, in terms of perceived expectations to date earlier and to act older, there is some, but not overwhelming evidence, that early developing boys are more likely to be subject to such expectations, especially from friends. Part, but not all, of this pattern appears due to the fact that early developers are taller.

Plans for the Future

Table 6.1 shows significant clusters related to aspiration level in Grades 7 and 10. There is no support, however, for the hypothesis that children who are more mature biologically will have a greater desire to assume adult roles. In fact, early developers are least likely to want to get married in the future (Table 6.5A: Grade 10, $p < .10$; and after height and weight are controlled: Grade 7, $p < .10$). They are also least likely to want children (Table 6.5A: Grade 7, $p < .10$; and after height and weight are controlled: Grade 10, $p < .10$).

Just as students were asked whether they perceive that significant others expect them to date and to act older, they were asked whether they were expected to make career plans. For girls, Chapter 5 reported that teachers were more likely to expect career planning of early maturing girls. However, for boys findings are inconsistent across variables with neither teachers nor friends showing this pattern.[26]

In sum, only in terms of opposite-sex relationships is there very con-

TABLE 6.4. Independence Variables—Deviations from Grand Mean According to Timing of Pubertal Development for Boys[a]

	Grade 6			Grade 7			Grade 9			Grade 10		
	Early (91)	Middle (77)	Late (103)	Early (90)	Middle (73)	Late (103)	Early (55)	Middle (50)	Late (69)	Early (58)	Middle (52)	Late (73)
A. *Independence from parents*												
Times per month baby-sit	+.14***°	+.03	−.14	n.s.			n.s.			n.s.		
B. *Perception that others expect older behavior*												
Parents	n.s.			n.s.			n.s.			−.28***	+.19	+.08
Friends	n.s.			+.01**	+.18	−.13	+.18***	.00	−.13	n.s.		
C. *Value independence*	n.s.			n.s.			−.05**°	+.23	−.13	n.s.		

[a]Deviations from the mean are reported in cases where the unadjusted relationship (with height and weight uncontrolled) are statistically significant (p ≤ .10). Where no deviations are reported, findings do not reach significance. A One-Way ANOVA and MCA are used each year.
*$p < .01$; **$p < .05$; ***$p < .10$; °homogeneity of variance problem.

TABLE 6.5. Aspirational Variables—Deviations from Grand Mean According to Timing of Pubertal Development for Boys[a]

	Grade 6			Grade 7			Grade 9			Grade 10		
	Early (91)	Middle (77)	Late (103)	Early (90)	Middle (73)	Late (103)	Early (55)	Middle (50)	Late (69)	Early (58)	Middle (52)	Late (73)
A. *Educational, occupational, and marital aspirations*												
Want to get married	n.s.			n.s.			n.s.			$-.10$***º	$+.01$	$+.07$
Want to have children	n.s.			$-.08$***	.00	$+.07$	n.s.			n.s.		
SES of ideal job	n.s.			n.s.			n.s.			$-.29$***	$-.01$	$+.21$
B. *Perception that others expect career planning*												
Parents	n.s.			$+.14$*	$+.08$	$-.08$	n.s.			n.s.		
Teachers	$-.06$**	$+.21$	$-.10$	n.s.			n.s.			n.s.		
Friends	n.s.			n.s.			n.s.			$-.01$*	$+.28$	$-.18$

[a]Deviations from the mean are reported in cases where the unadjusted relationship (with height and weight uncontrolled) are statistically significant ($p \leq .10$). Where no deviations are reported, findings do not reach significance. A One-Way ANOVA and MCA are used each year.
*$p < .01$; **$p < .05$; ***$p < .10$; º homogeneity of variance problem.

185

sistent support for the overall hypothesis that boys who look older earlier will act older, develop less childish values, and be more exposed to expectations for older behavior.

Conformity Issues

School Problem Behavior. In adolescence, the student has to choose whether or not to conform to adult regulations and values. We found that early developing girls were less likely to perform well academically in Grades 6 and 7 and more likely to show problem behavior in school. No such difference appears for boys, however. Neither the clusters nor the individual variables related to school problem behavior and academic performance show significant effects of pubertal timing. It should be noted there are studies that show that boys who become early developers score more favorably in academic and achievement measures than their later developing peers (Douglas and Ross, 1964; Gross, 1984). Since these correlations predate adolescence, there is some question whether in the population studied poor health or unfavorable socioeconomic factors may be retarding both physical and intellectual development. In any case, our data show no such relationship.

Relationship with Parents. Frequently, disengagement from parents and movement to peers in adolescence has been described as a task full of conflict. While we did not direct major attention to this area every year, we did ask two questions repeatedly to tap this process. In every grade we asked:

How much do your parents like your close friends?
Do your parents like your close friends
_____ Very much
_____ Somewhat
_____ A little, or
_____ Not at all
How much do your close friends like your parents?
Do your close friends like your parents
_____ Very much
_____ Somewhat
_____ A little, or
_____ Not at all

In tenth grade, this cluster indicates a significant relationship to pubertal development according to the MANOVA analysis (Table 6.1); and the constituent items show significant effects in earlier years as well, according to the analyses of variance and covariance. Table 6.6 presents the results unadjusted for height and weight; and, since there is an additional significant result when height and weight are controlled, Figure 6.1 presents

TABLE 6.6. Conformity Variables—Deviations from Grand Mean According to Timing of Pubertal Development for Boys[a]

	Grade 6			Grade 7			Grade 9			Grade 10		
	Early (91)	Middle (77)	Late (103)	Early (90)	Middle (73)	Late (103)	Early (55)	Middle (50)	Late (69)	Early (58)	Middle (52)	Late (73)
A. *Problem behavior*												
B. *Victimization*												
C. *Academic performance*												
D. *Perception that adults evaluate one highly*												
Parents	n.s.			n.s.			n.s.			+ .28***	− .22	− .06
E. *Perception of parent– peer relationship*												
Parents like close friends	n.s.			− .14***	+ .10	+ .05	n.s.			+ .04**	+ .15	− .13
Close friends like parents	− .14***	+ .07	+ .07	n.s.			n.s.			n.s.		

[a]Deviations from the mean are reported in cases where the unadjusted relationship (with height and weight uncontrolled) are statistically significant (p ≤ .10). Where no deviations are reported, findings do not reach significance. A One-Way ANOVA and MCA are used each year.
 *p < .01; **p < .05; ***p < .10.

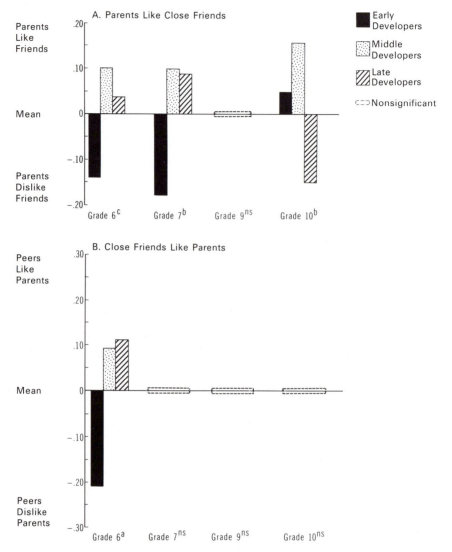

FIGURE 6.1. Effects of early development on parent–peer relations for boys: adjusted deviations from the grand mean. (A separate grand mean is used for each year and each variable, and an Analysis of Covariance performed.) Significance of relationship between puberty and variable: [a] $p \leq 0.01$; [b] $p \leq 0.05$; [c] $p \leq 0.10$; [ns] not significant.

the results controlled for height and weight. Figure 6.1 shows that in the early years early developers indicate more of this conflict, and in Grade 10 later developers report more conflict. In Grades 6 and 7 early developers are the most likely to say parents do not like their friends (in Grade 6 the early developers report their friends as reciprocating this dislike); while in Grade 10, it is the late developers who report this enmity. These findings are the first that could support the hypothesis that change has negative ramifications. During the years of greatest pubertal change, boys perceive their parents as disliking their friends—for the early developers, this problem occurs in Grades 6 and 7; for the late developers in Grade 10.

In addition, by Grades 9 and 10, early developing boys, the most adult-looking and the most likely to be beyond peak pubertal change, report the highest evaluations from parents. Statistically significant findings are shown for the MANOVA cluster "Perception that adults evaluate one highly," which contains perceived "Mother's evaluation" in Grade 10 (Table 6.1).[27] Statistically significant results are also shown for the parental evaluation scale in the analysis of variance in Grade 10 (Table 6.6D) and in the Analysis of Covariance in Grades 9 and 10 (Figure 6.2).

Although only these few questions were asked all 4 years relative to the relationship with parents, in Grades 9 and 10 a battery of additional questions was asked. These 15 questions are listed in Tables 3.9 and 3.10 and focus on conflict with parents and engagement with parents (participating in joint activities, seeking parental advice). When pubertal timing is related to these variables, there is only 1 significant individual relationship in Grade 9 and 2 in Grade 10. And, in only one of the three questions do late developers indicate the most difficulty with parents and/or early developers the least.[28]

Thus, there is no evidence of a generalized problem with parents for late developers close to the time of pubertal change (Grade 9–10). However, in terms of perceived parental evaluation and peer/parent's liking one another in Grades 9–10, the early developing boys seem to have the smoothest relationship with parents; a smoothness that on those particular variables was likely to be absent during their years of peak pubertal change (Grades 6 and 7).

In summary, developmental timing has only a few, very specific effects upon boys' social–psychological reactions in adolescence. There is virtually no consistent impact of early, middle, and late development upon global self-image, feelings of academic competence, same-sex peer relations, allowed independence, problem behavior, or academic behavior. There is some effect upon body image, sex role self-image, relationship with the opposite sex, perceived expectations by significant others, and perhaps relationship with parents. Early developers are more satisfied with their height because they are taller and with their muscular development and athletic ability, presumably because of their greater muscu-

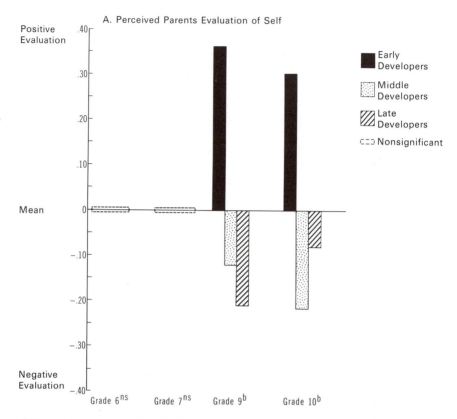

FIGURE 6.2. Effects of early development on perceived adults' evaluation of self for boys: adjusted deviations from the grand mean. (A separate grand mean is used for each year and each variable and an Analysis of Covariance performed.) Significance of relationship between puberty and variable: [a] $p \leq 0.01$; [b] $p \leq 0.05$; [c] $p \leq 0.10$; [ns] not significant.

larity. However, these specific attitudes do not generalize to a greater satisfaction with their looks. In part because of their heavier weight, they are less satisfied in general with their looks. Early developers, however, do show more positive attitudes toward being a boy, and data could be interpreted to indicate greater ease and less defensiveness with their masculinity. Like girls, they date earlier, but only in Grade 6. These findings tend to support the cultural ideal hypothesis that certain characteristics are valued in our society—greater height and muscularity and less fat—and individuals who come close to this ideal will show some benefits.

Virtually the only findings that support the hypothesis that change is stressful or that being deviant is disadvantageous are those involving relationship with parents. There is some evidence of greater problems close to the time of pubertal change for early developers in Grade 6–7 when they are deviant and for late developers in Grade 10 when they are deviant. However, since very few indicators are involved, these results have to be regarded as suggestive rather than conclusive.[29]

The Deviance Hypothesis Examined More Closely

In testing the deviance hypothesis we have assumed that early developers will be at risk in Grade 6 and perhaps Grade 7 when they are in the minority, and late developers will be at risk in later years. However, one could also hypothesize on the basis of the deviance hypothesis that middle developers (who are never deviant) will fare the best in all years. In fact, if one examines Tables 6.2–6.6, there are 12–15 significant relationships for variables that have a clear positive or negative meaning.[30] On only 4 of these relationships do middle developers score the most positively (involving club membership, parents liking friends and friends liking parents). Thus, there is no evidence that middle-developing boys by and large are doing better than other groups on variables that show significant differences among the groups.

Extreme Pubertal Development

A better test of the deviance hypothesis is possible, however. As noted earlier, our first split of the boys into early, middle, and late development attempts to divide them into equal thirds in order to have a high enough number of cases in all cells. Another split can be made that isolates young men who are more deviant relative to peers. In this case, we attempt to split the cases into 20% of earliest developers, 60% middle developers, and 20% latest developers in order to be comparable to other studies in this area (Gross, 1984; Duke et al., 1982). Due to the way the cases distribute, however, the closest split we could get that was not identical to the prior less extreme split was 10% of early developers (whose peak height growth was before Grade 7), 78% middle developers, and 12% of late developers (whose peak height growth occurred after Grade 9).[31]

Just as for girls, we tested the deviance hypothesis by positing that those students who were deviant in the timing of their development should score more negatively across the dependent variables. If early, middle, and late development have no consistent positive or negative effect, then each of the three groups should score the most negatively on about one-third of the variables. On the other hand, if the deviance hypothesis is accurate, then (1) in Grades 6 and 7 the extreme early developers should be the most likely group to score negatively and (2) in Grades 9 and 10 it should be the extreme late developers.

As noted in the discussion of female puberty, there were from 25 to

27 dependent variables that carried a positive or negative meaning. In Grades 6 and 7 the proportion of these variables in which early developers scored most negatively can be compared to the 33% that would be expected by chance. In Grades 9 and 10, the comparison will involve the proportion of times the late developers score most negatively. A one-tail significance test based on the binomial expansion will be used.[32] When unadjusted mean scores are used, we find no significant differences in Grades 7, 9, and 10. However, in Grade 6 extreme early developers as the "deviant" group do score most negatively on 13/26 of the variables as predicted (p = .05), while extreme late developers (as part of the majority of non-pubertal boys in Grade 6) are the group to score most negatively on only 3/26 of the variables. If height and weight are controlled and adjusted mean scores used, the findings are in the same direction, but there are no significant findings for binomials any year.

If one utilizes our less extreme split, as in the beginning of this chapter, no significant differences are found in Grades 6, 7, or 9; but in Grade 10, as predicted, the deviant group of late developers are significantly more likely than chance to score most negatively on the dependent variables, both before and after height and weight are controlled (for unadjusted scores, 13/27 of the variables, $p < .10$; for adjusted, 15/27, $p = .01$).[33] In Grade 10 then, there is some evidence that the deviant group is reacting more negatively. In fact, while findings reach significance only for the regular, rather than the extreme split in Grade 10, they are in the same direction in both cases.[34]

In sum, while the data for girls did not lend much support for the deviancy hypothesis, there is some indication that for boys it might apply. For girls, we found only that early developing girls in Grades 6 and 7 scored negatively across variables; in later grades there was no comparable disadvantage for late developing girls. For boys, as we have just noted, extreme early developers show negative effects in early years; late developers in later years. Yet, even then, there are few variables considered on their own where differences reach statistical significance either before or after controlling for height and weight. Thus, while there is some support for the deviancy hypothesis in these data, it is not easy to find.

The reason extreme late developing girls do not show negative effects in late years, however, may be related to the timing of the measurement. By Grade 9 when we measured the students, only four girls did not have their period (too few cases to investigate). Even the late developers had almost all attained menarche. Measurement in Grade 8, when there were sufficient numbers of extreme late developers without periods, would have provided a more adequate test for girls. The fact that boys' pubertal calendar starts and ends later allows the Grade 9 and 10 measurement to be a better test for them.

Eighth Grade

While we do not have extensive measurement in Grade 8, we have measured the students' self-esteem. As we noted earlier, girls in eighth grade do not demonstrate a pattern in line with the deviance hypothesis. Boys also show no significant effects of puberty on self-esteem in Grade 8, regardless of whether the regular puberty or the extreme puberty split is used.

Social Class and Pubertal Change

As noted in Chapter 5, Clausen (1975) found that early development was more of an advantage for working than for middle class boys. One might expect that the earlier entry to adulthood in the working class would lead these boys to regard early development more favorably. One might also expect a greater valuation of physical strength to occur in the working class, rendering the muscularity and greater height of the early developers to be regarded with special favor. However, there were relatively few significant interactions between pubertal timing and social class in regard to our dependent variables, and no pattern emerged across these significant findings. There was no real evidence that early development was more of an advantage for working than middle class boys, or that early development was more likely to translate into more adult attitudes, behaviors, or expectations.[35]

Summary

How Substantial Are the Effects of Pubertal Development?

For boys, like girls, developmental timing has only a few, very specific effects, primarily involving body image. We have seen in Chapter 5 that later developing girls show greater satisfaction with their height and weight and in later years with their figure as well. Early developers were more satisfied with their figure solely in the one year (Grade 6) when they were the only ones to have much of a figure. In contrast to the pattern of less favorable body image of the early developing girl, early developing boys showed some advantages. They were more satisfied than late developers with their height, muscles, and in Grade 10 with their athletic ability.

However, neither for boys nor girls do these attitudes generalize very well, even to an overall satisfaction with looks or rating of the self as "good-looking." In fact, for boys, the late, not the early developers, are most positive to their looks in general, despite the fact that the early developers are more satisfied with height and muscles. We suggested that the greater heaviness of the early developers may have been responsible for these last findings since they disappeared when height and weight were controlled.

For both sexes, developmental timing also affects relationships with the opposite sex. Early developers of both genders appear to start dating earlier. However, while early developing or pubertal girls continue to date more in all years than their late developing counterparts and/or perceive themselves as more popular with the opposite sex, early developing boys show this difference in Grade 6 only. To some extent this greater activity with the opposite sex among early developers may reflect a tendency of others to treat the older looking children as older. Some findings suggest that peers may involve them in dating for this reason; parents may allow dating for the same. In addition, students who are more developed—a figure for girls, muscularity and height for boys—may be more attractive to the opposite sex. Finally, their internal hormonal development may increase their libido and their own attraction as well as attractiveness to the opposite sex.

In addition, early developing boys showed some sign of greater comfort with and more positive attitude toward their own gender-role after Grade 6.[36]

For girls, but not for boys, developmental timing also had effects on independence behavior and on conformity. Early developing girls were allowed more independence from chaperonage and were less conforming in school than later developing girls. They performed less well academically and exhibited more problem behavior in early years when their differential development was evident to themselves and to others.

For boys, but not for girls, a few aspects of the relationship to parents, other than allowed independence, appeared to be affected by pubertal timing. At the time of pubertal development, whether that be early or late, parents and peers were seen as less approving of one another. And in Grade 10 late developers perceived parents as rating them less highly. These are virtually the only findings that could support, even weakly, the hypothesis that pubertal change is difficult for the youth at the time it is occurring.

For both sexes there was little, if any, evidence of significant effects of pubertal timing upon the global self-image—upon self-esteem, self-stability, etc.

Is Early Pubertal Development Advantageous or Disadvantageous?

For girls, the effects of early pubertal development were primarily, but not solely, negative in direction for those specific variables affected. Early pubertal development was a disadvantage for the girls' body image, school performance, and school behavior, but was an advantage for opposite-sex popularity (although there is some question whether opposite-sex popularity at this early age is, in fact, an advantage). For boys, as prior literature suggests (Petersen and Taylor, 1980), early development has more advantageous effects for those few variables affected. During some years there is indication of greater satisfaction with height, muscular development, and athletic ability; and a more positive attitude toward being a boy. Like girls, early developing boys date sooner, although it is not clear whether early dating, in fact, is an advantage. On the other hand, early development in Grade 7 is associated with lower satisfaction with looks in general until height and weight are controlled; early development has mixed effects upon parental relationships depending on the grade at issue. All of the previous findings are based on a trichotomy of approximately equal thirds. When a more extreme split is made, extreme early developers in Grade 6 (when they are deviant) are more likely to be the group to score most negatively across variables. It should be recalled that in these last findings we are talking about the 10% of boys who mature earliest, in fact who are maturing in elementary school.

Thus, while in general early development can be considered to have some disadvantages for girls and some advantages for boys, most variables studied here are unaffected by timing of pubertal development, and there are a few findings contradictory for both genders.

Are Early Developers More Adultlike?

Chapter 5 showed that in Grades 6 and 7 there was some evidence that early developing girls and/or those who reached menarche at a given time were allowed more independence, treated as older by significant others, dated earlier, and were more likely to adopt adolescent values—to care more about body image and opposite-sex popularity. For boys the findings are mixed. In Grade 6 early developers date more and value opposite-sex relationships more than do late developers. In some years, but not others, friends and parents are perceived to expect early developers to date more. On the other hand, findings were contradictory in regard to certain significant others' expectations for older behavior and for career planning; there was little or no indication that early developing boys were allowed more independence by parents; there was some evidence that early developing boys were less, rather than more, likely to aspire to adult future roles; and findings were inconsistent in relation to adoption of certain adolescent values (valuation of physical appearance and independence).

Thus, for both genders there is evidence that early developers become oriented earlier to opposite-sex relationships. For girls, but not boys, earlier movement away from childish roles and perceived expectations is evident for a wider variety of variables as well.

How Long Lasting Are the Effects of Pubertal Development?

For girls there was some evidence that the impact of early development occurred primarily in Grades 6 and 7 when these girls looked different from their peers, although an unfavorable body image and a greater propensity to date persist into Grades 9 and 10. For boys, the few findings that occur are spread over the 4 years of measurement; no less evident in Grades 9 and 10 than in Grades 6 and 7. This difference between boys and girls may be due to the fact that early developing boys, unlike early developing girls, still look older than their peers in Grades 9 and 10. Early developing boys, in both Grades 9 and 10, are still taller, as well as heavier, than their peers. In contrast, early developing girls in Grades 9 and 10 are no longer taller than their late developing counterparts and are no longer the only ones to have a developed figure.

Support for Alternate Hypotheses

In terms of support for the hypotheses introducing this chapter, there is little support in the boys' data for the hypothesis that pubertal change is inherently stressful and has widespread negative effects whenever it occurs. For boys, what few differences do occur between early and late developers are likely to favor, not disfavor, the early developers at the time they are changing in Grades 6 and 7. Only in relationship to parents is there any suggestion of support for the "change is stressful" hypothesis for boys, and this evidence is weak. For girls, while early developers do show more problems in early years, later developers do not demonstrate negative effects in later years when they are the ones closest to pubertal change. Also, girls closer to menarche hardly ever scored significantly more negatively on a dependent variable than did girls who were further removed from the onset of menstruation.

On the other hand, there is some, but not overwhelming support for the deviance hypothesis. Boys who are in the earliest 10% of developers are the group to score most negatively in Grade 6 on more variables than would be expected by chance; and late developers show most negative effects by the same test in Grade 10. Thus, boys who show asynchronies between their biological development and their grade level show some negative results.[37] There is no such pattern for girls—while early developers (extreme and otherwise) score more negatively in Grades 6 and 7 than would be expected by chance, late developers do not score more negatively in later years when they are in the minority. The absence of eighth grade data, though, makes our test for girls incomplete.

As for the adult resemblance hypothesis, there is some support in these data. There are two aspects of this hypothesis—first, individuals who resemble adults more will show some advantages; second, they will be treated as older and act older than peers who look more childish. In fact, early developing boys (but not girls) do demonstrate advantages. In addition, in terms of the second part of the hypothesis, early developers of both genders move faster into the new adolescent behavior of dating; and early developing girls perceive that others expect older behavior from them, and they, in fact, report older behavior and values along several dimensions in addition to dating.

The developmental readiness hypothesis also fits with some of the data, but only for girls. According to this hypothesis early development would be difficult because it thrusts the youngster into more change before he or she is ready for it. Early development does seem to have a variety of negative attitudinal and behavioral consequences for girls, but not for boys. The question then arises as to why the sexes react differently.

First, the hypothesis itself predicts a stronger effect for girls than for boys, since girls' pubertal development begins earlier than does boys'. Girls are thus more likely at a younger age to find childhood truncated and themselves catapulted into adolescence.

Second, the cultural ideal hypothesis could explain the discrepancy of findings. The society's high evaluation of male height and muscularity favors the early developing boys; societies' high evaluation of a slim but developed female figure favors the late developing girl especially in later years.

In conclusion, the boys' data point to some very specific advantages for the early developing boy, although extreme early developers show some negative effects in Grade 6 when they are in a very small minority. For girls a variety of specific advantages accrue less to the early maturer than to the late maturer. In addition, there is some evidence that children who appear older (early developers) act older in these years, particularly in relationship to the opposite sex.

Footnotes

[1]See Petersen and Taylor (1980).

[2]For reviews of this literature, see Eichorn (1963, 1975), Dwyer and Mayer (1968–1969), Clausen (1975), White and Speisman (1977), Jersild, Brook, and Brook (1978, Ch. 4), Petersen and Taylor (1980), Livson and Peskin (1980), and Blyth, Simmons, Bulcroft, Van Cleave, Felt, and Bush, 1981a). For information about the Fels studies, see Reynolds and Wines (1951), and Kagan and Moss (1962).

[3]Mussen and Jones (1958).

[4]Jones and Bayley (1950), Eichorn (1963), and Jones (1965).

[5]Jones and Bayley (1950), Latham (1951), Mussen and Jones (1958), Mussen and Boutourline-Young (1964), Clausen (1975), and Savin-Williams (1979, 1980).

[6]Jones and Bayley (1950).

[7]Jones and Bayley (1950), Dwyer and Mayer (1968–1969), and Clausen (1975).

[8]Jones and Bayley (1950), Mussen and Jones (1957), and Weatherley (1964).

[9]Douglas and Ross (1964).

[10]The family observation studies of Steinberg and Hill (Steinberg and Hill, 1978; Steinberg, 1981) are also very important pieces of contemporary research in this field.

[11]Tobin-Richards et al. (1983), Dornbusch et al. (in press), and Petersen et al. (1983).

[12]Duke et al. (1982).

[13]Duke et al. (1982).

[14]Dornbusch et al. (in press).

[15]Throughout Chapter 6, as in Chapter 5, we have done a separate analysis controlling for the ponderal index, with findings virtually identical to those reported when controlling for height and weight (see Chapter 5, footnote 13).

[16]Prior to the collection of the Grades 8–10 data, we utilized rate of height growth as a preliminary indicator of pubertal growth in Grades 6–7. (Only with the addition of later years of measurement could we ascertain when the peak rate of height growth occurred.) This preliminary analysis showed that once height and weight were controlled, boys who were growing more rapidly showed a higher level of self-esteem (Blyth et al., 1981a).

[17]However, in the "longitudinal sample" of children present all 4 years in the study, the difference does not become nonsignificant when height and weight are controlled.

[18]For similar results based on rate of height growth in Grades 6–7, see Blyth et al. (1981a).

[19]However, it should be noted that there are no bivariate significant effects of pubertal timing on satisfaction with weight.

[20]When height and weight are controlled, Grade 10 late developing boys also care significantly less than early developing boys about school work ($p < .10$) and about competence in general (being "the best in the things you do" versus being popular or independent—$p < .10$). However, it should be noted that in Grade 6 the direction of findings related to valuation of school work is not the same ($p < .05$ when height and weight are controlled).

[21]After height and weight are controlled, Grade 9 differences in the same direction also become significant. All other differences between early and other developers remain significant with height and weight controlled. However, in the "longitudinal sample" (the sample of children interviewed in all 4 years), the early developers in Grade 6 are significantly more, not less, likely to say it is important not to act like the opposite sex.

[22]There are homogeneity of variance problems with these items. Early developers show the greatest variances, middle the least on questions about acting like the opposite sex. Middle developers show the greatest variance when asked about their positive or negative attitude toward being a boy.

[23]When height and weight are controlled, the difference remains in the same direction but no longer reaches significance.

[24]In fact, once height and weight are controlled, the following finding emerges in Grade 7: early developers become significantly less likely, rather than more likely, to perceive that their parents expect them to date ($p < .10$).

[25]The only other significant relationship in Table 6.3 involves Grade 10 in school extracurricular memberships and appears to be idiosyncratic rather than consistent. While early developers are more active in clubs in Grade 10, both before and after covariates are controlled, in Grade 7 once height and weight are controlled, early developers are least active.

[26]In Grade 7, however, parents are perceived as expecting more career planning of early developing boys, a finding that disappears when height and weight are controlled.

[27]For the MANOVA analysis, we used only mother's evaluation rather than parent's evaluation in order to minimize the impact of missing data from children without fathers.

[28]Late developers were the least likely in Grade 10 to seek advice about dating ($p = .05$); early developers were the most likely.

[29]Also, findings involving club membership might be consistent with the deviance and change is stressful hypothesis. While the cluster is not significant (Table 6.1), the analysis of covariance shows early developers in Grade 7 and late developers in Grade 9 to be significantly less likely to be in clubs.

[30]In some cases the same variable is significant for more than 1 year. Dating and independence variables are not included here, since it is not clear that early behavior of this type has a positive meaning (see Simmons *et al.*, 1979; in press a). However, inclusion of these variables would not change the foregoing conclusion. See Chapter 5, footnote 44 for a total list of variables. In this case, parents liking friends and friends liking parents are also included.

[31]Only those boys whose height curves were clear and for whom there was little missing data were utilized for this analysis ($N = 153$). Boys who had to be classified with the discriminant function analysis for the trichotomy into equal thirds are thus excluded from this analysis (see Chapter 2).

[32]In cases of ties, the result is considered as nonsupportive of the hypothesis.

[33]In contrast, as predicted, the early developers who are now part of the majority of pubertal boys in Grade 10 score most negatively on only 7/26 of the variables where scores are unadjusted and 4/27 when adjusted.

[34]In Grade 10 the extreme late developers (the deviant group) score most negatively on 12/27 of the variables both before and after controls, while the extreme early developers (as part of the majority at this point) score most negatively in only 6/27 of the variables before controls are instituted and 5/27 afterward.

[35]Based on two-way analyses of variance, we found 1 significant interaction between social class and pubertal timing in Grade 6 out of 68 possibilities, 2 significant interactions in Grade 7 out of 69 possibilities, and 2 significant interactions in Grade 9 out of 63 possibilities. In Grade 10 there were 7 significant interactions, however. In no case was the same variable involved in more than one year. In Grade 10, in 3 cases the early developers scored less favorably (relative to later developers) in the working but not the middle class (perceived self-stability, satisfaction with looks, opposite sex popularity); in 3 cases they scored more favorably (depressive affect, participation in activities, and problem behavior).

[36]For girls, findings were inconsistent. Late developers were significantly more positive to being a girl in Grade 7, early developers in Grade 9.

[37]See Frisk *et al.* (1966) for evidence in Finland in support of the deviance hypothesis.

IV

THE IMPACT OF SCHOOL ENVIRONMENT

This volume opened with a puzzle—why in the original Baltimore study was there a drop in self-esteem and a generally less favorable self-image at the entry to adolescence in Grade 7? Could such findings be replicated? What role did biological change (i.e., pubertal development) play; what role did changes in school environment play?

As noted in Part II, when we ignore differences in pubertal development and school environment and look at all youngsters as a group, the findings do not replicate. No overall negative turn appears in early adolescence. When differences in pubertal development are examined, a complex set of results occurs. Consequences of pubertal development are specific rather than general. Body image, popularity with the opposite sex, and deviant behavior are affected, but global self-esteem is not.

In the earlier Baltimore study, however, all children transferred from an intimate elementary school to a large, impersonal junior high school at the entry to adolescence. In the present study, only some of the children make this same transition. Do the earlier findings of a negative turn in early adolescence replicate for the group moving into junior high school? Is this effect stronger for girls than for boys, as it was in the earlier research? If there are negative effects, are they short-lived or long-term in their impact, and how widespread and sizable are the effects?

It is to these questions that Part IV turns. Chapters 7 and 8 discuss the direction of effects of school transition on various tasks of adolescence for boys and for girls as groups. Chapters 9 and 10 investigate the extent of the effects, and look at the issue of individual recovery for variables impacted negatively in Grade 7.

At some time the individuals living in modern urban centers have to move out of "primary" or small and intimate environments into the large, impersonal, "secondary" type organizations that are so characteristic of the larger society. For many children, the first such transition occurs with the movement out of elementary school into junior high. The question is whether the coincidence of this transition with the entry into adolescence is difficult for the youngster.

It should be noted that other investigators with a different focus have questioned the impact of between-school characteristics. Influenced by Coleman, Campbell, Hobson, McPartland, Mood, Weinfeld, and York (1966), several studies in the last decade concluded that between-school differences, especially differential resources, had little effect on educational achievement. What did have an impact were the background characteristics children brought to the school or the within-school differences (see Alwin and Otto, 1977; Hauser, Sewell, and Alwin, 1976).

Some critics of this conclusion argue that the importance of school factors should not be dismissed despite their small effects since such factors can be altered, unlike the background variables that have larger effects (Sumners and Wolfe, 1977; Rowan et al., 1983; Purkey and Smith, 1983). Other critics claim that the right type of school characteristics were not examined. While major structural characteristics and resources had little consequence, effects were produced by status-composition factors (ethnic and social class proportions), by microstructural or more proximate characteristics (such as tracking, departmentalization, ability grouping, degree of teacher control, classroom characteristics, stability of student body), and by climate or school culture.[1]

Our data do not allow the detailed examination of the many microstructure or status-composition factors that might be relevant. In later chapters (12, 13), however, we will utilize those school characteristics for which we have measures to analyze the causal processes at work. At this point, though, our focus is on the effects of discontinuity in school-transition, on the direction, persistence, and extent of differences between our K–8/senior high school cohort and our K–6/junior high school/senior high school (K–6/JH/SH) cohort in terms of the many outcome variables at issue. Does the discontinuity of a transition to a new school bring with it disruption in psychosocial development?

As noted in Chapter 1, a discontinuous or abrupt change into a new period in the life course is expected to cause more difficulty than a more gradual transition (Benedict, 1954). The move into junior high school involves a dramatic and abrupt change into adolescence. On the other hand, the individual in a K–8 school in Grade 7 enters adolescence in a protected environmental context. He or she gradually can become accustomed to the new age-role expectations of adolescence and to some pubertal changes before having to cope with a major environmental transition.

In the next two chapters we examine the extent to which these two different sequences of environmental context affect the student from Grades 6 to 10. The following sets of generic hypotheses involving short- and long-term effects guide the research.

Short-Term Positive versus Negative Effects

1. Being in a small elementary school will be more beneficial for the early adolescent than being in a large, impersonal environment.

2. Changing from a small elementary school to a large junior high school in Grade 7 will have a negative impact on the early adolescent child (the discontinuity hypothesis).
3. Being "top" dog (among the oldest children in the school) will be more beneficial than being "bottom" dog (among the youngest).

The first two hypotheses are based on the expectation that intimate environments and gradual, rather than discontinuous, change is beneficial for children of this age as they enter a new period in the life course. In terms of the third hypothesis, the principle of social comparison (Rosenberg, 1979) leads us to expect that youngsters who rank high, rather than low, in a social system (the "top" versus the "bottom dogs") will feel better about themselves and will react more positively in general. Mastery of the environment and comfort with it are also likely to be higher when one ranks high in a social system, especially when the system is familiar and one has moved upward through its ranks. For all of these reasons we expect evidence of a "top dog/bottom dog" effect.

Short-Term Socialization Effects

All effects are not positive or negative in nature. Some involve acceptance of new age-related values and exposure to age-related expectations; that is, to values and expectations appropriate to adolescence. We hypothesize that: Children will assume adolescent values if they are in a school with older, adolescent children (adolescent socialization hypothesis). Therefore, Grade 7 children will be treated as older and subjected to more adultlike expectations in junior high school than in a K–8 school.

Long-Term Positive and Negative Effects

In addition to the short-term effects at the entry to adolescence, longer term consequences are of great interest. Particularly, if there are negative short-term effects, the issue of recovery is then raised. Several alternate hypotheses can be posed.

1. *Change is stressful hypothesis.* Change into a new and larger school will be stressful whenever it occurs, with few long-term effects.
2. *Developmental readiness hypothesis.* Environmental change into a new and larger school is negative only if it occurs in early adolescence when children lack the maturity to cope with it. Early negative reactions at this young age will have long-term unfavorable consequences.
3. *Stress inoculation hypothesis (or experience hypothesis).* Whatever the short-term effect of the first transition, simply experiencing such a transition will prepare children to cope better with later transitions of similar type.

If the first hypothesis, that change is stressful whenever it occurs, is accurate, then the cohort moving from a K–6 to a junior high school and then to a senior high school (K–6/JH/SH cohort) should score more negatively in Grades 7 and 10 when they change schools; the K–8 cohort should show more negative effects in Grade 9 when they are the ones to change schools. If, instead, the developmental readiness hypothesis is accurate, the K–6/JH/SH cohort will score more negatively than the K–8 cohort not only in Grade 7 when they first change school but persistently thereafter in Grades 9 and 10. They will not recover. According to the developmental readiness hypothesis, the K–8 cohort, however, will not do badly when, at a later age, they first change schools. They will not be the ones to score more negatively in Grade 9, for at this older age they will be more ready developmentally for the change. They will not have been propelled too soon out of intimate into impersonal contexts.

According to the first two hypotheses, the K–6/JH/SH cohort should be doing relatively badly in Grade 10 at the time of transition into senior high school (but for different reasons). The third hypothesis, the stress inoculation hypothesis predicts instead that this cohort will show a more favorable transition to senior high school than the K–8 cohort. In Grade 10 the K–6/JH/SH cohort will be changing schools for the second time. They will have prior experience with such change and, therefore, will not react negatively; they may even score more positively than the K–8 cohort. It will be as if they have been inoculated or prepared for stress. On the other hand, when the K–8 cohort changes into senior high school (Grade 9), those children, inexperienced with change, will score particularly negatively. Table IV.1 summarizes these alternate hypotheses concerning long-term reactions.

TABLE IV.1. Guiding Theories and Specific Predictions Concerning Long-Term Reactions

Alternate hypotheses	Hypothesized long-term reactions (K–8 versus K–6/JH/SH cohort)	
	Grade 9	Grade 10
Change is stressful	K–8 cohort worse than K–6/JH/SH	K–6/JH/SH cohort worse
Developmental readiness	K–6/JH/SH worse	K–6/JH/SH worse K–6/JH/SH worse than Grade 9 K–8
Stress inoculation hypothesis (experience hypothesis)	K–8 worse	No difference between cohorts or K–8 worse K–6/JH/SH better than Grade 9 K–8

Analysis Plan

The analysis in Chapters 7 and 8 takes four approaches. First, as in prior chapters, a Multivariate Analysis of Variance is used to examine the relationship of clusters of dependent variables to school context each year. The second approach is to examine relationships of school context to key specific variables in Grades 6 and 7 from those clusters where significant relationships are found.

Third, changes in these key variables between Grades 6 and 7 will be analyzed, controlling for initial differences. Grade 6 scores will be controlled through an Analysis of Covariance, and adjusted mean changes between Grades 6 and 7 will be compared for boys and girls in different school contexts. In essence through this procedure all children are treated as if they started out in Grade 6 at the same score prior to any transitions. We then can compare the relative changes of various subgroups to one another with less worry about ceiling or floor effects or regression toward the mean (Bohrnstedt, 1968).[2] For example the Grade 6–7 adjusted change score in self-esteem for junior high school girls tells us whether after the transition into junior high, girls lost or gained self-esteem relative to the other subgroups of students and net of what could be predicted from their initial scores. For the key variable of self-esteem, corrections for reliability and correlated error have been made in the change score analyses (see Simmons et al., 1979, in press b; Carlton-Ford, Simmons, and Blyth, 1983; and Chapter 9 for further discussion).[3]

Fourth, change over the full 5 years of the study will be examined for each of these same variables. Simple trends will be analyzed (i.e., differences in means among boys and girls in the two school cohorts will be investigated over the 5-year period). In addition, adjusted mean changes between Grades 6 and 9 and Grades 6 and 10 will be constructed. Again the Grade 6 score will be controlled through an Analysis of Covariance. The Grades 6–9 and 6–10 adjusted change scores will allow us to compare differential change among the groups in later years, net of what would have been expected simply from their original scores in Grade 6 at the beginning of the quasi-experiment. For example, compared to other groups, have the junior high school girls in Grade 9 changed differently over 3 years? Compared to other groups in Grade 10 have they changed differently after 4 years?[4] These issues will be investigated in Chapters 7 and 8.[5]

Footnotes

[1]For studies or reviews of school climate, microstructure, and/or status composition factors, see Kelly (1968), McDill and Rigsby (1973), Rosenbaum (1976), Epstein and McPartland (1976, 1979), Rutter and Hersov (1977), Lipsitz (1977), Hindelang and McDermott (1977), Boesel et al. (1978), Rutter et al. (1979),

Gottfredson and Daiger (1979), Berkovitz (1979), Brookover *et al.* (1979), Eckland and Alexander (1980), Gottfredson *et al.* (1981), Coleman, Hoffer, and Kilgore (1982), Epstein and Karweit (1983); Eccles (1984), Reuman (1984), Feldlaufer (1984), and Midgley (1984). For in-depth studies of outlier schools with excellent reputations, see Lightfoot (1983) and Lipsitz (1984).

[2]That is, otherwise children with initially low scores (e.g., in self-esteem) will have more room than other children for improvement, while children with initially high scores will have more room than others on the self-esteem scale to move downward.

[3]In general, an Analysis of Covariance in regression format was used to construct these change scores. The dependent variable in Grade 7 is the raw change score, the sixth grade score on the same variable is the covariate, and the independent variables (sex and school type) are "effect coded" and treated as dummy variables. From this procedure, adjusted mean scores for boys and girls in the two school types can be constructed (that control for the Grade 6 score). In order to express change for each subgroup in terms of overall gain and loss, we have added the grand mean change itself to the subgroup deviation from the grand mean change.

Of course, the estimated effect of an independent variable (as indicated by an unstandardized regression coefficient and significance level) on an adjusted Time 1–Time 2 change-score will be identical to the estimated effect of that variable on an adjusted Time 2 score. The R^2 will also be identical. The identity of these values can be proved algebraically. That is, the use of the adjusted change scores does not double adjust for differences at Time 1 (see Bock, 1975:505; Carlton-Ford *et al.*, 1983). The only estimate that will be different in the two approaches involves the effect of the Time 1 score itself. We chose to utilize adjusted change scores rather than adjusted posttransition scores to focus attention on the fact we are studying change and for greater ease of communication and graphic representation. For the self-esteem change scores, a LISREL measurement model was used to correct for reliability and correlated error over time (see Appendix E). That is, individual corrected self-esteem scores for each grade were constructed, and these values were used to derive "corrected" subgroup mean scores and then "corrected" adjusted mean scores (see Chapter 9 for more detail). Because of these corrections, the figures reported here are slightly different from the uncorrected change scores reported in prior publications (Simmons *et al.*, 1979; Blyth *et al.*, 1983). Conclusions, however, are the same.

In all cases, we have tested for significant covariate-factor interactions and report these.

[4]See Chapter 9 for more elaborate analyses at the individual level.

[5]We will not present here an analysis of absolute change such as that used in Chapter 4. This analysis was performed but failed to turn up consistent differences between the school types in either Grades 6–7 or Grades 9–10. However, among boys and girls in both school types the degree of absolute change and the absolute standard deviations were higher at entry to adolescence in Grades 6–7 than in middle adolescence (Grades 9–10) for most variables. These findings are consistent with the conclusions in Chapter 4.

THE EFFECT OF TYPE OF SCHOOL ENVIRONMENT UPON ATTITUDES TOWARD SCHOOL AND UPON THE SELF-IMAGE

Chapter 7 will deal with the effects of school environment upon certain attitudes toward school and upon establishment of the self-image. Chapter 8 will look at effects upon the other tasks of adolescence.

Attitude toward School

In addition to our usual set of outcome variables, certain attitudes toward school have been investigated and will be analyzed in relation to school context and school transition. Our focus is on attitudes that indicate feelings of discomfort, impersonality, and anonymity in the school. We have investigated (1) the degree of anonymity felt, (2) the perception that school is different this year from last, (3) the extent to which the student likes or dislikes being in the present grade, and (4) the degree of worry about the movement next year into the next highest grade.

As in prior chapters, a Multivariate Analysis of Variance was first performed. Table 7.1 shows that there is a significant relationship between school context and the cluster of attitudes toward school each year.

In terms of the specific variables in the cluster, one of the most important involves the level of anonymity experienced in the school. Children were asked to agree or disagree with the following:

This school has so many students in it that I feel I don't know lots of kids.

Lots of kids don't know me at my school because it is so large.

At this school the teachers don't seem to know who you are or what your name is.

At this school most students don't seem to know who you are or what your name is.

(See Appendix G for a description of the resultant scale.)

Table 7.2 shows the effects of school type on felt anonymity and on the other measured attitudes toward school. In general, when they are

TABLE 7.1. MANOVA—Relationship between Cluster of School Attitude Variables and School Type for Boys and Girls[a]

	Boys				Girls			
Cluster	Grade 6 (N = 148) Significant canonicals (p =)	Grade 7 (120)	Grade 9 (121)	Grade 10 (88)	Grade 6 (145)	Grade 7 (114)	Grade 9 (123)	Grade 10 (82)
School attitudes[b]	.29 (p = .01)	.64 (p < .001)	.50 (p < .001)	.36 (p < .05)	.39 (p < .001)	.60 (p < .001)	.49 (p < .001)	.37 (p < .05)

[a]Significance of the relationship of school type (K–6/JH/SH versus K–8/SH) on Cluster.
[b]Included in this cluster are the following variables: Perception of this grade as very different from last year's grade, liking of this grade, worry about school next year, and perceived school anonymity. Since perceived anonymity and perception of school as different were asked of only a random half of the youngsters in Grades 6 and 7, MANOVAS in these 2 years are based on smaller Ns than usual.

208

TABLE 7.2. School Attitude Variables—Means for Boys and Girls According to School Type[a]

	Cohort	Boys				Girls			
		Grade 6 (323)	Grade 7 (279)	Grade 9 (123)	Grade 10 (89)	Grade 6 (271)	Grade 7 (241)	Grade 9 (124)	Grade 10 (82)
1. Anonymity[c]	K–8/SH	1.09*	.53*°	1.40****°	1.07***	1.45*°	.40*°	1.24****	.89***°
	K–6/JH/SH	.77	2.51	.76	1.51	.74	2.13	1.19	1.67
2. School is different this year[c]	K–8[b]	2.54**	2.64*†††	3.46*°	2.32*	2.69**	2.87*†††	3.55*	2.41*
	JH	2.46	3.44	2.42	2.69	2.30	3.19	2.53	3.04
3. Like this grade	K–8	3.29**	3.48	3.74	3.68†††°	3.51**	3.61	3.55	3.37†††
	JH	3.51	3.50	3.57	3.30	3.63	3.65	3.48	3.45
4. Worry about next year	K–8	1.68*††††	1.71*°	1.60†††°	1.32	1.65*††††	1.69*	1.50†††	1.37
	JH	1.82	1.63	1.52	1.37	2.02	1.60	1.90	1.38

[a]According to a Two-Way ANOVA (school type and gender as independent variables). School type main effect is significant: *$p \leq .001$; **$p \leq .01$; ***$p \leq .05$; ****$p \leq .10$. School type by gender interaction is significant: †$p \leq .001$; ††$p \leq .01$; †††$p \leq .05$; ††††$p \leq .10$. °Homogeneity of variance problems within that gender.

[b]In the table, K–8/SH is abbreviated to K–8; K–6/JH/SH to JH.

[c]These questions were asked of a random half of the total sample for Grades 6 and 7 but for the full sample in Grades 9 and 10. Grade 6: Ns = 148 males and 120 females; Grade 7: Ns = 145 males and 114 females.

nearer to top in their school in Grades 6 and 7, youngsters regard the school as less anonymous, less different, and they like the school better. In Grade 6, the K–6 youngsters (who are "top dogs" in their school) are significantly less likely than those in K–8 schools to feel anonymous and unknown and to see the school as different from last year; and they are more likely to indicate they like their grade in school. In Grade 7, when this same cohort of youngsters make the transition to a new, large junior high school where they are the youngest (the "bottom dogs") and where there are many more students in their own grade, the situation is reversed. They feel more anonymous and unknown than they did before and significantly more anonymous than their seventh grade counterparts who have remained in the same, small K–8 school. As expected, they are significantly more likely to perceive the new grade as different. Finally, in terms of liking "this grade," the junior high school students remain about the same on average in Grades 6 and 7, while the K–8 youth increase their liking. The net result is that the K–6 cohort's advantage in Grade 6 is eroded almost completely, and the two cohorts end up about the same in this regard.

The findings regarding anonymity are particularly interesting. Table 7.3 shows that in seventh grade, the junior high schools are considerably larger than the K–8 schools. They are larger overall plus there are more than five times as many students in one's grade (Grade 7), and more than nine times as many students one's age and older. Therefore it is not surprising that students feel that they do not know others in their school and others do not know them (see Chapter 2 for more discussion of school differences).

However in Grade 6, the findings are a bit surprising: the K–8 youngsters feel more anonymous than those in K–6 schools even though the overall difference in mean school size is fairly small. There is also very little difference in the number of students in one's grade (Grade 6); and, if anything, there are more younger children in the K–6 school than in the K–8 school. Where there is a big difference, of course, is in the number of children in one's grade or older. The K–8 school has almost four times as many students in this category as the K–6 school. What this finding suggests is that students older than oneself are more likely than younger ones to assume significance. Thus, if K–8 sixth grade students do not know the seventh and eighth graders personally, this fact may shape their picture of the school environment more than will any number of unknown first and second graders. The sixth grade K–8 students probably are neither very well recognized by nor likely to be well acquainted with the students who "matter in the school." Whereas the K–6 sixth grade students know everyone who "matters" in their school.

Size of school and the "top dog" phenomenon presumably are operating together here. The sixth graders in a K–6 school are the ones who matter

TABLE 7.3. Size and Grade Level Composition of Schools[a]

	Grade 6 (1974)		Grade 7 (1975)			Grade 9 (1977)		Grade 10 (1978)	
	K–8	K–6	K–8	K–6/7–9	K–8/9–12	K–8/9–12	K–6/7–9	K–8/9–12	K–6/7–9/10–12
Mean number of students in school (SD)	544.8 (157.0)	465.6 (100.9)	497.3 (140.3)	1307.0 (192.5)	1876.2 (718.7)	1876.2 (718.7)	1245.1 (149.8)	1760.8 (706.1)	2275.0 (321.0)
Mean number of students in own grade (SD)	59.0 (28.4)	59.1 (19.1)	79.0 (34.2)	402.9 (70.1)	343.8 (154.1)	343.8 (154.1)	388.0 (70.5)	521.2 (162.6)	716.7 (144.4)
Mean number of students in own or higher grades (SD)	199.7 (73.2)	59.1 (19.1)	143.5 (54.6)	1307.0 (192.5)	1876.2 (718.7)	1876.2 (718.7)	388.0 (70.5)	1395.6 (634.8)	2275.0 (321.0)
Mean number of students in lower grades (SD)	345.2 (99.6)	406.5 (86.9)	353.8 (108.3)	—	—	—	857.1 (108.7)	365.2 (157.8)	—

[a]Values are secured for each relevant school attended by a member of our sample who moves either from a K–8 school to a 9–12 school or from a K–6 school to a junior high school and then a 10–12 senior high school. The values are summed over schools and divided by the number of schools in the category.

most. Whether or not they know most of the younger children by name, they know each other, and it is likely that as "top dogs" they are also recognized by the students in the younger grades. The K–8 sixth graders, in contrast, are not the school leaders and therefore are probably less well known by younger as well as older students.

Adjusted Change Score: Grades 6–7

If we turn from a within-grade comparison to a longitudinal focus on change and look at adjusted change scores, the findings are consistent with the previous discussion. Figure 7.1 presents the mean adjusted change scores between Grades 6 and 7 for perceived anonymity for boys and girls in each of the school types. In this analysis, individual's initial attitudes in sixth grade are controlled; that is, individuals are used as their own controls. Therefore we can see which groups are experiencing relative increments in attitude and which are showing relative decrements, above and beyond initial differences. In Figure 7.1 we find that controlling for Grade 6 score, children's own felt anonymity increases relatively in junior

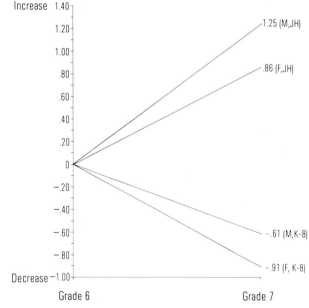

FIGURE 7.1. Change in perception of school anonymity by sex and school type. Mean adjusted change scores, Grades 6–7 (Analysis of Variance with Grade 6 score as the covariate: school type main effect, $p \leqslant .001$; gender main effect, n.s.; gender by school type interaction, n.s.) ($N = 119$). F, females; M, males.

high and decreases in K–8 schools. Similarly, children's view of whether school is different this year increases relatively more in junior high school.[1] (There is no significant adjusted change difference, however, in regard to liking this grade.)

Trend over Five Years

Table 7.2 presents data not only for the 2-year change between Grades 6 and 7, but also for the entire four points in time of the study (Grades 6, 7, 9, and 10). In all years, we find that perceptions of school are very responsive to changes in school environment. Every scheduled school transition involves a switch into a larger school with older children (see Table 7.3). Every year that the students switch schools, their perception that they are in an anonymous environment increases substantially.

In Grade 9 when K–8 students make the transition to senior high schools, their perception of anonymity increases dramatically, while the Grade 9 junior high school students, who are now the oldest students in their school, become less likely than before to characterize the environment as anonymous (Table 7.2). Again, it is possible that the junior high ninth graders do not really know the seventh graders in their school any better than they knew the older students when they were in Grade 7. However, as the oldest students in the school (the "top dogs"), they know everyone who "matters," and many of them are probably recognized by younger students. Feelings of anonymity are probably produced by failure to recognize and be recognized by those who hold equal or higher rank in an environment rather than by the proportion of all members who are known.

In Grade 10, it is the turn of the K–6/JH cohort to make the switch into senior high school with its larger and older population. And in Grade 10, this cohort shows an upswing in feelings of anonymity (Table 7.2), while the original K–8 cohort now in the second year of high school shows a downswing.

An adjusted change score analysis controlling for the Grade 6 score and looking at change from Grade 6 to 9 and Grade 6 to 10 shows results in the same direction as the foregoing trend analysis, although the results do not reach significance. Similarly, perceptions that their new grade is different from the one before are likely to be more frequent in all years where children have changed schools. Both the trend analysis (Table 7.2) and adjusted change analysis (from Grades 6–7, 6–9, and 6–10) show significant changes in line with this summary.

Despite the feelings of greater anonymity among the K–8/SH cohort in Grade 9 when they switch into senior high school, the K–8/SH cohort does not, on average, report liking their grade less (Table 7.2). In Grade 10 there is also no clear pattern of children in one type of school liking their grade better—boys and girls appear to react differently in this regard (Table 7.2).

In summary, these data suggest that being a top dog in a K–6 school engenders relatively favorable attitudes toward school. However, this advantage over the K–8 cohort is eroded upon transition into junior high school where students feel more anonymous and no longer like their grade better than do the K–8 students. In all years, movement into a new and larger school, with greater numbers of higher ranking (older) students, produces increased feelings of anonymity. Being in the lowest ranking age-group in the school organization ("bottom dog") is associated with more anonymity. Being in the highest ranking group ("top dog") is associated with less feeling of anonymity. However, liking one's grade in school is not so clearly associated with school transition and one's age-rank in the school.

One final variable worth examining in terms of attitude toward transition involves the degree to which students worried about the year to come. We asked:

> How worried are you about going into (7th) grade next year? Are
>> you . . .
>> very worried
>> pretty worried
>> a little worried, or
>> not at all worried?

We would expect more worry the year before a major transition. Since we did not measure the K–8 cohort in eighth grade, the year before members moved into senior high school, we cannot test the hypothesis on this cohort. However, for the K–6/JH/SH cohort, we can see if these children were the ones to exhibit more worry in Grade 6 and Grade 9, the years prior to the junior and senior high school transitions, respectively. In fact, girls in this cohort in both Grades 6 and 9 were more likely to be worried about next year than were girls in the K–8 cohort. K–6/JH/SH boys were more worried than their K–8 counterparts in Grade 6 prior to junior high, but not in Grade 9. Thus, at least for girls, there is evidence that some anticipatory anxiety is occurring the year prior to a major school transition.

While students' attitude toward school is of interest to us, their attitude toward themselves is the more central issue in this study. How does transition into an impersonal environment affect the accomplishment of the first task of adolescence—the need to establish a positive self-image?

Self-Image

Table 7.4 shows that some self-image clusters are affected by school type but not others (according to a Multivariate Analysis of Variance), and that there are differences between the genders and between the grades

TABLE 7.4. MANOVAs—Relationship of Self-Image Variable Clusters to School Type for Boys and Girls[a]

Cluster	Boys				Girls			
	Grade 6 ($N=323$) Significant canonicals ($p =$)	Grade 7 (279)	Grade 9 (123)	Grade 10 (89)	Grade 6 (271)	Grade 7 (241)	Grade 9 (124)	Grade 10 (82)
I. Establish Self-Image								
Global self-image	n.s.	n.s.	n.s.	n.s.	n.s.	.16 ($p < .10$)	n.s.	.30 ($p < .10$)
Body-image	.17 ($p < .10$)	n.s.	n.s.	n.s.	n.s.	n.s.	n.s.	n.s.
Concern with body-image	.23 ($p < .01$)	n.s.	n.s.	n.s.	n.s.	n.s.	n.s.	n.s.
Perceived self-competence	.23 ($p = .001$)	n.s.	n.s.	n.s.	n.s.	n.s.	n.s.	.34 ($p < .05$)
Concern with competence	.17 ($p = .05$)	n.s.	n.s.	n.s.	n.s.	n.s.	.36 ($p < .01$)	.33 ($p < .10$)
Gender-role attitudes	.18 ($p < .05$)	n.s.	n.s.	n.s.	n.s.	n.s.	.23 ($p = .10$)	n.s.
Depressive-affect	—	—	—	—	—	—	—	—

[a]Significance of school type (K–6/JH/SH versus K–8/SH) on variable clusters related to self-image.

TABLE 7.5. Self-Image Variables—Means for Boys and Girls According to School Type[a-c]

		Boys				Girls			
	Cohort	Grade 6 (323)	Grade 7 (279)	Grade 9 (123)	Grade 10 (89)	Grade 6 (271)	Grade 7 (241)	Grade 9 (124)	Grade 10 (82)
A. Global self-image									
Self-esteem	K–8/SH	3.63	3.69††	4.21	4.61**	3.00	3.39†††	3.76	4.24**
	K–6/JH/SH	3.69	3.77	4.36	4.32	3.06	2.83	3.32	3.15
Self-consciousness	K–8	1.70***	1.72	1.91	1.71****°	1.98***°	2.04	2.15	2.18****°
	JH	1.79	1.81	2.05	2.02	2.22	2.07	2.29	2.26
B. Perceived self-competence									
Perceive self as smart	K–8	2.94**	3.01	3.03	3.00°	2.93**°	2.95	2.93	2.92
	JH	3.08	3.02	3.02	3.03	2.99	2.98	2.98	2.97
Good at school work	K–8	2.88*	2.99°	2.89****	3.00	2.95*°	2.98	2.82****	2.78
	JH	3.11	2.98	2.93	2.89	3.05	3.00	3.07	2.89
Good at sports	K–8	3.16***	3.16	3.09***††	3.14**	2.85***	2.78	3.03***††	3.00**
	JH	3.28	3.19	3.10	3.02	2.96	2.78	2.58	2.55
C. Body-image									
Perceive self as good looking	K–8	2.82***	2.86°	2.91°	2.96	2.54***	2.61	2.61	2.73
	JH	2.93	2.89	2.95	2.95	2.66	2.64	2.66	2.70
Satisfaction with looks	K–8	3.17†††	3.24	3.23°	3.14	3.16†††	3.12	3.00	3.08
	JH	3.31	3.26	3.22	3.23	3.04	3.05	2.97	2.93
Satisfaction with weight	K–8	3.13	2.82	3.00	3.21†††	2.54	2.67	2.36	2.30†††
	JH	3.24	2.87	3.01	2.97	2.58	2.74	2.56	2.58
D. Concern with body-image									
Care about looks	K–8	2.72††	2.77***	2.85	2.89	2.94††	2.90***°	3.00	3.00
	JH	2.97	2.93	2.92	2.95	2.84	3.05	3.16	3.04
Care about weight	K–8	2.59	2.47	2.48	2.18***	2.97	3.11	3.09°	3.04***
	JH	2.79	2.59	2.49	2.33	2.96	3.11	3.32	3.29
Care about height	K–8	2.50**	2.54°	2.34	2.21***	2.30**	2.32	2.21	3.04***
	JH	2.74	2.59	2.45	2.46	2.48	2.47	2.34	3.29
Care about body build	K–8	2.89**	2.78***	2.60	2.56	2.69***	2.80***	3.33	3.11
	JH	3.17	2.90	2.88	2.74	2.77	2.99	3.30	3.20

E. Concern with competence

Care about intelligence	K–8	3.46***	3.47	3.14***	3.07	3.44***	3.38	3.09***	3.22
	JH	3.58	3.47	3.35	3.28	3.51	3.45	3.26	3.33
Care about school work	K–8	3.53	3.49°	3.34†††	3.18	3.60	3.55	3.15††††	3.18°
	JH	3.60	3.57	3.26	3.20	3.68	3.60	3.36	3.42
Care about good at sports	K–8	3.28	3.17	2.85****††	3.04****°	2.90	2.80	3.09****††	2.89****°
	JH	3.32	3.10	2.97	3.03	3.02	2.82°	2.57	2.44

F. Gender role attitudes

How feel about being a boy or girl	K–8	3.42****†††°	3.43	3.46	3.39	3.24****†††	3.30	3.36	3.44
	JH	3.63	3.56	3.49	3.61	3.22	3.27	3.35	3.47
How important not to act like opposite sex	K–8	2.51****	2.69†††	2.57**	2.46***	1.86****	1.84†††	1.81**	1.67***°
	JH	2.60	2.64	2.69	2.59	1.99	2.05	2.18	2.05

[a]In this table K–8/SH is abbreviated to K–8; K–6/JH/SH to JH.

[b]Findings are reported for a specific variable for all years if there are significant effects in at least 1 year for either gender. For a total list of variables tested, see Table 1.1(1).

[c]According to a Two-Way ANOVA (school type and Gender as independent variables): School type main effect is significant: *$p \leq .001$; **$p \leq .01$; ***$p \leq .05$; ****$p \leq .10$. School type by gender interaction is significant: †$p \leq .001$; ††$p \leq .01$; †††$p \leq .05$; ††††$p \leq .10$. ° Homogeneity of variance problems within that gender.

217

in school. In Grade 6, before the major transitions, the self-image clusters of the boys are often different in the two school types. But the girls are the ones to be affected by school type differences in later grades. While Table 7.4 indicates which clusters of variables are significant, Table 7.5 presents the effects of school type on those specific self-image variables that demonstrate a significant effect in at least one year for either gender.

Global Self-Image: Self-Esteem

We showed in earlier chapters that whatever effects pubertal timing had, they did not involve the global self-image as a cluster or self-esteem as a key variable. In contrast, school type affects girls' global self-image, in general, and self-esteem, in particular. Table 7.4 demonstrates a significant effect for the global self-image cluster for girls in Grade 7 (the year the K–6/JH/SH cohort shifts into junior high school) and in Grade 10 (the year the same cohort shifts into senior high school), but not for boys.

Within the global self-image cluster, it is the key variable of self-esteem that appears to be affected (Table 7.5). In terms of this central dimension of the self-image, junior high schools appear detrimental for girls, but not for boys (see our earlier publications: Simmons *et al.,* 1979; Blyth, 1977). In Grade 6, there is little difference in self-esteem of girls in the two school types; but whatever advantage exists is in favor of the K–6 girls. However, for the Grade 7 girls who have entered junior high school, self-esteem becomes relatively low. Mean self-esteem is only 2.83 for Grade 7 junior high girls compared to 3.39 for seventh grade girls in K–8 schools ($p <$ .05). No such significant difference appears for boys.

Adjusted Change Scores Grade 6 to 7

This vulnerability of the girls is a consequence of differential change in self-esteem as they move from sixth to seventh grade in the different types of schools. Figure 7.2 presents the mean adjusted change-scores in self-esteem for boys and girls in each of the school types, adjusting for their self-esteem in sixth grade. Comparison of the adjusted mean change score allows us to see which groups are experiencing relative increments in self-esteem and which are showing relative decrements.

This longitudinal analysis points to the junior high school girl as being at special risk. As Figure 7.2 clearly indicates, only junior high school girls experience an adjusted mean loss in self-esteem between sixth and seventh grade. All other groups appear to increase their level of self-esteem. Thus, the results of our earlier study in Baltimore in 1968 have been partially replicated here with a better test of the impact of environment upon self-esteem.

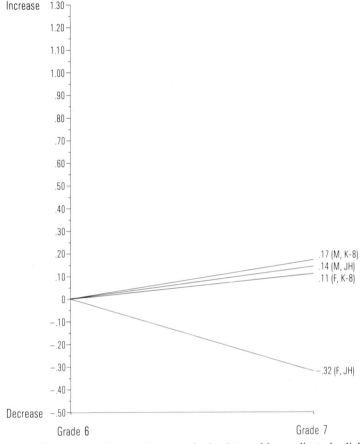

FIGURE 7.2. Change in self-esteem by sex and school type. Mean adjusted reliability-corrected change scores, Grades 6–7 (Analysis of Variance with Grade 6 score as the covariate: school type main effect, $p \leq .05$; gender main effect, $p \leq .05$; gender by school type interaction, $p \leq .10$) ($N = 517$).

Trends over Five Years

Figure 7.3 presents the trends for self-esteem graphically over the 5 years of the study. The dotted line represents the average pattern for the girls in the K–8/SH cohort. The regular line represents the girls who move from a K–6 school to a junior high school to a senior high school. As noted earlier, the K–6 girls show slightly higher average self-esteem than the K–8 girls in Grade 6, but when they move into junior high school their self-esteem declines considerably below that of the K–8 cohort. As evident in Figure 7.3, the self-esteem of these girls rises again between seventh

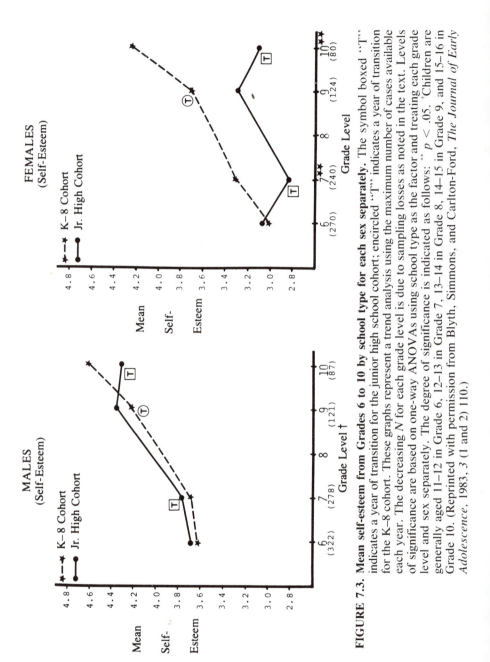

FIGURE 7.3. Mean self-esteem from Grades 6 to 10 by school type for each sex separately. The symbol boxed "T" indicates a year of transition for the junior high school cohort; encircled "T" indicates a year of transition for the K–8 cohort. These graphs represent a trend analysis using the maximum number of cases available each year. The decreasing N for each grade level is due to sampling losses as noted in the text. Levels of significance are based on one-way ANOVAs using school type as the factor and treating each grade level and sex separately. The degree of significance is indicated as follows: ** $p < .05$. †Children are generally aged 11–12 in Grade 6, 12–13 in Grade 7, 13–14 in Grade 8, 14–15 in Grade 9, and 15–16 in Grade 10. (Reprinted with permission from Blyth, Simmons, and Carlton-Ford, *The Journal of Early Adolescence,* 1983, *3* (1 and 2) 110.)

and ninth grade as they become the oldest students in the junior high school. Yet, on the average the gain is not enough for them to completely catch up with the K–8 cohort; the seventh grade experience has left its residue on the girls. The junior high school girls are still at a relative disadvantage compared to girls who have not been subjected to this environmental experience. And compared to boys, they are at a particular disadvantage. The boys in both the K–8 and junior high school environment show a steady rise in self-esteem from sixth to seventh and then to ninth grade. There is no significant difference between the two groups of boys through Grade 9.

The advantage of the K–8/SH girls over the junior high school girls in

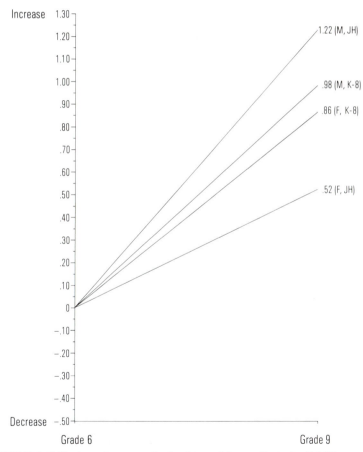

FIGURE 7.4. Self-esteem by sex and school type. Mean adjusted reliability-corrected change scores Grades 6–9 (Analysis of Variance with Grade 6 score as the covariate: school type main effect and interaction are not significant; gender main effect, $p \leq .10$) ($N = 245$).

Grade 9 occurs despite the fact that the K–8 girls have just made their first transition into a large, impersonal organizational context. According to these results, transition at this later age does not appear to have the negative consequences for girls that the earlier transition has. However, it is possible that there was a drop in self-esteem for the K–8/SH cohort between eighth and ninth grade that these data cannot tap, since we had no identical measure of self-esteem in eighth grade. In any case, if a drop occurred, it was not sufficient to lower their self-esteem below their sixth and seventh grade level. Nor was it sufficient to erase all of the advantage of the K–8 girls over the junior high school girls.

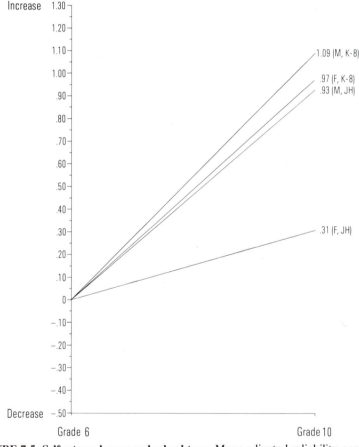

FIGURE 7.5. **Self-esteem by sex and school type.** Mean adjusted reliability-corrected change scores, Grades 6–10 (Analysis of Variance with Grade 6 score as the covariate: school type main effect, $p \leq .05$; gender main effect, $p \leq .05$; gender by school type interaction, n.s.) ($N = 166$).

What happens to the K–6/JH/SH cohort when they make their second major school transition into senior high school? Do they, once again, show a negative change as they move from top to bottom dog? Or, instead, do they show a benefit from having experienced one transition already (stress inoculation hypothesis)? For boys, the entry into senior high school in tenth grade provides the only noticeable interruption of the general upward trend in self-esteem. There we find a leveling off in self-esteem, while the self-esteem of the K–8 cohort of boys continues to rise between Grades 9 and 10.

For girls, this second switch of schools results in a second down turn in self-esteem, rendering them significantly lower in self-esteem than the K–8/SH girls whose self-esteem is rising at the same grade. Just as they were starting to recover in Grade 9, they are hit with what could be described as a ''double whammy.'' This group of girls appears at some risk with lower self-esteem than any other group of boys or girls, though on average their self-esteem is higher than it was in seventh grade.

Figures 7.4 and 7.5 present mean adjusted change scores from Grades 6 to 9 and from 6 to 10. Here, initial differences between the groups are controlled. Again, we see that the girls who moved in and out of junior high school are the most vulnerable group. All of the other groups show greater improvement between the initial measurements in Grade 6 and later years; these girls show the least improvement.

Global Self-Image: Other Variables

There are no significant differences involving perceived stability of the self. There are significant differences involving self-consciousness, with the Grade 10 K–6/JH/SH cohort scoring more negatively than the K–8/SH cohort. However, differences in the same direction were already present in Grade 6, and the adjusted change score analysis does not show significant differences in change among subgroups.

Specific Self-Evaluation Variables

The K–6 school has several advantages over the K–8 school for the sixth grade child, in addition to benefitting global self-esteem. The cluster of variables relevant to feelings of competence in Grade 6 shows significant school effects (Table 7.4). In specific (Table 7.5), the K–6 sixth graders are significantly more likely than their K–8 counterparts to rate themselves as smart, as good at school work, and as good at sports. These advantages are similar for both genders.

In addition, in the K–6 school, children are also more likely to perceive themselves as good-looking, although the findings for girls are not consistent across similar variables. In general then, being the oldest children in a small school appears to have several self-image advantages.

In Grade 7, when the children become "bottom dogs" in a junior high school, these advantages disappear. There are no significant differences and hardly, if any, difference in mean values between children in the two types of schools. In Grade 9, once again, the "top dogs"—the junior high school students—rate themselves significantly better at school work. For both genders, the junior high ninth graders rate themselves higher in this regard than the K–8 ninth graders who have just switched schools. In tenth grade, when members of neither cohort are "top dog," significant differences are absent once again. Self-rating of athletic ability appears more complex in later years and does not follow a clear pattern.

Self-Values

Students' self-values were measured as well as their positive and negative self-evaluations. We investigated the extent to which they cared about their body image, competence, and gender-role behavior. While there are some significant school differences related to these areas, the differences do not follow a clear-cut pattern. The adolescent socialization hypothesis would suggest that students in schools with older students would come to value body image more. Findings are not in line with this prediction. Although aspects of body image become more important to girls in general as they move out of childhood into adolescence (see Table 3.2B), the value placed on body image is not consistently greater in schools with large numbers of older students.[2]

In very few of these specific self-evaluation or self-value areas do the adjusted change score analyses show significant school effects, and these few form no pattern.

Fall–Spring Analyses

One of the central hypotheses being tested throughout this book involves the issue of whether change is stressful for the child's adjustment and self-image. If changing into a new, impersonal organization context is stressful, one might expect it to be more so in the fall of the year than in the spring. In Grades 6–7 a random half of the children were interviewed in the fall of each year and the other random half were interviewed in the spring of each year. For all variables that were measured in both seasons, a Repeated Measures Analysis of Variance was run. Where there was a significant interaction involving the seasons of the interview, an adjusted change score analysis was then performed.

For our key variable of self-esteem there are significant interactions involving season in the Repeated Measures Analysis of Variance and a significant season effect in the adjusted change scores. In general, self-esteem shows less positive change in the spring than in the fall (Figure 7.6). It is particularly interesting, that self-esteem in junior high school was more negatively affected in the spring, rather than in the fall, for both genders (Figure 7.6). The analysis in the first part of this chapter has shown girls to be at risk when they enter junior high school. Figure 7.6 indicates they are at more risk than their K–8 counterpart in both the fall and spring—in both seasons they show greater relative decreases in self-esteem than the K–8 girls as well as greater decreases than all groups of boys.[3] However, females in junior high school in the spring indicate a greater drop in self-esteem than does any other group in either season or either school type. These findings suggest that whatever negative change in self-esteem has occurred persists throughout the year; it is not a transitory phenomenon.

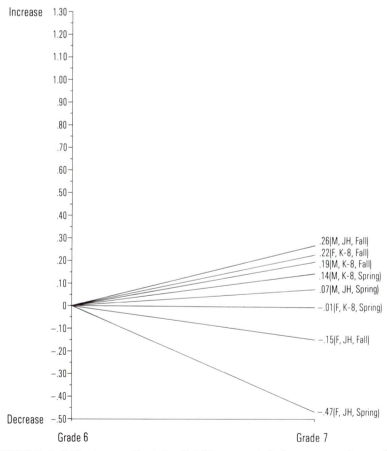

FIGURE 7.6. **Self-esteem: adjusted reliability corrected change score by gender, school type, and season, Grades 6–7.** (Analysis of variance with Grade 6 score as the covariate: school type main effect, $p \le .10$; gender main effect $p \le .05$; gender by school type interaction, $p \le .10$.)

There are several self-image variables that show both significant interactions involving season in the Repeated Measures ANOVA and significant season effects in the adjusted change score analysis. However, no clear pattern emerges across variables and/or across genders implicating one season versus another. There is certainly no clear pattern of difficulties in self-image adjustment occurring soon after entry to junior high school and then reversing later in the same academic year.

Summary

In this chapter we have looked at the effects of school type and school transition upon attitudes toward school and upon the self-image. In regard to our initial hypotheses, there is some evidence that a small elementary school is more beneficial for the early adolescent than a large, impersonal environment; that being a member of the highest ranking cohort (being "top dog" in terms of age) is more beneficial than ranking the lowest (being "bottom dog"), and that the change from a small elementary school to a large impersonal junior high school has a negative impact on the early adolescent child. In the sixth grade, the students in a K–6 school are the "top dogs." They like their grade in school better and perceive school as a less anonymous and impersonal place than do their K–8 counterparts, who are not "top dogs" in school that year. Furthermore, compared to their K–8 peers in Grade 6, the K–6 girls show slightly higher self-esteem, and both genders rate themselves higher in intellectual and athletic competence and, to some extent, in looks.

All of these advantages disappear abruptly the next year when the same children suddenly become "bottom dogs" in a large, impersonal junior high school. In fact, change score analysis indicates relative increases in anonymity upon entry to junior high school and decrements in self-esteem for girls. The K–8 students in seventh grade, who are moving into "top-dog" status in a small and intimate school, are the ones now at an advantage.

These findings partially replicate those of the earlier Baltimore study. It should be noted, however, that there are several self-image variables that are unaffected in this current research that appeared affected in the earlier investigation.

Short-term change is only part of the concern here. Also, of major interest is the longer term impact of those transitions made in early adolescence. At the beginning of this chapter, three alternate hypotheses relative to the senior high school transition were advanced: (a) the stressful change hypothesis; (b) the developmental readiness hypothesis; and (c) the stress inoculation hypothesis. In fact, there is some evidence that change itself is stressful for some variables—over the short but not the long term. In particular, feelings of anonymity increase for a short while every time there is a switch of schools. In contrast, there is no evidence to support the stress inoculation or experience hypothesis—the hypothesis that one transition into a larger, impersonal context prepares children better for the next transition. The K–6/JH/SH cohort does not do better upon transition into senior high school (their second transition) than does the K–8/SH cohort who makes only one change.

In fact, for the key variable of self-esteem there is some evidence for the alternate "developmental readiness" hypothesis, at least for girls. According to this hypothesis, environmental change will have negative effects primarily if it occurs in early adolescence when the children lack the maturity (are not "ready") to cope with it. Such negative effects are likely to persist, and children are unlikely to recover rapidly or completely. In terms of self-esteem the K–6/JH/SH girls never recover from the seventh grade drop in self-esteem, at least in terms of the mean scores and average change scores presented so far. In fact, when they make their second transition, their average self-esteem drops not only below their own score the year before and below the Grade 10 score for the K–8 cohort, but also below the score of the K–8 cohort the year they switched into senior high school (Grade 9). Thus, they respond more, not less, negatively to the transition into senior high school than does the cohort who has to make only one change at a more mature age. Even the year the K–8 cohort switches into senior high school (Grade 9), they score more favorably than the K–6/JH/SH cohort of girls, despite the fact that the latter group are "top dogs" in their school.

The underlying idea behind the "developmental readiness" hypothesis is one of asynchrony of development (Eichorn, 1975; Faust, 1983). Although many students begin to mature physically by Grade 7, it is possible they are not equally mature emotionally and socially. Their emotional maturity may not be sufficient for such a discontinuous, environmental change. The discontinuous change not only places the youngsters in their first major impersonal environmental context, but would appear to be a dramatic marker alerting youth, parents, and teachers that a major status-passage had occurred—the transition out of childhood into adolescence. It is possible the girls are not "ready" emotionally for such a clear change in status and self-definition.

The issue for Chapter 8 is whether these conclusions are compatible with the findings for the outcome variables related to the other tasks of adolescence.

Footnotes

[1]However, a significant covariate factor interaction renders this last analysis tentative. Furthermore, if the longitudinal sample is used (just those children for whom we have data all 4 years), Grade 7 junior high school girls do not see their school as more different from their K–8 counterparts.

[2]In fact, there is some suggestion that the K–6 cohort, particularly the boys, care about body image more in all years, starting with Grade 6.

[3]For the "longitudinal sample" the JH girls in the spring still show the greatest relative drop in self-esteem. In addition, the JH girls in the fall still score less favorably than the K–8 girls in the same season. However, the fall JH girls no longer score more negatively than all groups of boys.

8

THE EFFECTS OF TYPE OF SCHOOL ENVIRONMENT UPON PEER RELATIONSHIPS, INDEPENDENCE, FUTURE PLANS, AND CONFORMITY BEHAVIOR

In Chapter 7, data suggested that students' attitudes toward school and self-images were affected by school context. Negative effects were demonstrated as students moved from "top-dog" status in a small, intimate K–6 school into a large, impersonal junior high school as "bottom dogs." This chapter examines the impact of school context upon the other tasks of adolescence—the intensification of peer relations, establishment of independence, planning for the future, and dealing with conformity/deviance issues.

Table 8.1 shows the clusters that are significantly related to school type. If a cluster is significant at any point for either gender, as almost all clusters are, we will present the specific variables within the cluster that at any point indicate significant relationships for either gender, as we did in Chapter 7. Values for all 4 years for each of these variables are presented, whether all years are significant or not, so that trends can be noted. In the few cases where the cluster fails to ever show significant relationships, that fact will be mentioned.

Peer Relationships

As the second task of adolescence, we have emphasized the intensification of positive peer relationships. Table 8.2 presents the specific variables that indicate statistically significant relationships at any grade level.

Perceived Popularity

First, the sixth grade findings are similar to those just presented for the self-image. Not only do K–6 students rate themselves more highly than the K–8 sixth graders in intelligence, school work, sports, and looks, they also see themselves as more popular with their own sex. Once this K–6 cohort moves into Grade 7 in a junior high school, their significant advantage over the K–8 youngsters disappears and never reappears. These

TABLE 8.1. MANOVAs—Relationship of Variable Clusters to School Type for Boys and Girls[a]

	Boys				Girls			
Cluster	Grade 6 (N = 323)	Grade 7 (279)	Grade 9 (123)	Grade 10 (89)	Grade 6 (271)	Grade 7 (241)	Grade 9 (124)	Grade 10 (82)
II. Establish Peer Relationships								
Peer popularity[b]	.15 ($p < .05$)[c]	n.s.	n.s.	n.s.	n.s.	n.s.	n.s.	n.s.
Value popularity	n.s.	.19 ($p = .05$)	n.s.	n.s.	n.s.	n.s.	n.s.	n.s.
Dating behavior	n.s.	n.s.	n.s.	n.s.	n.s.	n.s.	n.s.	n.s.
Others' expectations regarding opposite sex relationships[d]	n.s.	.17 ($p < .10$)	n.s.	n.s.	n.s.	n.s.	n.s.	n.s.
Participation in activities[e]	.17 ($p < .05$)	.29 ($p < .001$)	.23 ($p < .10$)	.43 ($p = .001$)	n.s.	.47 ($p < .001$)	n.s.	.42 ($p < .01$)
III. Establish Independence								
Independence from parents[f]	.27 ($p < .01$)	.24 ($p < .05$)	.35 ($p < .05$)	n.s.	.34 ($p < .001$)	.33 ($p < .001$)	n.s.	n.s.
Perception that others expect older behavior	n.s.	.17 ($p < .10$)	n.s.	.33 ($p < .05$)	n.s.	n.s.	n.s.	n.s.
Value independence	.16 ($p < .05$)	n.s.	n.s.	n.s.	n.s.	n.s.	n.s.	.32 ($p = .05$)

IV. Plan for Future

Educational, occupational and marital aspirations	n.s.	n.s.	n.s.	n.s.	n.s.	n.s.	n.s.	n.s.
Perception that others expect career planning	n.s.	n.s.	n.s.	n.s.	n.s.	n.s.	n.s.	n.s.

V. Deal with Conformity/ Deviance Issues

Problem behavior	n.s.	n.s.	n.s.	n.s.	n.s.	.22 ($p < .01$)	n.s.	n.s.
Victimization	—	—	—	—	—	—	—	—
Academic performance	n.s.	.22 ($p < .05$)	—[g]	n.s.	n.s.	.23 ($p < .01$)	—	n.s.
Perception that adults evaluate one highly	n.s.	n.s.	.21 ($p < .10$)	n.s.	.15 ($p = .05$)	n.s.	.20 ($p < .10$)	n.s.
Perception of parent–peer relations	n.s.	n.s.	.20 ($p < .10$)	n.s.	n.s.	n.s.	n.s.	n.s.

[a] Multivariate analysis of variance—significance of school type (K–6/JH/SH versus K–8/SH) on variable clusters.

[b] The peer popularity and dating cluster contain a common item—opposite sex popularity (see Table 3.1).

[c] Significant canonicals ($p =$).

[a] This cluster has four items in Grades 6 and 7; two in Grades 9 and 10 (see table 3.1).

[e] In Grades 6 and 7, this cluster contains four items; in Grades 9 and 10, three items (see Table 3.1).

[f] This cluster has eight items in Grades 6 and 7; seven in Grades 9 and 10 (see Table 3.10).

[g] No reading or math achievement tests were given in Grade 9, so only GPA remains as a variable in this cluster.

TABLE 8.2. Peer Relationship Variables—Means for Boys and Girls According to School Type[a-c]

		Boys				Girls			
	Cohort	Grade 6 (323)	Grade 7 (279)	Grade 9 (123)	Grade 10 (89)	Grade 6 (271)	Grade 7 (241)	Grade 9 (124)	Grade 10 (82)
A. *Peer popularity*									
1. Same-sex	K–8/SH	3.06**	3.03	3.15°	3.07	3.06**	3.13	3.06°	3.11°
	K–6/JH/SH	3.21	3.10	3.08	3.08	3.17	3.15	3.10	3.05
B. *Value popularity*									
2. Care about same-sex popularity	K–8	2.94	2.73****	2.48****	2.74	3.11	3.03****	2.88	2.67
	JH	2.99	2.84	2.69	2.70	3.13	3.18	3.07	2.85
3. Care about opposite-sex popularity	K–8	2.12	2.29****	2.83	3.00	2.24	2.46****	2.82	2.78
	JH	2.07	2.52	2.89	2.93	2.24	2.49	2.80	2.82
4. Value popularity more than competence or independence	K–8	.93††††	.99	1.10***	1.34†††°	1.32†††	1.27	.93***	.79†††
	JH	1.06	1.02	1.26	1.08	1.13	1.31	1.35	1.06
C. *Others' expectations regarding opposite-sex relationships*									
5. Same-sex peers expect interest in opposite sex	K–8	.14	.14**	—	—	.24	.25**	—	—
	JH	.17	.32	—	—	.26	.35	—	—
D. *Participation in activities*									
6. Total in-school clubs and sports	K–8	1.05	1.36*	.94	1.32*††††°	.96°	1.30*°	1.33	2.19*††††°
	JH	1.05	.71	.91	.79	.91	.49	.88	.87
7. Total out-of-school clubs and sports	K–8	.55	.49††°	.40	.57	.59	.73††°	.67°	.81°
	JH	.59	.60	.58	.49	.49	.47	.58	.56
8. Coed clubs (in and out of school)	K–8	.45†††°	.87*†°	—	—	.86†††°	1.55*†°	—	—
	JH	.68	.49	—	—	.76	.41	—	—
9. Leadership in clubs and sports	K–8	.30	.28***	.17††	.04†°	.30	.25***°	.36††	.30††°
	JH	.33	.25	.36	.13	.26	.12	.22	.11

[a]In this table K–8/SH is abbreviated to K–8; K–6/JH/SH to JH.
[b]Findings are reported for a specific variable for all years if there are significant effects in at least 1 year for either gender. For a total list of variables tested, see Table 1.1(2).
[c]Two-Way ANOVA (school type, gender as independent variables). School type main effect is significant: *$p \leqslant .001$; **$p \leqslant .01$; ***$p \leqslant .05$; ****$p \leqslant .10$. School type by gender interaction is significant: †$p \leqslant .001$; ††$p \leqslant .01$; †††$p \leqslant .05$; ††††$p \leqslant .10$. °Homogeneity of variance problems within that gender.

232

findings suggest once again the advantage of being a "top dog" in one's school and the disadvantage of being the "bottom dog" in a larger, new school.

The adjusted change analysis, however, shows no significant effect for perceived popularity. Also, there are no significant effects of school context on opposite-sex popularity or on dating any year (either in terms of the cluster—see Table 8.1—or in terms of absolute effects for specific variables or of adjusted change scores). Thus, in this respect, the data do not support our initial "adolescent socialization" hypothesis that students in a school with older children will be more likely to adopt adolescent behavior and attitudes.

Values and Expectations

This adolescent socialization hypothesis can also be tested in regard to values and the perceived expectations of others. As will be recalled from Chapter 7, children in schools with older children were no more likely to place high value on their body image. But do children in schools where there are greater numbers of older students come to value opposite- and same-sex popularity more, and are they more likely to perceive that others expect them to be interested in the opposite sex? In sixth grade, no such findings occur. In seventh grade, however, youngsters in junior high school, where there are more older children, are significantly more likely to adopt adolescent values and to perceive others as holding adolescent-appropriate expectations of them. The junior high school seventh graders are significantly more likely than their K–8 counterparts to value same- and opposite-sex popularity and to report that their peers expect them to be interested in the opposite sex. However, these findings do not reverse in Grade 9 when the K–8/SH cohort moves into senior high school and members confront many older children.[1]

Thus, in regard to the adolescent socialization hypothesis, findings are mixed.

Participation in Extracurricular Activities

The clearest effects of school type on matters involving peers are found with regard to participation in extracurricular clubs and sports. For all 4 years, there are significant cluster effects (Table 8.1). The results are presented numerically in Table 8.2 for specific variables and graphically in Figure 8.1 for overall participation in school clubs and activities. Because this is one of the few variables for which we have Grade 8 data, we have entered these data on the graph. Figure 8.1 shows that sixth graders participate in extracurricular activities about the same amount, regardless of school environment. However, in seventh grade, the junior high school students, who have suddenly become "bottom dogs," react by decreasing

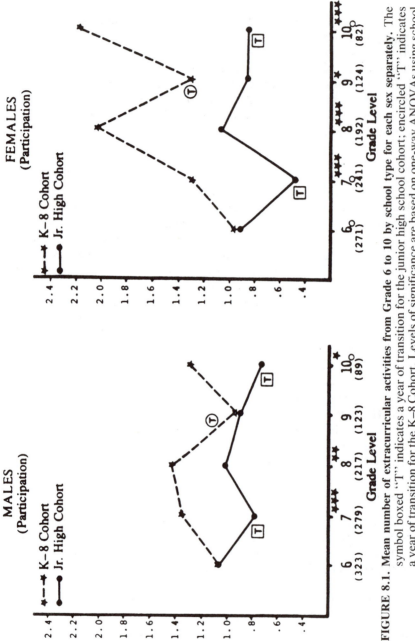

FIGURE 8.1. Mean number of extracurricular activities from Grade 6 to 10 by school type for each sex separately. The symbol boxed "T" indicates a year of transition for the junior high school cohort; encircled "T" indicates a year of transition for the K–8 Cohort. Levels of significance are based on one-way ANOVAs using school type as the factor and treating each grade level and sex separately. The degree of significance is indicated as follows: ° p less than .10; * p less than .05; *** p less than .01; ° indicates that there was a significant lack of homogeneity in the variances.

their participation at the same time as the K–8 youngsters are increasing theirs.[2] The seventh grade junior high students, both boys and girls, not only are less likely than K–8 students to participate in extracurricular activities, they also are less likely to be leaders (particularly the girls— Table 8.2, Row 9). The adjusted change analysis also supports this view of junior high school students decreasing participation and leadership relative to other groups (Figure 8.2).

Interestingly, the lower participation of seventh graders in school activities in junior high school is not because there are less activities available nor because there are more children in the school for each activity that is available. In fact, Table 8.3 shows that there are more activities available in junior high school than in the K–8 school in absolute terms. If we consider the ratio of total number of children to activities available, we find that there are fewer, not more, children per activity in the junior high schools than in the K–8 schools (Median of 98.6 versus 114.0).[3] However, if we look just at the number of seventh graders for each activity available, the possible reasons for lower junior high school participation becomes clearer. In the junior high school there is one activity available for every 30.4 seventh grade children, whereas in the K–8 school there is one activity available for every 17.0 children.

What is probably happening here is that the youngest children in the school have less access to these activities. In our K–8 schools, seventh graders, as a favored and small older group, are apparently among the ones to participate and lead in whatever activities exist. In junior high school, the seventh graders in the lowest-ranking age-group may feel less free to participate in activities, and furthermore, there are more seventh grade students for each activity. Certainly, it is not surprising they are less likely to be chosen as leaders. Barker and Gump (1964) have also shown that fewer students participate in extracurricular activities in a large school despite the fact that there are more activities.

Trend over Five Years

In Grade 8, both cohorts increase their participation, as they move into higher ranking age cohorts in the school (Figure 8.1). However, the gradual recovery shown by the junior high school cohort is insufficient to allow them to catch up to the K–8 youngsters. In ninth grade, the junior high school students once again become "top dogs," and they continue to participate more on the average than they did in Grade 7 (Figure 8.1). This greater participation allows the boys to catch up with the K–8 senior high school cohort, since the latter decreases participation their first year in high school. However, the K–8/SH girls, once accustomed to extracurricular participation, continue to participate at a high rate, and the junior high school girls are still unable to catch up. The adjusted change analysis

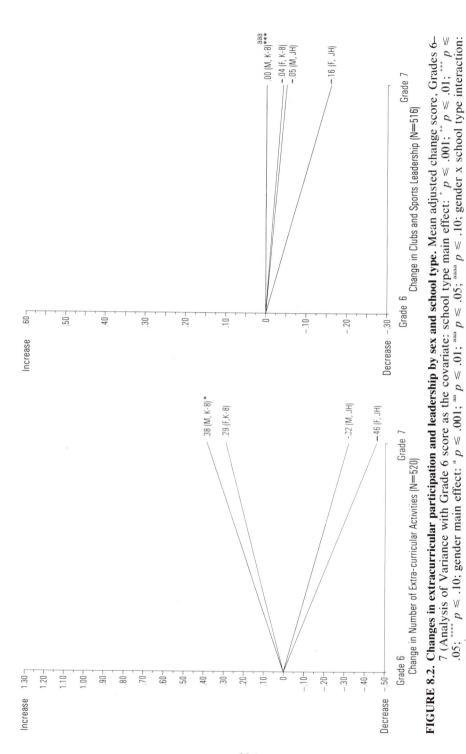

FIGURE 8.2. Changes in extracurricular participation and leadership by sex and school type. Mean adjusted change score, Grades 6–7 (Analysis of Variance with Grade 6 score as the covariate: school type main effect: [*] $p \le .001$; [**] $p \le .01$; [***] $p \le .05$; [****] $p \le .10$; gender main effect: [a] $p \le .001$; [aa] $p \le .01$; [aaa] $p \le .05$; [aaaa] $p \le .10$; gender x school type interaction: n.s.).

TABLE 8.3. Principals' Reports of Extracurricular Activities in Their School

	Type of school[a]		
	K–6	K–8	Junior high school (7–9)
Median number of activities available (range)	10.0 (2–14)[b]	3.5 (1–6)	13.5 (8–28)
Median ratio of total number students in school/ number of activities	51.8 (35–220)[b]	114.0 (93–461)	98.6 (40–148)
Median ratio of seventh graders/activities	—	17.0 (12.3–131.0)[b]	30.4 (10.9–49.2)

[a]The measurement for the K–6 schools occurred when the subjects were in grade 6; the measurements reported for the K–8 and JH schools occurred when the subjects were in grade 7.
[b]Numbers in parentheses represent the range.

between Grade 6 and 9 shows significant differences consistent with the trend analysis (Figure 8.3A).

Although in seventh grade, the K–8 students were significantly more likely than the junior high school students to attain leadership positions in extracurricular activities, in Grade 9 junior high school boys are more likely to be leaders than are the K–8/SH boys who have just entered the lowest grade of senior high school (Table 8.2). Among Grade 9 girls, however, those in junior high school are less likely to be leaders than those in the first year senior high school, just as they are less likely to participate at all[4] (Table 8.2). Girls seem unable to make up the deficiency created by the early adolescent transition into a large junior high school and the initial drop in participation and leadership.

In Grade 10, when the K–6/JH/SH cohort once again changes into a new and larger school with many older children, the effect is once again like a "double whammy." In the discussion of self-esteem, we noted that while junior high school girls started to catch up in Grade 9, movement into Grade 10 hit them once again negatively, leaving the K–8/SH cohort much better off. With extracurricular participation we see similar effects but this time for both genders, although exaggerated for girls (Figure 8.1). The increase in participation after Grade 7 has reversed by Grade 10 for K–6/JH/SH boys and halted for girls. Boys' participation drops to a particularly low point in Grade 10. At the same time the K–8/SH cohort, which has moved into second year high school, shows sizable increases in participation—especially the girls. Thus, this K–8/SH cohort ends up in Grade 10 with much higher rates of extracurricular participation. For girls, but not boys, members of the K–8/SH cohort are significantly more likely to be extracurricular leaders in school as well.

The adjusted change scores from Grade 6 to 10 (Figure 8.3B) also illustrate the negative impact of the K–6/JH/SH experience upon participation. Comparing individuals' scores in Grade 10 to their own scores in

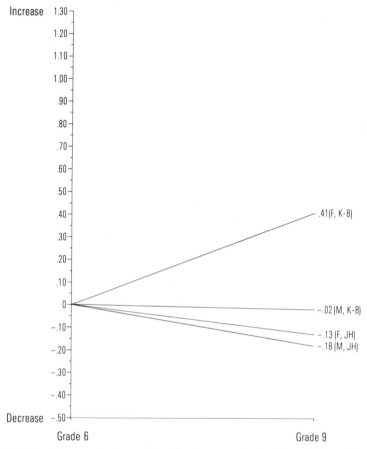

FIGURE 8.3A. Extracurricular participation by sex and school type. Mean adjusted
change scores, Grades 6–9. (Analysis of Variance with Grade 6
score as the covariate: school type main effect, $p \leq .10$; gender
main effect, n.s.; gender by school type interaction, $p \leq .10$.)
($N = 247$).

Grade 6 (controlling for initial Grade 6 differences among groups), we find
that the K–6/JH/SH boys and girls show a relative reduction in participation, whereas the K–8/SH boys and girls show a relative increase in
participation over the years.

In summary, although both cohorts of students start out at about the
same level of extracurricular participation in sixth grade, they end up radically different. A transition into a new school almost always results in a
decreased level of participation. However, the early adolescent transition
has persistent long-term consequences. The K–6/JH/SH cohort, which
has experienced a loss in participation in moving from Grade 6 to 7 in

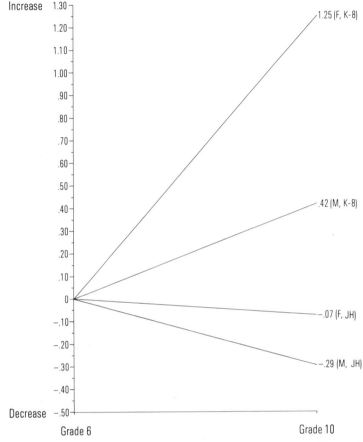

FIGURE 8.3B. Extracurricular participation by sex and school type. Mean adjusted change scores, Grades 6–10. (Analysis of Variance with Grade 6 score as the covariate: school type main effect, $p \leq .001$; gender main effect, $p \leq .05$; gender by school type interaction, n.s.) ($N = 171$).

early adolescence, never fully recovers from this loss. The K–8/SH students (particularly the girls), who show increases in extracurricular activity in early adolescence, continue to demonstrate an advantage, even in the years they switch schools and their participation declines. Extracurricular participation can be regarded not only as an index of the student's integration into peer society, but also as an index of integration into activities approved of by adults in the larger culture. These findings indicate that the level of such integration is considerably affected over the short and long term by the type of school context.

TABLE 8.4. Independence Variables—Means for Boys and Girls According to School Type[a-c]

		Boys				Girls			
	Cohort	Grade 6 (323)	Grade 7 (279)	Grade 9 (123)	Grade 10 (89)	Grade 6 (271)	Grade 7 (241)	Grade 9 (124)	Grade 10 (82)
A. Independence from parents									
1. Take bus without adult	K–8/SH	1.09***†††	1.39*	—	—	1.31***†††°	1.46*	—	—
	K–6/JH/SH	.89	1.14	—	—	.74	1.00	—	—
2. Go places without parents' permission	K–8	.20	.29**	.43	.43†††	.14	.25**°	.39	.52†††
	JH	.20	.23	.38	.64	.10	.08	.23	.35
3. Left home alone	K–8	2.11	2.34	2.91°	2.89††††°	2.06	2.40	2.81	2.96††††°
	JH	2.17	2.42	2.83	2.92	2.06	2.31	2.72	2.78
4. Parent permission not required after dark	K–8	.27****	.46***†††	.31	.43	.15****	.19***†††	.21	.33
	JH	.38	.60	.39	.48	.16	.20	.19	.18
5. Baby-sit	K–8	.36	.88°	.44†††°	.55	1.62	2.98	3.76†††	3.16
	JH	.43	.70	1.36	.55	1.90	2.71	3.40	2.73
6. Job	K–8	.34**	.41**	.54***	.42	.22*°	.29*°	.36***	.44
	JH	.22	.34	.44	.46	.12	.16	.19	.29
7. Perceived independence from parents	K–8	2.96**	2.95°	2.97	2.96††††	2.97**	3.04	3.15	3.30†††
	JH	3.13	3.07	3.11	3.18	3.11	3.01	3.13	3.16
8. Perceived independent decision making	K–8	2.05†††	2.20°	2.29	2.25	2.19†††	2.15	2.18	2.46
	JH	2.21	2.24	2.38	2.36	2.16	2.22	2.25	2.31

240

B. *Perception that others expect older behavior*

9. Teachers expect older behavior	K–8	2.67	3.46°	3.82	3.35**	2.86	3.54	3.51	3.18**
	JH	2.78	3.42	3.76	3.82	2.97	3.38	3.78	3.67
10. Friends expect older behavior	K–8	3.37	2.68**	2.71	2.61**	3.20	2.80**	2.81	2.48**
	JH	3.46	2.91	2.93	2.98	3.18	2.97	2.92	2.85

C. *Value independence*

11. Value independence	K–8	3.25***††††	3.24	3.06	3.21	3.37***††††	3.23°	3.39	3.25
	JH	3.47	3.25	3.12	3.11	3.37	3.29	3.42	3.40
12. Value independence vs. competence or popularity	K–8	.34****	.29***	.37	.32	.28****	.19***	.41	.36
	JH	.39	.39	.31	.33	.39	.27	.31	.31

[a]In this table K–8/SH is abbreviated to K–8; K–6/JH/SH to JH.

[b]Findings are reported for a specific variable for all years if there are significant effects in at least 1 year for either gender. For a total list of variables tested, see Table 1.1(3).

[c]Two-Way ANOVA (school type, gender as independent variables). School type main effect is significant: *$p \le .001$; **$p \le .01$; ***$p \le .01$; ****$p \le .10$. School type by gender interaction is significant: †$p \le .001$; ††$p \le .01$; †††$p \le .05$; ††††$p \le .10$. °Homogeneity of variance problems within that gender.

241

Independence

If the adolescent socialization hypothesis is to be confirmed, indications of independence should be affected by school context. According to this hypothesis, children in schools with larger numbers of older children should be encouraged to behave in a less childish and a more adolescent fashion. Furthermore, the change into a junior or senior high school should act as a cue to parents that their child had attained a new age status. First, then, in Grade 6, the students in a K–8 school should be allowed to act in a more independent manner by parents, and in Grade 7 the situation should reverse. In fact, as Table 8.4 shows, there is little consistent difference in either Grade 6 or 7, and in Grade 7 several findings are contrary to the hypothesis.

Trend over Five Years

In Grade 9, we might expect the K–8/SH cohort, which has just switched to senior high school, to show more independence. There are few significant differences save those involving jobs; those few are in line with predictions (Table 8.4). Girls from the K–8/SH cohort baby-sit more, and boys from that cohort are more likely to hold part-time jobs. In Grade 10, both groups are now in senior high school and exposed to two higher grade levels. Thus, it is difficult to predict differences in independence between the two groups. For K–6/JH/SH boys we do see higher independence on several indicators in Grade 10 compared to K–8 boys (going places without parental permission, being left home alone, and perceiving oneself as independent). However, there is no such pattern for girls—whatever differences in independence occur in tenth grade are in favor of the K–8/SH cohort.

In terms of valuing independence, only in Grade 6 and 7 do we see significant differences, and these results are inconsistent across years (Table 8.4C). While the Grade 7 results are in line with predictions, in Grade 6 the K–6 youth value independence more, contrary to predictions. We also have asked students about the expectations of their significant others—parents, teachers, friends. With multiple choice questions, we have asked whether these significant others expect the child to act alot differently and a lot older this particular year. There are no significant differences in regard to perceived parental expectations. However, the years that the K–6/JH/SH cohort changes school (Grades 7 and 10), members are significantly more likely to perceive their friends as expecting much older behavior; and in Grade 10 they are significantly more likely to report such expectations from teachers than are their K–8/SH counterparts (Table 8.4B). The findings from Table 8.4 are, by and large, reflected in the change analysis.

In sum, while some significant differences are in line with predictions, many are in the reverse direction. And the change analysis shows no other significant differences once initial differences between the cohorts are controlled. The results do not appear to support in any clear way the hypothesis that school context affects the child's level of independence.

Plan for the Future

One might also expect that children in schools with older cohorts of children would expend more energy on setting future career and family plans and to perceive that others expect them to do so. Such findings would support the adolescent socialization hypothesis. However, as noted in Table 8.1, there are no significant results found for clusters of variables involving future plans as related to school type.

Dealing with Conformity/Deviance Issues

Victimization and Problem Behavior

Boesel *et al.* (1978) have reported that younger adolescents are more likely to be victimized in school than are older adolescents; and that students are victimized primarily by children their own age and only secondarily by older schoolmates. We show no such decline in victimization with age. Our study indicates, however, that school type affects level of victimization. In fact, in Grade 7, junior high school students, particularly boys, are victimized significantly more than their K–8 counterparts (Table 8.5). Early adolescent boys who have just moved into a new school and are the youngest in the school are more likely to be victims than are boys who remain in a protected elementary school.[5] Unlike Boesel *et al.* (1978), we did not ask the children for the age of the person victimizing them and therefore cannot replicate or refute their data. However, the fact that the Grade 7 youngsters in junior high school are not more likely than the K–8 students to be involved themselves in problem behavior would be compatible with the alternate hypothesis that it is the older children who victimize the younger.

Up to this point in the analysis, seventh grade children in the junior high school have demonstrated several disadvantages that they did not exhibit the year before. Compared to the K–8 students, they show less favorable attitudes toward school, lower self-esteem for the girls, less participation and less leadership in extracurricular activities, and greater victimization, especially among boys. Involvement in problem behavior presents the first exception to this pattern. Junior high school seventh graders report less, rather than more, involvement in problem behavior than their K–8 peers (Table 8.5) and show more negatively adjusted change on this variable as well ($p = .001$). However, there are no significant differences in suspension or probation.

TABLE 8.5. Conformity Variables–Means for Boys and Girls According to School Type[a-c]

		Boys				Girls			
	Cohort	Grade 6 (323)	Grade 7 (279)	Grade 9 (123)	Grade 10 (89)	Grade 6 (271)	Grade 7 (241)	Grade 9 (124)	Grade 10 (82)
A. *Victimization*									
1. Victimization	K–8	—	.29**†††††	.49	.61*	—	.32**†††††	.42	.56*°
	JH	—	.46	.43	.38	—	.35	.31	.11
B. *Problem behavior*									
2. Problem behavior	K–8	6.74	6.63****	6.37	6.21	5.66	5.66****	6.03	5.92
	JH	6.88	6.42	6.71	6.06	5.75	5.30	5.68	5.65
3. Suspension or probation	K–8	1.11°	1.16	1.23††††°	1.21	1.04°	1.00°	1.30††††	1.29°
	JH	1.17	1.15	1.34	1.13	1.03	1.07	1.16	1.22
C. *Academic performance*									
4. GPA	K–8	2.38	2.44**	2.15****††††	1.85	2.70	2.79**	2.04****††††	2.20
	JH	2.41	2.16	2.16	1.73	2.71	2.65	2.59	1.98
5. Reading achievement	K–8	-.29	.11	—	.27****	-.11	.05	—	.28****
	JH	-.27	.16	—	-.05	-.05	.24	—	.14
6. Math achievement	K–8	-.32***	.09	—	.49****°	-.43***°	.18	—	.29****
	JH	-.21	.04	—	.08	-.25	.16	—	.24

244

D. Perception that adults value one highly							
7. Parents' evaluation	K–8	1.00††††	.82	1.00	.62	1.14††††	.71	.95
	JH	1.05	.85	.71	.56	.90	.89	1.07
8. Teachers' evaluation	K–8	2.84***	2.89	2.66**°	2.81	2.95***	2.82**	3.04
	JH	2.93	2.89	2.87	2.90	3.04	2.94	2.96
E. Perception of parent/peer relations							
9. How much parents like close friends	K–8	3.45	3.42	3.29***	3.25	3.51	3.24***	3.44
	JH	3.43	3.38	3.40	3.45	3.46	3.48	3.50
10. How much close friends like parents	K–8	3.35	3.32	3.15***	3.42	3.44	3.22***°	3.60	3.48°
	JH	3.42	3.40	3.40	3.41	3.54	3.36	3.52	3.41

[a] In this table K–8/SH is abbreviated to K–8; K–6/JH/SH to JH.

[b] Findings are reported for a specific variable for all years if there are significant effects in at least 1 year for either gender. For a total list of variables tested, see Table 1.1(5).

[c] Two-Way ANOVA (school type, gender as independent variables). School type main effect is significant: *$p \leq .001$; **$p \leq .01$; ***$p \leq .05$; ****$p \leq .10$. School type by gender interaction is significant: †$p \leq .001$; ††$p \leq .01$; †††$p \leq .05$; ††††$p \leq .10$. ° Homogeneity of variance problems within that gender.

245

Trend over Five Years

In later years, there are no significant differences between the cohorts in problem behavior, in terms of the cluster of variables (Table 8.1) or the specific problem behavior score itself (Table 8.5).[6] In Grade 9, there are no significant differences in victimization either.

In Grade 10 both cohorts are in high school. We have shown many advantages for the K–8/SH group in Grade 10—lower feelings of anonymity, higher self-esteem for girls, greater participation in activities, more leadership for girls. However, there appears to be one disadvantage. These students in their second year of a 4-year high school are more likely to report being victimized (Table 8.5). Whether the reason for this finding is idiosyncratic to our sample is, of course, unclear. It cannot be due to differences in presence of older children in the school. Both types of schools—the 3-year and the 4-year senior high school—have large numbers of older children. Furthermore at this age the older children are not necessarily stronger. Boesel *et al.* (1978) question whether older children are the prime victimizers even in junior high school when they are stronger. Whatever the case for junior high school, the greater victimization of tenth graders in a 4-year high school is unlikely to be the responsibility of the older students in the school. The 3-year and 4-year senior high schools differ not so much in the numbers of older students but in the numbers of younger ones. Boesel *et al.*'s findings (1978) suggest that younger adolescents are more likely than older adolescents to be both the victims and the victimizers. While their data do not point to younger students attacking older ones, it is possible that in this case the ninth graders in the 4-year high school are an important source of the problem. This ex post facto explanation remains conjecture, of course.

Adjusted change scores show no consistent school effects across genders for problem behavior between Grades 6 and 9 and no significant findings for Grades 6–10.[7]

Academic Performance

The negative impact of the movement into junior high school goes beyond decreased self-esteem for girls and participation in activities and beyond the greater victimization and negative attitudes toward school. In addition, in seventh grade, the junior high school students, both boys and girls, earn less high GPAs (Table 8.5, $p < .01$).[8] There are no significant differences in GPAs the year before (although the K–6 group shows a significant advantage in math achievement test scores). It is upon entry to junior high school that the academic performance cluster becomes significant (Table 8.1), that the disadvantage in GPA appears, and that the initial Grade 6 advantage in math achievement disappears (Table 8.5).

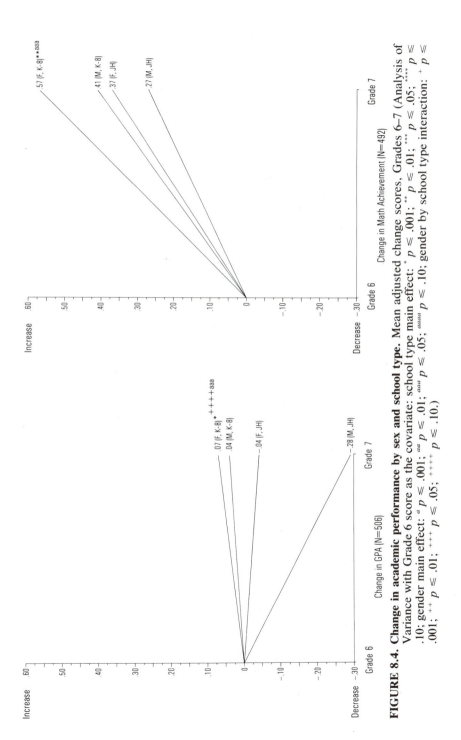

FIGURE 8.4. Change in academic performance by sex and school type. Mean adjusted change scores, Grades 6–7 (Analysis of Variance with Grade 6 score as the covariate: school type main effect: * $p \leq .001$; ** $p \leq .01$; *** $p \leq .05$; **** $p \leq .10$; gender main effect: [a] $p \leq .001$; [aa] $p \leq .01$; [aaa] $p \leq .05$; [aaaa] $p \leq .10$; gender by school type interaction: + $p \leq .001$; ++ $p \leq .01$; +++ $p \leq .05$; ++++ $p \leq .10$.)

247

Adjusted Change Score

The adjusted change score analysis shows significantly greater reductions in GPA from Grade 6 to 7 for the K–6/JH cohort and significantly lower increases in math achievement scores (Figure 8.4).[9] There are no significant school effects in regard to adjusted changes in reading achievement.

Trends over Five Years

Figure 8.5 graphs the 5-year change in GPA for males and females. The first observation worth noting is the general decrease in GPA as one goes up in grade level. Second, each school transition appears to be associated with a steeper decline. We have already noted the greater negative change upon entry to junior high school. It is difficult to be sure that the K–8 students experience a drop in GPA as they make the transition into senior high school between eighth and ninth grade, because we do not have an eighth grade data point. Nevertheless, the ninth grade GPA for the K–8 cohort is much lower than it was in Grade 7; whereas the junior high school cohort remains about the same between Grades 7 and 9. The net result is that for boys the two cohorts are earning about the same GPA in Grade 9; whereas for Grade 9 girls, the K–8 cohort is doing considerably worse.

In Grade 10, it is the K–6/JH/SH cohort, who have just entered senior high school, who are showing a steeper decline in GPA and therefore end up somewhat worse off (n.s.). The K–8 cohort of girls now in their second year of high school have started to recover as their GPA rises a bit.

The adjusted change scores from sixth to ninth grade also indicate that the GPA of the K–8 cohort suffers upon entry to senior high school. The K–8/SH students show a statistically significant ($p < .01$) greater decrease in GPA, compared to the K–6/JH/SH cohort. There were no significant adjusted mean changes in GPA between sixth and tenth grades.

These results may be due to the fact that a change of school is stressful academically whenever it occurs. Alternatively, it is likely that standards become more difficult as children move into new secondary schools, and that secondary school teachers are tougher in grading and therefore GPA declines. Achievement test scores are independent of changes in teacher standards. Thus if students in one cohort do less well than students in the other cohort in the year of transition, we could conjecture that the transition was academically stressful. We have already noted that in Grade 7 the cohort that is changing schools (the JH cohort) improves less in math achievement scores than the cohort remaining in the same school (K–8 students); and thus the advantage the JH cohort had the year before is eased in Grade 7.

Students were not given achievement tests in Grade 9. However, we

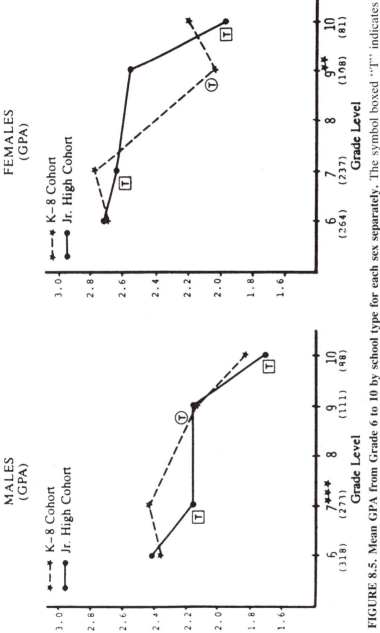

FIGURE 8.5. Mean GPA from Grade 6 to 10 by school type for each sex separately. The symbol boxed "T" indicates a year of transition for the junior high school cohort; encircled "T" indicates a year of transition for the K–8 Cohort. Levels of significance are based on one-way ANOVAs using school type as the factor and treating each grade level and sex separately. The degree of significance is indicated as follows: ** *p* less than .05; *** *p* less than .01.

do have Grade 10 scores (see Table 8.5). In Grade 10, the K–6/JH/SH cohort, which has just switched into senior high school, is scoring significantly lower in both math and reading achievement tests than is the K–8/SH group. This result occurs despite the fact that this same cohort (K–6/JH/SH) started out in Grade 6 scoring higher than K–8 students in achievement tests and despite the fact that there was no difference in Grade 7 in mean test scores. Adjusted change score analyses are consistent; they also show significantly less favorable change from Grade 6 to 10 in the K–6/JH/SH cohort. (For math achievement, $p < .08$; for reading $p < .05$.)

These results then are compatible with the hypotheses that change into a new and larger school is academically stressful and that children do not perform so well as they could at that time. However, without test scores for Grade 9, the year the K–8 cohort switches schools, our conclusions must remain tentative. It is, of course, possible that both processes occur— that changing schools is stressful academically and at the same time grading standards are becoming more difficult. In fact, the tougher grading standards may be a stressor in their own right, exacerbating the difficulty, at least temporarily.

Perception of Adults' Evaluation and Parent–Peer Relationship

In terms of relations with significant adults, Grade 6 and especially Grade 9 are the only years in which we see significant effects of school type on clusters of the variables or on the specific variables measured (Tables 8.1 and 8.5). In these years when the K–6/JH/SH children are "top dogs" in the school they are more likely than the K–8 youngsters (who are not "top dogs") to perceive the teachers as evaluating them highly (Table 8.5). In Grade 9 junior high school students also are more likely to report that their parents and peers like one another.

The adjusted change score analysis is consistent with these findings. There are no significant effects for Grade 6–7 or 6–10 change; but, according to the 6–9 change analyses, junior high school students show significant increases in perceived teacher evaluations and in peer and parents liking one another.[10]

Fall–Spring Differences

As discussed in Chapter 7, half the students in Grades 6 and 7 were randomly measured in the fall of the year, half in the spring. The first issue is whether there is any evidence that adjustment to junior high school is more difficult initially, that is, in the fall rather than in the spring. In Chapter 7 we showed no evidence that the self-image was more detrimentally affected in fall than spring. For variables discussed in this chapter that are relevant to positive versus negative adjustment (e.g., peer popularity, extracurricular participation, problem behavior, parent evaluation), there is also no indication that fall is significantly worse than spring in the JH versus the K–8 school.

Several of the variables discussed in this chapter involve socialization to adolescent behavior and attitudes. It was hypothesized that students might adopt attitudes and behaviors more typical of adolescence and less typical of childhood in a school with greater numbers of older children (e.g., in a junior high school in Grade 7). Little evidence to support this hypothesis has been found in general. The question here is whether the season of the year would affect these findings.

As one would predict, in general students interviewed in the spring are significantly more likely to report adolescent attitudes and behavior than students interviewed in the fall—in terms of caring about opposite-sex popularity; reporting that friends expect them to date and expect interest in the opposite sex; dating more; being allowed to take the bus alone and to go places after dark without parent permission; valuing independence; reporting that parents and teachers expect older behavior this year and that parents, teachers, and peers expect career planning this year. For these variables, a Repeated Measures Analysis of Variance showed significant season effects in this direction; in the remainder of variables there were no contradictory findings consistent across genders and school types.

While students interviewed in the spring were thus more likely to report adolescent rather than childish behaviors and expectations, there is no evidence from these analyses that the K–8 and junior high school differ consistently in this respect or in any way related to season.

Summary of Chapters 7 and 8

This analysis has investigated the impact of social structure on the mental health and adjustment of children as they move into and through adolescence. The structure of school transitions does appear to have an effect on individuals at this period in the life course. Certain school environmental contexts appear more favorable than others each year. In Grade 6, the K–6 school seems to benefit the child more than the K–8 school; the child holds more positive attitudes toward school, a more positive self-image in several specific regards (a high self-rating of looks, sports ability, schoolwork ability, and intelligence, and a high self-rating of popularity), and a higher teacher evaluation and better mathematics achievement scores.

The next year (Grade 7), the situation is reversed when the K–6 cohort makes the transition into a large junior high school and the K–8 children remain in elementary school. In Grade 7 the junior high school seems to be the less favorable context. School attitudes are less favorable than in the K–8 school; self-esteem is lower for girls, as is leadership in extracurricular activities; participation in extracurricular activities, GPAs, and math achievement scores are less high and/or change less favorably for both genders; and victimization levels are worse for boys. (School problem behavior, however, is worse in the K–8 school.) In Grade 9, the year the K–8 cohort makes the transition into senior high school and the K–6/JH cohort becomes the oldest in junior high school, findings are mixed. Along some variables the junior high school appears more beneficial, while along other variables it is the 4-year senior high school that seems more favorable.

In Grade 10, a year of school transition for the K–6/JH/SH cohort and stability for the K–8/SH cohort, the latter appears to benefit. Students in the second year of a 4-year high school report fewer feelings of anonymity, greater extracurricular participation, higher achievement test scores, and, for girls, higher self-esteem and leadership. (The only area of disadvantage involves victimization.)

Our initial hypotheses should be examined in light of these findings. First, in terms of short-term effects, we predicted that a small elementary school would be more beneficial for the adolescent than a large, impersonal environment, and that changing from an intimate elementary school to a large junior high school would have unfavorable consequences. The advantage of the K–8 school over the junior high school in Grade 7 and the negative changes shown by the K–6 cohort as they move into junior high school are compatible with these hypotheses.

Second, it was posited that being among the oldest children in the school ("top dog") would be beneficial and being among the youngest ("bottom dog") would be disadvantageous temporarily. There are many data that fit with this hypothesis. The advantages shown by the K–6/JH/SH youngsters in Grade 6 and the disadvantages shown by them in Grades 7 and 10 are in line with this hypothesis. On the other hand, the K–8/SH cohort does not show a clear disadvantage in Grade 9 when they are "bottom dogs" for the first time and when the junior high school cohort are "top dogs." If we had data in Grade 8 when the K–8 students were the oldest in the school, the pattern may have been clearer.

Alternative Hypotheses Concerning Long-Term Effects

In terms of long-term positive and negative effects, several alternate hypotheses were raised. The underlying issue is whether the negative changes shown upon entry to junior high school are simply temporary effects or whether they have longer ranging consequences. If the problem is only temporary, then it is of less concern, of course. Two of the alternate hypotheses posit temporary effects, but for different reasons. The first predicts that change into a larger, impersonal environment will be stressful temporarily whenever it occurs. Thus, the K–6/JH/SH cohort will have difficulty in Grades 7 and 10, but the K–8/SH cohort will have problems in Grade 9. The second hypothesis—stress inoculation hypothesis—goes further. It predicts that the experience of an early change (Grade 7) will, in fact, help the child to cope with the later transition (Grade 10). Thus whatever advantage occurs early for the group that experiences no change will be counteracted by later difficulties. The K–8 cohort when switching for the first time in Grade 9 with no prior experience of change or of exposure to a large school context will have particular problems. At time of entry to senior high school, they will react with more distress than will the K–6/JH/SH cohort.

The final alternate hypothesis (the developmental readiness hypothesis) posits longer ranging negative consequences of the early transition. Instead of the early change making the next transition easier, it will render it more difficult. If children switch environmental contexts before they are developmentally ready to do so, they will show negative effects from which they will be less likely to recover. (See Table IV.1 for an outline of these specific predictions.)

The assessment of these alternative hypotheses raises some problems. First, we are dealing with many dependent variables, and they do not all operate in the same way. Consequently, it is necessary to see whether there are broad patterns across variables and also to focus on key variables of interest to ourselves and policy makers—self-esteem, GPA, extracurricular participation, school problem behavior, felt anonymity. Another difficulty stems from our missing Grade 8 data, which prevents us from comparing Grade 8 to Grade 9 change in the two school cohorts; the K–8 cohort is changing into senior high school in Grade 9; the JH/SH cohort is not. A final problem arises because more than one hypothesis can explain some broad directions of findings—for example negative effects for the K–6/JH/SH cohort in Grade 10 can be explained by the "top–bottom dog" hypothesis, by the change is stressful hypothesis, and by the developmental readiness hypothesis. Our conclusions have to be impressionistic rather than precise. Are the findings for key variables and the broad sweep of findings compatible or incompatible with these various hypotheses?

First, what about the stress inoculation hypothesis that posits that one copes better with a second change if one has experienced a first? According to this hypothesis, the K–6/JH/SH cohort will find their transition to senior high school less difficult because it is their second transition. In fact there is no evidence for this hypothesis. The K–8 cohort, when going through their first change in Grade 9, is not coping less well across the board than is the junior high school cohort in Grade 9. In Grade 10, the K–6/JH/SH cohort, who now are experiencing their second transition, are not doing as well or better than the K–8 cohort of tenth graders; they are doing worse. We can also compare absolute mean scores of the two cohorts across grades, looking at each the year that they switch into senior high school, that is, the K–6/JH/SH cohort in Grade 10 (when they make their second change) can be compared to the K–8 cohort in Grade 9 (when they make their first change). The experience hypothesis predicts that the

K–6/JH/SH group would fare better than the K–8/SH group during the year of transition into senior high school. No such pattern of findings is evident. Whatever slight differences exist sometimes favor one group, sometimes the other.[11]

In fact, for key variables the alternate hypotheses appear to fit better. Several findings are in line with the alternate hypotheses that change into a new, larger impersonal context will be stressful whenever it occurs. Feelings of anonymity, of not knowing anyone, and not being known increase temporarily whenever a cohort makes one of these school transitions. In addition, participation and leadership in extracurricular activities go down whenever a transition occurs (although in Grade 9 only for boys) as do GPAs and achievement test scores.

In sharp contrast to the stress inoculation hypothesis is the developmental readiness hypothesis. This hypothesis predicts that if the first major environmental change occurs too early before the children have the maturity to cope with it, the effects may be long lasting. Thus, according to this hypothesis, the K–6/JH/SH cohort will score more negatively in later years than the K–8 cohort; they will not recover. They certainly will not react more favorably during the next transition, as the stress inoculation hypothesis predicts. For girls along two key variables, the developmental readiness hypothesis appears particularly relevant. Girls suffer a loss in self-esteem in Grade 7 and a reduction in extracurricular participation and leadership from which, on average, they do not recover. In Grade 9 they still report lower levels of self-esteem and participation than their K–8/SH counterparts. When the second change occurs in Grade 10, instead of showing benefits from the early experience they react as if hit by a "double whammy." The average self-esteem and leadership of K–6/JH/SH girls drops considerably below that of their K–8/SH counterparts in Grade 10, and the participation of both genders also turns out to be significantly lower. (These scores in the Grade 10 transition year are also less favorable than those of the K–8/SH cohort in Grade 9 when the latter changed schools.)

The idea that it is advantageous to protect children from too early change is given some, though not overwhelming, support by these data. Chapters 9 and 10 will deal in more detail with the question of the number of children suffering from the early transition into junior high school and with the issue of recovery.

A final hypothesis guiding the analysis in Chapters 7–8 was the adolescent socialization hypothesis. It was predicted that in schools with more older adolescent students, children would assume adolescent values earlier, be treated as older, and be subjected to more adultlike expectations. Findings were mixed and give no clear, consistent support for this hypothesis.

In summary, organizational context (type of school) and timing of organizational transition have social–psychological effects upon the children.

Hypotheses compatible with these effects have been inspected and tentative conclusions drawn. The importance of these findings will be explored in the following chapter.

Before turning in greater detail to further exploration of these findings, an aside related to sample drop-out is in order.

An Aside on Children Who Change School Unexpectedly

As noted in Chapter 2, not all children remain in the expected school types over the 5 years of the study. Some youngsters leave the public school system or the community; others simply switch out of the expected school sequence.[12] While there is little of this movement in Grade 7, there is more by Grades 9 and 10. On the one hand, these children who move raise potential biasing problems for the analysis; on the other hand, they could be interesting in their own right.

From the point of view of potential bias, as indicated earlier, we have taken several precautions. To review briefly, we have reanalyzed the data just for those youngsters who remain in the sample over the course of the study to better ensure that our conclusions are not due to differential drop-out. No major differences in conclusions emerge from this reanalysis, and minor differences are reported. Also, within social class categories, we find that key results have been replicated. That is, middle- and working-class youngsters react similarly to school differences in regard to felt anonymity, self-esteem, extracurricular participation, leadership, and GPA.[13] Of course, despite these efforts, we cannot be certain that the children who left the sample would have reacted the same way to school transition as did students who remained in the sample. Our concern must be on the effect of school type on the students who did attend the schools of interest.

Above and beyond the methodological issues, there are interesting substantive questions in regard to the students who leave the expected schools. Could the pattern of leaving the expected school sequence be a response to the child's adjustment level? Children clearly change schools due to factors not directly related to their own performance—the break-up of the parental marriage, change in parental jobs, social-class related aspirations and difficulties. Furthermore, children who show severe delinquency may be removed from a regular public school, and children with particularly low GPAs will fail to be promoted. But, in addition, is there evidence that parents try to cope with children's difficulties in adjustment by removing them from the type of school they are attending?

In fact there is some evidence that is consistent with such a process, although (as we shall discuss) other explanations are also possible. This evidence involves a comparison of the students in the expected schools and the students who switched out of the expected school sequence but remained in the proper grade in Milwaukee. The students who by Grade 9 were switched out of the expected sequence were the ones who had originally scored lower in GPA in Grade 6 ($p = .001$). The students who had switched by Grade 10 were the ones who had initially in Grade 6 demonstrated lower self-esteem ($p = .07$). These patterns were evident in both the K–6 and K–8 schools.[14] (We see no such pattern for the few children who switched as early as Grade 7, nor does school problem behavior in Grade 6 seem to lead children to be switched to other schools in Milwaukee, although it does lead them to drop out of the school system and sample all together.) It is possible that factors in the parents' lives (e.g., an impending divorce) lead independently to the school move and to the child's difficulties (in GPA and self-esteem), with the child's problems having little to do with the reason for the change. However, it is also possible that parents are coping directly with their child's difficulty by alteration of his or her environmental context.

Thus, without forgetting that youngsters and families can cope with stressors by exiting from the school environment, we turn to a further analysis in Chapter 9 of school type upon those students who remained in the two cohorts.

Footnotes

[1]By and large, adjusted change score analyses also show significantly greater increase in valuation of peer relations in the junior high school cohort for these variables from Grade 6 to 7 (although the "value popularity versus competence and independence" changes significantly in the opposite direction). The 6–9 change scores are mostly nonsignificant, and the 6–10 findings form no clear pattern relevant to the adolescent socialization hypothesis.

[2]In the "longitudinal sample" (the sample of students who remain in the study for 4 years), the change from Grade 6 to 7 is even more dramatic. For in Grade 6 in the longitudinal sample the K–6 students (both boys and girls) participate in significantly more activities than their K–8 peers ($p < .05$). In Grade 7, this situation is reversed, and, as in the larger sample, the junior high school students participate significantly less than the K–8 students ($p < .05$).

[3]Medians have been used here instead of means since there is one K–8 outlier—a school with one activity for its 461 children.

[4]The adjusted change analysis from 6 to 9 shows no consistent school effects across gender, and the 6 to 10 results show no significant results in regard to leadership.

[5]Boesel et al. (1978) show somewhat less victimization of seventh graders in schools attended by adolescents of senior high school age (Grades 7–12 schools) but little difference between middle schools and junior high schools. They hypothesize that the older students are a moderating influence, and that segregating early adolescent children in their own schools may lead to more problems. Thus, it may be that in terms of victimization it is better for the early adolescent to be in a protected elementary school or to be in the same environment as older teenagers, rather than to be age-segregated with 11–14 year olds.

[6]The findings for suspension are inconsistent across the genders.

[7]Victimization was not measured in Grade 6; thus change scores cannot be calculated.

[8]As in all cases in this analysis (unless otherwise noted), such differences are not a function of those students who drop out of the study over time. Basic con-

clusions do not change if we consider just those students who were present at all the time periods that are being compared. In this case, the findings dealing with Grades 6 and 7 are virtually identical if we look just at the students present both these years (see footnote 14 for more detail).

[9]Since different achievement tests were used at different grade-levels, we cannot compare absolute scores over the years. Instead, we compare percentile scores based on the total population.

[10]There is one finding where the direction of difference changes between the maximum sample reported here and the 4-year "longitudinal" sample; this finding involves Grade 6–7 adjusted change. In the sample of children with data for all 4 years rather than the Grades 6–7 sample reported in the foregoing text, Grade 7 parents are seen as increasing their liking of friends significantly more in junior high school than in the K–8 school.

[11]The K–8 cohort does significantly better in terms of liking this grade, sports' self-rating, school extracurricular participation, boys' perception of parental rating. The K–6/JH/SH cohort does significantly better in terms of perception of teachers' rating and on two variables measuring parent–peer relationship (see Tables 7.2, 7.5, 8.2, and 8.5).

[12]The differences in sample size between these analyses in Chapters 7 and 8 and those in Chapter 3 is primarily due to the children who switch out of the expected school sequence but remain in our sample at another Milwaukee school. Also, this analysis does not include the white children attending heavily black schools, although such children are in the puberty and gender-role analyses (see Chapter 2 for further discussion).

[13]There were not enough cases of children from broken families to duplicate these analyses for parental marital status in Grades 9 and 10. In Grade 7, where there is only a small degree of drop-out, there were no significant interactions with marital status for these key variables. Also note that the adjusted change score analyses in Chapters 7 and 8 control for the Grade 6 score on the relevant outcome variables.

[14]For self-esteem there was no significant difference between the school types in this respect. That is, there were no significant school type by school-switcher interactions. For GPA, the drop-out of low performing students by Grade 9–10 occurred in both school types but was more likely to occur in the K–8 school. However, as indicated previously, if we just look at the students who remained in the sample for 5 years, basic conclusions reported in the text about students in the two school types persist. Furthermore, the change analyses are based only on students who were present at both the time periods being considered, and therefore could not be distorted by differential drop-out in the two school types. In addition, the Grade 6–7 findings are not affected by this differential drop-out, since in Grade 7 there was very little drop-out. In fact, if we exclude from the Grade 6–7 analysis those few students who will drop out in Grade 7, the mean GPAs in the two school types remain identical for boys and almost identical for girls.

9

INDIVIDUAL CHANGE AND RECOVERY: SELF-ESTEEM*

The issue of the long-run effects of stress and change requires further examination. On three key dimensions it appears that students, especially girls, react unfavorably during early adolescence to the sudden change into an impersonal school environment. Their self-esteem, academic achievement, and participation in organized extracurricular activities decline with the move into seventh grade. Three years later in tenth grade the girls in this cohort (the K–6/junior high school/senior high school cohort) are still likely to have lower self-esteem, lower GPAs, and lower extracurricular participation than girls who did not change schools in Grade 7. In terms of self-esteem and extracurricular participation, these "junior high school"[1] girls, once hurt in seventh grade, never recover enough to show average scores equal to those of the K–8 girls, even in ninth grade when they are "top dogs" in junior high school and the K–8 girls themselves have just entered into an impersonal high school environment as freshmen.

Both the trend analysis and the mean adjusted change-score analysis support these conclusions. Also, GPA appears more continually responsive to change in school environments, with students declining in whatever years they change schools. That is, the K–8 cohort shows the greatest losses in GPA the year they change schools (ninth grade); it is not simply the junior high school cohort that reacts negatively to change.

These analyses suggest that early adolescent experiences affect some key dimensions of psychological adjustment in relatively long-lasting ways. The girls, in particular, do not appear to recover from the environmental transition in seventh grade; and they appear more vulnerable to the new transition in tenth grade. However, in both the trend analysis and the adjusted change analysis, we have been examining means. Since changes in mean scores can be produced by several alternate processes, we cannot really be certain that the junior high school girls who show unfavorable self-esteem in Grade 9 and Grade 10 are the same ones who reacted unfavorably in Grade 7. We wish to know if the negative experience of Grade

*By Roberta G. Simmons, Steven L. Carlton-Ford, and Dale A. Blyth.

7 is a transitory one; that is, whether it is or is not one from which young-sters recover. Thus, we need to know whether individuals who showed a drop in self-esteem in Grade 7 are less likely to recover if they were in junior high school rather than in a K–8 school that year.

In addition, we need to have some idea what proportion of junior high school girls experience these negative effects. Is it simply a very few girls who show extreme negative effects, while the bulk of junior high school girls cope well with the environmental transition? Or is it that there are a lot of girls affected but each only slightly? If either of these two pos-sibilities is accurate, one might worry less about the junior high school environment than if there is a general and substantial negative shift among the junior high school girls.

In order to explore these questions—the pervasiveness of negative change among junior high school girls and the extent of recovery after seventh grade—we need indicators more specific than mean group change scores. We need to be able to characterize each individual in terms of change, both to see how many individuals changed in a relatively negative direction and to see if those girls who changed negatively in Grade 7 re-covered in later years. Once again, a simple raw change score might be misleading because of the effects of measurement error.[2] For this reason, individual adjusted change scores were created utilizing essentially the same analysis of covariance logic that created the group adjusted change scores. These scores control for the individual's sixth grade initial scores. In essence, they tell us how much the children would have changed relative to one another if they all started out with the same scores in Grade 6. That is, a certain amount of the raw change between Grade 6 and Grade 7 can be predicted simply because a given individual started out higher or lower than the mean in the total sample. The logic in effect subtracts that amount of "automatic" or predicted change from the actual change, leaving the change not due to a child's initial sixth grade score. Individuals then can be compared to one another to see how they would have fared had they all scored the same in Grade 6.

Thus, in Chapters 9 and 10 individual adjusted change analyses will be presented. For each set of time-periods the largest samples possible will be used. (And, where appropriate, corrections for unreliability and cor-related error will be made.) However, in order to be sure of our findings, the same analyses have also been performed in two additional ways: (1) with raw, unadjusted, and uncorrected change scores and (2) with adjusted change scores for the "longitudinal" sample of cases.[3] The longitudinal sample consists of the cases for whom we have data all 4 years.[4] In fact, in most instances the conclusions are the same no matter which way the analyses are done; basic differences shall be reported.

Our emphasis is on change relative to the child's starting point in Grade 6. After 1 year's time, what is the net effect of school type transitions (the Grade 6–7 change score)? Furthermore, what is the net effect after 3 years (the Grades 6–9 change score) and after 4 years (the Grades 6–10 change score)? While other approaches are possible, our focus on recovery to initial levels of well-being and performance encouraged this approach[5] (see below).

In Chapters 9 and 10 we focus only on a few key variables. Since we are interested in recovery, we look only at variables that can be described as positive or negative, favorable or unfavorable. Also we will look only at variables that emerged from previous chapters as important in distinguishing the effects of the different school environments and for which we have measures in Grades 6, 7, 9, and 10.[6] Self-esteem, GPA, extracurricular participation, leadership, and certain attitudes toward the school itself (especially felt anonymity) are variables of this type that seem most affected by school environment.

For this analysis, we decided to concentrate on those variables that can be thought of as characteristics of the individual—self-esteem, GPA, participation in activities, and leadership—rather than on attitudes toward school. Leadership was ultimately eliminated as a variable in the analysis, since only a minority of children were leaders in any year between Grades 6 and 10. The present chapter will focus on self-esteem; Chapter 10 will deal with GPA and extracurricular participation. Since junior high school girls are the most vulnerable group in terms of self-esteem, this chapter will emphasize these girls; since the GPA and extracurricular changes affect both boys and girls in junior high school, Chapter 10 will have a more equal emphasis on both genders.

Self-Esteem Change Scores: Corrections for Reliability and Correlated Error

Since self-esteem is measured by six independent multiple-choice questions, the individual, adjusted change scores for self-esteem can be corrected for unreliability and correlated error based on a LISREL analysis (Jöreskog and Sörbom, 1981, 1983). For the analysis in this chapter, such a correction was made. First, measurement models were constructed in order to make such corrections and to thus estimate the "corrected" self-esteem scores each year. Importantly, the same LISREL measurement model was a good fit and suitable for self-esteem for all four grades (Grades 6, 7, 9, and 10) and for both the junior high school sample and the total sample.[7] After the measurement models were constructed with LISREL, estimated "corrected" self-esteem scores were secured for each individual in each of the 4 years.

Second, individual difference scores were computed between the Grade 6 "corrected" self-esteem score and each of the "corrected" self-esteem scores in later grades.[8] Finally, these difference scores were adjusted for the individual's "corrected" Grade 6 self-esteem score, utilizing the co-variance logic described previously. The resultant individual, adjusted scores represent an estimate of the relative degree this individual would have changed in self-esteem had all children started out in Grade 6 with the same score.[9] (For more detail, see Carlton-Ford et al., 1983.)

Caveats

Two caveats are in order here before presentation of results. First, we are asking questions about change in these and later chapters that are not frequently asked and for which the methods have not been worked out. As Rogosa, Brandt, and Zimowski (1982) say, "many crucial aspects of the measurement of change have been overlooked . . . in previous in-vestigations" (p. 726). We are concerned here (1) with the extent of neg-ative change among individuals in different subgroups had they all started out the same and (2) with the extent of recovery to initial levels of well-being from negative change. Our attempt to deal with these issues has to be regarded as a first step, and one that might encourage others to wrestle with these problems as well.

A second caveat involves the size of the sample in comparable school types in Grades 9 and 10. Because the sample for whom we have data all 4 years begins to become small, particularly in the K–8 cohort, some of the findings involving the latter years have to be considered suggestive rather than conclusive.

Self-Esteem: Pervasiveness of Negative Change

To recapitulate, the junior high school girls appeared to be a vulnerable group whatever one's vantage point. This group was the most likely to show an average drop in self-esteem after sixth grade, whether one com-pared the sixth grade score to that in seventh, ninth, or tenth grade. The first question to be addressed is whether many or only a few girls are responsible for this negative group change.

It is, of course, possible that a difference in a mean score will be pro-duced solely by a few extreme cases—in this case a few girls could be showing large drops in self-esteem. The median, however, would not be so affected by a few extreme scores. Table 9.1A, B, and C shows the medians and ranges of the individual adjusted change scores for girls and boys in the two different school types. Each year, the medians for the junior high school girls are lower than the median for the K–8 girls (as were the means); that is, the cohort of junior high school girls show less positive change in self-esteem. And for the changes based on Grade 6–7 the junior high school girls show a negative median, whereas the K–8 girls show a positive median. For example, from Grade 6 to 7 the median in-dividual adjusted change score in self-esteem is $-.350$ for the junior high

TABLE 9.1. Individual Adjusted Change Scores in Self-Esteem[a]

| | A. Grade 6–7 Score | | | | B. Grade 6–9 Score | | | | C. Grade 6–10 Score | | | |
| | Girls | | Boys | | Girls | | Boys | | Girls | | Boys | |
	K–8	JH	K–8	JH	K–8	JH	K–8	JH	K–8	JH	K–8	JH
Mean	.110	−.321	.167	.143	.861	.522	.979	1.219	.970	.306	1.085	.925
Median	.400	−.350	.511	.400	1.748	1.196	1.719	1.719	1.374	.383	1.324	1.315
Range	5.480	6.331	6.331	6.272	5.701	6.129	4.817	6.078	4.184	4.278	4.376	4.496
Minimum	−2.995	−3.386	−3.386	−3.327	−2.692	−3.013	−1.764	−3.025	−1.769	−2.002	−1.853	−1.973
Maximum	2.485	2.945	2.945	2.945	3.009	3.116	3.053	3.053	2.415	2.276	2.523	2.523
SD	1.290	1.309	1.339	1.134	1.781	1.789	1.451	1.432	1.205	1.242	.964	.941
(N)	(93)	(146)	(111)	(167)	(33)	(91)	(34)	(87)	(25)	(54)	(28)	(59)

[a]Unrecoded scores, reliability corrected.

263

TABLE 9.2. Change in Self-Esteem, Grade 6–7, Percentage Scoring in Four Categories of Adjusted Individual Change Scores[a]

	Girls		Boys	
	K–8 (93)	JH (146)	K–8 (111)	JH (167)
Very negative change	24% ⎫ 40	26% ⎫ 56	18% ⎫ 39	18% ⎫ 35
Moderately negative change	16 ⎭	30 ⎭	21 ⎭	17 ⎭
Moderately positive change	25 ⎫ 60	25 ⎫ 44	24 ⎫ 61	37 ⎫ 65
Very positive change	35 ⎭	19 ⎭	37 ⎭	28 ⎭
	100%	100%	100%	100%

[a]Reliability corrected scores, Chi Square: $p = .003$ (four category change); $p = .002$ (two category change).

school girls, while the median for K–8 girls is .400 (Table 9.1A).[10] For each year, the medians for boys are always positive and higher than medians for the junior high school cohort of girls.[11] Thus, it would appear that the difference between the junior high school and K–8 girls is not due solely to a few girls with extremely negative changes.

Table 9.1 does show a greater range in scores for the junior high school girls than for the K–8 girls in all 3 time periods. For two time periods the maximum score (the greatest gain in self-esteem in that subgroup) is higher for the junior high school girls than for the K–8 girls (Tables 9.1A and

TABLE 9.3. Change in Self-Esteem, Grade 6–9, Percentage Scoring in Four Categories of Adjusted Individual Change Scores[a]

	Girls		Boys	
	K–8 (33)	JH (91)	K–8 (34)	JH (87)
Very negative change	15% ⎫ 30	15% ⎫ 36	3% ⎫ 24	7% ⎫ 14
Moderately negative change	15 ⎭	21 ⎭	21 ⎭	7 ⎭
Moderately positive change	24 ⎫ 70	38 ⎫ 64	29 ⎫ 76	45 ⎫ 86
Very positive change	46 ⎭	26 ⎭	47 ⎭	41 ⎭
	100%	100%	100%	100%

[a]Reliability corrected scores, Chi Square: $p = .016$ (four category change); $p = .007$ (two category change).

TABLE 9.4. Change in Self-Esteem, Grade 6–10, Percentage Scoring in Four
Categories of Adjusted Individual Change Scores[a]

	Girls		Boys	
	K–8 (25)	JH (54)	K–8 (28)	JH (59)
Very negative change	4% ⎤ 28	22% ⎤ 35	4% ⎤ 11	7% ⎤ 14
Moderately negative change	24 ⎦	13 ⎦	7 ⎦	7 ⎦
Moderately positive change	20 ⎤ 72	41 ⎤ 65	39 ⎤ 89	44 ⎤ 86
Very positive change	52 ⎦	24 ⎦	50 ⎦	42 ⎦
	100%	100%	100%	100%

[a]Reliability corrected scores, Chi Square: $p = .007$ (four category change);
$p = .015$ (two category change).

9.1B); in all three time periods the minimum score (the greatest loss in
self-esteem in that subgroup) is lower for the junior high school girls. That
is, among girls no one in the K–8 group shows as great a reduction in
self-esteem as does the lowest junior high school girl.[12]

In Tables 9.2, 9.3, and 9.4 we have divided the adjusted change scores
into four categories. For the Grade 6–7 change scores we created the four
categories in the following fashion: (1) We first divided the scores into
positive and negative changes (there were no students with exactly zero
adjusted change). (2) Each subgroup (positive and negative) was divided
into roughly equal halves (''very'' versus ''moderately'' positive or negative). For Grades 6 to 9 and 6 to 10, we used the same process. Table
9.2 presents the Grade 6–7 change; Table 9.3, the Grade 6–9 change; and
Table 9.4 the Grade 6–10 change.[13]

These tables also show that the differences between K–8 and junior
high school girls are not the result of a few more junior high school girls
at the extreme negative end; rather, much of the distribution is affected
in each table. In no case does the entire difference appear to be produced
by a few junior high school girls at the negative extreme (nor by a few
K–8 girls at the positive extreme).[14] And, in general, fully 56% of junior
high school girls show a negative adjusted change score from Grade 6 to
7 (''very negative'' or ''moderately negative'') compared to only 40% of
the K–8 girls and 35–39% of the boys (see Table 9.2).[15]

This question interests us because of our desire to evaluate the implications of the mean reduction in self-esteem among junior high school
girls. If only a very small proportion of girls were producing the difference,
then the issue would be less worrisome for policymakers and less interesting for theoreticians.

Our overall theoretical aim is to investigate the effects of environmental structures and changes in environmental context on mental health. The more pervasive the effect, the more interesting the phenomenon to be explained.

How Substantial is the Change?

In this light, we want to know if the entire difference is produced by slight change or by more substantial change. We already know that more than a few girls are involved, but are these girls changing only slightly or a "substantial" amount? Since scores on the self-esteem scale have only a relative rather than absolute meaning, it is difficult to answer the question. However, utilizing our four-category breakdown we can define "very" negative or positive change as more substantial than "moderate" losses and gains. Thus, we can get some initial handle on the issue by looking again at the four-category breakdowns in Tables 9.2, 9.3, and 9.4. If the change is only a slight one, then the entire difference between the two groups of girls should show up in the middle categories; the extremes should be quite similar. However, each year at least one of the extremes reveals differences, to the disadvantage of the junior high school cohort.

Thus, the problem with junior high school girls appears neither to be solely a case of a very small proportion changing a lot nor a case of a large proportion changing only slightly. Of course, the fact that neither self-esteem scores nor self-esteem change scores have an absolute meaning prevents us from characterizing the severity of the problem as precisely as we or policymakers would wish.[16]

Figure 9.1 graphs the entire distribution of Grade 6–7 change scores for the K–8 and junior high school cohort of girls. Most obvious in the graphing is the high degree of overlap. While the junior high school curve has a higher proportion of its cases at the negative end than does the K–8 cohort, there is a great deal of overlap; the schools do not produce totally discrepant or disjunctive experiences. It is not a case of negative reactions occurring almost only in junior high school or positive reactions occurring almost only in the K–8 environment. In both environments substantial numbers of girls experience either losses or gains in self-esteem. It is just that losses are more likely to occur in the junior high school, and gains in the K–8 school.

And, in summary, insofar as we can measure, these differences appear substantial enough, both in pervasiveness and size, to be of concern.

Recovery

Since the loss in self-esteem among junior high school girls appears to be substantial enough for concern, the next issue involves recovery. Are the girls who show loss in self-esteem from Grade 6 to 7 the same ones

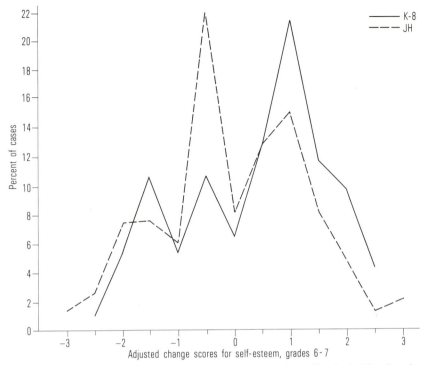

FIGURE 9.1. Individual adjusted change in self-esteem from Grade 6–7 for females by school type. (Reliability corrected.)

who show loss from the vantage points of ninth and tenth grades? Or is the loss a transitory one from which they recover (at least to initial Grade 6 levels)? If the loss is transitory and the girls recover completely we should not be able to predict the Grade 6–9 or Grade 6–10 change scores from the Grade 6–7 change scores. That is, if the girls bounce back completely, then change between Grades 6 and 9 will be independent of what happened between Grades 6 and 7; by Grade 9 the Grade 6–7 problem will be invisible and without trace. However, if the girls do not recover to initial levels, the girls who end up showing a loss in self-esteem from Grade 6 to 9 should be the same ones who initially lost self-esteem between Grades 6 and 7.

Is There a Lack of Recovery?

Results from analyses of variance are presented in Table 9.5. We attempted to predict the Grades 6–9 change score from the Grade 6–7 change score. Presented in the top half of the table are the Grade 6–9 and Grade 6–10 means of individual adjusted change scores, representing the overall

TABLE 9.5. Relationship of Grade 6–7 Adjusted Change in Self-Esteem to
Later Adjusted Individual Change[a]

	Change Grade 6–7 (range)			
	Very negative (−3.386 to −.942)	Moderately negative (−.942 to 0)	Moderately positive (0 to .678)	Very positive (.678 to 2.945)
Grade 6–9 adjusted means (N = 244)	−.21	.56	1.31	1.42
Grade 6–10 adjusted means (N = 166)	.41	.55	.72	1.19

One-Way analysis of variance and R^2
  Independent variable: change Grade 6–7
  Dependent variable:
  Grade 6–9 individual adjusted change
    $p = .0001$
    $R^2 = .147$[b]
  Grade 6–10 individual adjusted change
    $p = .010$
    $R^2 = .067$[b]

[a]Reliability corrected scores.
[b]Based on unrecoded scores in each case.

relationship between change in Grades 6–7 and change in later years.
Clearly, students who changed very negatively from Grade 6 to 7 are also
more likely than others to be classified as changing negatively from Grade
6 to 9 (Table 9.5). Students who changed very negatively from Grade 6
to 7 have a mean change score of −.21 from Grade 6 to 9; those who
changed moderately negatively from Grade 6 to 7 have a mean change of
.56 from Grade 6 to 9; however, those who changed moderately or very
positively from Grade 6 to 7 have mean change scores of 1.31 and 1.42,
respectively, from Grade 6 to 9. The more positively one changed from
Grade 6 to 7, the more positively one also changed from Grade 6 to 9
($p = .0001$). The second column in Table 9.5 again leads to the same
general conclusion—students who changed more positively from Grade
6 to 7 also changed more positively from Grade 6 to 10 ($p = .01$).[17]

Thus, in summary, these findings indicate that students who show negative changes in self-esteem between Grades 6 and 7 are still likely to be
the same ones who at a later vantage point (Grade 9 or Grade 10) indicate
loss in self-esteem from childhood (Grade 6). Clearly there is not complete
recovery from the Grade 6–7 loss nor complete erasure of Grade 6–7 gains.
Further analysis indicates that by and large in all subgroups the Grade 6–
7 change has left its mark: For both sexes and for both school types,

children who indicated negative change in Grade 6–7 are less likely than those who showed positive change to demonstrate improvements from Grade 6 to 9 or Grade 6 to 10. Thus, the identification of children showing losses in self-esteem in Grade 7 could have policy implications. If extra help were provided for such children early, perhaps a better chance for recovery would result.

How Substantial Is the Lack of Recovery?

We have demonstrated up to now that the differential self-esteem loss from Grade 6 to 7 among junior high school girls is not merely a transitory one. There is significant lack of recovery from the loss, with the same students likely to be in difficulty in Grades 9 and 10. We still do not know how substantial the continued lack of recovery is, however. How high is the relationship between loss in seventh grade and loss seen at a later vantage point? Of what proportion of youngsters are we talking?

One way of examining the issue is to present the proportion of young-sters who do and do not recover from a negative change in Grade 6–7. There are not enough cases to present a cross-tabulation involving four categories of Grade 6–9 change by four categories of Grade 6–7 change by sex and school-type. However, we can present the dichotomized data for the junior high school girls versus every one else combined. As Table 9.6 (Column 1) shows, 57% of the junior high school girls who showed negative Grade 6–7 change also show negative Grade 6–9 change (very or moderately negative change). But among junior high school girls who started out with positive Grade 6–7 change, nowhere near so high a pro-portion end up with negative change scores in Grade 9: Only 19% of them demonstrate negative change from Grade 6 to 9 (Table 9.6, Column 1 versus 3). And among "other students" who begin with Grade 6–7 negative

TABLE 9.6. Grade 6–9 Individual Adjusted Change Scores in Self-Esteem According to Level of Grade 6–7 Individual Adjusted Change[a]

	Negative change Grade 6–7		Positive change Grade 6–7	
	1 JH girls (42)	2 All other students[b] (58)	3 JH girls (48)	4 All other students (96)
Change Grade 6–9				
Negative	57%	31%	19%	13%
Positive	43	69	81	87
	100%	100%	100%	100%

[a]Reliability corrected scores.
[b]Junior high school boys, K–8 girls and boys.

changes, they again are less likely than the junior high school girls to end up with negative change scores in Grade 9. Only 31% of these "other students" persist in showing negative change in Grades 6–9 (Column 2) versus the 57% of junior high school girls (Column 1).

In tenth grade we have a similar phenomenon (Table 9.7). Of junior high girls who showed negative change in Grade 6–7, 39% also show negative (very or moderate) change from Grade 6 to 10 (Column 1) compared to 31% of the junior high school girls who originally demonstrated positive change from Grade 6 to 7 (Column 3) and compared to only 22% of "other students" who started out with negative change Grade 6–7 (Column 2). Thus, 39–57% of junior high school girls who show negative change from Grade 6 to 7 are still demonstrating negative change between sixth grade and later years; but among other students who start out with negative losses between Grades 6 and 7, a much smaller proportion persist with negative change in later years. And less than one-third of junior high school girls who originally gained in self-esteem between Grades 6 and 7 end up in Grade 9 or 10 showing a loss since Grade 6.[18]

Thus, a substantial proportion of youngsters, and certainly a substantial proportion of junior high school girls, who indicate self-esteem losses from Grade 6 to 7 still appear to be at risk 2 and 3 years later in terms of their self-esteem. They are still likely to be showing losses in self-esteem from childhood (Grade 6), despite the fact that the overall sample demonstrates a gain in self-esteem between sixth grade and ninth grade and between sixth grade and tenth grade (see Table 9.1B and C). However, substantial does not mean total; there are sizable proportions of junior high school girls and of other students who recover from very negative changes in Grade 6–7 self-esteem—who show positive adjusted gain scores between Grades 6 and 9 and Grades 6 and 10.

TABLE 9.7. Grade 6–10 Individual Adjusted Change Scores in Self-Esteem According to Level of Grade 6–7 Individual Adjusted Change[a]

| | Negative change Grade 6–7 | | Positive change Grade 6–7 | |
	1 JH girls (28)	2 All other students[b] (41)	3 JH girls (26)	4 All other students (71)
Change Grade 6–10				
Negative	39%	22%	31%	13%
Positive	61	78	69	87
	100%	100%	100%	100%

[a]Reliability corrected scores.
[b]Junior high school boys, K–8 girls and boys.

Summary

In prior chapters we indicated that the movement of early adolescent girls from sixth grade into junior high school was detrimental to their self-esteem. On the average, junior high school girls showed lower self-esteem than K–8 girls and than all boys in Grade 7; and the average self-esteem of the junior high school female cohort in Grades 9 and 10 remained lower than that of all other children. However, merely comparing subgroup averages and average change-scores did not answer several important questions; namely, were few or many girls affected, was the effect minor or substantial, and did girls recover in later years? In order to answer these questions the change analysis had to be brought down from the group average to an individual level; that is, we needed to characterize each individual's change between Grade 6 and subsequent years. Individual adjusted change scores for self-esteem were therefore created; these scores controlled for differences among individuals in initial self-esteem (Grade 6).

According to this analysis, the environmental discontinuity experienced by girls moving into junior high school has fairly substantial effects. The average pattern was not produced by a few extreme individuals, nor solely by many individuals changing only a small amount. On the other hand, the two environmental experiences—the nonchanging, small K–8 school versus the transition into a large impersonal junior high school—are not completely discrepant. There is much overlap among the two groups of girls in terms of change in self-esteem. Many girls who attend junior high school show self-esteem gains in Grade 7; many girls who attend K–8 demonstrate losses. Nevertheless, the girls who switch into junior high school are at greater risk than are other students.

More important, this risk does not appear to be transitory (although small numbers of cases in some cells render these conclusions tentative). A high proportion of junior high school girls who show negative change in self-esteem between Grades 6 and 7 are the same ones who show negative change at later vantage points; that is, between Grades 6 and 9 or Grades 6 and 10. Recovery to initial levels of well-being fails to occur for a sizable proportion of these girls, despite the rise in self-esteem with age for the total sample.

Thus, identification of the particular girls who demonstrate loss in self-esteem as they move out of childhood (Grade 6) into early adolescence (Grade 7) may have implications for policy; these girls seem to be a group at risk, at least in terms of self-esteem and at least for the next 3 years. It is possible that they may benefit from extra support and help.

While the certainty of our conclusions is limited by sampling loss,[19] the findings appear to have relevance for theory as well. In fact, the findings illustrate the impact that environmental context can have upon the mental health of individuals. Although the existence of a relationship between environmental structure and individual well-being is almost a tenet of so-cial–psychology, actual empirical evidence of this association is still in great need. We have shown here that a discontinuous environmental transition at a key time in the life cycle can produce lasting negative changes for the self-picture. Changing from a protected, small, stable elementary school to a large, impersonal, and anonymous junior high school in early adolescence is detrimental for girls for at least the next few years, regardless of subsequent environmental changes. Whether the negative effects last into late adolescence and adulthood is a matter for future research.

Footnotes

[1]To simplify discussion in this chapter, the cohort of students who progress from K–6 schools to junior high schools (7–9) then to senior high schools (10–12) will be termed "junior high school" cohort. The students who move from a K–8 school to a 4-year senior high school (9–12) will be termed the "K–8" cohort.

[2]See Simmons et al. (1979), Bornhstedt (1968), Rogosa et al. (1982), and Chapters 7 and 8.

[3]Where reliability is corrected for the analyses in the body of the chapter (i.e., for self-esteem), it is corrected for the "longitudinal" sample as well. The raw change analysis does not correct for reliability.

[4]As in the other chapters, the main analysis in Chapters 9 and 10 is based on the maximum number of cases possible—that is, for the change score from Grade 6 to 7 we used all children present in both Grade 6 and Grade 7 for whom we had self-esteem scores. It is also possible just to look at that subsample for whom we have data in Grades 6, 7, 9, 10 (the "longitudinal subsample"). In general, our tactic in this book is to first present data on the greatest number of cases possible, in order to maximize our N and to keep the sample as close to the original random sample as possible (to enhance generalizability). However, in order to see if any differences between 6–7, 6–9, and 6–10 findings are due to selective drop-out in later years, we have redone the analyses on the smaller, longitudinal sample.

[5]A Grades 7–9 or 9–10 change score would also have interest; however, such scores would not tell us whether years after the Grade 7 transition the individual had bounced back and recovered to initial Grade 6 levels.

[6]For example, reading and math achievement test scores are not available in Grade 9.

[7]These individual "corrected" scores were created using the following three step procedure: (1) The mean of each self-esteem indicator was subtracted from each individual's score on the variable. This yielded a new variable with a mean of zero. (2) These new indicators were then multiplied by the factor score regression coefficients obtained from LISREL VI analyses and summed. (See Appendix E for more detail and the measurement model.) (3) The mean of the reference indicator, which defines the mean of the factor scores (see Schoenberg, 1982), was then added into the scores resulting from step (2). However, the self-esteem scale as used up to this point in this book is based on six indicators with a range of 0 to 6; while this new score, based on the range of the reference indicator, can vary only from 0 to 1. Therefore, in order to make the new "corrected" score comparable to the original scale values, all scores were multiplied by 6 at this point. Note that the measurement models on which these scores are based correct for correlated error over time between indicators. (See Appendix E.)

[8]To estimate these adjusted change scores, an OLS regression was used with "corrected" change scores as the dependent variable and the Grade 6 "corrected" score, sex, and school type as independent variables. The resultant beta attached to the Grade 6 score could then be utilized in the covariance formula to construct the individual adjusted "corrected" change scores for self-esteem.

[9]If we compute a mean from the individual's adjusted change scores, for a subgroup, this subgroup mean will be the same as the adjusted subgroup mean derived directly from the Analysis of Covariance formula, as used in earlier chapters. Where reliability corrections are presumed unnecessary, as in the case of GPA and extracurricular participation, the resultant means will be identical to those presented in Chapter 8 (see Chapter 10). Where corrections have been made with LISREL VI, as in the case of self-esteem, a group-level adjusted mean change score based on "corrected" scores is identical to a mean of the individually adjusted reliability corrected change score within the same subgroup.

In addition, as with our other analyses involving analysis of covariance, we have tested for covariate-factor interaction using the estimated corrected Grade 6 score as a covariate and sex and school type and their interaction as factors. All tests for covariate factor interaction yielded nonsignificant results at the .05 level.

[10]If raw (unadjusted, uncorrected) change scores are used instead, the Grades 6–10 junior high school median for girls (.04) is lower than the K–8 median (.75) but not negative in direction.

[11]In the "longitudinal sample" of students, who were in the study all 4 years, in one case (from Grades 6–7), K–8 boys show the most negative median (but not mean) change.

[12]Despite this difference in range, however, a test for homogeneity of variances shows no significant differences among the four subgroups.

[13]The cut-off point within the positive category and within the negative category were thus somewhat different each year. In all years the positive-negative cut-off (above or below zero) was the same.

[14]The raw (unadjusted and uncorrected) change analysis leads to the same conclusions for Grade 6–7 change, but the Grades 6–9 and 6–10 change is primarily due to a difference at the negative extreme (Grade 9: 20% of the junior high school girls show extreme negative change versus 10% of the K–8 girls; Grade 10: the comparable figures are 26% versus 7%.)

[15]If raw (unadjusted and uncorrected) change scores are used, then 42% of the junior high school girls show negative change from Grade 6–7 compared to only 30% of K–8 girls and 21–28% of the boys. If adjusted reliability corrected change scores are used on the longitudinal sample, 57% of junior high school girls demonstrate negative Grade 6–7 change compared to 40% of K–8 girls and 36–50% of boys. In any case, at the least we are dealing with a large minority of junior high school girls and, at most, with a majority who show negative change between Grades 6 and 7 (and also between Grade 6 and later years).

It should be noted that from Grade 6–7 (but not Grade 6–9 or 6–10) in the "longitudinal sample" of children present all four years in the study, K–8 boys show almost as much negative change as junior high girls. However, the nonlongitudinal sample from Grade 6–7 is the better one, since it is closer to the original random sample.

[16]We can compare the difference between the change scores of the K–8 and junior high school girls to the standard deviation (Table 9.1). In terms of Grade 6–7, the difference is 1/3 of a standard deviation; in Grade 6–10, it is a little over 1/2 of a standard deviation.

[17]There is no inevitable artifactual correlation between the Grade 6–7 and 6–9

or 6–10 change scores. If completely different children were showing gains and losses between Grades 6 and 7 and Grades 6 and 9, no relationship between the two adjusted change scores would emerge. In order to demonstrate this fact, we did a simulation on random data for a case in which the Time 1, 2, and 3 scores were randomly generated and uncorrelated and in which there were two dichotomous independent variables uncorrelated with one another, with one of the independent variables significantly correlated with the Time 1 score (as sex is in our real case). The adjusted Time 1–2 change score and the adjusted Time 1–3 change scores showed a correlation close to zero ($r = -.04$, n.s.), whereas in our real case the correlation between the 6–7 and 6–9 adjusted change scores is .40 ($p \leq .001$) and the correlation between 6–7 and 6–10 is .29 ($p \leq .001$).

[18]The differences between originally negative junior high school girls and the others compared earlier appear even greater with the raw change analysis. For the raw unadjusted, uncorrected change analyses, approximately the same proportion of girls who originally showed negative Grade 6–7 change persist in demonstrating negative change in Grades 9 and 10.

[19]See Chapters 2 and 8.

10

INDIVIDUAL CHANGE AND RECOVERY: EXTRACURRICULAR PARTICIPATION AND GPA*

As noted earlier, the change into junior high school not only leads to lower self-esteem among seventh grade girls, but it is associated with a drop in GPA and extracurricular participation for both sexes. The questions at issue here are parallel to the ones we asked in Chapter 9 for self-esteem:

1. How pervasive are the changes that occur each year? Are they produced by a few children changing a great deal, or are the findings reflective of a differential change involving many students?
2. How substantial are the differential changes? Are they a result of many children changing a bit more in one environment than in another or are they a consequence of large differences in the degree of change?
3. To what extent do youngsters recover from the losses they sustain in Grade 7? Can we predict the children who will drop in grades and participation from Grades 6 to 9 or from 6 to 10 on the basis of knowledge about their loss or gain between Grades 6 and 7? Or have they recovered enough by the later vantage points so that their experience between Grades 6 and 7 is no longer predictive?

Once again, we use adjusted change scores and the largest sample possible. However, we have repeated the analysis with raw change scores and with just those cases for whom we have data all 4 years. For the most part the conclusions are the same; where there are important differences, they are reported.[1]

Extracurricular Participation

Since extracurricular participation seemed to show a similar pattern to self-esteem in the trend analysis in Chapters 7 and 8, we shall investigate it first here. As noted earlier, the question asked of the students was the following:

*By Roberta G. Simmons, Steven L. Carlton-Ford, and Dale A. Blyth.

> Do you belong to any clubs, sports, or activities at school? [IF YES] What
> sports, activities or clubs do you belong to at school? [LIST ALL MENTIONED]

Prior trend analysis indicated that each change in schools leads to a drop or leveling off of extracurricular participation, while longer tenure in the same school is associated with an increase in participation. When the child becomes the "bottom dog" in a junior high school (Grade 7 for the junior high school cohort) or in senior high school (Grade 9 for the K–8 cohort; Grade 10 for the junior high school cohort), participation is constrained for that year but begins to climb the next. Even so, however, the junior high school girls, whose average participation drops in Grade 7, do not seem to catch up later with the K–8 cohort even in Grade 9 when the K–8 cohort changes schools, and by Grade 10 the mean differences between the two cohorts for both sexes are considerable. Although the two cohorts started out almost the same in Grade 6, their subsequent history is very different.

These analyses in Chapter 8 are based on means, however, and group adjusted mean-change scores. The first issue is whether these mean differences are produced by a few or many students.

Pervasiveness of Change

Table 10.1 shows that the differences in adjusted median change between the two cohorts is similar in direction to the differences in adjusted means. Thus, it does not appear that the difference in means is produced by a few extreme cases. More evidence to this effect is presented in Tables 10.2, 10.3, and 10.4 where the adjusted change scores are split into four categories (using the procedure described in Chapter 9). In these tables related to extracurricular participation, it is also obvious that the differences in change scores between the K–8 and junior high school cohorts are not produced by a few children at the extremes. For example, in Table 10.2, we can see that between Grade 6 and 7 32% of the junior high school girls showed "large" drops in participation compared to only 10% of the K–8 girls, and 43% of the junior high school girls showed "moderate" drops in participation compared to only 28% of K–8 girls; on the other hand, only 19% of junior high school girls demonstrated moderate increases in participation compared to fully 36% of the K–8 girls, and finally only 6% of the junior high school girls indicated larger increases in participation compared to fully 27% of the K–8 girls.

Thus, for the most part, the difference between the two cohorts in extracurricular participation is due to the reaction of many students, not just a few.[2] It is also not a result of only "moderate" changes. For the most part for both genders (Tables 10.2, 10.3, 10.4), the difference between the two cohorts is reflected in the entire distribution. There are proportionately more junior high school than K–8 students showing "larger"

TABLE 10.1. Individual Adjusted Change Scores in Extracurricular Participation[a]

| | A. Grade 6–7 Score | | | | B. Grade 6–9 Score | | | | C. Grade 6–10 Score | | | |
| | Girls | | Boys | | Girls | | Boys | | Girls | | Boys | |
	K–8	JH	K–8	JH	K–8	JH	K–8	JH	K–8	JH	K–8	JH
Mean	.286	-.457	.379	-.320	.411	-.127	-.016	-.176	1.255	-.073	.416	-.287
Median	.062	-.572	.216	-.580	.317	-.628	-.622	-.645	1.271	-.727	-.241	-.729
Range	4.851	6.851	6.851	6.426	4.910	5.727	5.000	6.090	6.254	6.254	5.507	3.761
Minimum	-1.422	-2.273	-1.422	-2.273	-1.010	-1.737	-1.373	-2.100	-.987	-1.494	-1.241	-1.494
Maximum	3.429	4.578	5.429	4.152	3.900	3.990	3.627	3.990	5.267	4.759	4.267	2.267
SD	.999	.861	1.133	1.099	1.312	1.237	1.232	1.280	1.681	1.150	1.631	.982
(N)	(93)	(148)	(112)	(167)	(33)	(91)	(35)	(88)	(27)	(55)	(28)	(61)

[a]Unrecoded scores.

277

TABLE 10.2. Change in Extracurricular Participation, Grade 6–7, Percentage
Scoring in Four Categories of Adjusted Individual Change
Scores[a]

	Girls		Boys	
	K–8 (93)	JH (148)	K–8 (112)	JH (167)
Larger decrease (−2.28 activities to −.800)	10%	32%	11%	36%
	} 38	} 75	} 39	} 73
Moderate decrease (−.799 to −.001)	28	43	28	37
Moderate increase (000 to .799)	36	19	30	14
	} 63	} 25	} 62	} 27
Larger increase (.800 to 5.43)	27	6	32	13
	100%	100%	100%	100%

[a] $p < .001$ (Chi-square test).

decreases in participation, as well as proportionately more showing
"moderate" decreases. If only a few students were involved, or if differences turned up only among those who changed a very small amount,
then the issue could be dismissed as being of little concern. However,
neither situation appears to be the case. The data so far suggest that the
decrease in extracurricular participation among the junior high school students can be regarded as a relevant issue.

Yet, two qualifications must be made. First, despite these differences
between the cohorts, there is considerable overlap in the distributions
(note the standard deviations and minimum and maximum scores in Table
10.1).

Second, the absolute size of the mean differences and standard deviations is small. In Grade 6, 43% of the children belonged to no clubs or
activities at all, and the average number of activities was 1 (although the
maximum was 6). Whether we look at raw change or these adjusted change
scores (Table 10.1), the mean change between Grades 6 and 7 and between
Grades 6 and 9 is less than 1—that is, the average child changes by less
than 1 activity. Furthermore, the standard deviation also is between 1 and
1.5. However, for the youngsters in the extreme categories, the losses
and gains in activities are, of course, larger.

TABLE 10.3. Change in Extracurricular Participation, Grade 6–9, Percentage Scoring in Four Categories of Adjusted Individual Change Scores[a]

	Girls		Boys	
	K–8 (33)	JH (91)	K–8 (35)	JH (88)
Larger decrease (−2.28 to −.800)	12% ⎱ 48	29% ⎱ 71	31% ⎱ 60	33% ⎱ 71
Moderate decrease (−.799 to −.001)	36 ⎰	42 ⎰	29 ⎰	38 ⎰
Moderate increase (.000 to .799)	24 ⎱ 51	13 ⎱ 29	14 ⎱ 40	7 ⎱ 30
Larger increase (.800 to 5.43)	27 ⎰	16 ⎰	26 ⎰	23 ⎰
	100%	100%	100%	100%

[a]$p = .10$ (Chi-square test).

TABLE 10.4. Change in Extracurricular Participation, Grade 6–10, Percentage Scoring in Four Categories of Adjusted Individual Change Scores[a]

	Girls		Boys	
	K–8 (27)	JH (55)	K–8 (28)	JH (61)
Larger decrease (−2.28 to −.800)	7% ⎱ 26	22% ⎱ 58	21% ⎱ 53	31% ⎱ 70
Moderate decrease (−.799 to −.001)	19 ⎰	36 ⎰	32 ⎰	39 ⎰
Moderate increase (.000 to .799)	15 ⎱ 74	20 ⎱ 42	11 ⎱ 47	13 ⎱ 29
Larger increase (.800 to 5.43)	59 ⎰	22 ⎰	36 ⎰	16 ⎰
	100%	100%	100%	100%

[a]$p < .05$ (Chi-square test).

In any case, even one extracurricular activity, whether it be a club or a team sport, can assume a great deal of the youth's after-school time. Thus, while we are not always discussing large numbers of activities, we conclude that there is a real difference between the K–8 and junior high school cohorts—with substantially more of the former likely to increase their level of participation after Grade 6, and substantially more of the latter likely to decrease participation.

Recovery

Since the differential in extracurricular participation between the cohorts appears to be large enough and to affect enough students to be of concern, the next issue is that of recovery. Are the students who decrease their participation from Grade 6 to 7 the same ones who show loss from the vantage points of ninth and tenth grade? Or is the loss a transitory one from which they recover, bouncing back at least to Grade 6 levels of participation? If the loss is merely a transitory one, we should not be able to predict the Grade 6–9 or 6–10 change score from the Grade 6–7 change score. Table 10.5 shows, however, that one can predict the Grade 6–9 change score and the Grade 6–10 change score from the Grade 6 to 7 score ($p = .0001$ in both cases). The greater the loss in Grade 6–7, the greater the loss from the vantage point of later years as well. For example, those who showed a large decrease from Grade 6 to 7 had a decrease of $-.55$ from Grade 6 to 9, while those who showed a large Grade 6–7 increase demonstrated an increase of 1.08 from Grade 6 to 9 (Table 10.5).

Furthermore, in terms of the proportion of youngsters affected: among students who had shown an adjusted decrease in extracurricular membership between Grades 6 and 7, fully 75% of junior high school girls, 81% of junior high school boys, and 64% of K–8 students also demonstrated adjusted decreases between Grades 6 and 9. In comparison, only 38–56% of junior high school students and 46% of K–8 students who had started out with positive Grade 6–7 change showed decreases from Grade 6 to 9. Similarly, the majority who exhibited loss between Grades 6 and 7 were still showing loss in membership from the vantage point of Grade 10 (i.e., 68% of junior high school girls, 80% of junior high school boys, and 52% of K–8 students). In contrast, only a minority of those who had demonstrated gains from Grade 6 to 7 showed loss from Grade 6 to 10 (only 33% of each gender in the junior high school cohort, 29% in the K–8 cohort).[3] Thus, the vast majority of children who decreased their extracurricular participation as they moved from Grade 6 to 7 still showed these decreases when looked at in Grades 9 and 10. They did not bounce back enough to erase the difference between themselves and their peers who had not reduced participation at the entry to adolescence.

There is a moderate degree of persistence over the years for all groups in loss and gain in this realm, just as there was in self-esteem. Once again,

TABLE 10.5. Relationship of Grade 6–7 Adjusted Change in Extracurricular Participation to Later Adjusted Individual Change

| | Individual adjusted change in extracurricular participation Grade 6–7 (range) | | | |
	Larger decrease (-2.28 to $-.800$)	Moderate decrease ($-.799$ to $-.001$)	Moderate increase (.000 to .799)	Larger increase (.800 to 5.43)
Grade 6–9 adjusted means ($N = 247$)	$-.55$	$-.18$	.25	1.08
Grade 6–10 adjusted means ($N = 171$)	$-.59$	$-.01$	.66	1.43

One-Way analysis of variance and R^2
  Independent variable: Change Grade 6–7
  Dependent variable:
    Grade 6–9 individual adjusted change
      $p = .0001$
      $R^2 = .15^a$
    Grade 6–10 individual adjusted change
      $p = .0001$
      $R^2 = .24^a$

[a]Based on unrecoded scores.

however, there is some evidence that the junior high school cohort is at greater risk. Grade 7 may be a key time for an individual to adopt patterns of participation in activities.

Grade Point Average (GPA)

As noted in Chapter 8, there is an overall tendency for GPA to drop with time, particularly with the movement into senior high school (perhaps due to more difficult grading standards in later years). Also, transition into a new school is associated with especially steep drops in grade point average. To recapitulate briefly: in Grade 7 the students who have just entered junior high school demonstrate drops in GPA while the K-8 students improve; in ninth grade the K–8 students are the ones to show significantly more negative change as they make the transition into senior high school; in tenth grade, the group change analysis does not indicate significant differences between the two cohorts (although the junior high school cohort, which has just switched schools, once again has the lower GPA).

Pervasiveness of Change

To make certain that the differential change in Grade 7 and in Grade 9 between the two school cohorts in mean GPA is not produced solely by a few extreme cases, we investigated the medians (Table 10.6) as well

TABLE 10.6. Individual Adjusted Change Scores in GPA

| | A. Grade 6–7 Score | | | | B. Grade 6–9 Score | | | | C. Grade 6–10 Score | | | |
| | Girls | | Boys | | Girls | | Boys | | Girls | | Boys | |
	K–8	JH	K–8	JH	K–8	JH	K–8	JH	K–8	JH	K–8	JH
Mean	.067	−.036	.042	−.280	−.824	−.182	−.467	−.374	−.675	−.741	−.831	−.693
Median	.366	−.010	.120	.306	−1.050	−.024	−.411	−.376	−.662	−.718	−.860	−.624
Range	3.457	3.358	2.991	2.412	3.750	4.053	3.585	3.807	3.377	4.269	3.425	3.938
Minimum	−2.047	−2.032	−1.559	−1.642	−2.933	−2.411	−2.742	−2.373	−2.776	−3.338	−2.825	−2.749
Maximum	1.410	1.326	1.392	.769	.817	1.642	.842	1.433	.601	.931	.600	1.189
SD	.812	.607	.588	.557	.919	.782	.903	.711	.825	.860	.944	.831
(N)	(89)	(145)	(108)	(164)	(28)	(79)	(33)	(77)	(27)	(54)	(28)	(59)

282

as the total distribution (Table 10.7, Table 10.8). (Since the initial difference between school cohorts for change between Grades 6 and 10, as reported in Chapter 8, was not significant, these analyses are not relevant for that year of change.)

Inspection indicates that the conclusions drawn from a comparison of the medians and the means are basically the same; and that, for the most part, the differences between the K–8 and junior high school cohort are present at several points in the distribution, not only at the extremes.[4] However, according to this analysis, the greater drop in GPA from Grade 6 to 9 in the K–8/SH cohort is evident only for girls, not for boys.

Another issue is whether the difference between the groups is large enough to be of relevance, or whether it is produced solely by "moderate" changes—that is, by several youngsters changing only a small amount. Tables 10.7 and 10.8 demonstrate that with the exception of boys' Grades 6–9 change score, the difference between the cohorts does show up among those who change a "larger" amount as well as those who change a smaller amount. In this case a "larger" amount means a minimum of ± .4 of a GPA point to ± 2.05 points. Thus, what we are saying, for example, is that if all these youngsters began with the same GPA in sixth grade, by seventh grade the K–8 cohort would have been considerably more likely than the junior high school cohort to have improved their GPA by .4 of a point or more. Four-tenths of a GPA point is a sizable difference—it is

TABLE 10.7. Change in GPA, Grade 6–7, Percentage Scoring in Four Categories of Adjusted Individual Change Scores[a]

	Girls		Boys	
	K–8 (89)	JH (145)	K–8 (108)	JH (164)
Larger decrease (−2.050 to −.400)	21% ⎫	23% ⎫	22% ⎫	45% ⎫
	⎬ 41	⎬ 48	⎬ 42	⎬ 67
Moderate decrease (−.399 to −.001)	20 ⎭	25 ⎭	20 ⎭	22 ⎭
Moderate increase (.000 to .399)	11 ⎫	33 ⎫	32 ⎫	21 ⎫
	⎬ 58	⎬ 52	⎬ 57	⎬ 33
Larger increase (.400 to 1.410)	47 ⎭	19 ⎭	25 ⎭	12 ⎭
	———	———	———	———
	100%	100%	100%	100%

[a] $p < .001$ (Chi-square test).

TABLE 10.8. Change in GPA, Grades 6–9, Percentage Scoring in Four
Categories of Adjusted Individual Change Scores[a]

	Girls		Boys	
	K–8 (28)	JH (79)	K–8 (33)	JH (77)
Larger decrease (−2.050 to −.400)	71% ⎫	39% ⎫	52% ⎫	48% ⎫
Moderate decrease (−.399 to −.001)	7 ⎬ 78	14 ⎬ 53	6 ⎬ 58	22 ⎬ 70
Moderate increase (.000 to .399)	14 ⎫	24 ⎫	24 ⎫	17 ⎫
Larger increase (.800 to .400 to 1.410)	7 ⎬ 21	23 ⎬ 47	18 ⎬ 42	13 ⎬ 30
	100%	100%	100%	100%

[a]$p < .10$ (Chi-square test).

approximately half a letter grade. Thus, it is the difference between a B+
and A− average or between a B− and C+ average.

Recovery

We have already noted that on the group level, recovery appears to
occur. Junior high school students are at a disadvantage in seventh grade
but at an advantage in ninth, and the results are mixed in tenth grade.
Nevertheless, it is possible that there are still substantial numbers of individuals who do not recover from their seventh grade academic loss. It
is possible that the seventh grade adjusted change score predicts the Grade
6–9 and Grade 6–10 adjusted change scores for individuals. Table 10.9
indicates that the Grade 6–7 adjusted change score does indeed predict
the Grade 6–9 and Grade 6–10 change score ($p < .001$ in both cases).
Youngsters whose grades show a relative decline from Grade 6 to 7 are
the same youngsters whose grades decline more between Grades 6 and 9
and 6 and 10. For example (Table 10.9), youth who demonstrated a "larger" drop between Grades 6 and 7 dropped −.87 between 6 and 9 (an
entire letter grade), while those who showed a "larger" increase between
Grades 6 and 7 improved by .06 between Grades 6 and 9.

How substantial is this lack of recovery? There is little difference be-

TABLE 10.9. Relationship of Grade 6–7 Adjusted Change in GPA to Later Adjusted Individual Change

	Individual adjusted change in GPA Grade 6–7 (range)			
	Larger decrease $(-2.050$ to $-.400)$	Moderate decrease $(-.399$ to $-.001)$	Moderate increase $(.000$ to $.399)$	Larger increase $(.400$ to $1.410)$
Grade 6–9 adjusted means $(N = 216)$	$-.87$	$-.46$	$-.12$	$.06$
Grade 6–10 adjusted means $(N = 167)$	-1.12	$-.86$	$-.52$	$-.35$
One-Way analysis of variance and R^2				
Independent variable: change Grade 6–7				
Dependent variable:				
Grade 6–9 individual adjusted change				
$p = .0001$				
$R^2 = .23^a$				
Grade 6–10 individual adjusted change				
$p = .001$				
$R^2 = .14^a$				

[a]Based on unrecoded scores.

tween the junior high school and K–8 cohorts in this particular respect. Fully 78–79% of students who showed an adjusted drop in GPA from Grade 6 to 7 also show a drop from Grade 6 to 9, whereas only 40–60% of students who improved between Grades 6 and 7 indicate a Grade 6–9 drop. Furthermore, 91–96% of students whose grades dropped between Grades 6 and 7 also show a drop from Grades 6 to 10 compared to only 57–72% of students whose grades did not drop between Grades 6 and 7.[5]

Thus, recovery from an early loss in GPA is somewhat difficult at an individual level. This difficulty in recovery occurs despite the fact that on average each cohort is at a relative disadvantage the particular year a school transition occurs.[6] While GPA is declining for most students during the adolescent years, students who show an early loss at entry to adolescence are even more likely than others to demonstrate a loss in later years as well.

Summary

At a group level, both the trend analyses and group adjusted change analyses indicated that school context affected students' adjustment along three key dimensions: self-esteem, grade point average, and participation in extracurricular activities. In our opinion, self-esteem is the most significant of the self-image variables measured (see Rosenberg, 1979). And grade point average is perhaps the most important indicator of competence provided to the adolescent. It certainly is one of the most relevant indicators in the school culture at large with considerable import for future opportunities.

The trend and group change analysis suggested that at entry to junior high school girls were at risk in terms of their self-esteem and both sexes showed relative losses in GPA and extracurricular participation. While longer tenure in the same school was helpful for GPA and participation, subsequent transition into a new, larger senior high school was detrimental. The individual adjusted change analyses presented in Chapters 9 and 10 indicated that the differences between K–8 and junior high school cohorts were (1) not due to a few extreme cases and (2) not due solely to several children changing a very small amount (although caveats on this point are necessary due to the lack of absolute meaning of self-esteem scale points and the small number of extracurricular activities at issue). Finally, students do not appear to recover easily from losses entailed between Grades 6 and 7. Those individual students who showed relative losses between Grades 6 and 7 were the ones to still show loss from the vantage point of Grade 9 and Grade 10. Some evidence was presented to suggest that junior high school students were less likely than K–8 students to recover in the area of extracurricular participation, and that junior high school girls were particularly unlikely to recover in self-esteem.

Footnotes

[1]Since these dependent variables are indexed by single items, reliability corrections are not possible. In addition, these variables are not treated as indicators of an underlying construct but as measures of actual, observable behavior—the actual GPA on file and the actual number of extracurricular activities. Therefore, reliability corrections are less relevant.

[2]Note that fully 73–75% of junior high school students show negative change. However, if raw change scores are used, then 40% of the junior high school girls and 42% of the junior high school boys show negative changes from Grade 6 to 7 compared to 20% of the K–8 girls and 20% of the K–8 boys. For the Grades 6–9 analyses there is a small difference in conclusion when the raw change scores are used. Junior high school boys are no longer clearly likely to show more negative change than the K–8 boys, although they are still less likely to show positive change.

[3]If raw change scores are examined, the tendency persists for the vast majority of those who decreased participation in Grades 6 and 7 to still show decreases in Grades 6–9 and 6–10. From 63 to 85% of junior high school boys and girls who showed a negative Grade 6–7 change persisted in demonstrating negative change in Grades 9 and 10 when raw change scores are used. But in Grades 6–9 this tendency is not greater in the junior high school cohort than in the K–8 cohort. For Grades 6–10 the raw change analysis leads to the same conclusions as the adjusted change analyses; differences reported earlier are, if anything, greater in the raw change analyses.

[4]In terms of the proportion indicating negative change between Grades 6 and 7: if unadjusted, raw change scores are used instead of the adjusted change scores in Table 10.7, 41% of the junior high school girls, 59% of the junior high school

boys, 36% of the K–8 girls, and 40% of the K–8 boys show negative change in GPA between Grades 6 and 7. Also, the raw change analysis for girls in Grades 6–9 is somewhat different from the adjusted change analysis in that most of the difference between school cohorts appears at the extremes.

[5]If raw change scores are used, most of the conclusions remain the same as do the sizes of the proportions, at least for the junior high school cohort. However, the tendency for the Grade 6–7 loss to predict a Grades 6–9 loss is no longer clear for the K–8 cohort, although it is clear for the junior high school cohort.

[6]As indicated before, in Grade 9 this relative disadvantage is clearer for the girls in the K–8/SH cohort than for the boys.

V

FACTORS THAT MITIGATE OR AGGRAVATE THE EARLY ADOLESCENT TRANSITION

Up to this point we have investigated the impact of age, gender, pubertal timing, and school transition upon the early and middle adolescents. Pubertal change and the school transitions have been examined independently of one another and independently of other aspects of the child's life. In this section, we look at school and pubertal change together along with other factors that may affect the entry to adolescence.

The transition into junior high school has been shown to have negative effects for one or both genders for the key variables of self-esteem, GPA, and extracurricular participation. Chapter 11 asks to what extent these negative effects are aggravated by several cumulative changes in the child's life. Chapters 12 and 13 focus on the move into junior high school and identify some school properties that intensify difficulty as well as the individual resources that help.

Clearly, not all early adolescents react in the same way to school and pubertal change. Some children react negatively to the junior high school transition, but others do not. The focus of this section is on the factors that aid or hinder youngsters as they make the transition into adolescence, particularly when entry into a new environment is involved. If junior high school is a potential stressor, what factors make it more likely and what factors make it less likely that the student will succumb to the stress? Thus, this section of the analysis deals more with the process involved.

11

CUMULATION OF CHANGE*

Up to now we have examined the impact of one type of change at a time on the young adolescent. Yet, the adjustment to one transition may be affected by the number of other changes the youngster is experiencing at the same time, by the "cumulation" or "synchronicity" of life changes (Wells and Stryker, in press). In short, in this chapter we are interested in the effects of the cumulation of change and whether children find it more difficult to adjust to several changes simultaneously.

Much relevant work has been done in this area, due to the extensive research on life events.[1] However, the focus of the life event literature is somewhat different from ours. Relatively few studies in the life events area have dealt with normal adolescents (see Gad and Johnson, 1980; Padilla, Rohsenow and Bergman, 1976; Gersten, Langner, Eisenberg and Orzeck, 1974; Gersten, Langner, Eisenberg, and Simcha-Fagan, 1977; Newcomb, Huba and Bentler, 1981; Johnson and McCutcheon, 1980; Swearingen and Cohen, 1985a,b). Those few that have, by and large, do not focus on the normal, scheduled life event changes of adolescence— move into junior high, pubertal change, onset of dating (see Padilla's cross-sectional study of boys, 1976, for an exception).[2] Like Elder and Rockwell (1979), we think life changes have to be considered in the light of normative transitions in the life course, and it is in that context that we are concerned with the consequences of experiencing several changes at a time.

Coleman (1974) has proposed a "focal" theory of change, and in earlier publications we have developed similar propositions (Simmons *et al.,* 1979).[3] According to these theories, it is easier if the child goes through the various adolescent changes at different times rather than simultaneously. The attempt to cope with several major life changes at the same time is expected to cause difficulty. More time to adjust gradually to one change before confrontation with another should be beneficial.

Thus, it should be very difficult for a child to have to make the transition into a large junior high school at the same time as he or she is experiencing major pubertal changes, beginning the very new behavior of "dating," moving neighborhoods, and/or going through a major family disruption.

*By Roberta G. Simmons, Richard Burgeson, and Dale A. Blyth.

Children who experience several important life changes in coincidence are expected to be at greater risk.

To test this hypothesis, children have been classified as experiencing major change in or before Grade 7 along the following dimensions for which we have measures:

1. School change—movement into a junior high school versus remaining in a K–8 school.
2. Pubertal change—girls: Onset of menstruation within 6 months prior to seventh grade interview or up to 3 months after seventh grade interview ($N = 151$) versus onset at a greater time distance from the interview ($N = 56$); boys: Early developers, who have reached peak height growth prior to Grade 7 interview ($N = 83$) versus middle and late developers who attained peak height growth later ($N = 171$).
3. Early dating—children who have dated a member of the opposite sex alone or who go steady ($N = 57$ girls, 93 boys) versus those who have no dating experience or only group dating ($N = 144$ girls, 153 boys).
4. Geographical mobility—movement into a new neighborhood since starting Grade 6 or into a new school off-schedule in Grade 6 ($N = 30$ girls, 30 boys) versus residential and school stability ($N = 177$ girls, 224 boys).
5. Major family disruption[4]—major parental change since age 9 (death of a parent, divorce, or remarriage of a parent—$N = 23$ girls, 26 boys)[5] versus parental stability ($N = 184$ girls, 228 boys).

To test the effect of cumulative change, we shall focus on the same three dependent variables as in Chapters 9 and 10, the key adjustment variables we know to be affected by school type in Grade 7: self-esteem, GPA, and extracurricular participation.

The question then is whether the child shows more difficulty with the entry to adolescence in Grade 7 if he or she has experienced a greater number of these life changes recently.

Each Change Considered by Itself

We already know that the change into junior high has significant, negative effects on one or both genders in terms of self-esteem, GPA, and participation. In general, none of the other individual changes dealt with here significantly affects self-esteem for either boys or girls.[6] That is, when considered separately, neither recency of pubertal change, residential change, early dating, or parental marital disruption significantly affects self-esteem for either boys or girls. Extracurricular activity and GPA are negatively affected by some of the other, individual life changes.[7] The main issue to be addressed in this chapter is the effect of these changes as they cumulate.

Cumulation of Change

There were not enough cases to look at different, specific combinations and permutations of change separately. Nor were there enough cases to disaggregate types of family change and separately examine the impact of divorce, parental death, or remarriage.[8] Therefore, we categorized children simply according to the number of changes they had experienced. The scores ranged from no change (0) to four (no child had experienced all five changes). This analysis should be regarded as a first step, hopefully to be followed in future research by more intensive examination of particular combinations of change.[9]

It should be noted that school change, pubertal change, and onset of dating are more common than family disruption or geographical mobility; and therefore, each of the former three transitions are more likely to be the only transition encountered by the child, or to be included in combinations of two, three, and four changes. While family disruption and geographic mobility did occur in combination in some cases, each of these two transitions are more likely to appear without the other, regardless of the number of changes at issue (Simmons, Burgeson, Carlton-Ford, and Blyth, in press a). As will be discussed later in the chapter, several precautions have been instituted to make certain that the difference between few changes and many changes is not an artifact due to one specific change alone or in combination.

The focus of this chapter then will be on the effects of experiencing a smaller or greater number of life changes at entry to early adolescence. Specifically, for each dependent variable, the number of changes has been entered into a regression equation, and then it and its square have been entered into a second regression equation. Thus, both the linear and quadratic component of cumulative change can be examined. If either component shows significant negative effects, then the child experiencing several changes can be considered at risk, but for different reasons. If the linear component is negative and significant, then it is the simple cumulation of negative effects that is placing the child in jeopardy. In this case, it would not be so much that coping with one change made it more difficult to cope with a second, but rather that each transition had independent (perhaps small), negative consequences. And all these small disadvantages would be additive so that the child would score lower in self-esteem, GPA, or participation than children who have had fewer transitions with which to cope.

If the curvilinear or quadratic component is negative and significant, then there is evidence that, above and beyond the independent cumulation of disadvantages, the presence of one transition makes it difficult to cope with others. In fact, as we shall see, not any curvilinear relationship will do to support this hypothesis. We are looking for a situation in which the negative effect becomes sharper after there are two or more changes facing the adolescent. (See below for more explanation.)

Males

Table 11.1 shows that number of changes has significant, negative linear effects on extracurricular participation and GPA but not on self-esteem. There are no significant curvilinear (i.e., quadratic) relationships. Figures 11.1 and 11.2 plot the significant relationships. It is clear that as the number of transitions increase, GPA and extracurricular participation decrease. While we have no evidence that coping with one change complicates adjustment to another, it does appear that boys who have more changes within a short period of time are a group at greater risk.

For school grades we are talking about a difference of .89 GPA points which is the equivalent of almost one entire letter grade (e.g., the difference between a "B − " and a "C − "). For extracurricular participation, we are talking about a difference of one activity. Since the average child belongs to not quite one activity, this difference is a meaningful one.

Since some researchers have indicated a link between social class and reaction to life events (see Dohrenwend, 1973; Gad and Johnson, 1980; Meyers, Lindenthal, and Pepper, 1974), we replicated our analysis controlling for social class background to ensure that this factor was not confounding our interpretations. We also controlled for the individual's original Grade 6 score to make sure our observed differences were not due to the students' starting out at different levels. The findings remain identical.

TABLE 11.1. Effects of Multiple Transitions on Self-Esteem, GPA, and Participation for Grade 7 Boys[a]

	Bivariate linear regression		Quadratic controlling for linear	
	b (SE)	Beta	b (SE)	Beta
Self-esteem		.0315	.053	.127
($N = 245$)	(.101)		(.082)	
Extracurricular participation	−.166***	−.134	.033	.099
($N = 246$))	(.079)		(.064)	
GPA	−.197*	−.241	.011	.052
($N = 242$)	(.051)		(.042)	

[a]One-tail test: *$p \leqslant .001$; **$p \leqslant .01$; ***$p \leqslant .05$; ****$p \leqslant .10$.

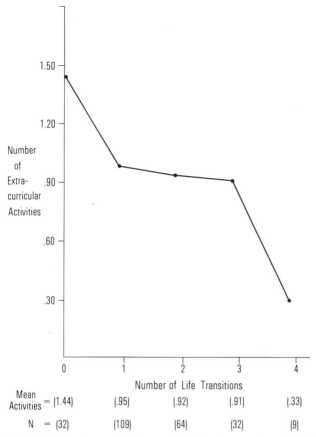

FIGURE 11.1. **Grade 7 extracurricular participation by number of life transitions for boys.**

Females

Table 11.2 shows significant, negative effects of number of changes upon self-esteem, GPA, and extracurricular participation.[10] For self-esteem and participation the effects are linear; for GPA they are curvilinear. Thus, the more changes the girl has experienced recently, the lower her self-esteem, club participation and GPA (see Figs. 11.3 and 11.4).

However, for GPA the effects are not merely reflections of a simple process of cumulative negative impact. For this variable, the experience of one change appears to make the others more difficult. Figure 11.5 plots the curvilinear pattern. For one change to interfere with the adjustment to a second change, the child obviously has to have experienced more than one change. Thus, we predicted curves in which the slope downward would become steeper at some point after one change. That is, whatever the slope between no changes and one change, we would see a steeper

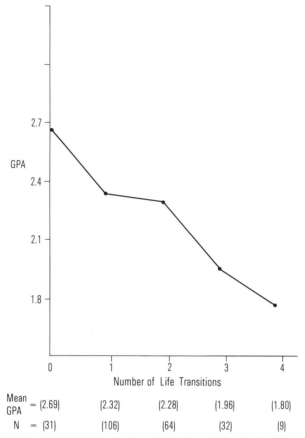

FIGURE 11.2. Grade 7 GPA by number of life transitions for boys.

TABLE 11.2. Effects of Multiple Transitions on Self-Esteem, GPA, and Participation for Grade 7 Girls[a]

	Bivariate linear regression		Quadratic controlling for linear	
	b (SE)	Beta	b (SE)	Beta
Self-esteem	$-.333^{**}$	$-.173$	$-.165$	$-.268$
($N = 200$)	(.135)		(.136)	
Extracurricular				
participation	$-.293^{*}$	$-.238$	.024	.062
($N = 201$)	(.085)		(.086)	
GPA	$-.238^{*}$	$-.275$	$-.152^{**}$	$-.594$
($N = 199$)	(.059)		(.059)	

[a]One-tail test: $^{*}p \leq .001$; $^{**}p \leq .01$; $^{***}p \leq .05$; $^{****}p \leq .10$.

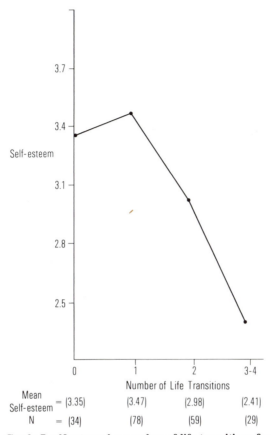

FIGURE 11.3. Grade 7 self-esteem by number of life transitions for girls.

descent at some point after that. The negative effects would become sharper once there were two or more changes. In fact, for both GPA and self-esteem we do see that pattern, although only in the case of GPA is the curvilinearity significant.

In terms of the size of the effects, we are talking about one-half of a standard deviation unit of self-esteem, more than one extracurricular activity (when the average number of activities is less than one), and .83 GPA units (or the difference between a "B" and a "C"). In other words, the differences appear sizable. As for boys, we entered the original Grade 6 score and social class background into the equations as control factors. The findings remain the same.

Effects Within Subgroups

As noted above, there are not enough cases here to compare the effects

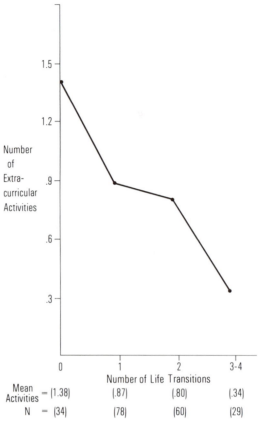

FIGURE 11.4. Grade 7 extracurricular participation by number of life transitions
for girls.

of various combinations and permutations of life changes. In order to rule
out the possibility that any one life change by itself or in combination is
responsible for these results, we have redone the analysis controlling for
each change in turn. In each case, we examined the findings for different
subgroups. (See Simmons *et al.*, in press a.) It is thus possible to determine
whether the negative effects of multiple changes are evident (1) among
students in junior high school as well as among students who attend K–
8 schools, (2) among those who have experienced pubertal changes more
recently as well as among those experiencing less pubertal change, and
(3) among those who have started dating as well as those who have not
entered into dating relations. There are too few youngsters who have experienced recent parental disruption or geographical mobility to perform
this analysis separately for such children. However, it is possible to determine whether the patterns are reproduced among those students who

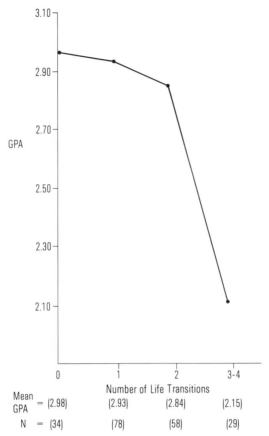

FIGURE 11.5. Grade 7 GPA and number of life transitions for girls.

have *not* experienced parental disruption and who have *not* been resi-
dentially mobile.

   In summary, to rule out the possibility that any one factor alone or in
combination is responsible for these results, we have controlled for each
factor in turn and investigated whether there is still a negative relationship
between the number of remaining changes and each of the outcome variables. In fact, Table 11.3 indicates that in most cases, the same coefficients
that were significant and negative in the full model remain so in the
subgroup models. Where significance disappears, all but one of the coefficients remain negative in direction. In fact, in one case (the effects of
life changes on extracurricular participation among K–8 girls), a significant
negative curvilinear relationship emerges showing the predicted pattern
($p < .05$).

   As an example, in Figure 11.6, we graph the patterns involving the
effect of life transitions upon girls' GPA for the two school cohorts, il-

TABLE 11.3. The Effect of Number of Transitions: Comparison of Significant Effects in Full Model with Models for Subgroups—Unstandardized Regression Coefficients from Subgroup Models[a]

	JH	K–8	Pubertal	Nonpubertal	Dating	Nondating	No family disruption[b]	No geographical movement[b]
Girls								
Self-esteem:								
linear	−.411***	−.095	−.939**	−.126	−.650***	−.275****	−.345**	−.404**
Extracurricular participation:								
linear	−.062	−.140	−.651*	−.272**	−.671**	−.411*	−.304*	−.269**
GPA:								
Linear	−.325*	−.197***	−.444*	−.248*	−.474*	−.106****	−.204*	−.188**
Quadratic	−.309***	−.151****	−.284*	−.144***	−.198	−.086	−.143***	−.133****
Boys								
Extracurricular participation:								
linear	.047	−.023	−.052	−.205***	−.444**	−.426*	−.131****	−.128****
GPA: linear	−.166**	−.180*****	−.294**	−.258*	−.126****	−.177***	−.158*	−.226*

[a]One-tail test: *$p \leq .001$; **$p \leq .01$; ***$p \leq .05$; ****$p \leq .10$.
[b]There are not enough cases with family disruption or geographical mobility to examine as a separate subgroup.

300

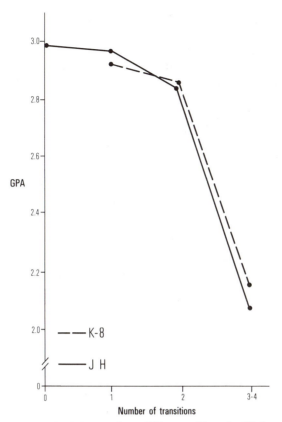

FIGURE 11.6. Grade 7 GPA by number of life transitions for K–8 and junior high school girls.

lustrating that the negative, curvilinear trend remains intact for both the junior high school and K–8 cohorts.

Recovery

The effects of cumulative change upon the entry to early adolescence have been examined. Children who have undergone multiple changes appear to be at risk in Grade 7 in general, in both school cohorts, and in the other relevant subgroups. Are these same children at any long-term risk? Analyses have been performed relating multiple changes in early adolescence (Grade 7) to later self-esteem, GPA, and participation in Grades 9 and 10.

In terms of GPA, especially for girls, these same children persist at risk in both Grades 9 and 10. For boys we still find significant negative linear relationships between number of changes and GPA—the greater the number of negative changes, the lower the GPA [Grade 9: b (S.E.) = −.26 (.10), $p \le .01$; Grade 10: b (S.E.) = −.16 (.12), $p \le .10$]. For girls, there is still a significant negative curvilinear relationship. After the first change, the more life changes there are, the ever steeper the drop becomes in Grade 9 and 10 GPA. Figure 11.7 presents these results [Grade 9: quadratic coefficient (S.E.) = −.29 (.12), $p \le .01$; Grade 10: quadratic coefficient (S.E.) = −.43 (.11), $p \le .001$].[11] Thus, children who experienced a greater number of major life transitions close to Grade 7 are still showing substantial negative effects in GPA 2 and 3 years later. In fact, in Grade 10 the differences between youngsters who have experienced no or one change and those who have experienced three or more changes are greater than one grade point difference apart. The average Grade 10 GPA for girls who experienced no changes would be a "C"; for girls who experienced one change, it would be a "C+"; whereas for girls subject to three to four changes it is a "D," at best.

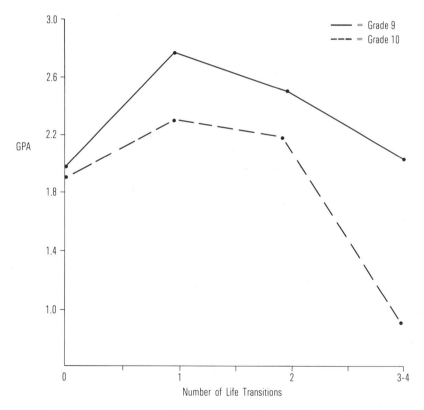

FIGURE 11.7. Grades 9 and 10 GPA by number of Grade 7 life transitions for girls.

For both boys and girls in Grades 9 and 10, these effects persist in the same direction even when Grade 6 GPA and social class are controlled, and, all but boys' Grade 9 findings remain statistically significant. Furthermore, for girls, the general direction of results is the same within both school type cohorts in Grades 9 and 10 (the K–8/SH cohort and the K–6/JH/SH cohort).[12] For boys, however, once cohort is controlled the differences are no longer clear.

In Grade 7, we saw that self-esteem also dropped as a function of number of changes for girls (but not for boys). In Grades 9 and 10 the same significant linear relationships still hold for girls ($p \leq .01$).[13] However, the relationship between the number of changes occurring close to Grade 7 and extracurricular participation does not persist in clear form for either gender in Grades 9 and 10.

Thus, girls who experienced multiple life changes in early adolescence in Grade 7 are still indicating negative outcomes in GPA 2 and 3 years later; in addition, they still show negative self-esteem effects. Extracurricular participation is no longer clearly affected, however, for either gender; and the long-term effect on boys' GPA is also not as clear as it was in Grade 7.

Senior High School Transition

We have examined the short- and long-term risk of multiple changes that occurred shortly before or at entry to Grade 7. It would be interesting to do a similar analysis for changes that occur close to the time of the transition into senior high school. However, there are comparatively few children in Grades 9 and 10 who experience the multiple life changes that we have measured. Our sample size has dropped in these years. In addition, parental disruption and geographical mobility, as is evident earlier, affect only a small proportion of those children who remain in the Milwaukee public school system in any 2–3 year period. Furthermore, changes important in early adolescence are no longer relevant. Most children (especially girls) will have attained puberty well before Grade 10. Thus, there are not enough cases to duplicate the analysis for children at the transition to senior high school.

Summary

The purpose of this analysis has been to test the notion that adolescents who experience multiple life changes within a relatively short time span will be at greater risk than those who have longer intervals in which to cope with these changes. Three out of the five possible changes at issue have been transitions (changing schools, onset of puberty, dating) which almost all adolescents must face at some point. Geographical mobility and parental marital change, on the other hand, are nonnormative and affect only a minority of children. Furthermore, these changes vary in the extent to which they are experienced as a group, rather than as individualized, unexpected occurrences (Wheeler, 1966). Change into junior high school is a group-scheduled occurrence. Onset of pubertal changes and dating are experiences that a sizable proportion of one's peers are confronting, although not all at the same rate. On the other hand, geographical mobility and parental marital change are likely to be experienced as lonely and unique events.

The findings support the idea that there are negative consequences for adolescents who must cope with several transitions at once. Girls suffer losses in self-esteem when the number of life change events they are exposed to increases. Both males and females exhibit declines in GPA and extracurricular participation the more of these transitions they encounter. Furthermore, for females the effect for GPA is curvilinear, indicating that after some point, each subsequent life change makes the overall coping process more difficult. Therefore, it does appear that facing multiple life changes simultaneously has deleterious effects on young adolescents. The fact that the proportion of students who experience 3–4 simultaneous transitions is relatively small makes it both easier and more compelling for schools to provide extra support at this time for such vulnerable youngsters.

The next question is the issue of recovery. Do individuals who react adversely to this initial combination of transitions continue to show negative effects? Or is there an adaptive process that allows them to recover? The findings of this chapter support the evidence presented in the two previous chapters—that is, it is apparently very difficult to recover from losses incurred in Grades 6 and 7. Negative consequences are still observed in Grades 9 and 10, especially in the area of academic performance. Thus, there are prolonged effects from undergoing multiple life changes at the same period when students are entering adolescence. These sustained effects hold for both genders, but females appear to be at greater risk than males.

In part (insofar as we find predicted curvilinear relations) these data also support the theory that we are postulating, that is, that the negative repercussions are sometimes not the mere result of the addition of many stressors. Rather, in addition, we emphasize the fact that multiple, key aspects of the child's life are changing at once. We suggest such a child cannot cope with one key change or one alteration in role relationships by withdrawing to a more comfortable, accustomed sphere or relationship when the latter is changing as well. When the child moves to a new school, he or she is suddenly faced with changes in peer networks, work habits, teacher relations, and extracurricular activities. In ordinary circumstances, the child might be able to withdraw temporarily to accustomed family relationships and there relax and become reenergized. However, if the parents are divorcing, remarrying, or changing residences at the same time, this sphere may be equally uncomfortable. Similarly, if one's physical appearance is changing dramatically, one may be able to cope with these alterations better if one's friendships, school life, and home are stable and comfortable and if one is not also altering the nature and importance of contact with the opposite sex.

The adolescent, like all persons, has multiple role relationships, identities, and aspects of the self-picture. To alter one such aspect should be easier if one still has "spheres of comfort," if one can feel "at home" in other life arenas and with other aspects of the self.

Footnotes

[1]See reviews of this approach and its controversies by Kessler (1979), Dohrenwend and Pearlin (1981), Newcomb, Huba, and Bentler (1981), Pearlin, Lieberman, Menaghan, and Mullan (1981), Tausig (1982), Zautra and Reich (1983), and Kessler, Price, and Wortman (1985).

[2]Most studies of adolescents do include a change of schools as a life event but do not distinguish between the normative scheduled change into junior high school and atypical school changes.

[3]Also, see Hetherington, 1979; Rutter, 1979, 1980; and Thoits, 1983.

[4]There were not enough cases to disaggregate these different types of family change look at them separately.

[5]It is assumed that short-term adjustment to such changes may take several years (Hetherington et al., 1982). In addition, if we used a more recent cut-off, we would not have enough cases of family disruption to analyze.

[6]In an earlier paper (Simmons et al., 1979), we did find early dating behavior negatively related to self-esteem for females in a bivariate cross-tabular analysis. However, in a subsequent regression analysis controlling for school type, the effect of dating behavior, although in the same direction, became nonsignificant. In addition, the dating variable used in the earlier analysis (based on three items) was somewhat different than the present version (based on six items). (See Appendix G.)

[7]See Simmons, Burgeson, Carlton-Ford, and Blyth (in press a). Extracurricular participation is negatively affected by geographic mobility for girls, and by early dating by boys. Girls' GPA is adversely affected by family disruption, geographic mobility, and early dating. Boys' GPA is negatively related to both family disruption and early dating behavior.

[8]See Hetherington et al. (1982), Rosenberg (1965), Rosenberg and Simmons (1972) for discussions of different effects of various types of family disruption.

[9]In general, in life event studies, a simple summation of positive and negative life events has yielded as strong relationships with outcome variables as have more complex attempts to weight the events according to perceived life change or impact (Johnson, 1982).

[10]Since there are only 3 girls who experience 4 changes, we have collapsed the categories of 3 and 4 changes for females.

[11]In Grade 9, but not Grade 10, the recovery findings are complicated by the fact that the K–8 cohort is now changing schools and their GPA drops that year. We are comparing children according to the number of transitions they experienced in Grade 7, and only the K–8 cohort had "0" transitions that year. Thus, the students with "0" transitions in Grade 7 (the K–8 cohort) will have particularly low GPAs in Grade 9. Therefore, the comparison between individuals with "0"

Grade 7 transitions and individuals with more transitions will be affected. However, the comparisons between students with "1" versus more Grade 7 transitions are not affected and are in the direction predicted for Grade 9 just as for the other years.

[12]In Grade 9, in both cohorts of girls, there is a drop in GPA for children with the greatest number of Grade 7 transitions. However, in the junior high school cohort, the effect is linear ($p < .05$), and for the K–8 cohort it is curvilinear with the predicted pattern ($p < .10$).

[13]With the exception of the K–8/SH cohort in Grade 10.

12

ADJUSTMENT TO THE JUNIOR HIGH SCHOOL TRANSITION: THE EFFECT OF SCHOOL PROPERTIES AND INDIVIDUAL RESOURCES ON SELF-ESTEEM*

The transition to junior high school has been shown to have some negative consequences, particularly for the self-esteem of girls. There are many youngsters who do not react unfavorably to this transition, however. Chapter 11 indicated that the reaction of the student is worse when he or she is experiencing many other life changes simultaneously. What other factors differentiate the students who find this environmental transition difficult from those who cope well?

The next two chapters will focus on two sets of factors: the characteristics of the junior high school that aggravate the difficulty, and the resources of the individual that aid adjustment to the junior high school transition. This chapter will examine effects upon self-esteem, while Chapter 13 will investigate interrelationships among these factors and other aspects of adjustment.

Problematic Characteristics of the Junior High School

The first question at issue here involves the aspects of the junior high school transition that might cause difficulty. In what key ways do K–8 schools differ from junior high schools in Grade 7? First, of course, the discontinuity of the change into junior high school is fundamental (see Benedict, 1954). As Hamburg (1974) theorizes, the coincidence of a major environmental change and new life cycle expectations may be particularly difficult.

Size

An important aspect of this environmental discontinuity involves the sudden change in school size. Children in our sample move from elementary schools in which there are, on average, 59 students at their grade-

*By Roberta G. Simmons, Steven L. Carlton-Ford, and Dale A. Blyth.

level to junior high schools in which there are 403 same grade students; K–8 students, however, remain exposed on average to only 79 students in Grade 7. It is possible that this sudden increase in classroom and school size in junior high has negative effects. Berkovitz (1979), however, posits contradictory effects of size on children. On the one hand, it may foster alienation, isolation, and difficulties with communication and intimacy.[1] On the other hand, there are many new opportunities, including the opportunity to meet a variety of peers from various backgrounds.

In terms of prior evidence, Barker and Gump (1964) note that fewer students participate in extracurricular activities in a large school (although there are more activities),[2] and Brookover et al. (1979) show mixed effects on academic self-concept.[3] A good number of studies, however, show no significant effects of school size on achievement or aspirations (McDill and Rigsby, 1973; Flanagan, Dailey, Shaycoft, Orr, and Goldberg, 1962; Ramsøy, 1961) or on a wider range of dependent variables (Rutter et al., 1979). We shall compare junior high schools of varying sizes to see if there are more negative effects at this age in the larger schools.

Departmentalization

Another discontinuous aspect of the move into junior high school involves a major increase in departmentalization. In the elementary and most K–8 schools, there is very little changing of classrooms or teachers. Children remain in a stable classroom context with exposure to relatively few people. In junior high schools, in contrast, students move from classroom to classroom and teacher to teacher. Although all junior high schools in our sample are departmentalized, in some the children move as a group from class to class while in others the movement is individualized. We have hypothesized that individualized movement in a large, new school will be more difficult for the child, having negative implications for the self-image. Group movement, by contrast, should be somewhat more protective.

Ethnic Heterogeneity

Just as small size and less individualized movement might be expected to be beneficial for the self-image, homogeneity among classmates might also be protective. In a more heterogeneous environment, the child might feel less comfortable and more alienated.

Several prior studies have concluded that status-composition factors in a school (ethnic and social class proportions) have an effect on the students above and beyond the student's own background. These factors affect achievement and college aspirations (McDill and Rigsby, 1973; Eckland and Alexander, 1980), victimization and delinquency (Gottfredson et al., 1981; Rutter et al., 1979), and academic self-concept (Brookover *et al.*, 1979; Alexander and Eckland, 1980). In general, these studies are not concerned with the role of heterogeneity in making children feel less comfortable or in challenging their self-pictures. Prior research focuses on (1) the extent to which students in middle-class and white schools will conform more to achievement norms and orient more to college; (2) on the extent to which students in lower class and minority schools will become more involved in deviant behavior; and (3) on the type of comparison processes that will occur among children who rank either higher or lower in ability, social class, and minority status when proportions in the school change (see Eccles, 1984; Rosenberg and Simmons, 1972).

We do not have information as to the socioeconomic heterogeneity in the various schools, but we do have information as to their relative ethnic heterogeneity, and we can compare changes in these white children's self-image in more and less heterogeneous schools.

In sum, we hypothesize that the child will find it more difficult to adjust to junior high school if the school is less intimate, if it is very large, ethnically heterogeneous, and if the student moves alone from class to class with constant changes of classmates. In such situations children will probably feel more anonymous, and their self-image should be challenged. This analysis will focus only on junior high school students. It would be highly desirable to be able to test whether differences between K–8 and junior high school students would disappear if size, heterogeneity, and departmentalization were all held constant. However, since each of the K–8 schools are smaller and involve less movement among classes than any of the junior high schools, it is impossible to make this test in this study.[4] As a result, in looking at the impact of these school characteristics, we are dealing with somewhat restricted ranges. In particular, the investigation of the impact of size compares junior high schools that range from 808 to 1590 students.

Individual Resources

Perhaps more important than the effect of the characteristics of the junior high school upon the children's adjustment is the effect of their own prior characteristics. A major purpose of this analysis is to identify those factors present in Grade 6 that help to predict higher self-esteem in Grade 7 and that affect other important outcome variables in junior high school. We predict that success in key areas in the elementary school years will act as a resource for the children and help them to maintain a higher level of self-esteem after the transition. For example, we predict that children who have had success with significant others (particularly peers) and who have done well in terms of physical attributes (looks, athletic ability) and academic achievement will react more favorably to the transition. Higher social class status and a high initial self-esteem might also act as resources.

In addition, since adolescence brings with it new rules of appropriate behavior, those youngsters who have already begun approximating such behavior might be expected to find the transition into junior high school less challenging for the self-picture. In particular, children who have already attained independence might fare better. Similarly, one might have expected that early pubertal developers and youngsters who are already popular with the opposite sex would find the change easier. However, we have just shown that while early pubertal development is favorable for boys by itself, it has mixed effects for girls and negative effects for both genders when it is combined with early dating and with school and other life changes (Chapters 5, 6, and 11). It is possible that instead of acting as a positive resource, early assumption of adolescent behavior and appearance may be premature. Many children may not be developmentally ready in Grade 6 for such a change. In any case, along with other potential resources, we shall investigate the effects of pubertal development, independence, and opposite-sex popularity.

In sum, then, the aim of the following analysis will be to help understand how certain school properties and potential resource variables, including timing of pubertal development, affect students' reaction to junior high school, first in terms of their self-esteem.

Analysis Plan

In order to understand the factors that help and hinder students in their transition to junior high school, we will undertake the estimation of a complex structural model that incorporates three types of variables: (1) resources that students had in sixth grade that might affect how they coped with the transition to seventh grade in the junior high school; (2) characteristics of the junior high school that might affect adjustment to the junior high school environment; and (3) a set of key outcome variables in Grade 7 (e.g., GPA, participation in school activities, and self-esteem), the most important of which is self-esteem. Sixth grade measures of these last variables are included as controls.

A LISREL VI (Linear Structural Relationships) analysis is used (Jöreskog and Sörbom, 1981, 1983; Kessler and Greenberg, 1981). The major virtues of LISREL for this analysis are: (1) it can allow one to examine and test many causal relationships simultaneously; (2) it can correct for measurement problems (for unreliability in the case of variables measured with multiple indicators and for correlated error when the same multiindicator variable is measured more than once over time).

In addition, LISREL allows the researcher to estimate the degree to which the hypothesized theoretical model[5] fits the information originally available from correlations among indicators.[6]

Construction and estimation of the causal model took place in three major steps: (1) selection of variables; (2) estimation of measurement models; and (3) estimation of the complete structural model. For a more detailed examination of these issues see Simmons *et al.* (in press b).

Selection of Variables

The major outcome variable for this analysis is global self-esteem measured in Grade 7 after the junior high school transition. Other dependent variables are those key behaviors shown to be affected by school type in prior chapters: GPA, participation in extracurricular school activities, and victimization.[7]

As already noted, we expected that certain seventh grade school structure variables would affect these dependent variables—(1) size of the junior high school; (2) movement from class to class in the school as a self-contained group rather than as isolated individuals; and (3) heterogeneity as indexed by proportion of ethnic minority students (the range is .9–48.9%).[8] Our choice of these Grade 7 school structure variables was dictated by theory and limited by data available from the school system. The general hypothesis was that adjustment would be higher in a smaller, more homogeneous, intimate environment.

Individual level resource variables were selected in a stepwise process. Before embarking on the LISREL analyses, we identified many Grade 6 factors that could be expected to act as resources in aiding the child to make the junior high school transition. In order to be included in the model, these variables had to show a significant (bivariate) correlation in either direction with the overall self-esteem scale[9] for at least one of the genders. The Grade 6 variables that survived this screening involved physical resources (perceived athletic ability, perceived good looks), perceived success with peers (high regard by peers, opposite-sex popularity), academic success (perceived teacher regard) and independence from parental supervision and chaperonage.[10]

To these variables we added a few others, either because they were central to this book (level of pubertal timing), because it seemed necessary to control for them (social class background), because their Grade 7 counterparts were key dependent variables (Grade 6 GPA and participation in activities),[11] or because the first LISREL runs yielded puzzling findings that suggested their addition (school problem behavior). All resource variables and dependent variables that were measured in both Grades 6 and 7 were, at first, included in the model at both time points. Then, if initial runs of the causal model yielded no significant causal paths to or from a Grade 7 variable, it was dropped from the model (Grade 7 independence and teacher evaluation).[12] For girls, opposite-sex popularity in Grade 7 was also dropped from the model due to technical difficulties (i.e., multicollinearity with Grade 6 opposite-sex popularity).

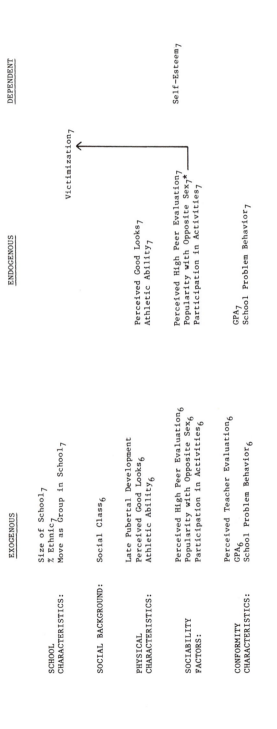

FIGURE 12.1. **Model: School factors and resource variables impacting on self-esteem.** (The subscript refers to the grade at school. For example, Perceived Good Looks$_7$ refers to perception of looks measured in Grade 7.) (The asterisk indicates dropped from the model for girls due to multicollinearity.)

312

The variables included in the final model can be seen in Figure 12.1.

Measures

Details about the measures for all variables are listed in Appendix G. However, the meaning of a few of the variables should be mentioned here also. A high peer regard indicates that schoolmates in one's class think of one as a "wonderful" or "pretty nice" person. Victimization is measured by self-reports of:

1. Being threatened with physical violence while having money stolen at school
2. Having something more than $1.00 in value stolen from one at school
3. Being "beaten up" at school

For two key variables, we were able to construct multi-item measurement models and thereby to correct for measurement problems (unreliability and correlated error over time). These two variables are self-esteem and opposite-sex relations[13] (see Appendix E[14]).

Structural Model

As can be seen in Figure 12.1, the Grade 6 resource variables and the Grade 7 school structure variables are treated as independent, or more properly, "exogenous" variables. Most of the Grade 7 individual-level variables are treated as intervening variables in a causal chain, with self-esteem in Grade 7 the ultimate dependent variable.

In testing the model we estimated the effects of all exogenous variables upon all intervening variables. We also estimated effects of exogenous and intervening ("endogenous") variables upon the dependent variable of self-esteem. However, where we had both Grade 6 and Grade 7 measures for a variable, we estimated only the effect of the Grade 7 variable on self-esteem. We postulated that a Grade 6 resource variable first affected its Grade 7 counterpart which then impacted on Grade 7 self-esteem. For example, we predicted that perceiving oneself as good-looking in Grade 6 leads one to perceive oneself as good-looking in Grade 7, and that this contemporaneous positive self-perception is what enhances one's self-esteem in Grade 7.

There is, of course, a possibility that some of the causal ordering is the reverse of our hypotheses, and that Grade 7 self-esteem causes changes in the intervening ("endogenous") variables. This problem is discussed later. One should note, however, that the major purpose of this analysis is to see whether knowledge of a child's value on a Grade 6 variable enables us to predict adjustment to the junior high transition. The effects of Grade 6 self-esteem on the Grade 7 endogenous variables are also reported.

For the most part, causal paths among the intervening, endogenous variables are not estimated.[15] There is one exception as noted in Figure 12.1: A causal path was estimated between participation in Grade 7 extracurricular activities and Grade 7 victimization at school. (Subscripts attached to the variables refer to the year in which the variable is measured.) It was hypothesized that children who remained after school for activities would be more likely to be in a situation to be victimized. (The questions ask only about victimization on school property.)[16]

In general, our statistical tests are two-tail tests. However, in order to avoid Type 2 error in this exploratory search for resource variables, we also show the reader which results are of borderline significance using a one-tail test, provided the direction of the relationship was hypothesized ahead of time.

The Adequacy of the Causal Models

Before turning to our findings, we have to answer a technical question about the adequacy of our models to represent the data. In fact, tests indicate that the causal model as estimated by LISREL fit the data fairly well.[17]

In addition, the proportion of variance explained in the Grade 7 variables appears substantial (see Appendix F, Tables F.1 and F.2). For self-esteem we have explained 77% of the variance that we would like to explain. Since many sociologists are pleased by explaining even 10% of the variance, these results are encouraging. In all cases, except for opposite-sex popularity, the proportion of variance explained by all the variables together is quite a bit higher than that explained simply by the Grade 6 version of the same variables alone. For example, Grade 6 self-esteem explains about 50% of the variance in Grade 7 self-esteem by itself; but we have increased this proportion to 77% by adding the other variables in the model (see Simmons *et al.,* in press b, for more details).

Impact of Factors on Grade 7 Self-Esteem

Structural models were estimated separately for males and females. In some cases, the variables function differently for the two genders. In the following discussion, which is organized in terms of the conceptual categories outlined earlier, we will highlight both the similarities and differences between the findings for females and males.

In order to facilitate the report for the reader, portions of the structural model will be presented along with the discussion of each conceptual category (Figures 12.2–12.7). The reader should keep in mind, however, that the relationships depicted in these submodels were estimated with all other variables in the model controlled. (See Appendix F, Figures F.1 and F.2

for a depiction of the significant paths in the full models; for all stand-ardized and unstandardized coefficients and significance levels, see Appendix F, Tables F.1 and F.2.)

The submodels (Figures 12.2–12.7) have been abstracted from the larger model in order to focus on the process by which sixth grade individual characteristics and seventh grade school characteristics are translated into increments or decrements in self-esteem. Only statistically significant findings are depicted. Both the direct and more indirect effects upon self-esteem will be discussed.

Impact of Grade 6 Self-Esteem

For both genders, as would be expected, the most powerful predictor of Grade 7 self-esteem is Grade 6 self-esteem (with a standardized coefficient of .656 for males and .601 for females, $p < .01$). The causal ordering between self-esteem and the other variables in the model will be discussed more fully below. At this point, our attention is focused on the effect of all other variables upon Grade 7 self-esteem, holding Grade 6 self-esteem constant. That is, above and beyond the student's self-esteem prior to the transition, what is the effect of the other variables?

Impact of School Structure Characteristics

Effects for Both Genders

We predicted that a less intimate school environment would have negative effects. In terms of school structure, the size of school has the predicted direct effect on Grade 7 self-esteem for both males and females, although the significance level is borderline for girls[18] (see Figure 12.2). The larger the school, the lower the self-esteem of the student. Ethnic heterogeneity in the school has a similar negative effect. Both genders are more likely to be victimized in schools with higher proportions of ethnic students, and for this reason their self-esteem is negatively affected.

Gender Specific

We have already noted that a large school has a detrimental direct effect on self-esteem. However, the story is more complicated than that for boys, where there is an interesting contrasting effect of large size. In a larger school there is some evidence that a boy can find someone who will evaluate him more highly. The larger the school, the more highly he feels evaluated by peers and, therefore, the higher his self-esteem. However, calculations indicate that the negative direct effect of the large-sized school outweighs the positive indirect effect.[19] There is no such indirect link between school size and self-esteem for girls.

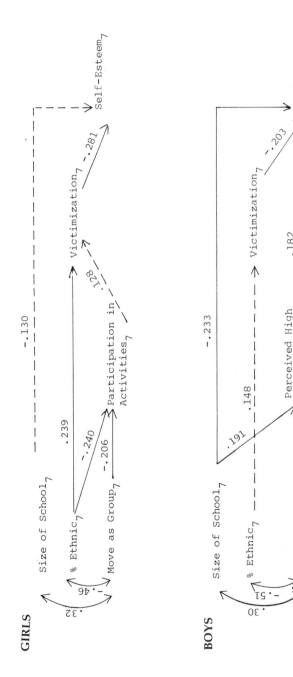

FIGURE 12.2. Significant effects of school characteristics on self-esteem: standardized coefficients. Within the diagram for one gender, LISREL estimates of standardized coefficients along the same causal route can be multiplied with one another in order to determine the strength of that route compared to other routes. The unstandardized coefficients would need to be used in making comparisons between boys and girls (see Appendix F, Tables 1 and 2). Dotted lines in all diagrams represent tests of borderline significance— one-tail tests ($p < .10$) where the direction was predicted ahead of time. Curved arrows indicate a correlation rather than a standardized coefficient that estimates effect.

We noted the negative link between a high ethnic proportion in the school and Grade 7 self-esteem for both genders. In addition, for girls, there is another indirect linkage that partly counteracts the negative effect. In schools with higher proportions of ethnic children, girls participate less in extracurricular activities. And girls who participate in fewer extracurricular activities in Grade 7 are, as predicted, somewhat less likely to be victimized in school, presumably because they do not remain after school for longer hours. Through this linkage, their self-esteem is protected. However, the participation–victimization link is of borderline significance, and the negative effect of a high ethnic proportion outweighs this protective effect.[20]

We predicted that movement from classroom to classroom in a group rather than as isolated individuals would be beneficial. In fact, group movement has positive, indirect links to self-esteem. However, these linkages represent accidental side effects of less positive processes. For girls, those who move in a group during the day participate less in extracurricular activities than those who have to move as individuals, perhaps because students moving as individuals have greater need to join activities than those encased in a familiar classroom group. In any case, the lower participation of girls who move in a group leads to less victimization and, thus, to higher self-esteem.

For boys, also, there is an indirect positive linkage between group movement and high self-esteem that is produced accidentally via negative effects of group movement. Moving in a group lowers boys' GPA in Grade 7; interestingly, individualized schedules are more beneficial for GPA. Because there is a puzzling negative relationship between Grade 7 GPA and self-esteem, the net indirect impact of group movement on self-esteem is positive. This puzzling relationship between GPA and self-esteem will be discussed later.

In sum, we predicted that less intimate, more heterogeneous environments would contribute to a more difficult adjustment to the junior high school transition. As predicted, large and ethnically heterogeneous schools have somewhat negative effects upon Grade 7 self-esteem. However, movement as an individual from classroom to classroom has complicated effects, rather than the simple negative impact upon self-esteem that was predicted.

Effects of Background Characteristics

Gender Specific

Throughout much of this book we have added social class as a control variable. We have shown that almost all important effects—whether they be of age, pubertal timing, school type, or cumulative change—persist when social class is controlled. However, here we wish to investigate the effect of class itself. One might expect that a higher social class background would act as a resource for the child and make it easier to cope with the junior high school transition. As can be seen in Figure 12.3, the effects of social class are quite different for the two sexes. For boys, this expectation is borne out. For boys a high social class has a solely positive effect, through an interesting causal route. Boys from a higher social class background are more likely to be well regarded by peers in Grade 7 and therefore to show higher self-esteem. For girls findings are more complex. On the one hand, there is a small indirect linkage favoring higher class girls. Girls from a higher social class are less likely to be involved in problem behavior in Grade 7, and thereby they improve their self-esteem. However, for some unexplained reason the direct relationship between social class and girls' Grade 7 self-esteem is negative, with girls of lower class status favored with high self-esteem. High social class is thus not a clear resource for girls at this age.

It is interesting that high class status is a clear resource for boys but not girls in early adolescence. Traditionally, social class has mattered more for the male in our society. In later adolescence a higher income has been beneficial to dating success when the boy is expected to pay for expenses; in adulthood social class has been a sign of male success in the key occupational role. It is interesting to find that early adolescent boys and girls differ in regard to the effect of social class status in the mid- to late 1970s.

Effects of Physical Characteristics

Effects for Both Genders

Good looks are an important resource for both genders. Children of either gender who rate themselves favorably on looks in Grade 6 perceive themselves as more highly evaluated by peers in Grade 7 and, therefore, have higher self-esteem (Figure 12.4).

Gender Specific

In addition to the common indirect pathway mentioned earlier, there are a series of other indirect ways in which good looks enhance Grade 7 self-esteem. These pathways are a bit different for males and females and are depicted in Figure 12.4. It should be noted that good-looking girls (Grade 6) are less likely to be victimized in Grade 7, and this association is protective of self-esteem. Also of interest is the fact that there is no indication of a causal relationship in the reverse direction for either gender—Grade 6 self-esteem is not related to Grade 7 perceived looks.

The effects of other physical characteristics—perceived athletic ability and timing of pubertal development on self-esteem—are indirect rather

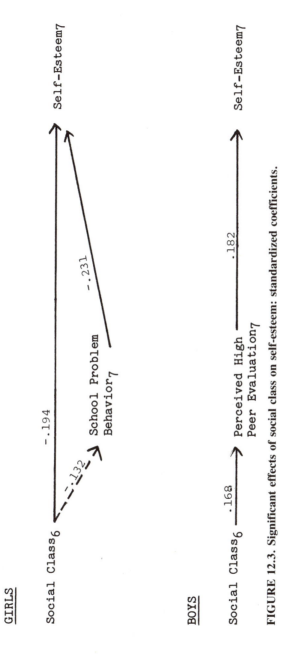

FIGURE 12.3. Significant effects of social class on self-esteem: standardized coefficients.

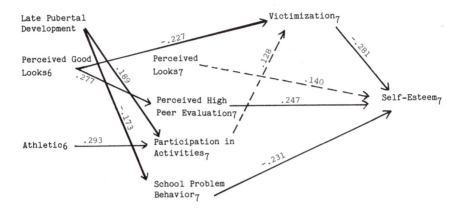

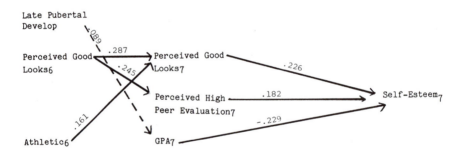

FIGURE 12.4. Significant effects of physical characteristics on self-esteem: standardized coefficients.

than direct and also somewhat different for the genders. The effect of perceived athletic ability in sixth grade for girls has a circuitous, weak negative effect on Grade 7 self-esteem. Athletic girls participate more in activities in Grade 7, and therefore (presumably because they stay after school more) they are more victimized, with resultant detriment to self-esteem. For boys, however, the effect was positive, via an indirect route through enhanced looks to self-esteem. Athletic boys are undoubtedly more muscular and therefore more likely to perceive themselves as good-looking, thus enhancing self-esteem.

While timing of pubertal development does not directly impact on self-esteem, late developers react in ways that have indirect effects on self-esteem in Grade 7. For boys, late developers have slightly higher Grade 7 GPAs than early developers, and because of the puzzling negative relationship between Grade 7 GPA and self-esteem, late development is negatively related to self-esteem. For girls, there are two contrasting effects. The larger relationship is the positive one[21]—late developers are less likely to be involved in problem behavior (as noted in Chapter 5) and therefore their self-esteem is protected. At the same time, however, late developers are more involved in after-school activities, and therefore, more likely to be victimized. And, as we have seen before, victimization hurts self-esteem.

In summary, physical characteristics of the children do affect Grade 7 self-esteem. Good looks are an important positive resource for both boys and girls. Athletic skill in Grade 6 is a positive resource for boys, but not girls. The effects of pubertal timing are indirect, complex, and relatively weak.

Effects of Peer Relations

Effects for Both Genders

Another key variable apparently affecting Grade 7 self-esteem for both genders is peer evaluation, the extent to which they perceive that other students in their class evaluate them highly (Figure 12.5). For girls, a high perceived peer evaluation in Grade 6 predicts a high evaluation in Grade 7, which in turn is associated with high seventh grade self-esteem. For boys, the association between perceived peer rating and global self-esteem is confined to Grade 7.

Gender Specific

The importance of peers is illustrated in another way. As noted earlier, victimization by other students is disadvantageous for the self-esteem of both genders. With Grade 6 self-esteem held constant, youngsters who have been victimized in their new schools in Grade 7 end up with lower self-esteem. Furthermore, for boys, students who perceive themselves more highly regarded by peers in Grade 6 are less likely to be victimized in Grade 7 and thus, by another route, their self-esteem is protected.

In addition to the general effects of peer relations, girls who perceive themselves to be popular with the opposite sex in Grade 6 are more likely to perceive themselves as good-looking in Grade 7, and this process aids self-esteem. For boys, opposite-sex popularity in Grade 6 affects the degree to which they feel that peers in general evaluate them highly in Grade 7 (a finding of borderline significance), and hence, opposite-sex popularity has some positive effect on self-esteem.

However, the situation in regard to opposite-sex popularity is actually

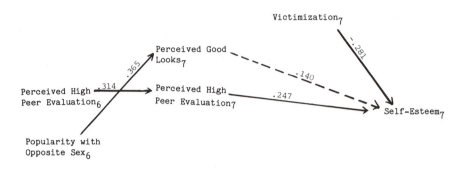

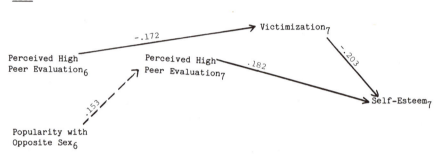

FIGURE 12.5. Significant effects of peer relations on self-esteem: standardized coefficients.

more complex than this. Opposite-sex popularity in Grade 6 is correlated with problem behavior in Grade 6 (for girls: .48, $p < .01$; for boys: .32, $p < .01$).[22] And, as we shall see later in this chapter, a history of problem behavior in Grade 6 appears to have negative causal effects on Grade 7 self-esteem for both genders. (This entire issue will be discussed more extensively in Chapter 13.)

Perceived peer evaluation and school victimization are two aspects of peer relationships; the extent to which the student participates in organized peer activities in and after school is another. Does extracurricular participation in Grade 6 prior to the transition predict the adjustment to the junior high transition? In fact, the effect of Grade 6 participation in extracurricular activities is quite different for girls than for boys (Figure 12.6). For girls there are two weak paths, one of which has a positive effect and one which has a negative effect. The positive effect is a result of the statistically marginal role that a history of participation in school extracurricular activities plays in reducing problem behavior (Grade 7)

GIRLS

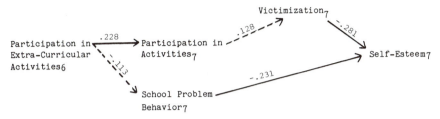

FIGURE 12.6. Significant effects of participation in extracurricular activities on self-esteem: standardized coefficients.

and, thereby, in enhancing self-esteem. The negative effect (which is weaker) takes the following route by now familiar to the reader: Grade 6 participation in extracurricular activities predicts Grade 7 participation; girls who stay after school in Grade 7 to participate in activities are more likely to be victimized, and for this reason their self-esteem is hurt.

For boys the process is much simpler. Boys who participate in school activities more in Grade 6 tend to have high GPAs in Grade 7. Because of the puzzling negative impact of Grade 7 GPA on self-esteem in Grade 7, the overall relationship is negative.

In summary, positive peer relations have a generally positive effect on Grade 7 self-esteem. A perceived high peer regard, perceived opposite-sex popularity, and low victimization by peers helps the students maintain high self-esteem in this transition year. Membership in organized peer activities has a more complex effect.

Conformity Characteristics and Independence

Effects for Both Genders

We predicted that a history of problem behavior would make the transition to junior high school more difficult; and this prediction was confirmed. For both genders school problem behavior in Grade 6 negatively affects self-esteem in Grade 7. On the other hand, we predicted that being allowed early independence in Grade 6 prior to the transition would aid with the transition to junior high school where older and more independent behavior was likely to be expected. In fact, however, being allowed early independence has negative results for both genders.

For both males and females, a greater tendency to be victimized is implicated in the causal process linking both school problem behavior and early independence to self-esteem (Figure 12.7). However, the causal routings are slightly different for boys and girls.

Gender Specific

Among girls, those who exhibit problem behavior in Grade 6 also reveal problem behavior in Grade 7 and therefore hold lower self-esteem. Furthermore, girls who are allowed early parental independence do not appear

GIRLS

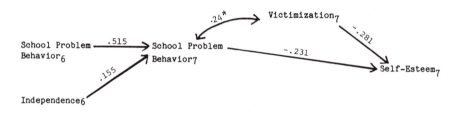

BOYS

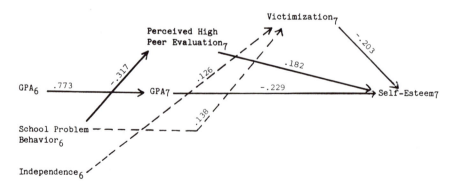

FIGURE 12.7. **Significant effects of conformity characteristics and independence upon self-esteem: standardized coefficients.** *Correlations between Grade 7 endogenous variables, represented by curved arrows, are estimated in the Psi Matrix (see Footnote 15).

to utilize this independence as a resource for high self-esteem. Instead, such girls are more likely to become involved in problem behavior in Grade 7 and, thereby, end up with lower self-esteem. Also, girls who show problem behavior in Grade 7 are the same ones who are more likely to be victimized; through this correlation,[23] then, problem behavior is again linked to low self-esteem.

The boys who are involved in problem behavior in Grade 6 are also more likely to be victimized, as are the boys allowed early independence by parents. For boys, problem behavior and early independence through this indirect linkage with victimization impact negatively on self-esteem in Grade 7 (although significance is borderline). Boys who show problem behavior in Grade 6 also are less highly evaluated by Grade 7 peers, and this fact also appears to hurt their self-esteem. Thus, youngsters who are the perpetrators of more deviant behavior are more likely to be its victims as well. Furthermore, as one might predict, children who are allowed early independence and freedom from supervision are more likely subsequently to become involved in trouble, either as agents or as victims. (See Chapter 13 for more discussion.) While the causal routings are slightly different for boys and girls, a negative impact on Grade 7 self-esteem appears to be the result.

There is one other gender specific result involving academic conformity. For females, GPA does not play an important role in affecting self-esteem; none of the paths for GPA are statistically significant. For males, on the other hand, GPA in Grade 6 is positively related to GPA in Grade 7 and, as indicated earlier, there is a puzzling negative relationship between Grade 7 GPA and self-esteem once the Grade 6 values are held constant.[24] Thus, in terms of self-esteem, a high GPA in Grade 6 does not act as a positive resource for either gender as children make the transition into junior high school.

In summary, being involved in school problem behavior and being allowed early independence from chaperonage from parents have negative effects on the self-esteem of both genders through indirect or direct routes. On the other hand, academic conformity, as indexed by a high GPA, does not act as a positive resource for either gender.

Evaluation by Teachers

While the perception that teachers rated one highly in Grade 6 does not have a direct or indirect causal impact on Grade 7 self-esteem, it does correlate with other Grade 6 factors that do act as resources for the child. (See Appendix F, Table F.3 for the correlations among Grade 6 variables.) Both boys and girls who perceive themselves as highly evaluated by teachers in Grade 6 are in an advantageous position in that grade. They are more likely to also rate themselves as good-looking in Grade 6 and as highly evaluated by peers, and they are less likely to be involved in problem behavior. All of these factors are ones that enhance Grade 7 self-esteem after the junior high school transition.[25]

Summary

There are several qualities that can be regarded as positive resources for the youth making the transition into junior high school. The key individual-level variables linked causally (either directly or indirectly) with high self-esteem in Grade 7, once all other variables are controlled, are the following: high self-esteem in Grade 6, perceived good looks in Grades 6 and 7, high perceived peer evaluations in Grades 6 and 7, absence of victimization in Grade 7, and absence of school behavior problems in Grade 6. For boys, but not girls, a high social class status and perceived athletic ability also have solely positive causal links to self-esteem. In addition, a high perceived teacher's evaluation in Grade 6, while not causally linked to high Grade 7 self-esteem, is correlated with variables that are positively linked for both boys and girls.

However, there are some potential resource variables that turn out to have negative effects on self-esteem or to be negatively associated with variables that enhance self-esteem. For both genders, early independence from parental chaperonage (Grade 6) has negative effects on self-esteem. For girls, athletic ability is involved in a negative causal chain, while the effects and correlations of social class, extracurricular participation, and opposite-sex popularity are mixed. In the case of girls, early pubertal development also has mixed effects. There is an interesting causal linkage of early puberty to higher problem behavior and thereby to lower self-esteem.[26] For boys the effects of GPA are complex, a point to be discussed further in the next chapter. And, for neither gender does Grade 6 or 7 GPA have consequences beneficial for Grade 7 self-esteem, once Grade 6 self-esteem is controlled.

In addition to individual-level resource variables, we have looked at the effects of environmental context. The structural properties of schools included in the model do show significant linkages to self-esteem. We predicted that self-esteem would suffer in a less intimate environmental context; that self-esteem would be lower in larger and more ethnically heterogeneous schools and among students who moved as individuals from classroom to classroom rather than in a self-contained group. The effects of size are somewhat complex. As predicted, larger size has a direct negative effect on the self-esteem of both boys and girls. However, in addition, in a larger school boys appear more able to locate peers who will evaluate them highly, and through this route enhance their self-esteem. The negative effect of size, however, outweighs the positive one.

Ethnic heterogeneity is associated with higher levels of victimization and is thereby detrimental for self-esteem, as predicted (see Chapter 13 for more discussion). Movement between classes as individuals, rather than in a group, does have negative indirect effects, but these linkages appear to represent accidental side effects. In fact, there are positive impacts of individual movement on variables other than self-esteem (e.g., GPA for boys, extracurricular participation for girls). It should be noted that larger and more ethnically heterogeneous junior high schools are the ones that generally move the children in groups from class to class.

Thus, while there is some evidence that the less intimate environment has negative consequences for self-esteem, the findings show some complexity as well.

A final point—the models presented are based on the view that: (1) self-perceived and actual success in specific areas in Grade 6 translate into success in the same areas in Grade 7; and (2) that above and beyond initial Grade 6 self-esteem, success in Grade 7 in these specific areas has a positive effect on Grade 7 self-esteem. It is also possible, however, that a generally high self-esteem affects actual and perceived success in specific areas. The models as presented allow us to look at the impact of Grade 6 self-esteem on the key variables in Grade 7, although they do not investigate reciprocal effects in Grade 7 (see Appendix F, Figures F.1 and F.2; Tables F.1 and F.2).[27]

These models clearly represent only a first step in delineating the many factors involved in the development of self-esteem during a transitional time period. We do believe, however, that they help one to gain a better understanding of the complexity of the process. The next chapter will examine the relationships that involve the outcome variables other than self-esteem.

Footnotes

[1]Also see Schmeideck (1979).

[2]Also see Morgan and Alwin (1980), Lindsay (1982, 1984), and Garbarino (1973).

[3]Also see Willems (1967), Schoo (1970), and Stemnock (1974).

[4]The largest K-8 school has 694 students and the smallest junior high has 808 students. There is more overlap in ethnic heterogeneity between K-8 and junior high schools. It also should be noted that there is only a slight increase in ethnic heterogeneity in our sample from K-6 elementary schools to junior highs.

[5]This model includes hypothesized factor structures, relationships among conceptual variables, and relationships among errors of measurement.

[6]There are of course a set of statistical assumptions about the measurement properties of the indicators. Indicators are assumed to be measured at the interval level. In addition, the distribution of these variables is assumed to be multivariate normal; the effects of violating these assumptions are not well understood.

For the analyses in this chapter and the next we have used Pearson correlation estimates of the relationships among our indicators, as well as standard deviations as input to the LISREL program. These inputs have been analyzed as a variance–covariance matrix, rather than as a correlation matrix.

[7]In Chapter 7 we show that perceived anonymity was also significantly impacted

by school type (also see Blyth *et al.*, 1983). However, this variable was not measured on the full sample, and, thus, to avoid case loss it is not included here.

[8]Neither social class heterogeneity nor heterogeneity in GPA in Grade 7 was available from the school system. Since the basis of our random sampling was the sixth (rather than the seventh grade) schools, we could not utilize our sample to derive estimates of these variables.

[9]For this screening analysis, the aggregated Rosenberg–Simmons self-esteem scale was used (see Appendix G). However, in the LISREL causal analysis itself, the scale was disaggregated to correct for reliability, as described in Appendix E and in Simmons *et al.* (in press b).

[10]It should be noted that perceived maternal evaluation did not survive this screening test.

[11]Victimization was measured only in Grade 7.

[12]As can be seen in Figure 12.1, this is a very large model, and the ability to run it seemed dependent on some paring.

[13]For other variables either we had only one relevant item or an adequate measurement model could not be constructed. In the case of problem behavior and victimization, the issue is whether the child had been involved in any behavior of this type. We did not expect high correlations among the various alternate problem behaviors or types of victimization.

[14]Each of these measurement models was first estimated separately for males and females with the measurement models free to vary across time. Then the models were estimated simultaneously for males and females, with the factor coefficients constrained to be equal at Time 1 and Time 2 and equal for males and females. For both self-esteem and opposite-sex popularity, comparisons indicated that the constrained models were not statistically significantly different from the unconstrained models. Therefore, the measurement models for males and females across the two time points can be treated as equal.

[15]Rather, the Psi matrix from the LISREL analyses estimates correlations among endogenous variables once the variance explained by hypothesized paths between exogenous and endogenous variables has been removed. Because of the estimation procedures used, the Zeta's (elements of the Psi matrix) are analogous but not identical to partial correlations.

[16]For other details about the model estimation, see Simmons *et al.* (in press b).

[17]In testing for the adequacy of a model, one does not wish to see statistically significant differences. And in fact, the goodness-of-fit tests indicate that the difference between this model and the data in the original variance–covariance matrix is not statistically significant. For boys $X^2 = 613.05$ with 587 degrees of freedom ($p = .22$) and for girls, $X^2 = 501.07$ with 465 degrees of freedom ($p = .12$). In general, the goodness-of-fit appears adequate (also see Simmons *et al.*, in press b). One caveat however: Hoelter (1983) has noted that the use of Chi-square fit statistics can be somewhat misleading, the smaller the sample size.

[18]It shows up only on a one-tail test at the .10 level. We looked only at such one-tail tests where we had a definite hypothesis about the direction of the relationship.

[19]To determine which route is more powerful, the standardized path coefficients along the same causal route can be multiplied and then compared to similar calculations for the other route. In this case, as diagrammed in Figure 12.2: $-.233$ (the direct effect) is stronger than the indirect effect of $(.191)(.182)$ or $.035$. Note that these coefficients are maximum likelihood estimates.

[20]Figure 12.2: $(.239)(-.281)$ or $-.067$ outweighs $(-.240)(.128)(-.281)$ or $.009$.

[21]Figure 12.4: $(-.173)(-.231) = .04$, while $(.189)(.128)(-.281) = -.007$.

[22]See Appendix F, Table F.3. These correlations are based on LISREL estimates since a measurement model is involved.

[23]This significant correlation ($p < .10$) between Grade 7 endogenous variables comes from the Psi Matrix. See Footnote 15.

[24]It should be noted that prior studies of the relationship between GPA and self-esteem in high school and college show a correlation. However the direction or even the presence of a causal connection has been debated. (See Bohrnstedt and Felson, 1981; Maruyama, Rubin and Kingsbury, 1981; Maruyama, Finch, and Mortimer, in press; Faunce, 1984). In our data there is not a significant correlation between Grade 6 GPA and self-esteem for either gender (see Appendix F, Table F.3). For boys only, as mentioned later, those with high Grade 6 self-esteem are significantly more likely to show a positive effect on GPA in Grade 7 (see Appendix F, Figure F.2, Table F.2).

[25]The inverse relationship shown in Appendix F, Table F.3 between social class and teacher evaluation for girls also works to benefit self-esteem due to the unexplained negative effect of social class on self-esteem.

[26]See Zakin, Blyth and Simmons (1984) for an analysis of the effect on self-esteem of the interaction of physical attractiveness and pubertal development.

[27]In terms of the effect of Grade 6 self-esteem on Grade 7 variables (controlling for the Grade 6 level of these variables), we found the following: for boys, those with high Grade 6 self-esteem are, in Grade 7, more likely to earn high GPAs, more likely to rate themselves as highly evaluated by peers, and less likely to be victimized (the statistical significances for the last two findings are borderline); for girls, those with high initial self-esteem in Grade 6 are less likely to score high in problem behavior in Grade 7 (borderline significance). There is a puzzling finding as well: girls with high Grade 6 self-esteem are less likely to regard peers as evaluating them highly in Grade 7 (holding the Grade 6 evaluation constant). The positive association between a high peer evaluation in Grade 7 and high self-esteem in Grade 7 is evident, despite these last findings.

13

ADJUSTMENT TO THE JUNIOR HIGH SCHOOL TRANSITION: OTHER INTERRELATIONSHIPS*

In the previous chapter, we described the factors that appear to impact on self-esteem for the junior high school students. But self-esteem is only one of the outcomes in early adolescence. We now turn to relationships among the other variables in the model that we estimated (Appendix F, Tables F.1 and F.2) in order to further examine the way in which adjustment to the junior high school transition is eased or impeded.

Utilizing the same model described in Chapter 12, we shall discuss the other statistically significant interrelationships. First, the effects of Grade 7 school characteristics and social class upon outcome variables other than self-esteem will be described; then we shall examine relationships involving the child's physical characteristics, peer relations, academic performance, independence, and problem behavior.

Since in many cases we have not predicted direction of causality among the variables, we shall examine correlates as well as causal effects in discussing relationships; and we shall discuss correlations among these variables both in Grades 6 and 7. In order to facilitate the substantive focus of this chapter, we shall not refer extensively to particular statistical analyses. The needed tables can be found in Appendix F.[1] Numbers reported in the text refer to statistically significant standardized coefficients derived from the full model unless otherwise noted. A full set of significant standardized and unstandardized coefficients and their levels of significance can be found in Appendix F, Tables F.1 and F.2.

Effects of School Structure

It was predicted that in a less intimate, more impersonal junior high school, students would have more difficulty adjusting to the transition. We have shown in Chapter 12 that the measured school properties had mixed effects on self-esteem. Overall, a large school was somewhat det-

*By Roberta G. Simmons, Steven L. Carlton-Ford, and Dale A. Blyth.

rimental for self-esteem. In one respect however, it was beneficial for boys: in a large school, boys were more likely to perceive themselves highly evaluated by peers. Large schools also have positive effects on some other variables. In large schools girls are somewhat more likely to earn higher GPAs (.145) and boys to report less problem behavior ($-.154$) than in smaller schools.

Ethnic diversity had primarily negative effects in the self-esteem analysis. In that analysis we also noted that in schools with a higher proportion of minority students, victimization of students worsened (although for boys, the significance level was borderline). In addition, we find that the participation of both boys ($-.211$) and girls ($-.240$) in extracurricular activities is less in such schools, and that white boys in an ethnically diverse school see themselves as less athletic ($-.184$). Because our sample for this analysis is all white, we did not determine the impact of ethnic diversity on nonwhite students.

An aside is relevant here. We wish to note that our measure—percentage ethnic—is an aggregate measure that applies to schools and provides no information about who victimizes whom. The relationships here are complex (see Blyth *et al.*, 1980), and clearly more research is needed in this area as our society moves toward more integrated school systems. In our view, if there are problems in the process of integration, the issue is not whether to integrate, but rather how to structure integrated schools so that they meet the mental health and intimacy needs of all children, provide them with equal opportunities to succeed, and present them with the chance to appreciate diversity.

In addition to school size and ethnic diversity, pattern of movement around the school was expected to affect adjustment. It was predicted that movement around the school in a group rather than as isolated individuals would be protective and beneficial. As noted in Chapter 12 there are some negative, rather than positive, effects of group movement on variables other than self-esteem. In fact, boys earn lower GPAs in these schools compared to schools with individualized class movement ($-.181$). Individually tailored schedules allow the boy to earn higher grades. In addition, girls who move in a group rather than as individuals are less likely to participate in extracurricular activities ($-.206$); that is, girls who move alone are more likely to join extracurricular activities. We suggested that this positive effect of individualized movement may be due to a greater need to find a small, intimate group with which to identify. The girl who stays with the same classmates all day may not need to join extra activities to find a group of friends.

In summary, the effects of large size and group movement are mixed in direction, although ethnic diversity shows negative impacts on the variables measured here.[2]

Effect of Social Class

We predicted that a higher social class background would serve as a resource to aid youngsters in their adjustment to junior high school. In fact, in terms of self-esteem, a higher social class origin was beneficial for Grade 7 boys (due to a higher peer evaluation), but for girls the effects of social class were mixed. Additional analysis indicates that boys from higher social class backgrounds not only see themselves as more highly evaluated by seventh grade peers in general (.168), but also as more popular with the opposite sex in particular (.138). Traditionally, as noted earlier, the male in our society with more financial resources has been better able to attract females; it is interesting that this phenomenon is evident as early as Grade 7 for this cohort. There are some additional advantages of high social class status for girls as well. Girls from higher class backgrounds are more likely to earn high GPAs in Grade 7 (.105) as well as to be less involved in problem behavior ($-.132$).

Relationships Involving Physical Characteristics

Timing of pubertal development had little effect on self-esteem, although late developing girls were less likely to be involved in problem behavior and therefore had higher self-esteem.[3] There is other evidence that in Grade 7 late developers are more oriented to academic conformity and to school activities than are early developers. While the findings are of borderline significance for males, late developing youngsters of both genders in Grade 7 are slightly more likely to earn high GPAs (.089 for boys and .151 for girls); furthermore, late developing girls are more likely to be active in extracurricular activities (.189). This tendency for late developers to be more conformist than early developers was suggested in Chapter 5; however, here the finding persists when all the other variables in the model are controlled. The only other findings of interest involve significant correlations between pubertal timing and Grade 6 variables, and these findings are expected ones: in Grade 6 late developing girls perceive themselves to have less athletic ability, and late developing boys are less likely to be popular with the opposite sex. In Grade 6 late developing girls are small and presumably therefore less athletic. Late developing boys are shorter and less muscular, and thus it is not surprising to find them less attractive to girls.

The self-esteem analysis identified perceived looks as one of the most important resources for children at entry to adolescence and certainly the most important "physical characteristic." A high opinion of one's looks benefited self-esteem directly and indirectly (through greater perceived popularity, and, for girls, through less victimization). Here we find that a perception that one is good-looking also has effects on, and relationships with, several other variables as well. Perceived good looks in Grade 6 leads boys in Grade 7 to indicate more popularity with the opposite sex (.179), less problem behavior ($-$.146), and a higher self-rating of athletic ability (.125). Furthermore, for both genders, perceived good looks in Grades 6 and 7 correlates significantly with several Grade 6 and 7 variables (see Appendix F, Tables F.3 and F.4). Children who perceive themselves as good-looking are likely to score positively on a wide variety of other variables in Grades 6 and 7, including perceived positive ratings from opposite- and same-sex peers as well as from teachers. Such children also appear more integrated in the social and academic fabric of the school showing greater extracurricular participation, less problem behavior,[4] and, for boys, a higher GPA. In addition, the association for boys between perceived good looks and perceived athletic ability is probably due to the greater muscularity of athletic boys.

In addition to the physical characteristics of pubertal timing and perceived looks, we can also look more specifically at self-evaluation of athletic ability. The role of athletic ability differs for the genders. For both genders there is a link of higher athletic ability with more problem behavior,[5] but for boys there also appear to be more significant positive effects and associations, as one might expect. According to Grade 6 correlations, athletic boys are significantly more likely to be well-regarded by Grade 6 peers. In addition, as noted previously, they are more likely to perceive themselves as good-looking. Furthermore, in Grade 7, athletic boys are more likely to be popular with the opposite sex and less likely to be victimized, perhaps because they are better able to defend themselves.

For girls, the findings are mixed. On the negative side, according to Grade 6 correlations, athletic girls not only show more school problems but also lower GPAs. On the other hand, Grade 6 correlations indicate that athletic girls perceive themselves to be more highly evaluated by teachers and opposite-sex peers. Finally, not surprisingly, girls who perceive themselves as more athletic in Grade 6 are also more likely to participate in extracurricular activities (clubs and sports) in Grade 7 (.293).

Relationships Involving Peers

The central role of peer relationships in affecting Grade 7 self-esteem was emphasized earlier. A high evaluation by peers in general seemed to have direct and indirect beneficial effects on self-esteem. In addition, a high peer regard is associated positively with many other variables, particularly for girls. As indicated earlier, for both genders (according to Grade 7 correlations), children who think they are well regarded by peers are the ones who perceive themselves to be better looking. Furthermore, especially for girls there is evidence in the Grade 6 correlations of an association between high peer regard and academic conformity and orientation to school activities. Specifically, girls who perceive themselves to be highly regarded by peers in Grade 6 also believe they are highly evaluated by teachers; and they earn higher GPAs, engage in less school problem behavior, and participate more in school extracurricular activities. In addition, these girls are more protected by parents and allowed less independence from parental supervision. Thus, at this age just prior to entry to junior high school, the girls who conform to adult expectations in school are the ones who appear to earn high peer evaluations.

For boys, there is also some evidence in the same direction, but it is less consistent. Most important, a perceived high evaluation by peers in Grade 6 predicts less school problem behavior in Grade 7 ($-.220$), even after Grade 6 problem behavior is controlled. That is, boys who prior to the transition feel well thought of by peers will adjust more favorably to junior high school after the transition in this very important respect—they are less likely to be involved in this type of deviant behavior. In addition, the Grade 6 correlations indicate that boys highly regarded by peers also report higher teacher evaluations. On the other hand, however, they are less likely to earn high GPAs in Grade 6.

Finally, it should be noted that in Grade 7 (according to correlations), boys who believe they are well regarded by peers in general perceive themselves as more popular with the opposite sex as well. In sum, children who believe they are popular with peers indicate academic conformity and/or lower problem behavior, as well as several other positive associations.

We have just shown that a high perceived evaluation by peers in general is associated with an absence of problem behavior for both genders and also that for boys, there is a linkage between general and opposite-sex popularity. Nevertheless, success with the opposite sex is found to be correlated with greater problem behavior for both genders and with low GPA for girls in Grade 6. Also, in Grade 7, according to the correlation analysis, boys who are more popular with the opposite sex are more likely to be involved in problem behavior and less likely to earn high GPAs. Thus, youngsters in Grade 6 who perceive themselves highly evaluated by peers, in general, resist nonconformist behavior in Grade 7; but children who at this early age are popular with the opposite sex, in specific, are more likely to be involved in nonconformist activity. These results raise the question of developmental timing—are Grades 6 and 7 too early for children to be involved in opposite-sex relations?[6]

There are some positive, as well as negative, associations involving opposite-sex popularity, however. According to the Grade 7 correlations, boys popular with girls are more likely to be athletic and to be involved in extracurricular activities. In addition, as mentioned earlier, girls popular with boys in Grade 6 are more likely to rate themselves as good-looking in Grade 7, as one might expect.

In addition to general peer evaluation and opposite-sex popularity, another aspect of peer relations involves organized participation in school extracurricular activities. As noted before, participation in extracurricular activities had the inadvertent effect of exposing girls more to the possibility of victimization (.128). The causal analysis in Chapter 12, however, indicated some positive effects of participation as well: Active girls in Grade 6 were less likely to become involved in problem behavior in Grade 7 ($-.113$), and active boys earned higher GPAs after the transition (.141). Similarly, the Grade 6 correlations show that girls involved in school extracurricular activities are the ones earning higher grades; they also rate themselves as more highly regarded by peers and as better looking.

Interestingly, girls active in extracurricular clubs report less independence from parental chaperonage according to the Grade 6 correlations. Parents who are supervising their daughters more closely may approve of organized school activities, but not of their daughters going places unchaperoned without specific permission. Furthermore, involvement in activities organized by the school may commit the child to more academic conforming behavior. The correlations in Grade 7 show some contrasting effects for boys, however—with the more active boys being more, not less, involved in problem behavior as well as more popular with the opposite sex and better looking.

In summary, extracurricular participation and opposite-sex popularity have both positive and negative associations with other variables. However, perceiving oneself as held in high regard by peers in general appears to have positive impact.

Relationships Involving School Performance

Being a good student in school—earning high GPAs and being highly evaluated by one's teachers—did not have clear-cut positive effects in the self-esteem analysis. School performance is, however, related to other variables in more interesting ways. If favorable school performance can be regarded as a type of conformity to adult standards, then it is not surprising to find an association between high GPA and low problem behavior. It is not surprising to find that boys with high Grade 6 GPAs are less likely to be involved in problem behavior in Grade 7 ($-.131$), and that there is a negative correlation for both genders in Grade 6 and Grade 7 between GPA and problem behavior.

There are also other suggestions that a high GPA is associated with a commitment to the school. The causal analysis indicates that boys with higher GPAs in Grade 6 participate more in school activities in Grade 7 (.278); the Grade 6 correlations for girls also show a positive association with school extracurricular activities.

In terms of the association between GPA and peer relationships, both genders show that a low GPA is related to high opposite-sex popularity (Grade 6 correlation for girls, Grade 7 correlation for boys). When looking at peer relations generally, as noted previously, we find that boys who are excellent students are also less likely in Grade 6 to report that they are held in high regard by peers. However, as discussed earlier, girls with high grades are more likely to report high peer regard. It also should be noted that girls with higher GPAs are less likely to see themselves as athletic in Grade 6. Thus, being a good student appears linked (though not necessarily causally) to some types of school conformity, to absence of success in peer relations for boys, and to less positive opposite-sex relationships and athletic self-evaluations for girls.

Relationships Involving Independence

We hypothesized that early experiences of independence would better prepare children to make the transition into adolescence, in general, and into junior high school, in particular. Being allowed independence from chaperonage by parents this early does not appear, however, to have positive effects. In fact, it appears to hurt the adjustment to junior high school. As noted earlier, girls who are allowed more independence in Grade 6 are more likely to be involved in problem behavior in Grade 7 (.155), and more independent boys are somewhat more likely to be victimized in Grade 7 (.126). In addition, the girls who are more independent in Grade 6 are more likely to earn low GPAs in Grade 7 after the transition into junior high school (− .151). Furthermore, the Grade 6 correlations show that independent girls are the ones with less high peer evaluations and less participation in organized activities, and the independent boys are more involved in problem behavior.

The only positive effects of independence involve perceived athletic ability and opposite-sex relationships for boys. Boys who are allowed more independence in Grade 6 are the ones who rate their athletic ability more favorably in Grade 7 (.223) and who report greater opposite-sex popularity (.137). Thus, an association among early independence, problem behavior, athleticism, and opposite-sex popularity appears to have emerged from these data, especially for boys.

Relationships Involving Problem Behavior

The earlier self-esteem analysis indicated that involvement in problem behavior was detrimental to later self-esteem, directly for girls and indirectly for boys (through causal links with low perceived peer regard and greater victimization). As noted before, the Grades 6 and 7 correlations indicate many associations between problem behavior and other variables. According to the Grade 6 correlations: among both genders, students who exhibit high problem behavior earn a low teacher evaluation and demonstrate greater opposite-sex popularity; among girls, such students also attain less positive peer regard in general and rate themselves less favorably on looks but more favorably on athletics; among boys, those who are behavior problems also are the ones to earn lower GPAs. According to the correlations in Grade 7, both boys and girls involved in problem behavior earn less high GPAs; girls are more likely to be victimized; boys show less positive general peer regard[7] but greater success in opposite-sex relationships, more participation in extracurricular activities, and a higher athletic self-rating.

Summary

Many of the interrelationships among variables analyzed here are complex ones and resist oversimplification. Yet, underlying many of these findings seem to be issues of school conformity and nonconformity. Inspection of the data suggests a basic distinction between children who are conforming to adult standards in school and those who are not. For both boys and girls in Grade 6 and Grade 7, youngsters with low GPAs are also more likely to be involved in school problem behavior. Students allowed more independence from chaperonage by parents in Grade 6 are the ones more likely to show either low GPAs, or high problem behavior, or both. Children involved in problem behavior and those allowed more independence are also more likely to be victimized in Grade 7. That is, children who are perpetrators of problems are also more likely to be victims. In addition, for girls only, youngsters from lower social class backgrounds are more likely to score low in GPA and high in problem behavior. However, the associations among variables being discussed here persist when social class is controlled.

Furthermore, popularity with the opposite sex at this early age appears linked to this nonconformist pattern. In addition, for both boys and girls, early pubertal developers are more likely to show up as school nonconformists. They are less likely to earn high GPAs, and early developing girls are more likely to score high on problem behavior. Magnusson, Stattin, and Allen (in press) show similar relationships between early development and deviant behavior. In addition, Jessor and Jessor (1977) also show a linkage among problem behavior in general, early sexual relations, valuation of independence, and a low GPA. They, too, view a low GPA as a type of nonconventional behavior.

Not all of the variables associated with conformity–nonconformity relate in the same direction to activity participation, peer regard, teacher regard, athletic skill, or even self-esteem. Involvement in school problem behavior itself is, however, negatively associated with peer and teacher regard and with self-esteem for both genders.

In sum, certain characteristics tend to be correlated and to predict each other from Grade 6 to Grade 7, and many of these variables appear to be associated with conformity–nonconformity. And children who specifically exhibit school problem behavior in Grade 6 appear at greater risk in terms of the adjustment to junior high school in terms of their self-esteem.[8]

It is interesting that independence from chaperonage at this early age appears associated with negative, rather than positive, outcomes. In Grades 6 and 7 children apparently are not ready for such loose supervision from parents. The question arises whether it is early freedom of supervision itself that has negative effects, or whether the negative effects are due to the parents' general attitude toward the child. Perhaps parents who fail to supervise their children care less about them in general, and this lack of care is what produces the unfavorable consequences. Children were asked how highly they felt that their mothers regarded them.[9] They were asked,

> Would you say that your mother thinks of you as
>
> a wonderful person
> a pretty nice person
> a little bit of a nice person or
> not such a nice person

In fact, however, when perceived mother's evaluation is controlled, the negative relationships between early independence and Grade 7 difficulties persist for both genders to almost the same extent as before. At the same time, we controlled for single-parent marital status (living with a single mother vs. living with two parental figures), and the negative relationships between independence and Grade 7 difficulties remain by and large unaltered. Thus, it appears that the early independence itself may be responsible, at least in part, for the child's difficulty; the negative effects do not seem to be simply a consequence of a hostile maternal attitude or of a single parent family.[10]

In sum, there are several findings suggestive of the idea of "developmental readiness"—the idea that children can be pushed too early into behaviors appropriate to the next period in the life course, in this case, into adolescence. Early independence, early popularity with the opposite sex, and early pubertal development have some associations with school problem behavior and low GPA (see Simmons et al., 1983; Blyth et al., 1983).

To recapitulate briefly the findings of Chapters 12 and 13: we have identified several factors of relevance to adjustment in early adolescence, particularly adjustment to the very different environment of junior high school. Some of these factors appear to have a direct causal impact themselves on the reaction to the junior high school transition; others are associated with factors that have a causal effect. Without exaggerating the size of any one relationship, we find that among the most important positive resources for a successful transition are a high initial self-esteem, a high self-perceived peer regard, and a high self-rating of one's looks. Factors that hinder adjustment to the transition include early independence from parental supervision and a history of school problem behavior.

For other potential resources, however, effects are either mixed in direction or absent (at least in a causal sense): i.e., for potential resources such as popularity with the opposite sex, participation in extracurricular activities, teacher evaluations, and GPA. In fact, for boys a high Grade 6 GPA predicts not only a lower Grade 7 self-esteem but also less high peer regard. Excellence in school work is neither a totally positive resource nor a clear detriment.

Finally, in terms of the impact of Grade 7 school experience and school-level characteristics, this analysis points to several significant effects. Children who are victimized in school demonstrate lower self-esteem. In addition, as predicted, larger school size and greater ethnic heterogeneity appear to have negative impacts on key adjustment variables (although not all effects of size are negative). It was our original hypothesis that this first sudden and discontinuous transition from a small, intimate environment to a large, impersonal one would be made more difficult by the large numbers of people involved and the greater heterogeneity of those people. While these effects are not large, the direction of the effects is generally in line with these hypotheses. We are presuming, although we cannot test this presumption with these data, that a child suddenly confronted with great numbers of people at a time of a major life course transition will be likely to feel alienated, uncomfortable, and unsure of his or her own self-standing. In this situation, a lower self-esteem is likely to result, especially among children lacking in key prior resources and particularly among those who find themselves victimized or held in low regard by these new peers.

Footnotes

[1]In Appendix F, Tables F.1 and F.2 present standardized and unstandardized "causal" coefficients, Table F.3 shows the correlations among the Grade 6 variables, and Table F.4 indicates the correlations from the Psi Matrix among the Grade 7 intervening ("endogenous") variables. The latter are analogous to partial correlations; they are correlations among the endogenous variables once the variance explained by hypothesized paths between exogenous and endogenous variables has been removed. Whenever we mention Grade 7 correlations, we are referring to these estimates from the Psi Matrix.

[2]We did not explore the impact of ethnic diversity on the opportunities for minority students, neither did we look at the effects on prejudice, or on long- or short-term interethnic toleration or friendship.

[3]In Chapter 5, we have shown that early developing girls were more likely to date. In this analysis we show no significant effect of early development on op-

posite-sex popularity. In fact, in Grade 7 early developing girls are more likely than late developers to date, to perceive themselves as popular with the opposite sex, and to invite boyfriends over to the house. However, the difference becomes significant for dating and perception of popularity only when, as in Chapter 5, height and weight are controlled and/or when pubertal development is dichotomized so that girls who have and have not attained menarche are compared.

[4]For boys, the association between good looks and less problem behavior shows up as the "causal" coefficient, while for girls it shows up as a correlation in Grade 6.

[5]For boys, there is a causal link between Grade 6 athletic ability and Grade 7 problem behavior (.235); for girls there is a correlation in Grade 6 between the variables.

[6]See Magnusson, Stattin, and Allen (1985) for another view of this issue.

[7]Note that this relationship appears over the long term to be a mutual one. Grade 6 boys highly evaluated by peers are less likely to exhibit problem behavior in Grade 7, and Grade 6 boys who exhibit problem behavior in Grade 6 are less highly regarded by peers in Grade 7.

[8]See Rosenberg and Rosenberg (1978), Kaplan (1980), and Wells and Rankin (1983) for discussion of the causal relation of deviant behavior and self-esteem. Studies have been conducted to determine whether low self-esteem affects deviant behavior more than deviant behavior affects self-esteem. More detailed analysis of the reciprocal relations is needed to address this question with these data.

[9]As noted earlier, perceived maternal evaluation was not associated strongly enough with self-esteem to be included in the model.

[10]A series of relationships between Grade 6 independence and other variables were run controlling for perceived evaluation by mother in Grade 6 and for single-mother family-status. Relationships involving independence that were significant in the above analysis were run with these controls. For girls, partial regressions were run for each of the following Grade 7 dependent variables: GPA, school problem behavior, and self-esteem; and partial correlations were run with Grade 6 extracurricular participation and peer evaluation as the variables of interest. For boys, a partial correlation involving Grade 6 problem behavior was run, as well as a partial regression with Grade 7 victimization as the dependent variable. In essentially all cases, except the last, the relationship between independence and the other variable remains significant and very little changed from the zero-order relationship. In the case of the association between independence and victimization, a significant relationship appears only when the other variables in the causal model (Appendix F, Table F.2 and Figure F.2) are included; the zero-order correlation is not significant nor is the particular partial regression coefficient at issue here.

VI

CONCLUSION

14

SUMMARY AND CONCLUSION

This study has focused on the transition from childhood into early adolescence and then into middle adolescence. It has investigated the impact of age, gender, pubertal timing, and timing of school transition on the self-image and adjustment of white youth. Utilizing a stratified, random, cluster sample, we interviewed 621 white youngsters in Grade 6 in 1974 in 18 schools; and, if they remained in the Milwaukee public school system, we attempted to follow them each year through Grade 10 in 1979.

This research took advantage of a natural experiment to study the effects of the timing of school transitions. In the same city two school sequences existed side by side. This situation allowed us to use a quasi-experimental design and to compare outcomes for the two types of school transitions. Some of the children in the city experienced their first transition into a large, impersonal organizational context in early adolescence (Grade 7), whereas others at that age remained in a more intimate elementary school context. The former ("the junior high school cohort") moved from a K–6 to a 3-year junior high school and then to a 3-year senior high school. The latter stayed in a K–8 school until Grade 9, when as middle adolescents they moved into a 4-year senior high school. A central aim of this research has been to contrast the two experiences over the 5-year period of the study.

In terms of dependent variables the research has been organized around five tasks of adolescence: (1) the need to establish a positive self-image (global self-esteem is a key outcome variable); (2) the necessity of forging closer peer relationships; (3) the need to attain a higher degree of independence; (4) the establishment of plans for adulthood; and (5) the need to deal with conformity/deviance issues in school.

The Extent of Disturbance at Entry to Adolescence

As Vinokur and Selzer (1975) have noted, not all life changes generate distress. This study demonstrates a variety of reactions to a major transition in the life course: the transition out of childhood into adolescence. Both folk wisdom and early theory (Hall, 1904) identified this transition as tumultuous for high proportions of individuals. Like Offer and Offer

(1975), however, we show that in terms of the self-image and other key variables, tumult and negative change are not inevitable or even majority responses. Overall, there is no consistent evidence of a negative change upon entry to adolescence for most dependent variables or most adolescent tasks for either boys or girls. On the other hand, measures of 1 year change do indicate greater instability upon entry to adolescence (between Grades 6 and 7) than in middle adolescence (between Grades 9 and 10). Whether this greater instability is also characteristic of the younger childhood years or whether it emerges at the beginning of adolescence cannot be determined with our data.

But, in any case, adolescent changes do not involve widespread negative effects on average. What seems to be true is that adolescent changes are difficult for some children under some circumstances. Reaction depends on (1) characteristics of the change, (2) characteristics of the individual, and (3) the outcome area at issue.

Characteristics of the Change

Timing of the Change

The timing of the adolescent changes and transitions appears critical in terms of their social–psychological consequences. Timing can be considered relative to age and developmental maturity (the developmental readiness hypothesis); it also can be considered in relation to the trajectories of one's peers (being "off-time" or "on-time") and relative to the rank structure in the school ("top dog" versus "bottom dog").

The Developmental Readiness Hypothesis

Many of the key findings from this research are compatible with a developmental readiness hypothesis, a hypothesis that children can be thrust too early into the next period in the life course. In this case they can be thrust too soon out of childhood into adolescence, before they are emotionally ready for the change. There is evidence that transition into a large, impersonal junior high school at age 12–13 may be too early for many youngsters. The students who switch into a large junior high school in Grade 7 can be compared to Grade 7 peers in a K–8 school who are not required to make any switch into a large, new school until they are 2 years older. When this comparison is made in Grade 7, the junior high school students turn out to be at a disadvantage in several important ways that were not evident the year before the transition. In junior high school, key attitudes toward school become more negative than in the K–8 schools; self-esteem and leadership show declines for girls; participation in extracurricular activities, GPAs, and math achievement scores are less high and/or change less favorably for both genders, and levels of victimization are higher for boys.

Furthermore, in two key respects, youngsters, especially girls, do not recover in middle adolescence from these early losses. They do not recover in terms of their self-esteem and their extracurricular participation and leadership. In Grades 9 and 10 the girls who attended junior high school are still showing less favorable scores than their K–8 counterparts. The K–8 students appear to have gained an advantage from remaining in an intimate school until an older age, from switching for the first time into a new, large school in Grade 9 (age 14–15) rather than in Grade 7 (age 12–13).

These findings are compatible with a developmental readiness hypothesis but give no support to the alternate stress inoculation hypothesis. The stress inoculation hypothesis posits that, for most children, experiencing one environmental change will better prepare them for the next similar transition and will be more advantageous than protection from the early change. The children who have experienced the move into a large junior high school do not demonstrate a more favorable reaction to the senior high school transition than do the K–8 youth who have never made such a prior school change. In fact, on average, in terms of self-esteem and participation in activities, the junior high school cohort (especially girls) indicate more, not less, negative reaction after the entry to senior high school.

The reaction of youngsters to early pubertal change, as well as to early school transition, also is compatible with the developmental readiness hypothesis. While pubertal timing does not show widespread effects, there is evidence of some negative consequences of early development for girls, but not for boys. All 4 years of the study, early developing girls show less satisfaction with aspects of their body image. In addition, in Grades 6 and 7 when they look older than other girls, they perform less well academically and demonstrate more school problem behavior.

The difference between boys and girls can be explained, in part, by the developmental readiness hypothesis (and, in part, by a cultural ideal hypothesis to be discussed later in the chapter). For girls, early development may propel them too soon into adolescence before they are mature enough emotionally to cope well. For boys, except for the extreme early developers who do show negative reactions, early developers reach puberty approximately 1 year later than early developing girls and may be more ready for the change.

There are additional findings that are also compatible with the idea of developmental readiness. Early independence from parental supervision and chaperonage has been shown to have negative effects and associations as the youngster makes the transition into junior high school. Early independence prior to the transition is associated with low self-esteem, low GPA, problem behavior, and victimization after the transition for one or both genders. Children may not be mature enough at this age for such loose supervision by parents. Finally, while the effects of early popularity with the opposite sex and early dating are mixed, there is evidence of association with school problem behavior and with low GPAs. Being allowed to assume the role behaviors typical of adolescence too early appears to be associated with an increased likelihood of negative outcomes for youngsters. Early school transition, pubertal development, allowed independence, and dating all can be problematic.

"On-Time" versus "Off-Time"

The level of emotional readiness is not the only issue related to the timing of transitions. Where changes occur at different times for different individuals, social comparison processes become relevant. In terms of pubertal change, some youngsters are on-time, some are off-time; that is, they attain puberty earlier or later than their average peer. The deviance hypothesis predicts that being off-time, being in the minority in relationship to one's peers, will have negative effects. For girls we see no consistent evidence in support of this hypothesis (where there are differences, late developers score more positively all years). However, for boys, there is evidence that general negative effects are associated with extreme deviance in pubertal timing, in terms of both extreme early and extreme late development. (Moderately early developers, however, do especially well in those areas in which there are effects.)

"Top Dog" versus "Bottom Dog"

Social comparison processes are related not only to individual timing of pubertal development, but also to the timing of school transitions for the group. That is, the timing of the school transition places the entire cohort at a comparative advantage or disadvantage in any given year. The year prior to the school transition the cohort can be considered "top dogs" in their organizational environment; the year after the transition they suddenly become "bottom dogs." As "top dogs" and the oldest students in their school, they rank highest, are most likely to know a very high proportion of students who "matter," and should feel comfortable in their environment. As "bottom dogs" and the youngest students in the school, they rank lowest, are unlikely to know a large number of school mates, and are strangers in a new environment.

In fact, there was evidence, particularly in late childhood (Grade 6) and early adolescence (Grade 7) of positive outcomes for "top dogs" and negative outcomes for "bottom dogs." In Grade 6, the K–6 students as the oldest students in their school appeared better off on a variety of self-image and other variables than their counterparts in the K–8 schools. In Grade 7 the situation was reversed, especially for girls, with the students who moved into a large impersonal junior high school as "bottom dogs" showing more negative effects than their peers who remained in the intimate K–8 environment.

In later years, findings were more complex due, we think, to other processes besides the "top dog" "bottom dog" ones (i.e., as indicated earlier, the K–8 cohort may be at an overall advantage due to their higher level of developmental readiness for changes). In Grade 9, when the K–8 cohort made their first transition into a large impersonal school, effects were mixed. Despite the fact they were "bottom dogs," the K–8 students did not show clear-cut disadvantages across all key variables that year. However, in Grade 10 when the junior high school cohort made their second transition and once again became "bottom dogs," by and large they were again at a disadvantage and demonstrated negative changes along key variables.

Discontinuity of the Change

The timing of adolescent change is one factor that appears to affect social–psychological outcomes. The discontinuity of the change is another such factor (Benedict, 1954). A change is considered to be discontinuous if it is abrupt and sudden rather than gradual and if it involves great differences between the pre- and posttransition periods. The transition out of elementary school to junior high school is an example of a sharp discontinuity. It represents a sudden change from a "primary" to a "secondary" environmental context.

Primary versus Secondary Context

The distinction between primary and secondary groups has received major attention in classical sociological theory (Toennies, 1887/1940). It has a meaning above and beyond the usual definition in education of primary (early) and secondary (advanced) schools. It involves a contrast between intimate, intense, and total ("diffuse") relationships, on the one hand, and impersonal, superficial, discrete, and specific relationships, on the other. This contrast has been emphasized by many of sociology's most important theorists including, among others, Durkheim, Cooley, and Parsons. The nuclear family is one of the key examples of the primary group, and the large-scale bureaucracy is a frequent example of a secondary group.

We have pointed out that the movement from a more "primary" to a more "secondary" context is one of the many important changes that occur in adolescence, at least for children in large, urban settings. Children move out of an intimate, small school into a larger, more impersonal environment. They spend a high proportion of their time in this new secondary type context. Our study indicates that this aspect of the adolescent transition can be problematic for some children for whom it may occur too early. Future research will be needed to determine whether the transition into junior high school is less problematic in a smaller, suburban, or rural school system where there are fewer strangers overall in the community. In general, the finding that girls who attend junior high school in a large city are a group at risk at the entry to adolescence replicates, with better evidence, the findings of an earlier investigation conducted in 1968 in a different large city (Baltimore; see Simmons *et al.*, 1973).

While this study does not allow an extensive examination of the impact of within-school characteristics, there is evidence that large school size has a direct, small, negative impact upon the self-esteem of both male and female junior high school students in Grade 7. In addition, ethnic heterogeneity is associated with higher levels of victimization and, thus, indirectly with lower self-esteem. These findings provide some additional indication that movement from an intimate to a less intimate, larger, and heterogeneous environment is more difficult for the child.

Cumulation of Change (the Focal Theory of Change)

In this research, our main attention has focused on normative, socially expected and desired changes associated with entry to adolescence (i.e., puberty, school change, and, to a lesser extent, initiation of opposite-sex relationships). For school change, all members of the individual's cohort confront the same transition at the same time; for puberty and initiation of dating, the rate of change is individualized, though sizable proportions of peers change at about the same time. In conjunction with these socially expected changes at entry to adolescence, we have also examined the impact of less desirable or less expected changes (e.g., change in parental marital status, change of residence).

While the timing and level of discontinuity of each individual change is important for the adjustment of adolescents, also relevant is the cumulation of life changes at one point in time. Coleman (1974) has advanced the focal theory of change relative to this issue; he has posited that at entry to adolescence, it is easier to deal with life changes one at a time rather than with all transitions simultaneously. It is easier if one can focus on one major transition before tackling the next.[1] For example, it is easier to cope sequentially rather than simultaneously with environmental changes, physiological differences, the new definition of self as an adolescent, and the alteration in others' expectations.

Findings from this study support the focal theory. Among both boys and girls, those who experience a greater number of major life changes in early adolescence are at greater risk in terms of our key outcome variables. (As noted previously, the life changes at issue involve change into junior high school, recent pubertal change, early onset of dating behavior, geographic change, and changes in parents' marital status—including divorce, remarriage, parental death.) Grade 7 females who have recently experienced multiple life changes are at a substantial and significant disadvantage in terms of their self-esteem, GPA, and extracurricular participation. Grade 7 males show substantial negative effects for GPA and extracurricular participation, but not for self-esteem. The cumulation of change has more negative effects than does any one change itself. Not only are students who face more life changes as they enter early adolescence at greater risk in Grade 7, but the negative effects of this cumulation, or synchronicity of change, persist into middle adolescence (Grades 9 and 10). Furthermore, the effects on GPA for girls are significantly curvilinear; that is, after a certain point each subsequent life change makes academic coping even more difficult.

In sum, in early adolescence, social–psychological outcomes are affected in interesting ways by the nature of the changes themselves. There is evidence of detrimental effects if change occurs at too young an age, if it causes the individual to be extremely off-time in development, if the transition places the person in the lowest ranking cohort in the environment, if change is marked by sharp discontinuity, and if many significant changes cumulate and occur close together in time.

Arena of Comfort

The developmental readiness hypothesis and the focal change hypothesis have emerged as important in interpreting many of these data. At this point we would like to go a bit beyond our data and raise the idea that underlying both of these hypotheses is the notion of an "arena of comfort." If change comes too suddenly—that is, if there is too much discontinuity with prior experience—or if change is too early given the children's cognitive and emotional states, or if it occurs in too many areas of life at once, then presumably individuals will experience great discomfort. They will experience discomfort with self and discomfort with the world. Such children will not feel at one with themselves nor at home in their social environments. Individuals should do better both in terms of self-esteem and behavioral coping if there is some arena of comfort in their lives.

The need for an arena of comfort would explain why more gradual change upon entry to adolescence appears beneficial as do fewer simultaneous changes. If the individual is comfortable in some environments, life arenas, and role-relationships, then discomfort in another arena can be tolerated and mastered. It is understandable that youngsters are less able to cope if at one and the same time they are uncomfortable with their bodies, due to physical changes; with their family, due to changes in family constellation; with home, because of a move; with school, due to great discontinuity in the nature of the school environment; with peers because of the new importance of opposite-sex relationships and because of disruption of prior peer networks in a new school and the changes in peer expectations and peer evaluation criteria. There needs to be some arena of life or some set of role-relationships with which the individual can feel relaxed and comfortable, to which he or she can withdraw and become reinvigorated.

Two analogies are relevant: first, an analogy to a battle, and, second, an analogy to an electric battery. In the first case, one can envision the individual as if between battles and in need of a comfortable place to rest and become reenergized. Or an alternative analogy: the individual resembles an electric battery that expends energy for awhile but then must be recharged. The energy that is expended is more likely to be useful if it can be focused on one task at a time, rather than spread out over all life tasks. In other words, it requires some energy and tension arousal to cope with those areas of life that are uncomfortable and that are changing. In order to maximize the expenditure of energy and avoid overdemand, reduction of tension between challenges should be helpful.

Successful coping with change has properties of the dialectic. A balance or synthesis of opposites is probably optimal: a balance between tension arousal and tension reduction, between over- and understimulation, between being challenged and being comfortable, between too many and too few demands, between growth and stability. We have discussed the discomfort that is the cost of challenge and change. On the other hand, too much comfort and stability clearly also has costs, that is, the failure to grow to one's full potential and the acceptance of unnecessary restrictions and dependencies.

For optimal self-esteem and coping in the long run, the individual cannot be totally comfortable; he or she has to leave the securities of childhood and to enter adolescence. Thus, at some point, at least in an urban context, the child has to learn to cope with large-scale organizational environments with all their opportunities as well as their impersonality. The child has to detach emotionally and physically from parents and accept expectations from peers and parents more suitable for this new period in the life course. Physical changes are inevitable, and most youth will have to deal with the new type of romantic/sexual relationships.

Coping with all of these "normative" changes will necessarily involve some degree of discomfort, even if nonnormative and less desirable changes are absent. The issue we have emphasized involves timing and pacing. Gradual rather than discontinuous change, changes that are spread out and dealt with in turn, rather than simultaneously, appear recommended.

We are not saying simply that a greater number of stressors will result in more distress or that social support can buffer the distress from life stressors. Without at all discounting the validity of such statements, we are highlighting the multiplicity of arenas, role-relationships, and role-identities in a person's life. At issue here is the absence of stressors in at least one significant sphere.

The concept of life arena or arena of comfort is being used here rather than identity, or status, role-relationship, or environmental context in order to be able to subsume all of these aspects of multiplicity in an individual's life. In future work, a more precise examination of the nature of such an arena of comfort in light of these more traditional concepts will be needed, and a more extensive test of the hypotheses. One would expect it to be more difficult to cope with changes in an arena in which one spends more time or in which one is more invested psychologically (Stryker, 1980).

Characteristics of the Individual

Reaction to adolescence is determined not only by the characteristics of the different changes that are involved but also by the characteristics of the individual. Clearly, not all individuals react in the same way to school and pubertal transitions. For some types of youngsters, adolescent transitions are more difficult.

Gender Differences

We have shown that in the 1970s the two genders were still reacting differently from one another to the adolescent transition. Douvan and Adelson (1966) emphasize the difference between the male and female experience of adolescence based on a cohort measured in the mid-1950s. Our study 20 years later still identifies gender as one of the most important factors affecting outcomes and processes at this age. On almost all key outcome variables at all grades there are significant male–female differences, while pubertal status itself affects only a few such variables. Timing of school transition also has a less pervasive effect than does gender.

For the most part, gender differences evident in a study of adolescents conducted a decade earlier (Simmons and F. Rosenberg, 1975) persist in this research despite the growth of the Women's Movement by the mid- to late 1970s. Differences are present for all five of the adolescent tasks studied here. First, females score less favorably than males in terms of their self-image; including their self-esteem, attitude toward their own sex, and especially their body image. In addition, they care more than males about their body image, which makes their dissatisfaction more upsetting to them. Second, adolescent and preadolescent girls continue to place higher value on same-sex popularity than do boys. In terms of the third task of adolescence, boys are allowed earlier independence from adult supervision than are girls. Fourth, in regard to future plans, only a small minority of girls express the desire to work continuously as adults, including the time when they will have young children. Finally, in terms of academic conformity and deviance, boys are more likely than girls to be involved in school problem behavior (both as perpetrator and victim), and boys earn less high GPAs and verbal test scores (there are no significant gender differences on math achievement).

Most important in terms of their self-pictures, girls appear more vulnerable to the environmental and biological transitions of adolescence. At a time when self-esteem is rising among boys, girls who enter junior high school show a drop in self-esteem. Moderately early pubertal change has negative effects on a girl's body image but positive effects for a boy. In part, the reason for a girl's greater vulnerability may be that they and their friends are changing biologically at a younger age. Part of the reason may also be due to the differential change in values for girls versus boys as they enter adolescence. The greater tendency for girls (versus boys) to place high value on looks, aspects of body image, and same-sex popularity increases with movement out of childhood (Grade 6) and entry into adolescence. Thus, compared to her male counterpart, the girl in adolescence becomes relatively more and more oriented toward aspects of herself that might make her vulnerable. At a time that her looks and the looks of her peers are changing, her standing in a hierarchy based on looks would appear to be unstable, particularly in a new and larger school where her peers are not well known. To stake herself more on such an ambiguous criterion should make the entry to adolescence more difficult.

Similarly, by caring more than boys about peer popularity, girls are placing their self-evaluations more at the mercy of outside judges. Particularly, in a new school with lesser known peers, these judgments may be harder to control. Also since they care more about peers, girls may find it more difficult to adjust to the disruption of peer networks that occurs upon entry to junior high school (Epstein and Karweit, 1983). Thus, by accepting traditional gender-role values in early adolescence, girls appear to be placing themselves at greater risk during the transition.[2]

The Cultural Ideal Hypothesis

Part of the reason that girls may react more negatively than boys to moderately early pubertal development may be due to the values of the larger culture. Early developing girls become heavier in early adolescence, and, in middle adolescence, they remain heavier than the taller and slimmer late developer. Being heavy is certainly regarded as undesirable at present in our culture. In contrast, puberty renders boys more muscular, a very desirable change. The muscular male clearly approximates the American cultural ideal more than his less muscular counterparts.

Individual Resources

This study has also identified key individual resources and factors, other than gender, that appear to help some children make the transition without general tumult and without decline in self-esteem. These resources that help the children were found to be present prior to the transition. The importance of self-perceived high peer regard as a resource is compatible with all of the research indicating the significance of social support in mitigating the effects of a stressor (Pearlin *et al.*, 1981). It is also compatible with classic theories of the reflected self—theories that emphasize the impact upon self-esteem of the perceived views of others (Rosenberg, 1979). The interesting question, which these studies cannot address, is whether perceived high peer regard would be as important in helping younger children to cope with a major change in environmental context. Flavell (1974) and Rosenberg and Kaplan (1982) posit that in adolescence there is an increase in the extent to which the child can take the role of the significant other. Does social support, as a buffer to stressors, assume markedly greater importance in adolescence in general? Or, even if we narrow our focus to self-esteem and to the issue of the reflected self, is a favorable view of others' opinions more of a resource for maintaining high self-esteem in adolescence than earlier?

These studies also point to the importance of self-perceived physical attractiveness in helping the children to negotiate the transition to a new, larger environmental context, specifically in helping them to maintain a favorable perception of their evaluation from peers as well as a high self-esteem. Much research has documented the overwhelming social–psychological importance of physical attractiveness in late adolescence and adulthood (e.g., Berscheid and Walster, 1974). Our own prior work involving physical illness has shown that adolescents exposed to a major life-threatening chronic illness compare very well to normal controls when the symptoms are invisible; however, once the same illness becomes visible due to medication side-effects that distort appearance, adjustment and self-images worsen significantly (Simmons *et al.*, 1977; Ch. 4). Clearly the present study documents the importance of physical appearance as a resource at the entry to adolescence. Again, a question arises that cannot be answered with these data: in earlier childhood would perceived attractiveness also serve as a resource in adjusting to environmental change?

Thus, characteristics of the child (e.g., gender, self-perceived peer evaluations, and physical attractiveness) have meaningful effects on the child's adjustment to the adolescent transition.

The Outcome at Issue

Specific versus Global Reactions

This study not only documents characteristics of the individual and characteristics of change that render adolescence more difficult, it also reminds us that reactions are not necessarily global and widespread. Individuals are clearly more likely to show negative change in some areas than in others as they move into and through adolescence. In general, the one realm in which there is a definite negative trend in adolescence involves conformity to adult standards: that is, there are increases in probations and suspensions; drops in GPA; and, for boys, a negative turn in parental and teacher evaluation.

Furthermore, while some types of transition appear to affect global and key variables, others have more specific impacts. School change and cumulative change affect global self-esteem and the key behavioral variable of GPA. Pubertal timing, however, does not influence global self-esteem but rather more specific aspects of body image such as evaluation of one's weight and body build.

Similarly, effects vary in their longevity. Some are relatively long-lasting. (For example, school change and cumulative change in early adolescence have negative effects for girls that persist for 3 and 4 years.) Early pubertal development for girls results in increased dating behavior several years later, even at a time when all girls have developed a figure. Other effects are more short-lived. For example, early development for girls has some impacts that appear to last only temporarily. The early developers are different in these respects from their peers only during the time they look older than their less developed peers; such differences disappear once the later developers also reach puberty. In Grades 6 and 7, but not later, early developing girls are allowed more independence from adult supervision than late developers and face higher expectations for "older" behavior. Early developers are thus encouraged to move faster away from childhood roles, but differences in these respects vanish by middle adolescence.

As has been emphasized by many scholars who study the life course, adjustment clearly is multidimensional, not unitary (Baltes, Reese, and Lipsitt, 1980; and Brim and Kagan, 1980).

In sum, the overriding concern of this investigation has been with the effect of expected life transitions on individuals as they move out of childhood into early and middle adolescence. Before closing, however, we wish to make some comments relevant to the study of change and relevant to policy.

Contributions to the Methodology of Studying Change

There are several ways of studying change in longitudinal research (Mortimer, Finch, and Kumka, 1982). This study has asked many conventional questions and used many conventional ways of examining change—from comparisons of means over time to examination of rank order stabilities; from Repeated Measures Analysis of Variance to group adjusted change-scores to causal modeling of change.

In addition, however, several questions arose for which usual methods did not appear adequate and/or direct. In order to answer these questions, we devised new approaches or modifications of old techniques. While we have no doubt that the type of questions are important in the study of change, we regard our methods as only a first and exploratory approach to their answers. We hope that these initial steps might create interest in these questions and improvements in techniques for dealing with them.

For example, we wished to know whether the amount of change was greater for different subgroups at different ages, regardless of the direction of this change (and apart from the level of rank-order stability). Therefore, we compared mean absolute 1-year change and the associated standard deviations for boys versus girls in early versus middle adolescence. As another example of new types of questions that emerged from the analysis: The group-level change analyses indicated that on the average, junior high school and K–8 children changed differently between Grades 6 and 7 with the junior high school girls showing more negative adjusted mean change. In order to determine whether these differences were meaningful, we wished to know how pervasive and substantial the negative change was among the junior high school versus the K–8 girls. Were the differences in mean adjusted change scores caused by a very few junior high school girls who reacted extremely negatively while the bulk of girls coped well with the environmental transition? Or were a lot of girls affected, but each only slightly? In either of these cases (which did not appear to characterize the data), one might worry less about the junior high school environment. For all these questions, we wished, insofar as possible, to determine the effects that would occur had all children started at the same level.

In order to explore these questions, that is, in order to determine the proportion of girls showing various levels of negative adjusted change, it was necessary to characterize each individual in terms of change. Individual adjusted change scores were therefore created within an analysis of covariance framework (controlling for initial score on the variable); the distribution of the girls on this new score was described.

A final but central question involved the issue of recovery. While the average scores suggested that girls did not recover in later years from Grade 7 losses, we could not be sure that it was the same girls who showed losses in Grade 7 who were still demonstrating loss from the vantage point of later years. The individual adjusted change scores were also utilized for this analysis to see if negative change persisted or if girls tended to bounce back after the Grade 7 loss. By Grades 9 or 10 was the Grade 6–7 problem invisible and without trace? (In fact, it was not; there was evidence of lack of recovery.) In this analysis, the individual pattern of adjusted change in Grade 6–7 became the independent variable.

It is our hope that these explorations will produce interest in what we think are important questions relevant to the study of change—the degree of absolute change occurring at various transition points, the distribution of different individual trajectories of change above and beyond initial differences, the proportions of individuals recovering from initial negative change.

Conclusions Relevant to Policy

The evidence from this research points to some long-lasting disadvantages of the junior high school transition in a large city, especially for a substantial proportion of the girls. While these data suggest some advantages for the K–8 system, there are relatively few K–8 schools in the United States at the moment, and it is unlikely that the clock will turn backward to create them. Rather, middle schools are becoming more prevalent (Blyth, 1977; Blyth and Karnes, 1981; Lipsitz, 1977). Middle schools extend from Grades 5–7 or Grades 6–8 and thus involve an earlier, first transition. Based on our results, we would predict that middle schools with an earlier transition would be easier for the children, especially if they are smaller in size than the usual junior high school. There is an opportunity for the middle school transition to be perceived as more gradual than the junior high school transition; especially if the transition brings with it a less dramatic increase in numbers of peers and older children.

Aside from size, the earlier transition might have the advantage of coinciding less with other adolescent changes—there would be less cumulation of change. Although the definition of boundaries of adolescence are ambiguous in our society, entry to a new school in Grade 5 or 6 (age 10 or 11) is likely to be perceived as predating adolescence. Thus, the change is less likely to be treated symbolically as a movement into a very new age-period. It is less likely to trigger a new set of expectations by parents and teachers; the child is less likely to be pressured to adopt adolescent behaviors and relinquish childhood patterns. In addition, for most youngsters, especially boys, it will precede much of pubertal development. Most boys will not have entered their height growth spurt, and most girls will not have begun to menstruate, although other aspects of pubertal development will have begun. Thus, the children could accustom themselves to a change in schools before having to cope with pubertal changes and changes in others' expectations of them.

Whether, in fact, an earlier middle-school transition will present the urban youngster with a more gradual, less discontinuous change and with less cumulation of changes in different spheres can be determined only with additional research—research that hopefully can disentangle the effects of a large school from the effects of an early transition. Whether or not the middle school is a more favorable context, some suggestions can be advanced for the junior high school.

It should be recalled that, although many youngsters appear to have difficulty with entry to junior high school, a great many children (particularly among the boys) do cope well with the junior high school transition. Therefore, less dramatic recommendations for modifications within the existing junior high school system may be more relevant than fundamental attempts to change it.

First, since one problem seems to be impersonality, it should be possible to create smaller, more intimate subcommunities of peers and teachers within the school. (See Lipsitz, 1984, p. 182 and Lightfoot, 1983, p. 348). Such subcommunities could be set up immediately upon entry to the school and continue throughout the year at least, if not throughout the child's tenure in the school. Hawkins and Berndt (1985) show positive effects of one such system in a junior high school. At the higher education level, Yale College has attempted to create such subcommunities through its special type of 4-year assignment to a dormitory complex (called the "college" system).

The apparent negative effects of victimization, too early independence from parental chaperonage, and early dating also have policy implications. Parental supervision in general and adult supervision at the school in after-school hours in specific would appear advised in early adolescence. Of course, many of the issues related to school problem behavior and victimization defy an easy solution, and we recognize that. While our analysis indicates that the negative effects of too early independence from parental supervision persist even when perceived maternal regard is controlled, in some cases the lack of parental supervision will be due to lack of parental love. In these cases, the advice to parents to maintain supervision at this age will be unacceptable to just those families who are most in need of change.

This study also may be useful to school systems because of its identification of types of children more likely to be at risk and more likely to need extra help in the adjustment to change. To repeat, the following types of children appear to be at greater risk: girls, students experiencing many life changes simultaneously (including early developing girls), children who are allowed earlier independence from parents, children who have been victimized by peers, and children with certain disadvantages prior to the transition—low self-pictures in general, unfavorable perceptions of their looks and peer popularity in particular, and a history of problem behavior in elementary school. Among boys, those who are from the low SES backgrounds and those who are less athletic prior to the transition have somewhat more difficulty than do others with the transition.

Future Research

In the preceding segments of this chapter we have suggested areas to be addressed by future research. Some additional suggestions seem warranted. Obviously, the findings in this study need replication. We have attempted throughout to carefully indicate caveats, where ideal information was unavailable, where (as in Grade 9–10) there was sampling loss, or where techniques involved necessary assumptions. As noted in the beginning of this volume, we have included a wide variety of dependent variables and a generous level of statistical significance in order to explore the areas in which pubertal timing and school transition might have effects. Given the identification of probable areas of effects, replication would be especially valuable to test generalizability.

Not only would replication on similar populations be worthwhile, but also it would be of value to investigate other contexts and types of subjects. This study itself replicated major findings from a decade earlier—that is, findings showing greater vulnerability of girls in terms of their self-images in adolescence and greater risk of the junior high schools for girls. Whether these findings will continue to replicate in newer cohorts is, of course, an important issue.

Equally relevant is the extent to which black and other ethnic subgroups react in the same way. In Milwaukee there were not enough black children in the K–8 schools to be able to compare black adjustment in junior high school versus K–8 schools. Since the transition into junior high school may be particularly difficult for urban children, the reaction of black children is important to investigate. The public school systems in many of the nation's cities are becoming or have become black-majority, and thus the issue of the urban junior high school is a significant one for such youngsters. In general, the theories being advanced here concerning the difficulty of coping with impersonality or cumulative change should not apply differently to black versus white children. However, gender roles traditionally have been defined somewhat differently within the black versus white community (Simmons and F. Rosenberg, 1975; Bush et al., 1977–1978); it is possible that the relatively higher prestige of females among blacks might serve as better protection for the junior high school transition. Value changes in adolescence may also differ within black subcultures. We suggested that relative increase in valuation of looks and peer popularity rendered the white female more at risk than her male counterpart. The process and effect of value changes for black females in recent cohorts needs to be investigated.

In addition to the comparison of different ethnic groups within the United States, cross-national studies of the entry into adolescence also are important. For some societies, the preadolescent or young adolescent child is expected to take more major and less reversible life steps. The decision to head to the university takes the children to different secondary schools from those they might have attended had they decided to terminate education earlier, and it is difficult to switch school types. In some societies, the child's future is dependent on success or failure in tests taken as young as ages 11–13. While informal and formal "tracking" in the United States have very significant consequences, future repercussions may be less obvious to parents and children than the systems in the United

Kingdom, Japan, and Korea, for example (see Powers and Cotterell, 1981). If the developmental readiness hypothesis has generalizability, we would expect increased difficulty for those young adolescents for whom a real decision-point occurs at this time. It may be very difficult at this young an age to confront such important decisions and/or the potential for such an important failure.[3]

In addition to testing the generalizability of these results within similar and different populations, future research should attempt to gain further understanding of some of the underlying processes at work here. This research did not demonstrate the operation of the stress inoculation hypothesis in general relative to school transition. Experience with a prior transition (the junior high school transition) did not appear to help with adjustment at entry to senior high school. Meichenbaum (1977) and Elder (1974) place emphasis on the importance of successful coping with an earlier stressor for coping with later stressors (Elder and Liker, 1982; Elder, Liker, and Jaworski, 1984). A study utilizing a longer time frame and focusing in more depth on successful early coping processes might elicit results more compatible with this hypothesis. Another process that could be investigated in greater depth is the role played by socially supportive relationships in adolescence (with both parents and peers) and by the disruption of peer networks at the time of the transition.

In general, in this research we have been concentrating on processes of self-evaluation. We have assumed the importance of the principles emphasized by Rosenberg (1979) in his classic work on the self-image: the principle of social comparison and the principle of the reflected self as well as the importance of self-values. That is, children's evaluations of themselves are affected by comparisons of themselves with significant others and by their view of what significant others think of them. Specific evaluations (e.g., regarding sports, looks, schoolwork) impinge more on global self-esteem if the specific areas are highly valued by the individual.

At entry to adolescence, values, comparison points, perceived opinions by others are all changing, rendering self-evaluation more difficult. Different specific areas come to be valued more, especially for girls, and this change in valuation affects the overall view of self. Also, peers change in a new school, thereby making social comparisons less clear than the year before. Furthermore, the child himself or herself is changing, especially in the realm of looks, and thus must compare new self-characteristics not only to those of peers who are also changing but also to "cultural ideals."

In addition, in terms of the reflected self, the fact that peers are changing may also make it more difficult to ascertain their opinions of one. On the other hand, due to cognitive maturation, adolescents may be better able to take the role of the significant other than they were previously and, therefore, may perceive more clearly what these others think of them

(Rosenberg and Kaplan, 1982). In fact, this greater accuracy may lead to a less inflated view of aspects of the self than is characteristic of younger children (Rosenberg and Simmons, 1972).

These processes, which we have emphasized throughout, appear to help explain insecurity and negative change in the self-images of girls who enter junior high school. But why, despite these processes, does the self-esteem of boys and K–8 girls generally rise through adolescence? In these studies, we have not measured global self-efficacy. Yet many recent theorists have emphasized the importance of a sense of self-efficacy in coping with stressors (Gecas and Schwalbe, 1983; Mirowsky and Ross, in press). It is possible that with maturation, the adolescent feels more competent and efficacious. Feelings of self-efficacy may, in turn, work to produce higher self-esteem at the same time as other factors are threatening self-esteem.

Feelings of self-efficacy may also intervene and explain other of our key findings. We noted that, according to the models specified, victimization and early independence from parental supervision tended to produce lower self-esteem. The question is why? It is possible that being victimized by other children reduces one's sense of self-efficacy and therefore results in lower global self-esteem.[4] It is also possible that too early independence from parental supervision puts one in situations one cannot handle (developmental readiness). The result again is lower self-efficacy and therefore less favorable self-esteem.

A final question involves the process by which cumulative change affects self-esteem and behavior. While we have speculated that cumulative change results in discomfort and uncertainty, we have no direct measures of this discomfort. It is possible that the feelings of discomfort related to change produce a a sense of detachment from self, a sense of unreality. As one watches oneself in new and uncomfortable situations, one may feel what Rosenberg has called recurrent transient depersonalization (Rosenberg et al., in press). This self-detachment or feeling of depersonalization may in turn negatively affect self-esteem. It is also possible that self-efficacy once again plays a role. If one is involved at the same time in too many new situations and role relationships, one might perceive oneself as generally ineffective. In other words, the inability to perform easily in multiple important new domains may generalize to an evaluation of the self as inefficacious. Consequently, self-esteem may drop, as well as actual ability to perform well (as reflected in one's GPA).

In short, the transition out of childhood into early adolescence remains a fascinating area for research. As an entry into a new period in the life course, adolescence involves fundamental changes in multiple domains—biological and physical change, as well as change in the social structural contexts confronting the individual. The effect of all of these varied changes upon the social–psychological adjustment of the individual is both complex and of great theoretical and practical importance.

Footnotes

[1]See Wells and Stryker (in press) for discussion of cumulative change at later points in the life course. They term the problem one of "synchronicity." Also see Hetherington (1979), Rutter (1979, 1980), and Thoits (1983) for development of ideas similar to the "focal" hypothesis.

[2]See Rutter (1981), Werner and Smith (1982) and Bronfenbrenner (in press) who argue that, in general, males of all ages are at greater risk than females. See Kessler et al., 1985 for evidence that adult women react more negatively to the accumulation of negative life events, but not to many specific stressful events.

[3]Of course for many children, their future pathways will be taken for granted by family and self, particularly if their abilities or lack of same are clear. For such children no real decision-point may be perceived. Also, in some cases both in the United States and in other countries the child does not make these decisions but is channelled through different tracks by school authorities.

[4]It will be necessary in future analyses to investigate more specifically the causal ordering between self-esteem and victimization. It is possible that children with low self-esteem carry themselves in such a way that they are more likely to be victimized. Since we did not measure victimization in Grade 6, prior to the junior high school transition, our analyses in this regard have been limited.

APPENDIXES

APPENDIX A: Subject Attrition Throughout the Study (Whites Only)

	Grade 6 1974–1975		Grade 7 1975–1976		Grade 9 1977–1978		Grade 10 1978–1979		Longitudinal sample present all four times	
	N	%	N	%	N	%	N	%	N	%
Interviewed	621	100.0%	553	89.0%	361	58.1%	314	50.6%	310	49.9%
Student no longer in appropriate grade[a]	0		5	0.8	15	2.4	19	3.1	19	3.1
Habitually absent[b]	0		0	0.0	12	1.9	14	2.3	14	2.3
Not in suitable public school[c]	0		17	2.7	58	9.3	68	11.0	70	11.3
Not in any school[d]	0		1	0.2	9	1.4	12	1.9	13	2.1
Left Milwaukee school district[e]	0		41	6.6	118	19.0	134	21.6	135	21.7
Not in Milwaukee schools/location unknown[f]	0		4	0.6	28	4.5	34	5.5	34	5.5
Parental or student refusal[g]	0		0	0.0	20	3.2	26	4.2	26	4.2
Original sample size	621	100.0	621	100.0	621	100.0	621	100.0	621	100.0

[a]Includes subjects who failed or skipped a grade.

[b]Includes subjects who were in a Milwaukee public school but never present on any of the days we checked and (in Grades 9 and 10) an alternate appointment could not be made.

[c]Includes subjects who attended any private school in the city of Milwaukee or public schools where we were not permitted to work (by principal).

[d]Includes subjects who had died (2), were institutionalized, confined to "home instruction" for health reasons, or who had officially dropped out of school.

[e]Includes subjects who had moved out of the city either to another state, another part of Wisconsin, or a suburb of Milwaukee.

[f]Includes subjects who were no longer listed as attending Milwaukee public schools and whom we were unable to locate.

[g]Includes subjects whose parents refused permission for the later phase of the study or subjects who personally decided not to participate.

367

APPENDIX B: Correlations of Developmental Timing with Physical Characteristics and Self- and Stranger Perceptions of Physical Development by Grade for Girls

Characteristic measured or rated	Developmental timing (early[a], middle, late developer)				
	Grade 6	Grade 7	Grade 8	Grade 9	Grade 10
Physical characteristic					
Height (mm)	.48	.37	.06	−.01	−.11
Weight (lb)	.46	.41	.00	.26	.16
Ponderal index (ht/wt$^{1/3}$) measure of leanness	−.24	−.27	−.36	−.32	−.22
Rate of height growth (mm/yr)	−.33	−.51	−.70	−.47	−.36
Self-perceptions					
Presence of underarm hair	.22	.30	.11	.04	—
Presence of figure	.26	.26	—	—	—
Degree of physical changes	.23	.04	−.05	−.13	−.23
Strangers' perceptions[b]					
Presence of acne	.23(.19)	.30(.24)	.21	.22(.07)	.17(.11)
Rate child as fatter	.16(.23)	.26(.16)	.27	.27(.15)	.19(.18)
Rating of figure development	.48(.40)	.49(.50)	.46	.26(.22)	.25(.27)
Rating—relative physical maturity	.42(.38)	.44(.36)	.40	.23(.20)	.15(.06)
Average N	236	224	201	163	145

[a]Early developers were originally coded with the lowest number. The signs of relationships have been reversed so that a positive sign thus indicates a positive association between greater pubertal development and the characteristic at issue.
[b]Both the nurse and the interviewer rated these children. The interviewer's ratings are in parentheses.

APPENDIX C: Correlations of Developmental Timing (of Peak Rate of Height Growth) with Physical Characteristics and Self- and Stranger Perceptions of Physical Development by Grade for Boys

Characteristic measured or rated	Developmental timing (early[a], middle, late developer)				
	Grade 6	Grade 7	Grade 8	Grade 9	Grade 10
Physical characteristic					
Height (mm)	.36	.52	.65	.46	.20
Weight (lb.)	.32	.40	.44	.39	.33
Ponderal index (ht/wt$^{1/3}$) measure of leanness	-.18	-.11	-.02	-.16	-.30
Rate of height growth (mm/yr)[b]	.26	.73	.43	-.71	-.79
Self-perceptions					
Presence of underarm hair	-.05	.09	.43	.41	—
Presence of recent muscle growth	.11	.07	.21	.30	-.10
Degree of physical changes	.08	-.02	.08	-.11	-.18
Strangers' perceptions[c]					
Presence of acne	.08(.21)	.24(.24)	.20	.21(.15)	.03(.26)
Rate child as fatter	.12(.15)	.21(.17)	.13	.12(.16)	.24(.13)
Rating of masculinity	.27(.14)	.47(.24)	.45	.48(.30)	.32(.34)
Rating—relative physical maturity	.35(.19)	.40(.39)	.49	.52(.45)	.63(.48)
Average N	156	158	148	141	145

[a]Only males with clear height growth curves are used in this analysis. Early developers were originally coded with the lowest number. The signs of relationships have been reversed so that a positive sign thus indicates a positive association between greater pubertal development and the characteristic at issue. Sixth and seventh grade heights and weights are based on measurements made closest to date of interview.

[b]Rate of height growth measures for the period between sixth and seventh grades are reported under the Grade 7 heading, for 7 to 8 grade information obtained under the eighth grade heading, etc. Rate of height growth from Grade 5 to 6 was computed using fifth grade information obtained from school records and our sixth grade measurements. The rate of height growth between Grade 5 and Grade 6 when based completely on school data does not yield very different results.

[c]Both the nurse and the interviewer rated these children. The interviewer's ratings are in parentheses.

APPENDIX D: Pearson Correlations between Scores on the Same Variable in Grades 6–7 and between Scores on the Same Variable in Grades 9–10

	Grade 6–7		Grade 9–10	
	Boys (N = 294)	Girls (N = 259)	Boys (N = 164)	Girls (N = 150)
I. Establish Self-Image				
A. *Global self-image*				
1. Self-esteem	.46	.53	.48	.61
2. Self-consciousness	.29	.54	.38	.54
3. Self-stability	.29	.42	.40	.44
B. *Body-image*				
4. Perceive self as good-looking	.35	.45	.45	.50
5. Satisfaction with looks	.27	.47	.49	.52
6. Satisfaction with weight	.42	.52	.54	.68
7. Satisfaction with height	.37	.47	.43	.42
8. Satisfaction with body build	.39	.52	.27	.60
C. *Concern with body-image*				
9. Care about looks	.41	.39	.41	.38
10. Care about weight	.40	.44	.44	.68
11. Care about height	.46	.41	.48	.59
12. Care about body build	.43	.44	.53	.50
D. *Perceived self-competence*				
13. Perceive self as smart	.25	.45	.56	.44
14. Good at school work	.40	.42	.53	.44
15. Good at sports	.56	.58	.56	.66
E. *Concern with competence*				
16. Value competence versus popularity and independence	.13	.18	.30	.36
17. Care about being smart	.24	.25	.45	.28
18. Care about school work	.27	.29	.45	.39
19. Care about good at sports	.28	.31	.55	.55

F. *Gender-role attitudes*				
20. Positive feelings about being own gender	.28	.41	.45	.51
21. Care about not acting like opposite sex	.08	.47	.40	.51
22. How often act like opposite sex	.23	.46	.59	.56
G.23. *Depressive-affect*	.25	.45	.36	.51
II. Establish Peer Relationships				
A. *Peer popularity*				
1. Same-sex	.33	.32	.39	.29
2. Opposite-sex	.57	.48	.29	.49
B. *Value popularity*				
3. Care about same-sex popularity	.34	.32	.47	.37
4. Care about opposite-sex popularity	.39	.43	.44	.56
5. Value popularity more than competence or independence	.03	.23	.40	.67
6. Value opposite-sex popularity more than competence	.24	.36	.31	.37
C. *Dating behavior*				
7. Dating behavior	.44	.41	.55	.59
D. *Others' expectations regarding opposite-sex relationships*				
8. Parents expect to date	.35	.39	.27	.37
9. Same-sex friends expect dating	.25	.28	.35	.36
10. Parents expect interest in opposite sex	.32	.33	—	—
11. Same-sex peers expect interest in opposite sex	.26	.10	—	—
E. *Participation in activities*				
12. Total in-school clubs and sports	.37	.47	.51	.54
13. Total out-of-school clubs and sports	.47	.47	.45	.58
14. Coed clubs (in and out of school)	.18	.45	—	—
15. Leadership in clubs and sports	.34	.27	.51	.41

(Continued)

371

APPENDIX D: (Continued)

	Grade 6–7		Grade 9–10	
	Boys (N=294)	Girls (N=259)	Boys (N=164)	Girls (N=150)
III. Establish Independence				
A. *Independence from parents*				
1. Take bus without adult	.37	.40	—	—
2. Go places without parents permission	.33	.29	.53	.47
3. Parents permission not required after dark	.32	.32	.42	.46
4. Left home alone	.38	.34	.22	.43
5. Times per month baby-sit	.36	.42	.30	.43
6. Part-time job	.34	.29	.26	.24
7. Perceived independence from parents	.29	.23	.39	.42
8. Perceived independent decision making	.16	.19	.29	.40
B. *Perception that others expect older behavior*				
9. Parents	.29	.28	.22	.34
10. Friends	.11	.33	.27	.32
11. Teachers	.21	.28	.28	.41
C. *Value independence*				
12. Value independence from parents	.24	.25	.41	.50
13. Value independence versus competence and popularity	.17	.19	.28	.23

372

IV. Plan for Future

A. *Educational, occupational, and marital aspirations*

1. Plan to go to college	.41	.50	.56	.63
2. Want to get married	.49	.60	.72	.61
3. Want to have children	.53	.63	.72	.49
4. SES of ideal job	.51	.29	.49	.38

B. *Perception that others expect career planning*

7. Parents	.39	.32	.34	.48
8. Teachers	.33	.21	.29	.10
9. Friends	.27	.24	.23	.28

V. Deal with Conformity/Deviance Issues

A. *Problem behavior*

1. Problem behavior scale	.63	.54	.61	.72
2. Probations/suspensions	.27	.18	.31	.49
3. Truancy	.47	.25	.62	.72

B. 4. *Victimization*

	—	—	.22	.04

C. *Academic performance*

5. GPA	.71	.61	.78	.79
6. Reading achievement score	.69	.75	—	—
7. Math achievement score	.56	.66	—	—

D. *Perception that adults evaluate one highly*

8. Mother	.38	.42	.42	.48
9. Teachers	.27	.32	.32	.38

E. *Perception of parent–peer relationship*

10. Parents like close friends	.39	.32	.42	.36
11. Close friends like parents	.27	.47	.30	.65

APPENDIX E: LISREL Measurement Models for Self-Esteem and Opposite Sex Relations

In the analyses in Chapters 9, 12, and 13 we used the LISREL program to estimate relationships among conceptual variables. This appendix provides summary information for assessing the measurement models constructed for those analyses in chapter 9; the measurement models for self-esteem were examined over all four years. The same model was appropriate for all years. For chapters 12 and 13 (where only two years are considered), measurement models for both self-esteem and opposite-sex relations were estimated separately for boys and girls and then reestimated with paths for boys and girls constrained to be equal. The constrained model fits well in both cases. This means, for example, that the relationships among indicators of self-esteem are the same for both boys and girls. The same scale is appropriate for each. Even more important, the same scale can be used for children of different ages.

Self-Esteem

There are six items involved in the self-esteem measurement model. These are:

SE$_1$: A kid said, "I am no good." Do you ever feel like this? (If *YES*, ask): Do you feel like this *a lot or *a little? "I am no good."

SE$_2$: A kid said, "There's a lot wrong with me." Do you ever feel like this? (If *YES*, ask): Do you feel like this *a lot or *a little? "There's a lot wrong with me."

SE$_3$: Another kid said, "I'm not much good at anything." Do you ever feel like this? (If *YES*, ask): Do you feel like this *a lot or *a little? "I'm not much good at anything."

SE$_4$: Another kid said, "I think I am no good at all." Do you ever feel like this? (If *YES*, ask): Do you feel like this *a lot or *a little? "I think I am no good at all."

SE$_5$: Everybody has some things about him which are good and some things about him that are bad. Are more of the things about you good, *bad, or are they *both about the same?

SE$_6$: How happy are you with the kind of person you are? Are you very happy with the kind of person you are, pretty happy, a *little happy or *not at all happy with the kind of person you are?

Starred responses indicate low self-esteem. All items are coded as dichotomies.

Figure E.1 presents the measurement model for girls (the same as the one for boys). The fit statistics indicate that the model does a good job

FIGURE E.1. Self-esteem measurement model for girls ($N = 106$). Lambdas are constrained across time and group; Betas are constrained across groups. This model was estimated simultaneously with the one for boys. Unstandardized coefficients are without parentheses; standardized are within parentheses. The same measurement model for Self-esteem is suitable for boys and girls, and for Grades 6 and 7. Tests follow for significant differences between the unconstrained model and a model in which Lambda's and Beta's for males and females in Grades 6 and 7 are constrained to be equal.

Model	Chi-square	df	p
Constrained	120.04	110	
Unconstrained	109.19	94	
	10.85	16	N.S. (.80)

Fit statistics for constrained model: Chi-square: 120.04 with 110 degrees of freedom ($p = .24$); Chi-square/df 1.09.

	Goodness-of-fit	Root mean square residual	R^2
Boys	.931	.012	.56
Girls	.901	.015	.47

FIGURE E.2. Opposite-sex relations measurement model for girls ($N = 106$). Lambdas are constrained acrosss time and groups; Betas are constrained across groups. This model was estimated simultaneously with the one for boys. Unstandardized coefficients are without parentheses; standardized are within parentheses. The same measurement model for Opposite-sex relations is suitable for both boys and girls and for Grades 6 and 7. Tests follow for significant differences between the unconstrained model and a model in which Lambda's and Beta's for males and females in Grades 6 and 7 are constrained to be equal.

Model	Chi-square	df	p
Constrained	40.92	36	
Unconstrained	27.91	26	
	13.01	10	N.S. ($p > .20$)

Fit statistics for constrained model. Chi-square $= 40.92$ with 36 degrees of freedom ($p = .26$).

	Goodness-of-fit	Root mean square residual	R^2
Boys	.954	.032	.45
Girls	.958	.036	.51

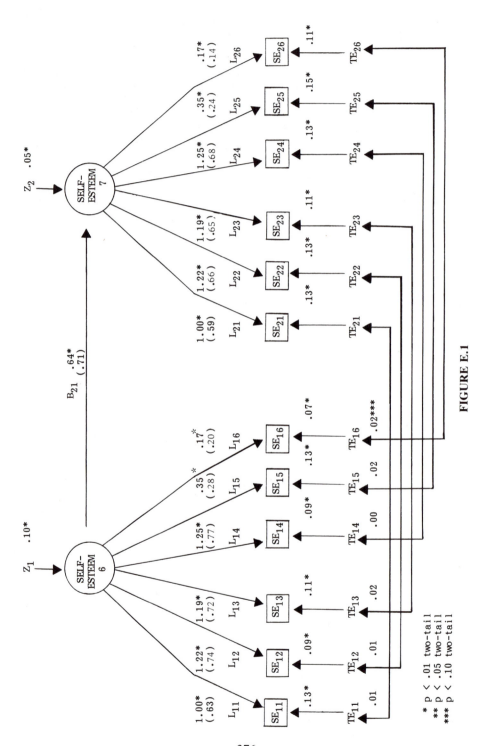

FIGURE E.1

* p < .01 two-tail
** p < .05 two-tail
*** p < .10 two-tail

376

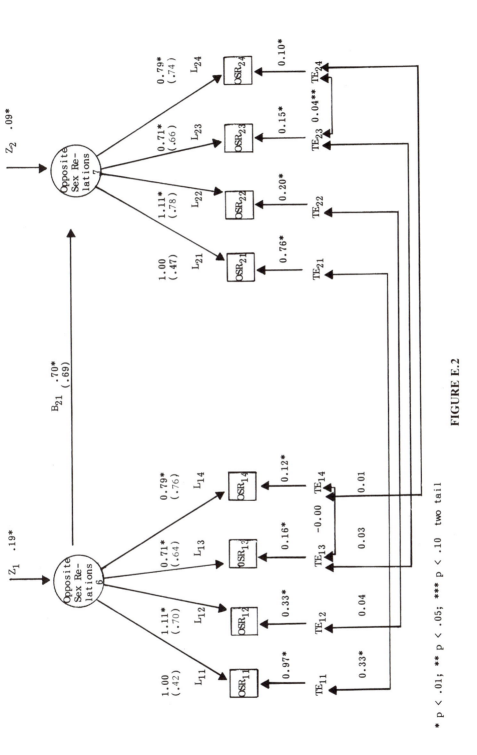

FIGURE E.2

* p < .01; ** p < .05; *** p < .10 two tail

377

of reproducing the relationships among the indicators. Although this model shows only Grades 6 and 7, our analyses demonstrate that the same model is applicable for Grades 9 and 10 as well.

Opposite-Sex Relations

Three items and a single variable index created from six items were used in the opposite-sex relations measurement model. All items involved were asked separately of boys about their relationships with girls and of girls of their relationships with boys. These items were combined to create measures of relations with the opposite sex. The exact wording of the questions employed is as follows:

OSR$_1$: "How much do the (girls/boys) at school like you? Do the (girls/boys) like you very much, pretty much, not very much, or not at all?" A variable was created with the following response categories: (1) not at all; (2) not very much; (3) don't know; (4) pretty much + very much.

OSR$_2$: Dating behavior—This is a complex indicator of dating with the following categories: (0) no dating; (1) goes out on dates with a group; (2) dates alone or goes steady (see Appendix G).

OSR$_3$: "Do you ever go over to a (girl's/boy's) house?" (0) no; (1) yes.

OSR$_4$: "Do you ever have (girlfriends/boyfriends) over to your house?" (0) no; (1) yes.

As with self-esteem, the measurement model for girls is presented in Figure (E.2). The fit statistics show that the model fits well for both boys and girls in Grades 6 and 7.

APPENDIX F: Tables and figures for Chapters 12 and 13

TABLE F.1. Effect of Predictor Variables on Adjustment in Grade 7—
Significant Coefficients for Junior High Girls[a]

	Unstandardized coefficient	Standard error	Standardized coefficient	p	R^2
Self-esteem$_7$					.77
School size$_7$	−.038	.025	−.130	$(< .10)^b$	
Self-esteem$_6$	.552	.086	.601	$< .01$	
Social class	−.073	.031	−.194	$< .05$	
Looks$_7$	.061	.038	.140	$(< .10)^b$	
Peer evaluation$_7$	.226	.073	.247	$< .01$	
Problem behavior$_7$	−.047	.020	−.231	$< .01$	
Victimization$_7$	−.141	.043	−.281	$< .01$	
Victimization$_7$					.18
Percentage ethnic$_7$	.140	.066	.239	$< .05$	
Looks$_6$	−.280	.136	−.227	$< .05$	
Participation in activities$_7$	.108	.083	.128	$(< .10)^b$	
Looks$_7$					.28
Opposite-sex relations$_6$	.445	.248	.365	$< .10$	
Athletic ability$_7$					.38
School size$_7$	−.082	.062	−.122	$(< .10)^b$	
Athletic$_6$	.396	.104	.429	$< .01$	
Perceived high peer evaluation$_7$					.19
Looks$_6$	.186	.076	.277	$< .05$	
Peer evaluation$_6$	.286	.102	.314	$< .01$	
Self-esteem$_6$	−.178	.107	−.178	$< .10$	
Participation in extracurricular activities$_7$					.21
Percentage ethnic$_7$	−.166	.076	−.240	$< .05$	
Move as Group$_7$	−.350	.206	−.206	$< .10$	
Late pubertal development	.155	.086	.189	$< .10$	
Athletic ability$_6$					
Participation in	.278	.122	.293	$< .05$	
activities$_6$	.195	.093	.228	$< .05$	
GPA$_7$					.59
School size	.118	.062	.145	$< .10$	
Social class	.109	.076	.105	$(< .10)^b$	
Late pubertal development	.145	.074	.151	$< .10$	
GPA$_6$	.631	.082	.566	$< .01$	
Independence$_6$	−.463	.224	−.151	$< .05$	

(Continued)

TABLE F.1. *(Continued)*

	Unstandardized coefficient	Standard error	Standardized coefficient	p	R^2
School problem behavior$_7$					.44
Social class	−.243	.155	−.132	$(< .10)^b$	
Late pubertal development	−.293	.151	−.173	$< .10$	
Participation in activities$_6$	−.200	.154	−.113	$(< .10)^b$	
Problem behavior$_6$	.478	.104	.515	$< .01$	
Independence$_6$	.841	.459	.155	$< .10$	
Self-esteem$_6$	−.540	.404	−.120	$(< .10)^b$	

[a] Dependent variables are indicated by italics. Variables listed under each dependent variable represent significant predictors. Subscript numbers refer to grade in school.

[b] One-tail test: $p < .10$. All other significance levels are two-tail tests.

TABLE F.2. Effect of Predictor Variables on Adjustment in Grade 7—
Significant Coefficients for Junior High Boys[a]

	Unstandardized coefficient	Standard error	Standardized coefficient	p	R^2
Self-esteem$_7$					.77
School size$_7$	−.058	.022	−.233	$< .01$	
Self-esteem$_6$	.565	.083	.656	$< .01$	
Peer evaluation$_7$	.101	.060	.182	$< .10$	
Looks$_7$	.156	.056	.226	$< .01$	
GPA$_7$	−.074	.032	−.229	$< .05$	
Victimization$_7$	−.072	.030	−.203	$< .05$	
Victimization$_7$					.21
Percentage ethnic$_7$	.104	.078	.148	$(< .10)^b$	
Peer evaluation$_6$	−.322	.185	−.172	$< .10$	
Independence$_6$	.248	.176	.126	$(< .10)^b$	
Problem behavior$_6$	.066	.050	.138	$(< .10)^b$	
Self-esteem$_6$	−.323	.249	−.132	$(< .10)^b$	
Looks$_7$					.19
Looks$_6$	.322	.105	.287	$< .01$	
Athletic$_6$	.088	.050	.161	$< .10$	
Athletic ability$_7$					.36
Percentage ethnic$_7$	−.122	.067	−.184	$< .10$	
Looks$_6$	.258	.172	.125	$(< .10)^b$	
Athletic ability$_6$	.417	.083	.416	$< .01$	
Independence$_6$	.411	.149	.223	$< .01$	
Self-esteem$_6$	.315	.211	.137	$(< .10)^b$	
Perceived high peer evaluation$_7$					.27
School size$_7$	.085	.044	.191	$< .10$	
Social class	.095	.048	.168	$< .10$	
Looks$_6$	.341	.123	.245	$< .01$	

TABLE F.2. *(Continued)*

	Unstandardized coefficient	Standard error	Standardized coefficient	p	R^2
Opposite-sex popularity$_6$	.142	.096	.153	$(< .10)^b$	
Problem behavior$_6$	−.096	.031	−.317	$< .01$	
Self-esteem$_6$	.211	.152	.136	$(< .10)^b$	
Opposite-sex popularity$_7$					.46
Social class	.080	.056	.138	$(< .10)^b$	
Looks$_6$	.256	.144	.179	$< .10$	
Opposite-sex popularity$_6$	.551	.115	.576	$< .01$	
Independence$_6$	.175	.125	.137	$(< .10)^b$	
Participation in extracurricular activities$_7$					.21
Percentage ethnic$_7$	−.157	.083	−.211	$< .10$	
Participation in activities$_6$	.130	.088	.144	$(< .10)^b$	
GPA$_6$	.297	.102	.278	$< .01$	
GPA$_7$					.63
Move as a group$_7$	−.394	.177	−.181	$< .05$	
Late pubertal development	.080	.056	.089	$(< .10)^b$	
Participation in activities$_6$	.130	.062	.141	$< .05$	
GPA$_6$	.850	.072	.773	$< .01$	
Self-esteem$_6$	.415	.185	.156	$< .05$	
School problem behavior$_7$					.42
School size$_7$	−.272	.155	−.154	$< .10$	
Looks$_6$	−.801	.435	−.146	$< .10$	
Athletic ability$_6$	.626	.209	.235	$< .01$	
Peer evaluation$_6$	−1.030	.397	−.220	$< .05$	
GPA$_6$	−.331	.206	−.131	$(< .10)^b$	
Problem behavior$_6$	.401	.108	.333	$< .01$	

[a]Dependent variables are indicated by italics. Variables listed under each dependent variable represent significant predictors. Subscript numbers refer to grade in school.

[b]One-tail test: $p < .10$. All other significance levels are two-tail tests.

TABLE F.3. Correlation Matrix–Grade 6 Variables[a]

	Social Class	Puberty	Looks	Athletics	Activities	Peer evaluation	Opp. sex[b]	Teacher evaluation	GPA	Independence	Problem behavior	Self-esteem[b]
Social class		.03	-.01	-.07	-.04	.15	-.00	-.22**	.02	.13	.05	-.14
Late puberty	.12		.06	-.18***	.07	.09	.12	.13	.08	-.12	-.08	-.09
Good looks	.05	.01		.10	.17***	.26*	.19***	.34*	.13	-.10	-.18***	.09
Athletic ability	.02	-.10	.18***		.13	.06	.44*	.17***	-.23**	.11	.28*	.09
Activities	-.04	.05	-.07	-.03		.18***	-.03	-.15	.17***	-.16***	.01	-.07
Peer evaluation	.10	.02	.11	.23**	.08		.08	.24**	.20**	-.23**	-.18***	.17***

382

Opposite sex relations[b]	.02	.48*	.01	−.26*	−.03		.11	.07	.10	.02	−.29*	−.11
Teacher evaluation	.28	−.22**	.15	.11		−.08	.20**	−.05	.01	.29*	.00	−.05
GPA	.05	−.38*	−.14		−.00	−.03	−.25*	.09	.08	.07	−.10	−.04
Independence	−.16	.07		−.09	−.10	.09	.11	.02	.13	−.08	−.15	.01
Problem behavior	−.09		.25*	−.16***	−.31*	.32*	−.02	−.02	.09	−.09	−.15	.15
Self-esteem[b]		−.07	−.04	−.06	.08	−.07	.25**	−.03	.19**	.19**	.05	.05

[a]JH boys below diagonal (N = 113), JH girls above diagonal (N = 106).
[b]These correlations are LISREL estimates, since measurement models are involved. Otherwise Pearson correlations are reported. *p < .01; **p < .05; ***p < .10.

TABLE F.4. Standardized PSI Matrix for Grade 7 Endogenous Variables.[a]

	Activities₇	Peer evaluation₇	Opposite sex relations₇	Looks₇	Athletics₇	GPA₇	Problem behavior₇	Victimization₇
Activities₇	.79 / .79	.05	—	.09	.20***	.02	−.06	—
Peer evaluation₇	−.03	.81 / .73	—	.26***	−.05	.06	.03	−.02
Opposite-sex relations₇	.25***	.22***	.54 / —	—	—	—	—	—
Looks₇	.13*	.13*	.04	.82 / .71	.07	.08	.02	−.15
Athletic ability₇	.08	−.07	.13*	.04	.64 / .62	.06	.02	.06
GPA₇	.13**	.05	−.13**	.13**	−.01	.41 / .37	−.11**	−.08
Problem behavior₇	.13*	−.14**	.12*	−.04	.10	−.11**	.58 / .56	.24***
Victimization₇	—	.11	−.01	−.02	−.13*	−.08	.03	.82 / .79

[a]The figures in the diagonal represent unexplained variance in the variable. JH boys below diagonal (N = 113), JH girls above diagonal (N = 106).

*p < .01; **p < .05; ***p < .10.

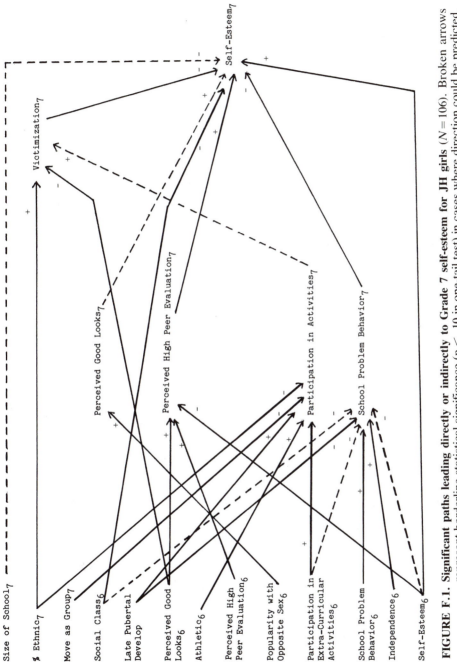

FIGURE F.1. Significant paths leading directly or indirectly to Grade 7 self-esteem for JH girls ($N = 106$). Broken arrows represent borderline statistical significance ($p < .10$ in one-tail test) in cases where direction could be predicted. Solid arrows represent $p < .10$ in two-tail test. The subscripts 6 and 7 attached to the variable names represent the grade level associated with the variable.

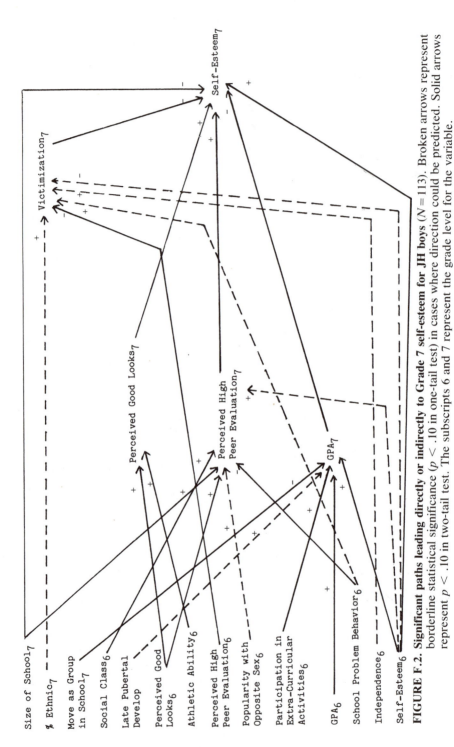

FIGURE F.2. Significant paths leading directly or indirectly to Grade 7 self-esteem for JH boys ($N = 113$). Broken arrows represent borderline statistical significance ($p < .10$ in one-tail test) in cases where direction could be predicted. Solid arrows represent $p < .10$ in two-tail test. The subscripts 6 and 7 represent the grade level for the variable.

APPENDIX G: Measurement of the Tasks of Adolescence, of School Structure and Perceptions, and of Socioeconomic Status

Variable	Description	Direction (range)	Source[a]	Years	N of Items
I. Establish Self-Image					
A. Global self-esteem					
1. Self-esteem	*a)* Additive scale: Simmons-Rosenberg modification of Rosenberg Self-Esteem Scale assesses global evaluation of self (Simmons *et al.*, 1973; Simmons *et al.*, 1979). (See items in Appendix E.)	High = high (0, 6)	I	6,7,9,10	6
			Q	8	6 Alpha = .72[b] Guttman scale Scalability (Scal.) = .75 Reproducability (Repro.) = .92
	b) See also the disaggregated LISREL measurement model in Appendix E.				
2. Self-consciousness	Modification of the Rosenberg-Simmons Self-Consciousness Scale (see Simmons *et al.*, 1973). The exact questions used here are: • "A young person said: 'When I'm with people I get nervous because I worry about how much they like me.' Do you feel like this often,[c] sometimes, or never?" • "Let's say some grownup or adult visitors came into class and the teacher wanted them to know who you were, so she asked you to stand up and tell them a little about yourself. Would you like that, not like it,[c] or wouldn't you care?"[c] • "If the teacher asked you to get up in front of the class and talk a little bit about your summer, would you be very nervous,[c] a little nervous, or not at all nervous?" • "If you did get up in front of class and tell them about your summer, would you think a lot about how all the kids were looking at you,[c] a little bit about how all the kids were looking at you, or wouldn't you think at all about the kids looking at you?"	High = high (0, 4)	I	6,7,9,10	4 Scal. = .76 Repro. = .95

(Continued)

APPENDIX G: *(Continued)*

Variable	Description	Direction (range)	Source[a]	Years	N of Items
3. Self-stability	Modification of the Rosenberg–Simmons Self-Stability Scale (see Simmons *et al.*, 1973). The exact questions used here are: • "How sure are you that you know what kind of person you really are? Are you . . . very sure,[d] pretty sure,[d] not very sure, or not at all sure?"[d] • "How often do you feel mixed up about yourself, about what you are really like? Often, sometimes, or never.[d] • "A kid said: 'Some days I am happy with the kind of person I am, other days I am not happy with the kind of person I am.' Do your feelings *change* like this? Yes, No.[d] • "A kid said: 'Some days I think I am one kind of person, other days a different kind of person.' Do your feelings *change* like this? Yes, No.[d]	High = high (0, 4)	1	6,7,9,10	4 Scal. = .82 Repro. = .95
B. *Body-image*					
4. Perceive self as good-looking	"How good-looking are you?"	High = very good-looking (1, 4)	1	6,7,9,10	1
5. Satisfaction with looks	"First, how happy are you with how GOOD-LOOKING you are?"	High = very happy (1, 4)	1	6,7,9,10	1
6. Satisfaction with weight	"How happy are you with how much you WEIGH?"	High = very happy (1, 4)	1	6,7,9,10	1
7. Satisfaction with height	"How happy are you with how TALL you are?"	High = very happy (1, 4)	1	6,7,9,10	1
8. Satisfaction with body build	"How happy are you with your (OVERALL MUSCLE DEVELOPMENT/FIGURE)?"[c]	High = very happy (1, 4)	1	6,7,9,10	1

C. Concern with body-image					
9. Care about looks	"How much do you care about how GOOD-LOOKING you are?"	High = very much (1, 4)	1	6,7,9,10	1
10. Care about weight	"How much do you care about how MUCH YOU WEIGH?"	High = very much (1, 4)	1	6,7,9,10	1
11. Care about height	"How much do you care about how TALL you are?"	High = very much (1, 4)	1	6,7,9,10	1
12. Care about body build	"How much do you care about your (MUSCLE DEVELOPMENT/FIGURE)?"[e]	High = very much (1, 4)	1	6,7,9,10	1
D. Perceived self-competence					
13. Perceive self as smart	"First of all, how SMART are you?"	High = very much (1, 4)	1	6,7,9,10	1
14. Good at school work	"How good are you at SCHOOL WORK?"	High = very much (1, 4)	1	6,7,9,10	1
15. Good at sports	"How good at SPORTS are you?"	High = very much (1, 4)	1	6,7,9,10	1
E. Concern with competence					
16. Value competence[f] versus popularity and independence	"Which would you most like to be? Would you like to be able to do things for yourself, well liked, or the best in things you do?"	High = competent (0, 1)	1	6,7,9,10	1
17. Care about being smart	"First, how much do you care about how SMART you are?"	High = very much (1, 4)	1	6,7,9,10	1
18. Care about school work	"How much do you care about how WELL you do in SCHOOL WORK?"	High = very much (1, 4)	1	6,7,9,10	1
19. Care about good at sports	"How much do you care about how GOOD AT SPORTS you are?"	High = very much (1, 4)	1	6,7,9,10	1

(Continued)

APPENDIX G: *(Continued)*

Variable	Description	Direction (range)	Source[a]	Years	N of Items
F. Gender-role attitudes					
20. Positive feelings about being own gender	"How do you feel about being a (BOY/GIRL)?"	High = great (1, 4)	I	6,7,9,10	1
21. Care about not acting like opposite sex	"How important is it for you NOT to act like a (GIRL/BOY)?"	High = very important (1, 3)	I	6,7,9,10	1
22. How often act like opposite sex	"Would you say you act like a (GIRL/BOY)?"	High = very often (1, 4)	I	6,7,9,10	1
G. 23. Depressive-affect	Modification of the Rosenberg-Simmons Depression Scale (see Simmons et al., 1973). The exact questions used here are: • "How happy are you today? Are you . . . very happy, pretty happy,[g] not very happy,[g] or not at all happy?"[g] • "How happy would you say you are most of the time? Would you say you are . . . very happy, pretty happy, not very happy,[g] not at all happy?"[g] • "A kid said: 'Other kids seem happier than I.' Is this . . . true[g] for you or not true for you?" • "Would you say that most of the time you are . . . very cheerful, pretty cheerful,[g] not very cheerful,[g] or not cheerful at all?"[g]	High = depressed (0, 4)	I	6,7,9,10	4 Scal. = .78 Repro. = .94
II. Establish Peer Relationships					
A. Peer popularity					
1. Same-sex	"How much do the other (BOYS/GIRLS) at school like you?"	High = very much (1, 4)	I	6,7,9,10	1
2. Opposite-sex	"How much do the (GIRLS/BOYS) at school like you?" See also the LISREL measurement model for Opposite-Sex Relations in Appendix E.	High = very much (1, 4)	I	6,7,9,10	1

	Question	Scoring		Grades	
B. Value popularity					
3. Care about same-sex popularity	"How much do you care about whether the (BOYS/GIRLS) at school like you?"	High = very much (1, 4)	1	6,7,9,10	1
4. Care about opposite-sex popularity	"How much do you care about whether the (GIRLS/BOYS) at school like you?"	High = very much (1, 4)	1	6,7,9,10	1
5. Value popularity[f] more than competence or independence	"Which would you most like to be? Would you like to be able to do things for yourself, well liked, or the best in things you do?"	High = well liked (0, 1)	1	6,7,9,10	1
6. Value opposite-sex popularity more than competence	"Which would you most like to be? Would you like to be well liked by (GIRLS/BOYS) or good at the things you do?"	High = well liked (0, 1)	1	6,7,9,10	1
C. Dating behavior					
7. Dating behavior	(A) Summary scale created as follows: The dating behavior scale was constructed through a multistage process including six questions. Each student was asked:	High = go steady (0,3)	1	6,7,9,10	6

(1) "Do you ever go out with another (boy/girl) and a couple of (girls/boys) or meet a group of boys and girls at night?"

(2) "Do you ever go to dances or parties where there are both boys and girls present?"

If they answered "No" to both they received a score of "0" on the dating scale, if they said "Yes" to either of these items but scored "low" on items 3–6, they received a "1." Students were also asked:

(3) "Do you ever go out with a (girl/boy) alone?"

(4) "Do you ever meet a (girl/boy) somewhere and then do something or go someplace together?"

Scal. = .93

Repro. = .98

(Continued)

APPENDIX G: (Continued)

Variable	Description	Direction (range)	Source[a]	Years	N of Items
	If they answered "YES" to either of these questions but scored "low" on either item 5 or 6, they received a score of "2" on the dating scale. Finally students were asked: (5) "About how often do you go out with or meet a (girl/boy) somewhere? $\underline{1}$ Once every 2 or 3 months $\underline{2}$ Once a month $\underline{3}$ Once every 2 or 3 weeks $\underline{4}$ Once a week $\underline{5}$ Once every 2 or 3 days $\underline{6}$ About once a day" (6) "How often do you and one special (girl/ boy) friend go somewhere? $\underline{1}$ Once every 2 or 3 months $\underline{2}$ Once a month $\underline{3}$ Once every 2 or 3 weeks $\underline{4}$ Once a week $\underline{5}$ Once every 2 or 3 days $\underline{6}$ About once a day" If they answered "once every 2 or 3 weeks" or more often to both, they were coded as "3" on the dating variable. (B) See also LISREL Opposite-Sex Relations Measurement Model in Appendix E.				
7a. Opposite-sex popularity	See II, A, 2				
D. Others' expectations regarding opposite-sex relationships					
8. Parents expect to date	"How much do your parents care about whether or not you go out with (GIRLS/BOYS)?" Multiplied by, "Would your parents like you to go out with (GIRLS/BOYS) or not like you to out with (GIRLS/ BOYS)?"	High = strongly want you to date $(-4, +4)$	I	6,7,9,10	2

392

Item	Question	Scoring			
9. Same-sex friends expect dating	"How much do your (BOYS/GIRL) friends care about whether you go out with (GIRLS/BOYS)?" Multiplied by, "Would your (BOY/GIRL) friends like you to go out with (GIRLS/BOYS) or not like you go out with (GIRLS/BOYS)?"	High = strongly $(-4, +4)$	1	6,7,9,10	2
10. Parents expect interest in opposite sex	"Do your parent(s) think you SHOULD BE INTERESTED IN (GIRLS/BOYS), SHOULD NOT BE INTERESTED IN (GIRLS/BOYS), or don't they care?"	High = should be interested $(-1, +1)$	1	6,7	1
11. Same-sex peers expect interest in opposite sex	"Do your (BOY/GIRL) friends think you SHOULD BE INTERESTED IN (GIRLS/BOYS), SHOULD NOT BE INTERESTED IN (GIRLS/BOYS), or don't they care?"	High = should be interested $(-1, +1)$	1	6,7	1
E. *Participation in activities*					
12. Total in-school clubs and sports	"Do you belong to any clubs, sports, or activities at school?" (if yes) "What sports, activities, or clubs do you belong to at school?"	High = many clubs $(0, 6)$	1	6,7,9,10	2
13. Total out-of-school clubs and sports	"Do you belong to any clubs, sports, or activities *other than* those at school?" (if yes) "What clubs, sports, or other activities do you belong to?"	High = many clubs $(0, 6)$	1	6,7,9,10	2
14. Coed clubs (in and out of school)	After the questions asked in 12 and 13, each student was asked: "Which of these clubs, sports, or activities have both boys and girls in them?"	High = many $(0, 10)$	1	6,7	3
15. Leadership in clubs and sports activities	After the questions asked in 12 and 13, each student was asked: "Have you ever been a leader in any of these groups or elected to a position like president, vice-president, or captain?"	Yes = 1 $(0, 1)$	1	6,7,9,10	3
III. **Establish Independence**					
A. *Independence from parents*					
1. Take bus without adult	"Do you ever go some place, other than school, in a bus without a grownup going along with you?" (If YES) "Do you do this a lot, a little, or hardly ever?"	High = a lot $(0,3)$	1	6,7	2

(Continued)

393

APPENDIX G: (Continued)

Variable	Description	Direction (range)	Source[a]	Years	N of Items
2. Go places without parents' permission	"Can you make plans to go somewhere like to a movie with a friend without your parent(s)' permission?"	High = yes (0,1)	1	6,7,9,10	1
3. Parents' permission not required after dark	"If you wanted to go more than a block away from home after dark, would you have to ask your parent(s)' permission?"	High = no (0,1)	1	6,7,9,10	1
4. Left home alone	"If your parent(s) aren't home, do they . . . leave you all by yourself, leave you by yourself but with someone around if you need help, or do they make sure someone older stays with you?"	High = home alone (1,3 in Grade 6 & 7) (0,1 in Grade 9 & 10)	1	6,7,9,10	1
5. Times per month baby-sit	"Do you ever baby-sit for children other than your brothers or sisters?" (If YES) "About how many times a month do you baby-sit for other children?"	High = 6 or more (0, 6)	1	6,7,9,10	2
6. Part-time job	"Do you have a part-time job or earn any other money?"	High = yes (0, 1)	1	6,7,9,10	1
7. Perceived independence from parents	"HOW INDEPENDENT FROM YOUR PARENTS are you? That is, how much can you do things on your own without your parents telling you what to do?"	High = independent (1, 4)	1	6,7,9,10	1
8. Perceived independent decision making	"Now I would like to know how you and your parent(s) make decisions about things." (give child card H) "Which number of this card best describes how important decisions are made between you and your parent(s)? 1. My parent(s) just tell me what to do. 2. I have many chances to make my own decisions, but my parent(s) always have the final OK.	High = student decides (1, 3)	1	6,7,9,10	1

3. I can make my own decisions but my parent(s) would like me to do what they say.
4. I can do what I want, even if my parent(s) do not want me to.
5. My parent(s) don't care what I do."

B. *Perception that others expect older behavior*

9. Parents

Answers to two items were summed:

- "Which one of these sentences do you think is the way your PARENTS feel about you?" (*repeat shortened sentences if necessary*). "Sixth grade is *very* different and kids should act MUCH OLDER. "Sixth grade is *not very* much different from other years, since kids should act a LITTLE OLDER each year."
- "Do your parent(s) expect you to act . . . a lot differently this year from the way you did last year, a little differently, or about the same as you did last year?"

1 High = expect different behavior (2, 5)

6,7,9,10 2

10. Friends

Answers to two items were summed:

- "Which sentence do you think is the way MOST KIDS in your school feel about being a sixth grader?" (*repeat shortened sentences if necessary*) "Sixth grade is *very* different and kids should act MUCH OLDER. Sixth grade is *not very* much different from other years, since kids should act a LITTLE OLDER each year."
- "Now I would like to ask you some questions about what your friends expect of you this year. Do your friends expect you to act . . . a lot differently, a little differently, or about the same as your friends last year expected you to act?"

1 High = expect different behavior (2, 5)

6,7,9,10 2

(Continued)

Variable	Description	Direction (range)	Source[a]	Years	N of Items
11. Teachers	Answers to two items were summed: • "And, which sentence do you think is the way that YOUR TEACHERS this year feel about sixth graders?" (*repeat shortened sentences if necessary*) "Sixth grade is *very* different and kids should act MUCH OLDER. Sixth grade is *not very* much different from other years, since kids should act a LITTLE OLDER each year." • "Now I would like you to think about the way your teachers this year expect you to act. Do your teachers this year expect you to act . . . a lot differently, a little differently, or about the same as the teachers last year expected you to act?"	High = expect different behavior (2, 5)	1	6,7,9,10	2
C. *Value independence*					
12. Value independence vs. popularity and competence	"Which would you most like to be? Would you like to be able to do things for yourself, well liked, or best in the things you do?"	High = independence (0, 1)	1	6,7,9,10	1
13. Value independence from parents	"How much do you care about how INDEPENDENT you are from your parents? That is, how much do you care about being able to do things on your own without your parents telling you what to do?"	High = very much (1, 4)	1	6,7,9,10	1
IV. **Plan for Future**					
A. *Educational, occupational, and marital aspirations*					
1. Plan to go to college	"Do you think you will finish high school?" (If YES or PROBABLY) "When you finish high school do you expect to . . . go to vocational school, go to college, go to work, or do something else?"	1 = College (0, 1)	1	6,7,9,10	2
2. Want to get married	"Do you want to get married when you get older?"	1 = Yes (0, 1)	1	6,7,9,10	1

396

3. Want to have children	(If DOES WANT TO GET MARRIED) "Do you want to have any children?"	1 = Yes (0, 1) (not want to get married = 0)	1	6,7,9,10	2
4. SES of ideal job	"Do you want to have a job when you are an adult?" (If YES) "If you could have any job that you wanted, what job would you *like* when you are an adult?" (Open-ended responses were then categorized.)	High = upper white collar (1, 4)	1	6,7,9,10	2
B. *Perception that others expect career planning*					
5. Parents	"How much do your PARENT(S) expect you to be thinking or planning about the kind of job you want when you get older?"	High = a lot (1, 3)	1	6,7,9,10	1
6. Teachers	"How much do your TEACHERS this year expect you to be thinking or planning about the kind of job you want when you get older?"	High = a lot (1, 3)	1	6,7,9,10	1
7. Friends	"How much do your FRIENDS expect you to be thinking or planning about the kind of job you want when you get older?"	High = a lot (1, 3)	1	6,7,9,10	1
V. **Deal with Conformity/ Deviance Issues** A. *Problem behavior* 1. Problem behavior scale	Scale covering both self-rated and perceptions of teachers ratings. The exact questions are: • "Do you get into a lot of trouble at school, a little trouble at school, or do you never get into trouble at school?" • "How much trouble do your teachers feel you get into at school? A lot of trouble, a little trouble, or no trouble at school?" • "Since you started __th grade, how many times have you been sent to the principal's office because you had done something wrong?" (never, 1 or 2 times, 3 or more)	High = problems (4, 12)	1	6,7,9,10	4 alpha = .71

397

(Continued)

APPENDIX G: (Continued)

Variable	Description	Direction (range)	Source[a]	Years	N of Items
	• "Since you started ___th grade, how many times have you been placed on school probation or suspended from school?" (never, 1 or 2 times, 3 or more)				
2. Probations/suspensions[h]	"Since you started ___th grade, how many times have you been placed on school probation or suspended from school?"	High = many (1, 3)	I	6,7,9,10	1
3. Truancy	"Since you started ___th grade, how many times have you skipped school or played hookey?"	High = many (1, 3)	I	6,7,9,10	1
B. *Victimization*	Summary score of the following items: "Since you started ___th grade, has anyone threatened to beat you up or hurt you if you didn't give them your money or something else that belonged to you?" "Since you started ___th grade, has anything that costs more than a dollar been stolen from your desk or locker when you weren't around?" "Since you started ___th grade, has anyone actually beaten you up or really hurt you?"	High = many times (0, 1)	I	7,9,10	3
C. *Academic performance* 5. GPA	Grade point average for academic subjects	High = A (0, 4.0)	S	6,7,9,10	Varies from year to year
6. Reading achievement score	Standardized reading achievement score Grade 6—Iowa Tests of Basic Skills (ITBS) Grade 7—Metropolitan Achievement Tests (MAT) Grade 10—Tests of Academic Skills (TASK)	High = above average (−3, +3)	S	6,7,10	1

		High =			
7. Math achievement score	Standardized Mathematics Achievement Score Grade 6—Iowa Tests of Basic Skills (ITBS) Grade 7—Metropolitan Achievement Tests (MAT) Grade 10—Tests of Academic Skills (TASK)	High = above average $(-3, +3)$	S	6,7,10	1
D. *Perception that adults evaluate one highly*					
8. Parents	• "Let's pretend your PARENT(S) wanted to tell someone about you. What would they say? What type of person would they say you were? (What else would they say?)" (Open-ended responses were categorized.) • "Would you say that your MOTHER thinks of you as . . . a wonderful person, a pretty nice person, a little bit of a nice person or, not such a nice person?" • "Would you say that your FATHER thinks of you as . . ." (as for mother)	High = all favorable (0, 2)	1	6,7,9,10	3 Alpha = .64
9. Teachers	"What if your TEACHERS wanted to tell someone all about you. What type of person would your teachers say you were? (What else would they say?)" (Open-ended responses were categorized.)	High = wonderful (1, 3)	1	6,7,9,10	1
E. *Perception of parent–peer relationship*					
10. Parents like close friends	"How much do your parent(s) like your close friends? Do your parent(s) like your close friends . . . very much, somewhat, a little, or not at all?	High = like very much (1, 4)	1	6,7,9,10	1
11. Close friends like parents	"How much do your close friends like your parent(s)? Do your close friends like your parent(s) . . . very much, somewhat, a little, or not at all?"	High = like very much (1, 4)	1	6,7,9,10	1

(Continued)

399

APPENDIX G: (Continued)

Variable	Description	Direction (range)	Source[a]	Years	N of Items
VI. School Structure and Perceptions A. *School structure variables*					
1. Move as a group	Junior high schools in our sample follow one of two organizational strategies. Either students move around with the same group of students when they change classes, or they are individually scheduled.	1 = Move as group (0, 1)	S	7	1
2. Percentage ethnic	This is the percentage of the student population that is either Native American, black Asian, or Hispanic in origin. These categories are the ones used by the U.S. Department of Health, Education and Welfare, Office of Civil Rights (see Milwaukee Public Schools, 1978).	High = large percentage ethnic (0, 100)	S	7	1
3. School size	This variable provides a measure of the number of students officially enrolled in the school as of late September or early October of the school year. When necessary, postgraduate students, exchange program students and Job Corps totals were subtracted.	High = large (333, 2716)	S	6,7,9,10	1
B. *Attitudes toward school*					
1. Anonymity	A scale composed of the following items (see Blyth *et al.*, 1978 and 1983): • "This school has so many students in it that I feel I don't know lots of kids." • "Lots of kids don't know me at my school because it is so large." • "At this school the teachers don't seem to know who you are or what your name is." • "At this school most students don't seem to know who you are or what your name is."	High = feel anonymous (0, 8)	I Q	6,7,9,10[i] 8	4 Alpha = .57 (Grade 6) .74 (Grade 7) .76 (Grade 9) .77 (Grade 10)

400

2. Like this grade	"How much do you like being in __ th grade this year?"	High = like very much (1,4)	6,7,9,10	1
3. Worried about next year	"How worried are you about going into __ th grade next year?"	High = very worried (1,4)	6,7,9,10	1
4. Perceive this grade as different	"Now I want to ask you some questions about school this year as compared to school last year. Is __ th grade very different than last year, pretty different than last year, a little different than last year, not at all different than last year."	High = very different (1, 4)	6,7,9,10[i]	1

VII. **Social Background**
A. *Socioeconomic status of head of household*
  1. SES

Students were asked a series of questions about the employment of their mother, father, or parental surrogate.
"Does your (FATHER/STEPFATHER/MOTHER/STEPMOTHER) now work at a job?
(If yes)
  "Does (s)he work full time or part?"
  "What kind of work does your (FATHER/STEPFATHER/MOTHER/STEPMOTHER) do?"
  "What is (his/her) job called?"
(If no)
  "Is your (FATHER/STEPFATHER/MOTHER/STEPMOTHER) unemployed, retired, disabled, or something else?"
  "What kind of work did your (FATHER/STEPFATHER/MOTHER/STEPMOTHER) do before he became ___?"

(Continued)

APPENDIX G: (Continued)

Variable	Description	Direction (range)	Source[a]	Years	N of Items
	Responses to these questions were combined to create an indicator of the socioeconomic status of the head of the respondent's household. The occupational status of each (step)parent was coded using the Hollingshead scheme. The father or stepfather's current occupation was used if possible, and the previous occupation was used if the (step)father was not currently employed. If there was no father or stepfather, the mother's occupational status was used.				

[a]I = interview; Q = questionnaire; S = school records.

[b]Cronbach's Alpha coefficient based on sixth grade measures for the longitudinal subsample. Guttman Scale characteristics noted are for sixth grade. Other grade levels had similar coefficients. Test-retest correlations between adjacent years averaged .54 while the sixth to tenth grade correlation was .36.

[c]Indicates higher self-consciousness. All items were dichotomized for Guttman Scale.

[d]Indicates higher stability on dichotomized item.

[e]The boys and girls were asked these questions in separate sex-specific sections of the interview schedule. The wording was identical except the use of different phrases about the body. The phrase for boys is presented first.

[f]This item is recoded three times in order to highlight each of the three possibilities and included under three different headings.

[g]Indicates higher depression on dichotomized item.

[h]This item is also included in the Problem Behavior Scale.

[i]Questions for the anonymity scale and the question about perceiving the grade as different were asked of random halves of the sample in Grades 6 and 7 and of all students in Grades 9 and 10.

Bibliography

Adams, G. R., and Montemayor, R. Identity formation during early adolescence. *Journal of Early Adolescence,* 1983, *3*(3), 193–202.

Aldous, J. *Family careers: Developmental change in families.* NY: Wiley, 1978.

Alexander, K. L., and Eckland, B. K. The "explorations in equality of opportunity" sample of 1955 high school sophomores. In A. C. Kerchoff (Ed.), *Research in sociology of education and socialization,* Vol. 1. Greenwich, CT: JAI Press, 1980, pp. 31–58.

Alwin, D. F., and Otto, L. B. High school context effects on aspirations. *Sociology of Education,* 1977, *50*(October), 259–273.

Apter, A., Galatzer, A., Beth-Halachmi, N., and Laron, Z. Self-image in adolescents with delayed pubertal and growth retardation. *Journal of Youth and Adolescence,* 1981, *10,* 501–505.

Attenborough, R. E., and Zdep, S. M. Self-image among a national probability sample of girls. *Proceedings of the Eighty-first Annual Convention of the American Psychological Association,* 1973, 237–238.

Bachman, J. G., O'Malley, P. M., and Johnston, J. *Adolescence to adulthood: Change and stability in the lives of young men.* Vol. VI: *Youth in transition.* Ann Arbor, MI: Institute for Social Research, 1978.

Baltes, P. B., Reese, H. W., and Lipsitt, L. P. Life-span development psychology. *Annual Review of Psychology,* 1980, *31,* 65–110.

Bamber, O. H. Adolescent marginality—Further study. *Genetic Psychology Monographs,* 1973, *88,* 3–21.

Bandura, A. The stormy decade: Fact or fiction? In D. Rogers (Ed.), *Issues in adolescent psychology,* 2nd ed. NY: Appleton-Century-Crofts, 1972.

Bardwick, J. M. *Psychology of women: A study of bio-cultural conflicts.* NY: Harper & Row, 1971.

Barglow, P., and Schaefer, M. The fate of the feminine self in normative adolescent regression. In M. Sugar (Ed.), *Female adolescent development.* NY: Brunner/ Magel, 1979.

Barker, R. C., and Gump, P. V. *Big school, small school.* Stanford, CA: Stanford University, 1964.

Becker, J. R., and Jacobs, J. E. Sex: Is it an issue in mathematics? *Educational Horizons,* 1983, *62,* 60–67.

Bell, R. R. *Worlds of friendship.* Beverly Hills, CA: Sage Publications, 1981, Ch. 3.

Bem, S. L. The measurement of psychological androgeny. *Journal of Consulting and Clinical Psychology,* 1974, *42,* 155–162.

Bem, S. L., and Bem, D. O. Training the woman to know her place: The power of a non-conscious ideology. In D. W. Johnson (Ed.), *Contemporary social psychology.* Philadelphia, PA: Lippincott, 1973.

Benedict, R. Continuities and discontinuities in cultural conditioning. In W. E. Martin and C. B. Stendler (Eds.), *Readings in child development.* NY: Harcourt, Brace & Jovanovich, 1954.

Berkovitz, I. H. Effects of secondary school experiences on adolescent female development. In M. Sugar (Ed.), *Female adolescent development.* NY: Brunner/ Magel, 1979.

Bernard, J. Adolescence and socialization for motherhood. In S. E. Dragasten and G. H. Elder, Jr. (Eds.), *Adolescence in the life cycle: Psychological change and social context.* Washington, D.C.: Hemisphere Publishing Co., 1975, pp. 227–252.

Berndt, T. J. The features and effects of friendship in early adolescence. *Child Development*, 1982, *53*, 1447–1460.

Berscheid, E., and Walster, E. Physical attractiveness. In L. Berkowitz (Ed.), *Advances in experimental social psychology*. NY: Academic Press, 1974.

Berzonsky, M. D., and Lombardo, J. P. Pubertal timing and identity crisis: A preliminary investigation. *Journal of Early Adolescence*, 1983, *3*(3), 239–246.

Block, J. H. Issues, problems and pitfalls in assessing sex differences: A critical review of "the Psychology of Sex Differences." *Merrill-Palmer Quarterly*, 1976, *22*, 283–308.

Block, J. H. Another look at sex differentiation in the socialization behaviors of mothers and fathers. In J. Sherman and F. L. Denmark (Eds.), *Psychology of women: Future directions of research*. NY: Psychological Dimensions, 1979.

Block, J. H. *Sex role identity and ego development*. San Francisco, CA: Jossey-Bass, 1984.

Blos, P. *On adolescence: A psychoanalytic interpretation*. NY: Free Press, 1962.

Blos, P. The child analyst looks at the young adolescent. *Daedalus*, 1971 (Fall), 961–978.

Blyth, D. A. *Continuities and discontinuities during the transition into adolescence: A longitudinal comparison of two school structures*. Unpublished Ph.D. dissertation, University of Minnesota, 1977.

Blyth, D. A., and Karnes, E. L. *Philosophy, policies, and programs for early adolescent education: An annotated bibliography*. Westport, CT: Greenwood Press, 1981.

Blyth, D. A., and Simmons, R. G. Puberty, achievement, and self-esteem among black and white adolescents. Part of a Division 7 Symposium entitled, "The Effects of Pubertal Timing on Achievement and Self-Image," presented at the Annual Meeting of the American Psychological Association, Anaheim, CA, September 1983.

Blyth, D. A., Simmons, R. G., and Bush, D. The transition into early adolescence: A longitudinal comparison of youth in two educational contexts. *Sociology of Education*, 1978, *51*(3), 149–162.

Blyth, D. A., Thiel, K. S., Bush, D. M., and Simmons, R. G. Another look at school crime: Student as victim. *Youth and Society*, 1980, *11*(3), 369–388.

Blyth, D. A., Simmons, R. G., Bulcroft, R., Felt, D., Van Cleave, E. F., and Bush, D. M. The effects of physical development on self-image and satisfaction with body-image for early adolescent males. In R. G. Simmons (Ed.), *Research in community and mental health*, Vol. 2. Greenwich, CT: JAI Press, 1981, pp. 43–73. (a)

Blyth, D. A., Hill, J. P., and Smyth, C. K. The influence of older adolescents on younger adolescents: Do grade-level arrangements make a difference in behaviors, attitudes, and experiences? *Journal of Early Adolescence*, 1981, *1*(1), 85–110. (b)

Blyth, D. A., Simmons, R. G., and Carlton-Ford, S. The adjustment of early adolescents to school transitions. *Journal of Early Adolescence*, 1983, *3*(1 and 2), 105–120.

Bock, R. D. *Multivariate statistical methods in behavioral research*. NY: McGraw Hill, 1975.

Boesel, D., Crain, R., Dunteman, G., Ianni, F., Martinolich, M., Moles, O., Spivak, H., Stalford, C., and Wayne, I. *Violent schools—Safe schools: The safe school study report to the congress*, (Vol. I). U.S. Department of Health, Education and Welfare, National Institute of Education. Washington, D.C.: U.S. Government Printing Office, 1978.

Bohan, J. S. Age and sex differences in self-concept. *Adolescence*, 1973, *8*, 379–384.

Bohrnstedt, G. W. Observations on the measurement of change. In E. F. Borgatta (Ed.), *Sociological methodology 1969*. San Francisco, CA: Jossey-Bass, 1968, pp. 113–133.

Bohrnstedt, G. W., and Felson, R. B. *Children's performances, perceptions of those performances and self-esteem: A comparison of several causal models.* Unpublished manuscript, 1981.

Bowerman, C. E., and Kinch, J. W. Changes in family and peer orientation between the fourth and tenth grades. *Social Forces*, 1959, *37*, 206–211.

Bowman, D. O. A longitudinal study of selected facets of children's self-concepts as related to achievement and intelligence. *The Citadel: Monograph Series* (No. XII), 1974, 1–16.

Bradburn, N. M., and Caplovitz, D. *Reports on happiness.* Chicago, IL: Aldine, 1965.

Braito, R., and Klundt, K. *Adolescents views of gender roles and appropriateness of varied family and work conditions.* Paper presented at the Western Social Science Association Meetings, April 1984, San Diego, Calif.

Brim, O. G., Jr., and Kagan, J. Constancy and change: A view of the issues. In O. G. Brim, Jr., and J. Kagan (Eds.), *Constancy and change in human development.* Cambridge, MA: Harvard University Press, 1980.

Bronfenbrenner, U. *Two worlds of childhood: U.S. and U.S.S.R.* NY: Russell Sage Foundation, 1970.

Bronfenbrenner, U. The ecology of the family as a context of human development: Research perspectives. *Developmental Psychology*, in press.

Bronfenbrenner, U. and Crouter, A. C. The evolution of environmental models in developmental research. In W. P. Kensen (Ed.), *History, theory, and methods*, Vol. 1, *Handbook of child psychology*, 4th Ed. (P. H. Mussen overall editor). New York: Wiley, 1983.

Brookover, W., Beady, C., Flood, P., Schweitzer, J., and Wisenbaker, J. *School social systems and student achievement: Schools can make a difference.* NY: Praeger, 1979.

Brooks-Gunn, J. The psychological significance of different pubertal events to young girls. *Journal of Early Adolescence*, 1984, *4*(4), 315–327.

Brooks-Gunn, J. The salience and timing of the menstrual flow. *Psychosomatic Medicine*, in press.

Brooks-Gunn, J., and Petersen, A. C. (Eds.). *Girls at puberty: Biological and psychosocial perspectives.* NY: Plenum Press, 1983.

Brooks-Gunn, J., and Petersen, A. C. Problems in studying and defining pubertal events. *Journal of Youth and Adolescence*, 1984, *13*(3), 181–196.

Brooks-Gunn, J., and Warren, M. P. *Physical and social maturity in early adolescents: The salience of different pubertal events.* Submitted for publication, 1985.

Broverman, I. K., Vogel, S. R., Broverman, D. R., Clarkson, F. E., and Rosenberg, P. S. Sex role stereotypes: A current appraisal. *Journal of Social Issues*, 1972, *28*(2), 59–78.

Bush, D. M. *Adolescent girls and attitudes toward violence: In the same voice or in another?* Paper presented at the American Sociological Association annual meeting, Detroit, MI, August 31–September 4, 1983.

Bush, D. M. The impact of changing gender role expectations upon socialization in adolescence: Understanding the interaction of gender, age and cohort effects. In A. C. Kerckhoff (Ed.), *Research in sociology of education and socialization*, Vol. 5. Greenwich, CT: JAI Press, 1985, pp. 169–197.

Bush, D. M. The impact of family and school on adolescent girls' aspirations and expectations: The public-private split and the reproduction of gender inequality. In J. Figueira-McDonnough and R. C. Sarri (Eds.), *The trapped woman: Catch-22 in deviance and control.* Beverly Hills, CA: Sage, 1987, pp. 282–323.

Bush, D. M., and Simmons, R. G. Socialization processes over the life course. In M. Rosenberg and R. H. Turner (Eds.), *Social psychology: Sociological perspectives.* NY: Basic Books, 1981, pp. 133–164.

Bush, D. M., and Simmons, R. G. Gender and coping with the entry into early adolescence. In R. Barnett, L. Biener, and G. Baruch (Eds.), *Gender, women and stress.* NY: Free Press, in press.

Bush, D. E., Simmons, R. G., Hutchinson, B., and Blyth, D. A. Adolescent perception of sex roles in 1968 and 1975. *Public Opinion Quarterly, 1977–1978, 41*(4), 459–474.

Campbell, A., Converse, P. E., and Rodgers, W. L. *The quality of American life.* NY: Russell Sage Foundation, 1976.

Campbell, E. Q. Adolescent socialization. In D. A. Goslin (Ed.), *Handbook of socialization theory and research.* Chicago, IL: Rand McNally & Company, 1969, pp. 821–859.

Carlson, R. Stability and change in the adolescent's self-image. *Child Development, 1965, 35,* 659–666.

Carlton-Ford, S., Simmons, R. G., and Blyth, D. A. *Analyzing longitudinal data from quasi-experimental designs: The analysis of change.* Paper presented at the American Sociological Association annual meeting, Detroit, MI, August 31–September 4, 1983.

Cherlin, A., and Walters, P. B. Trends in United States men's and women's sex-role attitudes: 1972–1978. *American Sociological Review, 1981, 46,* 453–460.

Chodorow, N. *The reproduction of mothering: Psychoanalysis and the sociology of gender.* Berkeley, CA: University of California Press, 1978.

Clausen, J. A. The social meaning of differential physical and sexual maturation. In S. E. Dragastin and G. H. Elder, Jr. (Eds.), *Adolescence in the life cycle: Psychological change and social context.* NY: Wiley, 1975, pp. 25–47.

Clifford, E. Body satisfaction in adolescence. *Perceptual and motor skills, 1971, 33,* 119–125.

Coleman, J. C. *Relationships in adolescence.* Boston, MA: Routledge & Kegan Paul, 1974.

Coleman, J. C. *The nature of adolescence.* NY: Methuen, 1980.

Coleman, J. S. *The adolescent society: The social life of the teenager and its impact on education.* NY: Free Press, 1961.

Coleman, J. S., Campbell, E. Q., Hobson, C. J., McPartland, J., Mood, A. M., Weinfeld, F. D., and York, R. L. *Equality of educational opportunity.* Washington, D.C.: U.S. Government Printing Office, 1966.

Coleman, J. S., Hoffer, T., and Kilgore, S. *High school achievement: Public, Catholic, and private schools compared.* NY: Basic Books, 1982.

Conger, A. J., Peng, S. S., and Dunteman, G. H. *National longitudinal study of the high school class of 1972: Group profiles on self-esteem, locus of control, and life goals.* Research Triangle Park, NC: Research Triangle Institute, 1977.

Cooley, C. H. *Human nature and the social order.* NY: Scribner's, 1912.

Comas, J. M. Personality characteristics of 18- to 22-year-old adolescent males self-rated as early, average, and late physical maturers. *Dissertation Abstracts International,* 1982, 3870-A.

Corder, J., and Stephan, C. W. Females' combination of work and family roles: Adolescents' aspirations. *Journal of Marriage and the Family,* 1984, 46(May), 391–402.

Crandall, V. C. The Fels study: Some contributions to personality development and achievement in childhood and adulthood. *Seminars in Psychiatry*, 1972, *4*(November), 383–398.

Cross, K. P. *Beyond the open door: New students to higher education*. San Francisco, CA: Jossey-Bass, 1971.

Cross, K. P. Women as new students. In M. T. S. Mednick, S. S. Tangri, and L. W. Hoffman (Eds.), *Women and achievement: Social and motivational analyses*. Washington, D.C.: Hemisphere Publishing, 1975, pp. 339–354.

Crowne, D., and Marlowe, D. *The approval motive*. NY: Wiley, 1964.

Davis, A. Socialization and adolescent personality. In *Adolescence, yearbook of the National Society for the Study of Education*, 1944, *43*, Part I.

Dohrenwend, B. S. Social status and stressful life events. *Journal of Personality and Social Psychology*, 1973, *28*, 225–235.

Dohrenwend, B. P., and Pearlin, L. I. *Report of the panel on life events from the committee for research on stress in health and disease*. Institute of Medicine, National Academy of Sciences, Washington, D.C., 1981, 150–169.

Dornbusch, S. M., Carlsmith, J. M., Gross, R. T., Martin, J. A., Jennings, D., Rosenberg, A., and Duke, P. Sexual development, age, and dating: A comparison of biological and social influences upon one set of behaviors. *Child Development*, 1981, *52*, 179–185.

Dornbusch, S. M., Gross, R. T., Duncan, P. D., and Ritter, P. L. Stanford studies of adolescents using the national health examination survey. In R. M. Lerner and T. T. Foch (Eds.), *Biological—psychosocial interactions in early adolescence: A life-span perspective*. Hillsdale, NJ: Lawrence Erlbaum, in press.

Douglas, J. W. B. *The home and the school*. London: MacGibbon and Kee, 1964.

Douglas, J. W. B., and Ross, J. M. Age of puberty related to educational ability, attainment and school leaving age. *Journal of Child Psychology and Psychiatry*, 1964, *5*, 185–196.

Douglas, J. W. B., Kiernan, K. E., and Wadsworth, M. E. T. A longitudinal study of health and behavior. *Proceedings of the Royal Society of Medicine*, 1977, *70*, 530.

Douvan, E., and Adelson, J. *The adolescent experience*. NY: Wiley, 1966.

Douvan, E., and Gold, H. Modal patterns in American adolescence. In L. Hoffman and M. Hoffman (Eds.), *Review of child development research*, Vol. 2. NY: Russell Sage Foundation, 1966.

Drummond, R. J., McIntire, W. G., and Ryan, C. W. Stability and sex differences on the Coopersmith self-esteem inventory for students in grades two to twelve. *Psychological Reports*, 1977, *40*, 943–946.

Duke, P. M., Carlsmith, J. M., Jennings, D., Martin, J. A., Dornbusch, S. M., Siegel-Gorelick, B., and Gross, R. T. Educational correlates of early and late sexual maturation in adolescence. *Journal of Pediatrics*, 1982, *100*(4), 633–637.

Duncan, O. D. *Introduction to structural equation models*. NY: Academic Press, 1975.

Duncan, B., and Duncan, O. D. *Sex-typing and social roles: A research report*. NY: Academic Press, 1978.

Dusek, J. B., and Flaherty, J. F. The development of the self-concept during the adolescent years. *Monographs of the Society for Research in Child Development*, 1981, *46*(4), Serial No. 191.

Dweck, C. S., Davidson, W., Nelson, S., and Enng, B. Sex differences in learned helplessness II. *Developmental Psychology*, 1978, *14*(3), 268–276.

Dwyer, J., and Mayer, J. Psychological effects of variations in physical appearance during adolescence. *Adolescence*, 1968–1969, *3*, 353–380.

Eccles, J. S. *Do students turn off to math in junior high school?* A paper presented in conjunction with a symposium on Early Adolescence: Attitudinal and Environmental Changes - AERA, New Orleans, LA, April 1984.

Eccles, J. S., and Hoffman, L. W. Sex roles, socialization, and occupational behavior. In H. W. Stevenson and A. E. Siegel (Eds.), *Research in child development and social policy*, Vol. 1. Chicago, IL: University of Chicago Press, in press.

Eccles, J., Adler, T. F., Futterman, R., Goff, S. B., Kaczala, C. M., Meece, J. L., and Midgley, C. Expectancies, values, and academic behaviors. In J. T. Spence (Ed.), *Achievement and achievement motivation.* San Francisco, CA: W. H. Freeman, 1983.

Eccles, J. S., Midgley, C., and Adler, T. F. Grade-related changes in school environment: Effects on achievement motivation. In J. G. Nichols (Ed.), *Advances in motivation and achievement: The development of achievement motivation*, Vol. 3. Greenwich, CT: JAI Press, 1984, pp. 283–331.

Eckland, B. K., and Alexander, K. L. The national longitudinal study of the high school senior class of 1972. In A. C. Kerckhoff (Ed.), *Research in sociology of education and socialization*, Vol. 1. Greenwich, CT: JAI Press, 1980.

Educational Research Service. *Organization of the middle grades: A summary of research.* Arlington, VA, 1983.

Eichorn, D. H. Biological correlates of behavior. In H. W. Stevenson (Ed.), *Child psychology, sixty-second yearbook of the N.S.S.E.*, Part I. Chicago, IL: University of Chicago Press, 1963.

Eichorn, D. H. Asynchronizations in adolescent development. In S. E. Dragastin and G. H. Elder, Jr. (Eds.), *Adolescence and the life cycle.* NY: Halsted, 1975, pp. 81–96.

Elder, G. H., Jr. Adolescent socialization and development. In E. F. Borgatta and W. W. Lambert (Eds.), *Handbook of personality theory and research.* Chicago, IL: Rand McNally & Co., 1968.

Elder, G. H., Jr. *Children of the great depression.* Chicago, IL: University of Chicago Press, 1974.

Elder, G. H., Jr., and Liker, J. K. Hard times in women's lives: Historical influences across forty years. *American Journal of Sociology*, 1982, *88*(2), 241–269.

Elder, G. H., Jr., and Rockwell, R. Economic depression and postwar opportunity in men's lives: A study of life patterns and health. In R. G. Simmons (Ed.), *Research in community and mental health*, Vol. 1. Greenwich, CT: JAI Press, 1979, pp. 249–303.

Elder, G. H., Jr., Liker, J. K., and Jaworski, B. J. Hardship in lives: Depression influences from the 1930's to old age in postwar America. In K. A. McCluskey and H. W. Reese (Eds.), *Life-span developmental psychology: Historical and generational effects.* NY: Academic Press, 1984, pp. 161–201.

Elkin, F., and Westley, W. A. The myth of adolescent culture. *American Sociological Review*, 1955, *20*(6), 680–684.

Elkind, D. Egocentrism in adolescence. *Child Development*, 1967, *38*, 1025–1034.

Engel, M. The stability of the self-concept in adolescence. *Journal of Abnormal and Social Psychology*, 1959, *58*, 211–215.

Epstein, J. L., and Karweit, N. *Friends in school: Patterns of selection and influence in secondary schools.* New York: Academic Press, 1983.

Epstein, J. L., and McPartland, J. M. The concept and measurement of the quality of school life. *American Educational Research Journal*, 1976, *13*, 15–30.

Epstein, J. L., and McPartland, J. M. Authority structure. In H. J. Walberg (Ed.), *Educational environments and effects.* Berkeley, CA: McCutchan Publishing, 1979.

Erikson, E. H. Identity and the life cycle. *Psychological Issues, I,* 1959, 1–171.

Erikson, E. H. *Identity: Youth and crisis.* NY: Norton, 1968.

Faunce, W. A. School achievement, social status, and self-esteem. *Social Psychology Quarterly,* 1984, *47*(1), 3–14.

Faust, M. S. Development maturity as a determinant in prestige of adolescent girls. *Child Development,* 1960, *31,* 173–184.

Faust, M. S. Somatic development of adolescent girls. *Monographs of the Society for Research in Child Development,* 1977, *42*(1), serial no. 169.

Faust, M. S. Alternative constructions of adolescent growth. In J. Brooks-Gunn and A. C. Petersen (Eds.), *Girls at puberty.* NY: Plenum, 1983, pp. 105–125.

Feather, N. T. Values in Adolescence. In J. Adelson (Ed.), *Handbook of adolescent psychology.* NY: John Wiley & Sons, 1980, pp. 247–294.

Feldlaufer, H. *Assessing changes in elementary and junior high school environments using observers' reports.* Paper presented as part of a symposium entitled Early Adolescence: Attitudinal and Environmental Changes at the American Educational Research Association Annual Meeting, New Orleans, LA, April 1984.

Fennema, E. Influence of selected cognitive, affective, and educational variables on sex-related differences in mathematics, learning and studying. In L. Fox, E. Fennema and J. Sherman, *Women and mathematics: Research perspectives for change.* Washington, D.C.: U.S. Department of Health, Education and Welfare, 1977.

Flanagan, J. C., Dailey, J. T., Shaycoft, M. F., Orr, D. B., and Goldberg, I. *Studies of the American high school.* Pittsburgh, PA: Project Talent Office, University of Pittsburgh, 1962.

Flavell, J. The development of inferences about others. In M. T. Michel (Ed.), *Understanding other persons.* Oxford: Blackwell, 1974, pp. 66–116.

Fox, L. The effects of sex role socialization on mathematics participation and achievement. In L. Fox, E. Fennema, and J. Sherman, *Women and mathematics: Research perspectives for change.* Washington, D.C.: U.S. Department of Health, Education and Welfare, 1977.

Freeman, F. N. Intellectual growth of children as indicated by repeated tests. *Psychology Monograph,* 1936, *47,* 20–34.

Freud, A. Adolescence. *Psychoanalytic Study of the Child,* 1958, *13,* 255–278.

Friedenberg, E. Z. *The vanishing adolescent.* Boston, MA: Beacon Press, 1959.

Frieze, I. H., Whitley, Jr., B. E., Hansuy, B. H., and McHugh, M. C. Assessing the theoretical models for sex differences in causal attributes for success and failure. *Sex Roles,* 1982, *8*(4), 333–343.

Frisk, M., Tenhunen, T., Widholm, O., and Hortling, H. Physical problems in adolescents showing advanced or delayed physical maturation. *Adolescence,* 1966, *1,* 126–140.

Gad, M. T., and Johnson, J. H. Correlates of adolescent life stress as related to race, sex, and levels of perceived social support. *Journal of Clinical Child Psychology,* 1980, *36*(Spring), 13–16.

Garbarino, J. High school size and adolescent social development. *Human Ecology Forum,* 1973, *4,* 26–29.

Garnier, M. A., and Hout, M. Schooling processes and educational outcomes in France. *Quality and Quantity,* 1981, *15,* 151–177.

Gatewood, T. E. What research says about the junior high versus the middle school. *North Central Association Quarterly,* 1971, *46*(2), 264–276.

Gecas, V., and Schwalbe, M. Beyond the looking-glass self: Social structure and efficacy-based self-esteem. *Social Psychology Quarterly,* 1983, *46*(2), 77–88.

Gersten, J. C., Langner, T. S., Eisenberg, J. G., and Orzeck, L. Child behavior and life events: Undesirable change or change per se? In B. S. Dohrenwend and B. P. Dohrenwend (Eds.), *Stressful life events: Their nature and effects.* NY: Wiley, 1974.

Gersten, J. C., Langner, T. S., Eisenberg, J. G., and Simcha-Fagan, O. An evaluation of the etiologic role of stressful life-change events in psychological disorders. *Journal of Health and Social Behavior,* 1977, *18,* 228–244.

Gilligan, C. New maps of development: New visions of maturity. *American Journal of Orthopsychiatry,* 1982, *52*(2), 199–212. (a)

Gilligan, C. *In a different voice: Psychological theory and women's development.* Cambridge, MA: Harvard University Press, 1982. (b)

Glaser, B. G., and Strauss, A. L. *Status passage.* Chicago, IL: Aldine-Atherton, 1971.

Glass, G. V., Peckham, P. D., and Sanders, J. R. Consequences of failure to meet assumptions underlying the fixed effects of analyses of variance and covariance. *Review of Educational Research,* 1972, *43,* 237–288.

Gold, M., and Douvan, E. *Adolescent development: Readings in research and theory.* Boston, MA: Allyn and Bacon, Inc., 1969.

Gold, M., and Tomlin, P. Skeletal and chronological age in adolescent development. Mimeographed manuscript, 1975. Ann Arbor, MI: Institute for Social Research.

Gottfredson, G. D., and Daiger, D. C. *Disruption in six hundred schools,* (Report No. 289). Baltimore, MD: Johns Hopkins University, Center for Social Organization of Schools, 1979 (ERIC No. ED 183 701).

Gottfredson, G. D., Joffe, R. D., and Gottfredson, D. C. *Measuring victimization and the explanation of school disruption.* (Report No. 306). Baltimore, MD: The Johns Hopkins University, Center for Social Organization of Schools, March 1981.

Gove, W., and Swafford, M. Sex differences in the propensity to seek psychiatric treatment: Prevailing folk beliefs and misused log-linear analysis—Comment on Kessler *et al. Social Forces,* 1981, *59*(4), 1281–1290.

Gove, W., and Tudor, J. F. Adult sex-roles and mental illness. *American Journal of Sociology,* 1973, *78,* 812–835.

Greenberg, D. F. Delinquency and the age structure of society. In D. F. Greenberg (Ed.), *Crime and capitalism.* Palo Alto, CA: Mayfield, 1981, pp. 118–139.

Greif, E. B., and Ulman, K. J. The psychological impact of menarche on early adolescent females: A review of the literature. *Child Development,* 1982, *53*(3), 1413–1430.

Grinker, R., Grinker, R., and Timberlake, J. A study of "mentally healthy" young males (homoclites). *American Medical Association Archives of General Psychiatry,* 1962, *6,* 405–453.

Gross, R. T. Patterns of maturation: Their effects on behavior and development. In M. D. Levine and P. Satz (Eds.), *Middle childhood: Development and dysfunction.* Baltimore, MD: University Park Press, 1984.

Gurin, G., Veroff, J., and Feld, S. *Americans view their mental health: A nationwide interview survey.* (Monograph Series, No. 4). NY: Basic Books, 1960.

Haan, N. *Coping and defending: Processes of self-environment organization.* NY: Academic Press, 1977.

Hacker, H. M. Women as a minority group. *Social Forces,* 1951, *30,* 60–69.

Hall, G. S. *Adolescence: Its psychology and its relations to physiology, anthropology, sociology, sex, crime, religion and education,* Vol. I and II. NY: D. Appleton, 1904.

Hamburg, B. A. Early adolescence: A specific and stressful stage of the life cycle. In G. V. Coelho, D. A. Hamburg, and J. E. Adams (Eds.), *Coping and adaptation*. NY: Basic Books, 1974.

Harter, S. The perceived competence scale for children. *Child Development*, 1982, *53*, 87–97.

Hartley, R. E. Sex role pressures and the socialization of the male child. *Psychological Reports*, 1959, *5*, 457–468.

Hathaway, S. R., and Monachesi, E. D. *Adolescent personality and behavior: MMPI patterns*. Minneapolis, MN: University of Minnesota Press, 1963.

Hauser, R. M., Sewell, W. H., and Alwin, D. F. High school effects on achievement. In W. H. Sewell, R. M. Hauser, and D. L. Featherman (Eds.), *Schooling and achievement in American society*. NY: Academic Press, 1976.

Havighurst, R. J. *Human development and education*. NY: Longmans Green, 1953.

Hawkins, J., and Berndt, T. J. Adjustment following the transition to junior high school. Presented at the Biennial Meeting of the Society for Research in Child Development, Toronto, Canada, 1985.

Helson, R. The changing image of the career woman. In M. T. S. Mednick, S. S. Tangri, and L. W. Hoffman (Eds.), *Women and achievement: Social and motivational analyses*. Washington, D.C.: Hemisphere Publishing Corporation, 1975, pp. 420–431.

Hersov, L. A. Refusal to go to school. *Journal of Child Psychology and Psychiatry*, 1960, *1*(1), 137–145.

Herzog, A. R. High school senior's occupational plans and values: Trends in sex differences 1976–1980. *Sociology of Education*, 1982, *55*(1), 1–13.

Hetherington, E. M. Divorce: A child's perspective. *American Psychologist*, 1979, *34*(10), 851–858.

Hetherington, E. M., Cox, M., and Cox, R. Effects of divorce on parents and children. In M. E. Lamb (Ed.), *Nontraditional families: Parenting and child development*. Hillsdale, NJ: Lawrence Erlbaum, 1982.

Heyns, B. *Summer learning and the effects of schooling*. NY: Academic, 1978.

Hill, J. P. *Some perspectives on adolescence in American society*. Position paper prepared for the Office of Child Development, United States Department of Health, Education and Welfare, 1973.

Hill, J. P. The family. In M. Johnson (Ed.), *Toward adolescence: The middle school years*. Seventy-ninth Yearbook of the National Society for the Study of Education. Chicago, IL: University of Chicago Press, 1980, pp. 32–55.

Hill, J. P., and Lynch, M. E. The intensification of gender-related role expectations during early adolescence. In J. Brooks-Gunn and A. C. Petersen (Eds.), *Girls at puberty: Biological and psychological perspectives*. NY: Plenum Press, 1983, pp. 201–228.

Hill, J. P., Holmbeck, G. N., Marlow, L., Green, T. M., and Lynch, M. E. Menarcheal status and parent–child relations in families of seventh-grade girls. *Journal of Youth and Adolescence*, 1985, *14*(4), 301–316.

Hindelang, M. J., and McDermott, M. J. *Criminal victimization in urban schools*, Criminal Justice Research Center, Albany, NY, 1977, Tables 2B, 2C, 2D.

Hoelter, J. W. The analysis of covariance structure: Goodness-of-fit indices. *Sociological Methods and Research*, 1983, *11*(3), 325–344.

Hoffman, L. W. Fear of success in males and females: 1965 and 1971. In M. T. S. Mednick, S. S. Tangri, and L. W. Hoffman (Eds.), *Women and achievement: Social and motivational analyses*. Washington, D.C.: Hemisphere Publishing Corporation, 1975, pp. 221–230. (a)

Hoffman, L. W. The employment of women, education, and fertility. In M. T. S. Mednick, S. S. Tangri, and L. W. Hoffman (Eds.), *Women and achievement: Social and motivational analyses*. Washington, D.C.: Hemisphere Publishing Corporation, 1975, pp. 104–122. (b)

Hoffman, L. W. Early childhood experiences and women's achievement motives. In M. T. S. Mednick, S. S. Tangri, and L. W. Hoffman (Eds.), *Women and achievement: Social and motivational analyses*. Washington, D.C.: Hemisphere Publishing Corporation, 1975, pp. 129–150. (c)

Hoffman, L. W. Changes in family roles, socialization, and sex differences. *American Psychologist*, 1977, *34*, 859–865.

Hollingshead, A. B., and Redlich, F. C. *Social class and mental illness*. NY: Wiley, 1958.

Horner, M. S. *Sex differences in achievement motivation and performance in competitive and noncompetitive situations*. Unpublished Ph.D. dissertation, Ann Arbor, MI, University of Michigan, 1968.

Horner, M. S. Femininity and successful achievement: Basic inconsistency. In J. M. Bardwick, E. Douvan, M. S. Horner and D. Gutman, *Personality and conflict*. Belmont, CA: Brooks Cole Publishing Company, 1970, pp. 45–74.

Hulbary, W. E. Race, deprivation, and adolescent self-images. *Social Science Quarterly*, 1975, *56*, 105–114.

Huston-Stein, A., and Higgens-Trenk, A. Development of females from childhood through adulthood: Career and feminine role orientations. In P. B. Baltes (Ed.), *Life-span development and behavior*, Vol. 1. NY: Academic Press, 1978, pp. 257–296.

James, W. *The principle of psychology*. NY: Dover (copyright 1890 by Henry Holt and Company), 1950.

Jersild, A. T., Brook, J. S., and Brook, D. W. *The psychology of adolescence* 3rd ed., NY: Macmillan Publishing Company, 1978.

Jessor, R., and Jessor, S. L. *Problem behavior and psychological development: A longitudinal study of youth*. NY: Academic Press, 1977.

Jöreskog, K. G., and Sörbom, D. *LISREL—Analysis of linear structural relationship by the method of maximum likelihood*. Chicago, IL: International Educational Services, 1981.

Jöreskog, K. G., and Sörbom, D. *LISREL VI: Supplement to LISREL V manual*, Chicago, IL: International Educational Services, 1983.

Johnson, J. H., and McCutcheon, S. Assessing life events in older children and adolescents: Preliminary findings with the life events checklist. In I. G. Sarason and C. D. Spielberger (Eds.), *Stress and anxiety*. Washington, D.C.: Hemisphere, 1980.

Jones, M. C. Psychological correlates of somatic development. *Child Development*, 1965, *36*, 899–911.

Jones, M. C., and Bayley, N. Physical maturing boys as related to behavior. *The Journal of Educational Psychology*, 1950, *41*(3), 129–148.

Jones, M. C., and Mussen, P. H. Self-conceptions and interpersonal attitudes of early- and late-maturing girls. *Child Development*, 1958, *29*, 491–501.

Jones, M. C., Bayley, N., MacFarlane, J. W., and Honzik, M. (Eds.), *The course of human development*. Waltham, MA: Xerox College Publishing, 1971.

Jorgensen, E. C., and Howell, R. J. Changes in self, ideal-self correlations from ages 8 through 18. *The Journal of Social Psychology*, 1969, *79*, 63–67.

Jourard, S. M., and Secord, P. F. Body size and body cathexis. *Journal of Consulting Psychology*, 1954, *18*, 184.

Kagan, J., and Moss, H. A. *Birth to maturity: A study in psychological development*. NY: John Wiley & Sons, 1962.

Kaplan, H. B. The self-esteem motive and change in self-attitudes. *Journal of Nervous and Mental Disease*, 1975, *161*, 265–275.

Kaplan, H. B. *Deviant behavior in defense of self*. NY: Academic Press, 1980.

Katz, P., and Zigler, E. Self-image disparity: A developmental approach. *Journal of Personality and Social Psychology*, 1967, *5*(2), 186–195.

Kelly, J. G. Toward an ecological conception of preventive interventions. In J. W. Carter, Jr. (Ed.), *Research contributions from psychology to community mental health*. NY: Behavioral Publications, Inc., 1968.

Kennedy, R. E. Which occupation? In *Life choices: A guide for your future*. NY: Holt, Rinehart and Winston, 1985, Ch. 4.

Kessler, R. C. A strategy for studying differential vulnerability to the psychological consequences of stress. *Journal of Health and Social Behavior*, 1979, *20*, 100–108.

Kessler, R. C., and Greenberg, D. F. *Linear panel analysis: Models of quantitative change*. NY: Academic Press, 1981.

Kessler, R. C., and McRae, J. A. Trends in the relationship between sex and psychological distress: 1957–1976. *American Sociological Review*, 1981, *46*, 443–452.

Kessler, R. C., Price, R. H., and Wortman, C. B. Social factors in psychopathology: Stress, social support, and coping processes. *Annual Review of Psychology*, 1985, *36*, 531–572.

Kett, J. F. *Rites of passage: Adolescence in America 1970 to present*. New York: Basic Books, 1977.

Koff, E., Rierdon, J., and Jacobson, S. The personal and interpersonal significance of menarche. *Journal of the American Academy of Child Psychiatry*, 1981, *20*, 148–158.

Kohlberg, L. A cognitive–developmental analysis of children's sex-role concepts and attitudes. In E. E. Maccoby (Ed.), *The development of sex differences*. Stanford, CA: Stanford University Press, 1966.

Kohlberg, L., and Gilligan, C. The adolescent as a philosopher: The discovery of the self in a postconventional world. *Daedalus*, 1971 (Fall), 1051–1086.

Latham, A. J. The relationship between pubertal status and leadership in junior high school boys. *Journal of Genetic Psychology*, 1951, *78*, 185–194.

Lecky, P. *Self-consistency*. NY: Island Press, 1945.

Lenney, E. Women's self-confidence in achievement settings. *Psychological Bulletin*, 1977, *84*(1), 1–13.

Lerner, R. M., and Karabenick, S. A. Physical attractiveness, body attitudes, and self-concept in late adolescents. *Journal of Youth and Adolescence*, 1974, *3*(4), 307–316.

Lerner, R. M., and Spanier, G. B. *Adolescent development: A life-span perspective*. NY: McGraw-Hill, 1980.

Lever, J. Sex differences in the complexity of children's play. *American Sociological Review*, 1978, *43*(4), 471–482.

Lightfoot, S. L. *The good high school: Portraits of character and culture*. NY: Basic Books, 1983.

Lindsay, P. The effect of high school size on student participation, satisfaction, and attendance. *Educational Evaluation and Policy Analysis*, 1982, *4*, 57–66.

Lindsay, P. High school size, participation in activities, and young adult social participation: Some enduring effects of schooling. *Educational Evaluation and Policy Analysis*, 1984, *6*, 73–84.

Lipman-Blumen, J., and Ticamyer, A. R. Sex roles in transition: A ten-year perspective. In A. Inkeles, J. Coleman, and N. Smelser (Eds.), *Annual Review of Sociology*, Vol. 1. Palo Alto, CA: Annual Reviews Inc., 1975, pp. 297–337.

Lipsitz, J. *Growing up forgotten*. Lexington, Mass.: Lexington Books, 1977.

Lipsitz, J. *Successful schools for young adolescents*. New Brunswick, NJ: Transaction Books, 1984.

Livson, N., and Peskin, H. Perspectives on adolescence from longitudinal research. In J. Adelson (Ed.), *Handbook of adolescent psychology*. NY: Wiley, 1980.

Long, B. H., Ziller, R. C., and Henderson, E. H. Developmental changes in the self-concept during adolescence. *School Review*, 1968, *76*, 210–230.

Lueptow, L. B. Social change and sex-role change in adolescent orientations toward life, work, and achievement: 1964–1975. *Social Psychology Quarterly*, 1980, *43*(1), 48–59. (a)

Lueptow, L. B. Gender wording, sex, and response to items on achievement value. *Psychological Reports*, 1980, *46*(1), 140–142. (b)

Lueptow, L. B. Social structure, social change and parental influence in adolescent sex-role socialization: 1964–1975. *Journal of Marriage and The Family*, 1980, *42*(1), 93–103. (c)

Lueptow, L. B. Sex-typing and change in the occupational choices of high school seniors: 1964–1975. *Sociology of Education*, 1981, *54*(1), 16–24.

Lueptow, L. B. *Adolescent sex-roles and social change*. NY: Columbia University Press, 1984.

McCarthy, J. D., and Hoge, D. R. Analysis of age effects in longitudinal studies of adolescent self-esteem. *Developmental Psychology*, 1982, *18*(3), 372–379.

McClelland, D. C., Atkinson, J. W., Clark, R. A., and Lowell, E. L. *The achievement motive*. NY: Appleton-Century-Crofts, 1953.

Maccoby, E. E., and Jacklin, C. N. *The psychology of sex differences*. Stanford, CA: Stanford University Press, 1974.

MacCorquodale, P. *The effect of the familial division of labor on sex-role attitudes*. Paper presented at the Western Social Science Association Meetings, San Diego, California, April 1984.

McDill, E. L., and Rigsby, L. C. *Structure and process in secondary schools: The academic impact of educational climates*. Baltimore, MD: The Johns Hopkins University Press, 1973.

MacFarlane, J. W. The impact of early and late maturation in boys and girls: Illustrations from life records of individuals. In M. C. Jones, N. Bayley, J. W. MacFarlane, and M. Honzik (Eds.), *The course of human development*. Waltham, MA: Xerox College Publishing, 1971, pp. 426–433.

Macke, A. S., and Morgan, W. R. Maternal employment, race, and work orientation of high school girls. *Social Forces*, 1978, *57*, 187–204.

McKee, J. P., and Sherriffs, A. C. The differential evaluation of males and females. *Journal of Personality*, 1957, *25*, 356–71.

McKee, J. P., and Sherriffs, A. C. Men's and women's beliefs, ideals, and self-concepts. *American Journal of Sociology*, 1959, *64*, 356–63.

Mackie, M. The domestication of self: Gender comparisons of self-imagery and self-esteem. *Social Psychology Quarterly*, 1983, *46*(4), 343–350.

Magnusson, D., Stattin, H., and Allen, V. L. Biological maturation and social development: A longitudinal study of some adjustment processes for mid-adolescence to adulthood. *Journal of Youth and Adolescence*, 1985, *14*, 267–283.

Magnusson, D., Stattin, H., and Allen, V. L. Differential maturation among girls and its relation to social adjustment in a longitudinal perspective. In D. L. Featherman and R. M. Lerner (Eds.), *Life-span development and behavior*, Vol. 7. NY: Academic Press, in press.

Marcia, J. E. Development and validation of ego identity status. *Journal of Personality and Social Psychology*, 1966, *3*, 551–558.

Marcia, J. E. Identity in adolescence. In J. Adelson (Ed.), *Handbook of adolescent psychology*. NY: Wiley, 1980, pp. 159–187.

Markus, G. B. *Analyzing panel data*. Beverly Hills, CA: Sage, 1979.

Maruyama, G., Rubin, R. A., and Kingsbury, G. G. Self-esteem and educational achievement: Independent constructs with a common cause? *Journal of Personality and Social Psychology*, 1981, *40*, 962–997.

Maruyama, G., Finch, M. D., and Mortimer, J. T. Processes of achievement in the transition to adulthood. In Z. S. Blau (Ed.), *Current perspectives on aging in the life cycle*. Greenwich, CT: JAI Press, in press.

Mason, K. O., and Bumpass, L. L. U.S. women's sex-role ideology, 1970. *American Journal of Sociology*, 1975, *80*(5), 1212–1219.

Mason, K. O., Czajka, J. L., and Arber, S. Change in U.S. women's sex-role attitudes, 1964–1974. *American Sociological Review*, 1976, *41*(4), 573–596.

Matteson, D. R. *Adolescence today: Sex roles and the search for identity*. Homewood, IL: The Dorsey Press, 1975.

Mead, G. H. *Mind, self and society*. Chicago, IL: University of Chicago Press, 1934.

Mead, M. *Coming of age in Samoa*. NY: New American Library, 1950.

Mednick, M. T. S., Tangri, S. S., and Hoffman, L. W. (Eds.) *Women and achievement: Social and motivational analyses*. Washington, D.C.: Hemisphere Publishing Corporation, 1975.

Meichenbaum, D. *Cognitive-behavior modification: An integrative approach*. NY: Plenum, 1977.

Metcalfe, B. M. A. Self-concept and attitude to school. *British Journal of Educational Psychology*, 1981, *51*, 66–76.

Meyer, B. The development of girls' sex-role attitudes. *Child Development*, 1980, *51*(2), 508–514.

Meyers, J. K., Lindenthal, J. J., and Pepper, M. P. Social class, life events, and psychiatric symptoms: A longitudinal study. In B. S. Dohrenwend and B. P. Dohrenwend (Eds.), *Stressful life events: Their nature and effects*. NY: Wiley, 1974.

Midgley, C. *The world of the early adolescent*. Paper presented as part of a symposium at the American Educational Research Association Annual Meeting, New Orleans, LA, April 1984.

Milwaukee Public Schools, Division of Relationships, *Enrollment by ethnic categories and schools*, September 15, 1978.

Mirowsky, J., and Ross, C. *Social Patterns of Distress*. Ms.

Monge, R. H. Developmental trends in factors of adolescent self-concept. *Developmental Psychology*, 1973, *8*, 382–92.

Montemayor, R. Parents and adolescents in conflict: All families some of the time and some families most of the time. *Journal of Early Adolescence*, 1982, *3*, 83–103.

Moos, R. H. A typology of junior high and high school classrooms. *American Educational Research Journal*, 1978, *15*(1), 53–66.

Morgan, D. L., and Alwin, D. F. When less is more: School size and student social participation. *Social Psychology Quarterly*, 1980, *43*(2), 241–252.

Morgan, R. (Ed.) *Sisterhood is powerful: An anthology of writings from the women's liberation movement*. NY: Random House, 1970.

Mortimer, J. T., Finch, M. D., and Kumka, D. Persistence and change in development: The multidimensional self-concept. In P. B. Baltes and O. G. Brim, Jr. (Eds.), *Life-span development and behavior*, Vol. 4. NY: Academic Press, 1982, pp. 263–313.

Moss, H. A., and Kagan, J. Report on personality consistency and change from the Fels longitudinal study. In D. R. Heise (Ed.), *Personality and socialization*. Chicago, IL: Rand McNally, 1972, pp. 21–28.

Murphy, G. *Personality*. NY: Harper, 1947.

Mussen, P. H. Early sex-role development. In D. A. Goslin (Ed.), *Handbook of socialization, theory and research.* Chicago, IL: Rand McNally and Co., 1969, pp. 707–732.

Mussen, P. H., and Boutourline-Young, H. Relationships between rate of physical maturing and personality among boys of Italaiana descent. *Vita Humana,* 1964, *7,* 186–200.

Mussen, P. H., and Jones, M. C. Self-conceptions, motivations and interpersonal attitudes of late- and early-maturing boys. *Child Development,* 1957, *28,* 243–256.

Mussen, P. H., and Jones, M. C. The behavior-inferred motivations of late- and early-maturing boys. *Child Development,* 1958, *29,* 61–67.

Nesselroade, J. R., and Baltes, P. B. Adolescent personality development and historical change: 1970–1972. *Monographs of the Society for Research in Child Development,* 1974, *39*(1), serial no. 154.

Nesselroade, J. R., and Baltes, P. B. (Eds.). *Longitudinal research in the study of behavior and development.* NY: Academic Press, 1979.

Newcomb, M. D., Huba, G. J., and Bentler, P. M. A multidimensional assessment of stressful life events among adolescents: Derivation and correlates. *Journal of Health and Social Behavior,* 1981, *22,* 400–415.

Newcombe, N., and Bandura, M. M. The effect of age at puberty on spatial ability in girls: A question of mechanism. *Developmental Psychology,* 1983, *19,* 215.

Newcombe, N., Bandura, M. M., and Taylor, D. G. Sex differences in spatial ability and spatial activities. *Sex Roles,* 1983, *9*(3), 377–386.

Newmann, J. P. Sex differences in depressive symptoms. In J. R. Greenley (Ed.), *Research in community and mental health,* Vol. 4 Greenwich, CT: JAI Press, 1984, pp. 301–323.

Nie, H., Hull, C. H., Jenkins, J. G., Steinbrenner, K., and Bent, D. H. *Statistical package for the social sciences,* 2nd ed. NY: McGraw Hill, 1975.

Nisbet, J. D., and Entwistle, N. J. *Age of transfer to secondary education.* London: University of London Press Ltd., 1966.

Nisbet, J. D., Illsley, R., Sutherland, A. E., and Douse, M. J. Puberty and test performance: A further report. *British Journal of Educational Psychology,* 1964, *34,* 202–203.

Nottelmann, E. D., Sussman, E. J., Blue, J. H., Inoff-Germain, G., Dorn, L. D., Loriaux, D. L., Cutler, Jr., G. B., and Chrousos, G. P. Gonadal and adrenal hormone correlates of adjustment in early adolescence. In R. M. Lerner and T. T. Foch (Eds.), *Biological psychosocial interactions in early adolescence: A life-span perspective.* Hillsdale, NJ: Lawrence Erlbaum, in press.

Oden, M. H. The fulfillment of promise: 40 year follow-up of the Terman gifted group. *Genetic Psychology Monographs,* 1968, *77,* 3–93.

Offer, D. *The psychological world of the teenager: A study of normal adolescent boys.* NY: Basic Books, 1969.

Offer, D., and Offer, J. *From teenage to young manhood: A psychological study.* NY: Basic Books, 1975.

Offer, D., Ostrov, E., and Howard, K. I. *The adolescent: A psychological self-portrait.* NY: Basic Books, 1981.

O'Malley, P. M., and Bachman, J. G. Self-esteem and education: Sex and cohort comparisons among high school seniors. *Journal of Personality and Social Psychology,* 1979, *37*(7), 1153–1159.

O'Malley, P. M., and Bachman, J. G. Self-esteem: Change and stability between ages 13 and 23. *Developmental Psychology,* 1983, *19*(2), 257–268.

Padilla, E. R., Rohsenow, D. J., and Bergman, A. B. Predicting accident frequency in children. *Pediatrics,* 1976, *58,* 223–226.

Parsons, T., and Bales, R. F. *Family socialization and interaction process.* Glencoe, IL: Free Press, 1955.

Pearlin, L. I. Sex roles and depression. In N. Datan and L. H. Ginsberg (Eds.), *Life-span developmental psychology: Normative life crises.* NY: Academic Press, 1975, pp. 191–207.

Pearlin, L. I., Lieberman, M. A., Menaghan, E. G., and Mullan, J. T. The stress process. *Journal of Health and Social Behavior,* 1981, *22,* 337–356.

Peskin, H. Pubertal onset and ego functioning. *Journal of Abnormal Psychology,* 1967, *72,* 1–15.

Peskin, H. Influence of the developmental schedule of puberty on learning and ego development. *Journal of Youth and Adolescence,* 1973, *2,* 273–290.

Peskin, H., and Livson, N. Pre- and postpubertal personality and adult psychologic functioning. *Seminars in Psychology,* 1972, *4,* 343–355.

Petersen, A. C. Biopychosocial processes in the development of sex-related differences. In J. E. Parsons (Ed.), *The psychobiology of sex differences and sex roles.* Washington, D.C.: Hemisphere Publishing Corporation, 1980, pp. 31–55.

Petersen, A. C. Pubertal change and cognition. In J. Brooks-Gunn and A. C. Petersen (Eds.), *Girls at puberty.* NY: Plenum, 1983, pp. 179–198.

Petersen, A. C., and Taylor, B. The biological approach to adolescence: Biological change and psychological adaptation. In J. Adelson (Ed.), *Handbook of adolescent psychology.* NY: Wiley, 1980, pp. 117–158.

Petersen, A. C., Tobin-Richards, M., and Boxer, A. Puberty: Its measurement and its meaning. *Journal of Early Adolescence: Biological and Psychosocial Perspectives.* 1983, *3*(1–2), 47–62.

Petersen, A. C., Schulenberg, J. E., Abramowitz, R., Offer, D., and Jarchow, H. A self-image questionnaire for young adolescents (SIQYA): Reliability and validity studies. *Journal of Youth and Adolescence,* 1984, *13,* 93–111.

Piers, E. V., and Harris, D. B. Age and other correlates of self-concept in children. *Journal of Educational Psychology,* 1964, *55*(2), 91–95.

Plake, B. S., Hoover, H. D., and Loyd, B. H. An investigation of the Iowa tests of basic skills for sex bias: A developmental look. *Psychology in the Schools,* 1980, *17,* 47–52.

Pleck, E. H., and Pleck, J. H. *The American man.* Englewood Cliffs, NJ: Prentice-Hall, 1980.

Poppleton, P. K. Puberty, family size and the educational progress of girls. *British Journal of Educational Psychology,* 1968, *38,* 286–292.

Powers, C., and Cotterell, J. Changes in students in the transition from primary to secondary schools. Education Research and Development Committee Report No. 27. Canberra, Australia: Australian Government Publishing Service, 1981.

Protinsky, H., and Farrier, S. Self-image changes in pre-adolescents and adolescents. *Adolescence,* 1980, *15*(6), 887–893.

Purkey, S. C., and Smith, M. S. Effective schools: A review. *The Elementary School Journal,* 1983, *83*(4), 427–452.

Radloff, L. S., and Rae, D. S. Components of the sex difference in depression. In R. G. Simmons (Ed.), *Research in community and mental health,* Vol. 2. Greenwich, CT: JAI Press, 1981, pp. 11–137.

Ramsøy, N. R. *American high schools at mid-century.* Unpublished, Bureau of Applied Social Research, Columbia University, 1961.

Rand, C. S., and Hall, J. A. Sex differences in the accuracy of self-perceived attractiveness. *Social Psychology Quarterly,* 1983, *46*(4), 359–363.

Reid, L. D. *Year of school transition and its effects on students.* Ph.D. dissertation, University of Minnesota, 1983.

Reuman, D. *Consequences of the transition into junior high school on social comparison of abilities and achievement motivation.* Paper presented as part of a symposium at the annual meeting of the American Educational Research Association, New Orleans, LA, April 1984.

Reynolds, E. L., and Wines, J. V. Individual differences in physical changes associated with adolescent girls. *American Journal of Diseases in Childhood,* 1948, *75,* 1–22.

Reynolds, E. L., and Wines, J. V. Physical changes associated with adolescence in boys. *American Journal of Diseases in Children,* 1951, *82,* 529–547.

Richardson, S. A., and Royce, J. Race and physical handicaps in children's preference for other children. *Child Development,* 1968, *39*(2), 467–480.

Richardson, S. A., Hastorf, A. H., Goodman, N., and Dornbusch, S. M. Cultural uniformity in reaction to physical disabilities. *American Sociological Review,* 1961, *26,* 241–247.

Rogosa, D., Brandt, D., and Zimowski, M. A growth curve approach to the measurement of change. *Psychological Bulletin,* 1982, *92*(3), 726–748.

Rosen, B. C., and Aneschensel, C. S. Sex differences in the educational–occupational expectation process. *Social Forces,* 1978, *57*(1), 164–186.

Rosenbaum, J. E. *Making inequality: The hidden curriculum of high school tracking.* NY: Wiley Interscience, 1976.

Rosenbaum, M. B. The changing body image of the adolescent girl. In M. Sugar (Ed.), *Female adolescent development.* NY: Brunner/Magel, 1979, pp. 234–252.

Rosenberg, F., and Rosenberg, M. Self-esteem and delinquency. *Journal of Youth and Adolescence,* 1978, *7,* 279–291.

Rosenberg, F. R., and Simmons, R. G. Sex differences in the self-concept in adolescence. *Sex-Roles: A Journal of Research,* 1975, *1*(2), 147–159.

Rosenberg, M. *Society and the adolescent self-image.* Princeton, NJ: Princeton University Press, 1965.

Rosenberg, M. Psychological selectivity in self-esteem formation. In C. Sherif and M. Sherif (Eds.), *Attitudes, ego-involvement and change.* NY: Wiley, 1967.

Rosenberg, M. *Conceiving the self.* New York: Basic Books, 1979.

Rosenberg, M., and Kaplan, H. B. (Eds.). *Social psychology of the self-concept.* Arlington Heights, IL: Harlan Davidson, Inc., 1982.

Rosenberg, M., and Simmons, R. G. *Black and white self-esteem: The urban school child.* Arnold and Caroline Rose Monograph Series. Washington, D.C.: American Sociological Association, 1972.

Rosenberg, M., Elliott, G., and Wagner, M. Self-esteem and transient depersonalization in youth: A causal inquiry. In T. H. Honess and K. M. Yardley (Eds.), *Self and identity.* Oxfordshire: Routledge and Kegan Paul, PLC, in press.

Rosenkrantz, P., Vogel, S., Bee, H., Broverman, I., and Broverman, D. M. Sex-role stereotypes and self-concepts in college students. *Consulting Clinical Psychology,* 1968, *32,* 287–295.

Ross, C. E., Mirowsky, J., and Ulbrich, P. Distress and the traditional female role: A comparison of Mexicans and anglos. *American Journal of Sociology,* 1983, *89*(3), 670–682.

Rossi, A. S. Transition to parenthood. *Journal of Marriage and the Family,* 1968, *30,* 26–39.

Rossi, A. S. A biosocial perspective on parenting. *Daedalus,* 1977, *106*(2), 1–31.

Rowan, B., Bossert, S. T., and Dwyer, D. C. Research on effective schools: A cautionary note. *Educational Researcher,* 1983, *12,* 24–31.

Rubin, L. *Intimate strangers: Men and women together.* NY: Harper and Row, 1983.

Ruble, D. N., and Brooks-Gunn, J. The experience of menarche. *Child Development*, 1982, *53*, 1557–1566.

Runyan, W. M. The life satisfaction chart: Perceptions of the course of subjective experience. *International Journal of Aging and Human Development*, 1980, *11*, 45–64.

Rutter, M. *Changing youth in a changing society: Patterns of adolescent development and disorder*. Cambridge, MA: Harvard University Press, 1980.

Rutter, M., and Hersov, L. *Child Psychiatry: Modern approaches*. Oxford: Blackwell Scientific Publications, 1977.

Rutter, M., Maughan, B., Mortimore, P., Ouston, J., with Smith, A. *Fifteen thousand hours: Secondary schools and their effects on children*. Cambridge, MA: Harvard University Press, 1979.

Rutter, M. Protective factors in children's responses to stress and disadvantage. In M. W. Kent and J. E. Rolf (Eds.), *Primary prevention of psychopathology*, Vol. III: *Social competence in children*. Hanover, NH: University Press of New England, 1979.

Savin-Williams, R. C. Dominance hierarchies in groups of early adolescents. *Child Development*, 1979, *50*, 923–935.

Savin-Williams, R. C. Dominance hierarchies in groups of middle to late adolescent males. *Journal of Youth and Adolescence*, 1980, *9*, 75–87.

Savin-Williams, R. C., and Demo, D. H. Conceiving or misconceiving the self: Issues in adolescent self-esteem. *Journal of Early Adolescence*, 1983, *3*(1–2), 121–140.

Savin-Williams, R. C., Small, S. A., and Zeldin, R. S. Dominance and altruism among adolescent males: A comparison of ethological and psychological methods. *Ethnology and Sociobiology*, 1981, *2*, 167–176.

Schmiedeck, R. A. Adolescent identity formation and the organizational structure of high schools. *Adolescence*, 1979, *14*(53), 191–196.

Schoenberg, R. Multiple indicator models: Estimation of unconstrained means and their standard errors. *Sociological Methods and Research*, 1982, *10*(4), 421–433.

Schonhaut, C. I. *An examination of education research as it pertains to the grade organization for the middle schools*. Ed.D. dissertation, Columbia University, 1967.

Schoo, P. H. *Students' self-concepts, social behavior, and attitudes toward school in middle and junior high schools*. Ph.D. dissertation, University of Michigan, Ann Arbor, Michigan, 1970.

Schwab, J. J., and Harmeling, J. D. Body image and medical illness. *Psychosomatic Medicine*, 1968, *30*, 51–61.

Seltzer, V. C. *Adolescent social development: Dynamic functional interaction*. Lexington, MA: Lexington Books, 1982.

Sherman, J. A. A summary of psychological sex differences. In M. T. S. Mednick, S. S. Tangri, and L. W. Hoffman (Eds.), *Women and achievement: Social and motivational analyses*. Washington, D.C.: Hemisphere Publishing Corporation, 1975, pp. 292–306.

Sherman, J. Mathematics, spatial visualization on related factors: Changes in girls and boys, grades 8–11. *Journal of Educational Psychology*, 1980, *72*(4), 476–582.

Silverman, C. *The epidemiology of depression*. Baltimore, MD: Johns Hopkins University Press, 1968, Ch. 4.

Simmons, R. G. Blacks and high self-esteem: A puzzle. *Social Psychology*, 1978, *41*(1), 54–57.

Simmons, R. G. (Ed.). *Research in community and mental health*, Vol. 1. Greenwich, CT: JAI Press, 1979.

Simmons, R. G. (Ed.). *Research in community and mental health,* Vol. 2. Greenwich, CT: JAI Press, 1981.

Simmons, R. G., and Rosenberg, M. Functions of children's perceptions of the stratification system. *American Sociological Review,* 1971, *36*(2), 235–249.

Simmons, R. G., and Rosenberg, F. Sex, sex-roles, and self-image. *Journal of Youth and Adolescence,* 1975, *4*(3), 229–258.

Simmons, R. G., Rosenberg, M., and Rosenberg, F. Disturbance in the self-image at adolescence. *American Sociological Review,* 1973, *39*(5), 553–568.

Simmons, R. G., Klein, S. D., and Simmons, R. L. *Gift of life: The social and psychological impact of organ transplantation.* NY: Wiley Interscience, 1977.

Simmons, R. G., Brown, L., Bush, D., and Blyth, D. A. Self-esteem and achievement of black and white early adolescents. *Social Problems,* 1978, *26*(1), 86–96.

Simmons, R. G., Blyth, D. A., Van Cleave, E. F., and Bush, D. M. Entry into early adolescence: The impact of school structure, puberty, and early dating on self-esteem. *American Sociological Review,* 1979, *44*(6), 948–967.

Simmons, R. G., Blyth, D. A., and McKinney, K. L. The social and psychological effects of puberty on white females. In J. Brooks-Gunn and A. Petersen (Eds.), *Girls at puberty: Biological and psychosocial perspectives.* NY: Plenum, 1983, pp. 229–272.

Simmons, R. G., Burgeson, R. and Blyth, D. A. Reaction to the cumulation of change in early adolescence. To be published in H. Stevenson and D. R. Entwisle (Eds.), *Child Development,* in press. (a)

Simmons, R. G., Carlton-Ford, S. L., and Blyth, D. A. Predicting how a child will cope with the transition to junior high school. In R. M. Lerner and T. T. Foch (Eds.), *Biological–psychosocial interactions in early adolescence: A life-span perspective.* Hillsdale, NJ: Lawrence Erlbaum, in press. (b)

Soares, L. M., and Soares, A. T. Self-concepts of disadvantaged and advantaged students. *Proceedings of the Seventy-eighth Annual Convention of the American Psychological Association,* 1970, pp. 653–654.

Stein, A. H., and Bailey, M. M. The socialization of achievement motivation in females. In M. T. S. Mednick, S. S. Tangri, and L. W. Hoffman (Eds.), *Women and achievement: Social and motivational analyses.* Washington, D.C.: Hemisphere Publishing Corporation, 1975, pp. 151–157.

Steinberg, L. D. Transformation in family relations at puberty. *Developmental Psychology,* 1981, *17*, 833–840.

Steinberg, L. D., and Hill, J. Patterns of family interaction as a function of age, the onset of puberty, and formal thinking. *Developmental Psychology,* 1978, *14*, 683–684.

Stemnock, S. K. Summary of research on size of schools and school districts. Research brief. Washington, D.C.: Educational Research Service, 1974.

Stipek, D. J. Sex references in children's attributions for success and failure on math and spelling tests. *Sex Roles,* 1984, *11*(11/12), 969–981.

Stockard, J., and Johnson, M. M. *Sex roles: Sex inequality and sex role development.* Englewood Cliffs, NJ: Prentice Hall, 1980.

Stolz, H. R., and Stolz, L. M. Adolescent problems related to somatic variation. In N. B. Henry (Ed.), *Adolescence: Forty-third yearbook of the National Committee for the Study of Education.* Chicago: Department of Education, University of Chicago, 1944.

Stolz, H. R., and Stolz, L. M. *Somatic development of adolescent boys.* NY: MacMillan, 1951.

Stone, A. A., and Onque', G. C. *Longitudinal studies of child personality.* Cambridge, MA: Harvard University Press, 1959.

Stone, C. P., and Barker, R. G. Aspects of personality and intelligence in post-menarcheal and premenarcheal girls of the same chronological ages. *Journal of Comparative Psychology*, 1937, *23*, 439–455.

Stryker, S. *Symbolic interaction: A social structural version*. Menlo Park, CA: The Benjamin/Cummings Publishing Company, 1980.

Summers, A. A., and Wolfe, B. L. Do schools make a difference? *The American Economic Review*, 1977, *67*, 639–652.

Swearingen, E. M., and Cohen, L. H. Measurement of adolescents' life events: The junior high life experiences survey. *American Journal of Community Psychology*, 1985, *13*(1), 69–85. (a)

Swearingen, E. M. and Cohen, L. H. Life events and psychological distress: A prospective study of young adolescents. *Developmental Psychology*, 1985, *21*(6), 1045–1054. (b)

Tanner, J. M. *Growth at adolescence*, 2nd ed., Oxford: Blackwell Scientific Publications, 1962.

Tanner, J. M. Sequence, tempo, and individual variation in the growth and development of boys and girls aged twelve to sixteen. *Daedalus*, 1971, Fall, 907–930.

Tausig, M. Measuring life events. *Journal of Health and Social Behavior*, 1982, *23*, 52–64.

Thoits, P. A. Dimensions of life events that influence psychological distress: An evaluation and synthesis of the literature. In H. B. Kaplan (Ed.), *Psychosocial stress: Trends in theory and research*. NY: Academic Press, 1983.

Thorne, B. Girls and boys together . . . but mostly apart: Gender arrangements in elementary schools. In W. W. Hartup and Z. Rubin (Eds.), *Relationships and development*. Hillsdale, N.J.: Lawrence Erlbaum, 1984.

Thornton, A., and Freedman, D. Changes in the sex role attitudes of women, 1962–1977: Evidence from a panel study. *American Sociological Review*, 1979, *44*(October), 831–842.

Thornton, A., Alwin, D. F., and Camburn, D. Causes and consequences of sex-role attitudes and attitude change. *American Sociological Review*, 1983, *48*(April), 211–227.

Tittle, C. K. *Careers and family: Sex roles and adolescent life plans*, Vol. 121. Sage Library of Social Research. Beverly Hills, CA: Sage Publications, 1981.

Tobin-Richards, M. H., Boxer, A. M., and Petersen, A. C. The psychological significance of pubertal change: Sex differences in perceptions of self during early adolescence. In J. Brooks-Gunn and A. C. Petersen (Eds.), *Girls at puberty: Biological and psychosocial perspectives*. NY: Plenum, 1983, pp. 127–154.

Toennies, F. *Geimeinschaft and gesellschaft* (1st ed., 1887). Translated and edited by C. P. Loomis. In *Fundamental concepts of sociology*. NY: American Book Co., 1940.

Tresemer, D. W. *Fear of success*. NY: Plenum, 1977.

Trowbridge, N. Self-concept and socio-economic status in elementary school children. *American Educational Research Journal*, 1972, *9*(4), 525–537.

Veroff, J., McClelland, L., and Ruhland, D. Varieties of achievement motivation. In M. T. S. Mednick, S. S. Tangri, and L. W. Hoffman (Eds.), *Women and achievement: Social and motivational analyses*. Washington, D.C.: Hemisphere Publishing Corporation, 1975, pp. 172–205.

Veroff, J., Douvan, E., and Kulka, R. A. *The inner American: A self-portrait from 1957 to 1976*. NY: Basic Books, 1981.

Vinokur, A., and Selzer, M. L. Desirable versus undesirable life events: Their relationship to stress and mental distress. *Journal of Personality and Social Psychology*, 1975, *32*(2), 329–337.

Watson, G. B., and Johnson, D. *Social psychology: Issues and insights*. Philadelphia, PA: Lippincott, 1972, Ch. 11.

Weatherley, D. Self-perceived rate of physical maturation and personality in late adolescence. *Child Development*, 1964, *35*, 1197–1210.

Weber, M. *The theory of social and economic organization*. Translated by A. M. Henderson and T. Parsons. NY: Oxford University Press, 1947.

Weiner, I. *Psychological disturbance in adolescence*. NY: Wiley Interscience, 1970.

Weitzman, L. J. *Sex role socialization: A focus on women*. Palo Alto, CA: Mayfield Publishing, 1979.

Wells, L. E., and Rankin, J. H. Self-concept as a mediating factor in delinquency. *Social Psychology Quarterly*, 1983, *46*(1), 11–22.

Wells, L. E., and Stryker, S. Stability and change in self over the life course. In P. B. Baltes, R. M. Lerner, and D. L. Featherman (Eds.), *Life-span development and behavior*, Vol. 8. Hillsdale, NJ: Lawrence Erlbaum, in press.

Werner, E. G., and Smith, R. S. *Vulnerable but invincible*. NY: McGraw Hill, 1982.

Wheeler, S. The structure of formally organized socialization settings. In O. G. Brim, Jr., and S. Wheeler (Eds.), *Socialization after childhood: Two essays*. NY: Wiley, 1966.

White, K. M., and Speisman, J. C. *Adolescence*. Monterey, CA: Brooks/Cole Publishing Company, 1977.

White, W. F., and Wash, J. A. Prediction of successful college academic performance from measures of body-cathexis, self-cathexis and anxiety. *Perceptual and Motor Skills*, 1965, *20*, 431–432.

Whiting, B. B., and Whiting, J. W. M. *Children of six cultures: A psychological analysis*. Cambridge, MA: Harvard University Press, 1975.

Willems, E. E. Sense of obligation to high school activities as related to school size and marginality of student. *Child Development*, 1967, *38*, 1247–1263.,

Wilson, E. O. *On human nature*. Cambridge, MA: Harvard University Press, 1978.

Wylie, R. *The self-concept theory and research: Vol. 2* (Rev. ed.). Lincoln, NE: University of Nebraska Press, 1979.

Yamamoto, K., Thomas, E. C., and Karns, E. A. School-related attitudes in middle-school age students. *American Educational Research Journal*, 1969, *6*(2), 191–206.

Yankelovich, D. *The new morality: A profile of American youth in the 70's*. NY: McGraw-Hill, 1974.

Youniss, J. *Parents and peers in social development: A Sullivan–Piaget perspective*. Chicago, IL: University of Chicago Press, 1980.

Zakin, D. F., Blyth, D. A., and Simmons, R. G. Physical attractiveness as a mediator of the impact of early pubertal changes for girls. *Journal of Youth and Adolescence*, 1984, *13*(5), 439–450.

Zautra, A. J., and Reich, J. W. Life events and perceptions of life quality: Developments in a two-factor approach. *Journal of Community Psychology*, 1983, *11*, 121–132.

AUTHOR INDEX*

*Numbers in italics indicate the page where the complete reference is given.

423

SUBJECT INDEX

A

Academic performance; *see also* Conformity/deviance, Grade point average; Achievement tests
as development task of adolescence, 15
effect on grade 7 self-esteem, 324–325, 336–337
effect of timing of pubertal development on
in females, 137, 154–156
in males, 187
gender differences in, 60, 81–84
measurement of, 398–399
school type, effect on, 231, 244, 246–250
score correlations between grades, 373
stability of, over time, 111, 117, 370–373
Achievement tests; *see also* Academic performance; Grade point average
as data source in study, 37
effect of timing of pubertal development, 152, 154
gender differences in, 60, 81, 82, 83–84
as indicator of academic conformity, 17
measurement of, 398–399
school type, effect on, 231, 241, 244
stability of, over time, 111, 117, 370–373

Adjustment
positive vs. negative, 114–119, 131–132, 162–163, 194–195, 202–204, 252–253
specific vs. global reactions, 355–356
Adolescence; *see also* Specific entries
disturbance. *See* Adjustment
division in developmental categories, 10
gender differences in early, 51–97
timing of changes during, 346
Adolescent socialization hypothesis, 203, 224, 243, 254, 256
Adult resemblance hypothesis, 132, 164, 171, 180
Age-effects, 103–129
Anonymity
effect of school type on feelings of, 207, 209–214, 327
measurement of, 400
Appearance. *See* Physical characteristics; Body-image
Arena of comfort, 351–353
Aspirations. *See* Planning for future
Athletic ability
effect on grade 7 adjustment, 379–380
effect on grade 7 self-esteem, 318, 320–321
effect of timing of pubertal development on 141, 178
gender differences, 61–62, 67–68
school type, effect on, 216

431